THE WHITE SHARKS OF WALL STREET

THOMAS MELLON EVANS
and the Original Corporate Raiders

DIANA B. HENRIQUES

A LISA DREW BOOK

SCRIBNER

NEW YORK LONDON TORONTO SYDNEY SINGAPORE

A LISA DREW BOOK/SCRIBNER
1230 Avenue of the Americas
New York, NY 10020

SCRIBNER and design are trademarks of
Macmillan Library Reference USA, Inc., used under license by
Simon & Schuster, the publisher of this work.
a lisa drew book is a trademark of Simon & Schuster, Inc.

Designed by Colin Joh

Set in Goudy Old Style

Manufacturued in the United States of America

1 3 5 7 9 10 8 6 4 2

Library of Congress Cataloging-in-Publication Data is available.

ISBN 0-684-83399-9

For my husband, with love,
And for his father and my friend,
Laurence Barlow Henriques (1906–1990)

ACKNOWLEDGMENTS

My agent, Denise Marcil, by happy coincidence, had actually met Thomas Mellon Evans long before I stumbled across him in the course of my research for my previous book, *Fidelity's World,* and her conviction that his story was worth telling sustained me at every step of this journey. So did the spirited, generous encouragement of Lisa Drew, my editor and the best friend any author could have.

I also owe special thanks to a small band of people who, in a very practical sense, made it possible for me to write this book. In late 1996, I incurred one of those stubborn repetitive-stress injuries that sometimes afflict journalists. Every extended bout of typing provoked a relapse; I feared not only for this book but for my very livelihood. Then, in the summer of 1997, a young man named Jeff Rutherford, who was working for Denise at the time, attended a technology fair and saw a demonstration of a new voice-recognition software program from Dragon Systems. He urged me to take a look, and I did, with the tireless help and support of Susan Fulton, Charles Rubin, Terry Schwadron, Ray Lewis, and all the wonderful people on the technology team at the *New York Times*. Susan was my teacher, cheerleader, trouble-shooter, and inspiration during the months I spent training myself to create by talking, not typing. She and the technology team literally gave me back my career, and this small "thank you" does not come close to expressing what is in my heart.

Through those months, I was comforted at every step by the unfailing support and kindness of Glenn Kramon and Alison Cowan, my editors in the business news department at the *Times*. Best of all, when I was adept enough at dictation to return to my normal duties, they promptly put me back to work, no questions asked, no allowances made. That was the greatest gift of all: they treated me like every other reporter on their team, demonstrating to me and to everyone that it was the quality of my work that mattered, not the technique I used to produce it.

Others have contributed enormously to the creation of this book. Barbara Oliver and Jack Begg, my research assistants, were creative, resourceful, and tireless. Sarah Weissman tracked down the atmospheric photographs. Floyd Norris, my friend and colleague, was my first reader and a wise and helpful critic. I am grateful, too, for the help of the priceless Donna Anderson at the *Times* and for her research counterparts at other publications, especially Charles Shipman at the *St. Louis Post-Dispatch* and Mary Danehy at Time Inc. And I appreciate so much the help of Lorie Olson of the American Heritage Center at the University of Wyoming and Alfons Landa Jr., who allowed me to be the first to explore his father's personal papers.

I would also like to thank all those who shared their memories of this remarkable man and the exciting days of the early takeover wars, especially John K. Foster, Elizabeth Parker Kase, Thomas Mellon Evans Jr., Joseph Flom, Sayre Rodman, Jack Markowitz, A. C. Pocius, and dozens of others who spoke to me on the record and in confidence.

And last but foremost, I thank my incredible husband, Larry, who never lost faith in my ability to overcome my injury and achieve my goals. He is, as I frequently tell him, the best thing that ever happened to me.

CONTENTS

THE
WHITE SHARKS
OF
WALL STREET

PROLOGUE: THE SECOND TIME AROUND

The Time: An evening in the early eighties.

The Place: A soaring hall in a famous Manhattan museum, set for dinner.

The Occasion: A private party hosted by Drexel Burnham Lambert, just emerging as the leading financier of the proliferating battles for control of America's largest corporations. Around the tables are men whose ambitions will chill the hearts of company executives, local mayors, labor leaders, and boardroom directors for years to come.

But at one table sits a man none of the celebrity-spotters recognize. He is Robert Sheldon Evans, an executive at the Crane Company, a polyglot industrial corporation whose last big headlines on Wall Street had come in the mid-seventies, when it made a bid to buy a stake in Anaconda Copper.

One of Evans's curious tablemates finally asks the question others at the table are clearly pondering. Why is he here? Where does he fit into this choreography of power?

"Oh," answers the low-key man from Crane, "I'm standing in for my dad, Tom Evans."

The questioner still looks blank. Who is this Tom Evans?

A brief coolness, then: "Well, I guess you could say, he started all this." His hand swept in the room full of strivers and acquirers, raiders and would-be raiders.

In the business world of the late fifties—that hazy fax-free and pre-laptop era when a round-trip to the Coast took days and takeover battles took months—Thomas Mellon Evans was a widely recognized figure. A Daddy Warbucks lookalike, he was so familiar that business writers could use his name unexplained, just as the names of investment wizard Warren Buffett and entrepreneur Donald Trump would be used decades later. He was a controversial figure as well—a New Jersey congressman would later brand him "the white shark" and *Forbes* magazine called him "the man in the wolf suit." Long before Drexel's Michael Milken became a household name in the eighties by facilitating the use of junk bonds to finance hostile corporate takeovers, Tom Evans had used debt, cash, and the tax code to seize control of more than eighty American companies, small and large. Long before giant pension funds and other institutional investors began to lobby for "shareholder rights," Tom Evans was demanding that public companies operate only for their shareholders—not for their employees or their executives, not for their surrounding communities, but for the people who owned their stock. His view seemed selfish and harsh in the pallid institutional community of that day, but he preached it fiercely and effectively.

By 1959, Tom Evans already had become the leading practitioner of a strange new form of corporate ruthlessness, one that squeezed "fat" out of profitable corporations in the relentless pursuit of greater profit. By 1968, the *Wall Street Journal* had declared Tom Evans "something of a legend for his tough methods of operating the company once he wins control. He demands prompt profit performance from both assets and men; if he doesn't get it, he sells the assets or fires the men."

Yet, despite the swath that Tom Evans cut across America's corporate landscape in the fifties and early sixties, most of the people who poured into Wall Street in the eighties to practice "M&A"—mergers and acquisitions—had no idea they were standing on anyone's shoulders. They thought they were part of a new age, engaged in something history had never seen before. They were wrong. Everywhere they strode, Tom Evans had been there ahead of them.

Although Tom Evans came to power in the blandly conformist Eisenhower years, few of the brash raiders of the eighties could match him for daring, cunning, or sheer exuberance. In a gray-flannel culture, Evans was a dapper maverick; in an age of polite corporate statesmanship, Evans spoke his mind, fiercely and fearlessly.

He was larger than life in his era—and he was not alone. Say "corporate raiders" to most baby-boomer Americans, and they will think of the colorful men whom Mike Milken bankrolled in the Drexel Decade. But the term, probably first coined for the robber barons of the nineteenth century, was commonly applied to the takeover artists of Tom Evans's generation—impatient, heart-scarred young men from the margins of American culture who were challenging their cautious mentors for a place at the top of American business. Besides Evans of Pittsburgh, they included Robert R. Young of Texas, Charles Green of New York, Lou Wolfson of Florida, Art Landa of Washington, D.C., and Leopold Silberstein of Berlin by way of London and the Far East—all once at least as famous as Evans, if not more so, and now all just as obscure.

Tom Evans's story was shaped partly by these remarkable men, for they were all more than coincidental fellow travelers through history. They followed one another's footsteps in a complicated dance, copying and sometimes improving on one another's tactics, publicly defending their common philosophy and business strategy. Among themselves, they were alternately allies and enemies as the occasion demanded, but always, in the public's mind, they were a unified force, viewed with fear and suspicion. Each, in his private life and public warfare, contributed to the controversial image that they all ultimately shared. One cannot understand the early postwar takeover era unless the strands of these men's lives are woven into the fabric of Tom Evans's story, just as their stories were woven together by the fascinated business writers who first recounted their exploits and made them famous.

Their challenges to the corporate Establishment, depicted in newspaper and magazine articles and even woven into Hollywood movie plots, made such a strong impression on the business community of their day that it seems almost inconceivable that they could have been so completely forgotten by the early eighties. Their exploits, after all, filled file upon file of clippings in the *New York Times* archives alone. They had been profiled by *Fortune*, featured in photo spreads in *Life* and *Look*, subjected to lengthy front-page scrutiny by the *Wall Street Journal*, vilified in Congress, quizzed on *Meet the Press*, and derided in *Barron's*. What had happened? How could Wall Street have entirely lost its memory of these remarkable boat-rocking men?

Their undeserved obscurity today is perhaps rooted in the cycles of the twentieth century's business literature. The golden-hued business world of the twenties attracted writers like honey attracts flies; there are a half-dozen excellent books, and probably dozens of mediocre ones, about the events that climaxed with the Great Crash of 1929. Indeed, one of the best books on that subject was published nearly a half-century after the fact, relying on the abundance of material produced in that era by dozens of fascinated scribblers. But during the Depression years, the writer's eye shifted firmly to Washington—and there it stayed, with a few brief exceptions, all through the forties, the fifties and the sixties. The New Deal, World War II, McCarthyism, the Cold War, the civil rights movement, the space race, and rock and roll all pulled the nation's literary and journalistic attention away from the prosperous and seemingly bland and unruffled world of Wall Street and corporate boardrooms. Only a handful of popular business books illuminate the first two postwar decades on Wall Street. The speculative market of the sixties attracted a few elegant mainstream writers. But then the dismal, colorless stock market of the seventies descended, and thousands of Wall Street veterans retired or found other lines of work, taking their memories with them. Soon, the grim attractions of Watergate and the Arab oil crises stole the spotlight once again. Thus, Thomas Mellon Evans and an entire generation of fascinating business figures from the two postwar decades have been largely neglected simply because the nation's attention was turned so firmly elsewhere. Piecing together the story of the early corporate raiders is like assembling a mosaic on some new archaelogical site; no doubt, key figures have been lost in the dust or smashed beyond recognition. One does the best that one can, however, in hopes that the incomplete outline will nevertheless be intriguing enough to attract fresh digging.

One could argue whether Tom Evans was, in fact, the "first corporate raider" of the postwar era or just one of the small band of pioneers who rushed onstage together as the great bull market of the fifties got rolling. But arguments about who went first—the most plausible cases can be made for Robert R. Young and Charles Green—miss the heart of what made Evans a lodestone figure in the evolution of American business.

He was a bridge of history—a man whose style, shaped by the business elite of his childhood, deeply frightened and angered most of his own contemporaries but appealed powerfully to the sons and grandsons of his generation. While most of his fellow mavericks focused on takeovers and had little interest in management, Evans went beyond his corporate raids— sometimes along rough and shadowy pathways—to reshape the way his companies did business with their workers, their vendors, their shareholders, their communities, even their senior executives. He called himself a "corporate rejuvenator," but he could almost be called the man who invented downsizing, one of the earliest promoters of the "lean and mean" business model. Back when most chief executives longed to appear statesmanlike, he relished his image of ruthlessness. When others sought to build up huge salaries and luxurious corporate empires, he often worked without a salary and pressed only toward the bottom line. And at a time when scattered shareholdings and passive institutional investors left most chief executives free of any serious concern about rewarding shareholders, Tom Evans seemed to care about only one thing: pushing up the value of his stockholders' investments. He waged corporate warfare with a brilliance and zest that few had yet mustered and built a "conglomerate" in the late forties before the media had even coined the term.

This was Tom Evans in the late forties and early fifties—and his approach to empire-building soon was so widespread that pundits found new names for him and the handful of men like him: Boardroom pirates. Proxyteers. Corporate raiders.

But unlike the more widely known mavericks of that era, Tom Evans endured. He stayed in the game well into the seventies, and the lessons that a younger generation of business leaders and advisers learned from his example echoed all across the corporate landscape.

His brusque and autocratic management style, once condemned by managers who were embracing "sensitivity training" and improving their "people skills," would ultimately be widely copied. In 1976, the midpoint of the "Me Decade," *Business Week* took stock of the Evans phenomenon, in an assessment that resonated two decades later. "Critics claim that Evans has worked extreme hardships on his managements, employees and the communities in which his companies operate," the magazine observed. "But one banker argues: 'It takes a strong man without too nice a conscience to build an empire. He's tough but he's honest. In this age of permissiveness, maybe he's a throwback, but a lot of stockholders out there could do a lot worse than have Tom Evans mind their money.' "

And in the world of Wall Street, he was a conduit between the business values of his mentors, the industrial barons of Mellon-era Pittsburgh, and those of his protégés, the young investment bankers and securities lawyers who trained on the deals of the seventies and dominated the decade of the eighties. He championed the rights of the shareholder when almost no one else was. Decades later, a nation of shareholders inherited the power he fought for—and profited immensely from the wealth their shareholdings produced.

To be sure, that power often had an ugly face—just as Tom Evans's squinty Santa Claus grin could vanish into an icy glare or a fiery tantrum. His life story is almost a summing up of all the ways that business can bruise society. The shareholder-first philosophy elbowed aside other important interests. Workers were abruptly fired or left ill or without pensions. Customers were cheated by illegal price-fixing schemes; suppliers were arm-twisted into improper reciprocal trade deals. Communities were polluted in the name of prosperity and then abandoned for the sake of profits. The Evans story reveals not only the ascendant power of the shareholder, but also the evolution of America's attitude toward the consequences of that power.

As the nineties ended, a prosperous and slightly smug America looked back on two decades that had been shaped by the values championed by Tom Evans and his fellow mavericks of the fifties. In the takeover-driven eighties, factories were closed, whole communities suffered, managers were stretched thin and then let go after years of service—all to generate a healthy return to newly alert and increasingly demanding stockholders. In the nineties, with the stock market soaring to a previously unimaginable altitude, corporate managers all across the country were learning to work for men like Tom Evans, tough men working for tough shareholders. And nations around the globe were wondering if they could possibly harness the magnificent wealth-producing power of the American capitalist model without enduring the harsh choices that men like Tom Evans symbolize.

It almost seems that Thomas Mellon Evans was a man so far ahead of his contemporaries that he had moved into the shadows before the full force of his business style had dawned on the rest of Corporate America. At every step of his career, he was barging in where few would follow—at first. But follow they did, at last. And their journey changed the face of American business, and American life.

CHAPTER ONE

STRANGER IN PARADISE

Early on a warm morning in late August 1931, two mismatched young men are piling themselves and their luggage into a taxi outside the American Hospital on the Boulevard Victor Hugo in a suburb on the northwestern edge of Paris.

One, tall and lanky, is moving gingerly, trying to avoid stretching the fresh stitches across his abdomen. Under a hank of unruly brown hair, John Kennedy Foster's long plain face shows the pallor of recent illness, and a dull weariness mutes his normally gregarious nature. The other young man, shorter and awkwardly built, glows like a new penny in the early morning light. At 5 foot 9, Thomas Mellon Evans's angular frame is topped by a head that is a little too large and a neck that is unequivocally too short. But his smooth, unlined face is almost pretty: a sensuously carved mouth, a soft cleft in his square chin, swelling cheekbones and arching brows. His fiercely intelligent brown eyes shine like searchlights from under a wide forehead crowned with sleek dark hair, parted high over his right eyebrow. As he impatiently slams the taxi door, a young man in a hurry, he seems to be wrapped in a magnetic field, crackling with possibilities. In schoolroom French polished almost into fluency by his long summer of practice, he directs the driver to the Gare Saint-Lazare, a few dozen blocks to the east. The magnificent liner, Holland America's *Statendam*, is waiting for them in Le Havre. It is time to go home—home to Pittsburgh.

As the two young men settle into their seats in the rail carriage, the train begins its rocking, rhythmic journey along the Seine to the sea. It was on just such a train trip—could it have only been a week ago?—that young

Foster began to feel feverish and queasy. He and Tom had traveled through the night in a third-class carriage from Nice to Paris. By the time that train had pulled into Paris, Tom Evans was genuinely alarmed about his child-hood friend. He sought out an American banker in the city, to whom he had a letter of introduction from home, and enlisted his help in getting Foster admitted immediately to the American Hospital. There, doctors promptly removed his dangerously swollen appendix—no trivial proce-dure in those pre-penicillin days. Foster later recalled that Tom Evans had been reassured to learn that his friend's nurse was a graduate from the nursing school at Yale, his own alma mater.

Just days after he had graduated from Yale in June 1931, Tom Evans and Johnny Foster, similarly furnished with a degree from Princeton, had set sail for Europe. They left behind a nation that was confused and increas-ingly anxious, as hardship tightened its grip and hope for better times grew weaker. President Herbert Hoover, unwilling to shrug with resigned patience in the face of panic or depression as earlier presidents had done, was encouraging the nation to be optimistic, to shake off the paralyzing fear that had grown steadily for more than a year. But by the spring of 1931, the giant steelmakers who dominated Pittsburgh had joined other key industries across the nation in cutting wages by as much as 20 percent. Layoffs had become common, spending had dried up, the prices for wheat and other farm products had plummeted. Like that prince of Pittsburgh, Treasury Secretary Andrew W. Mellon, most businessmen believed that hard times purged the toxic excesses from the nation's economy and left it stronger. Mellon, apparently secure in his own unimaginable wealth, faced the future unafraid, bemused and a bit scornful of his president's exertions.

Like Mellon, the two young men from Pittsburgh who had sailed to Europe in June of that foreboding summer also faced the future with opti-mism. Neither was rich enough to face hard times with indifference—indeed, Tom Evans had a keen sense of his own straightened circumstances, and their "grand tour" had been conducted on a shoestring. But both were too young and too enchanted with the freedom of their first post-college summer to dwell on the evidence of depression accumulating around them. They had toured Great Britain first, renting a cheap little car to travel to the Highlands. Then they had traveled to France, making their way south toward the fabled Riviera. On the way, they had gone to the races in Deauville on the coast of Normandy, and Tom Evans had gleefully spent his winnings on a fine new straw hat. They had found affordable off-season lodgings in the tony winter resort town of Juan-les-Pins, east of Cannes and just outside Cap d'Antibes. Tom always handled the hotel negotiations—John just grinned as his Pittsburgh buddy confidently exercised his French on the condescending clerks.

Like most American tourists of their day, they socialized mostly with other traveling Americans, who were still fairly numerous despite the gathering economic clouds at home. One couple and their two daughters, also staying in the popular Mediterranean resort, had befriended the two enthusiastic young men. When the daughters agreed to an evening expedition to the elegant casinos at Monte Carlo, the father volunteered his gleaming low-slung Hispano Suiza automobile for the trip along the cliff-hugging roads. Driving that magnificent vehicle substantially softened the car-crazy Tom Evans's disappointment when he found that, still shy of his 21st birthday, he was too young to be admitted to the main casino.

It had been a golden, joyful holiday—until that alarming trek on the night train from Nice to Paris. Once John Foster was installed at the American Hospital, Tom Evans had alerted Foster's mother, who was escaping the sooty summer heat of Pittsburgh at her family's rustic West Virginia farm. The farm had no telephone service, so it had taken considerable ingenuity to keep the alarmed Mrs. Foster posted on her son's progress. But Tom had set pre-arranged times for his calls, and each day Mrs. Foster traveled nearly twenty miles to the nearest telephone to receive the brief and appallingly expensive transatlantic reports. Traveling to her son's side was impossible, as the journey from remote West Virginia to Paris would take considerably more than a week. But she was tortured by worry—her brother had died of a ruptured appendix—and she clung to the confidence and optimism in young Evans's voice.

After a day or so, Tom became increasingly content to spend his final days in Paris at his friend's bedside. In a nearby room on the same ward, another American patient, a remarkably pretty teenaged girl from California, was recovering from an intestinal ailment, and she was visited daily by her beautiful sister and warm, gracious mother. It was inevitable that Tom Evans would become acquainted with the Parker family from Pasadena, California. Mrs. Elizabeth Parker, an animated and competent woman, was the wife of a successful lawyer whose clients included the heirs to some of southern California's well-known fortunes. Like her tall handsome husband, she was a graduate of the University of Michigan, and she had a sturdy midwesterner's sense of her own place in the world. She also had a relaxed, easy-going attitude about the stuffy social proprieties, and she extended her motherly attention to these two young men who were coping so cheerfully with a serious crisis far from home.

Mothers were an ambient theme for Tom Evans in that hectic week. By telephone, John Foster's mother exuded tenderness and concern. At the hospital, Mrs. Parker was a solid source of calm reassurance. But Evans, however worldly and mature he might seem on the boulevards of Paris, still could not think of his own mother without a disabling lump in his throat.

The lovely Martha Jarnagin Evans had been the daughter of Milton Jarnagin, whom one descendant described as "about as big a wheeler-dealer as a very rural Eastern Tennessee could hold right after the Civil War."[1] His grandfather, Captain Thomas Jarnagin, had served in the Revolutionary Army and afterward had settled a large track of river delta land near Lone Pine, Tennessee. The Jarnagin family lived comfortably, and their daughters were well-educated. Martha was beautiful and cultivated, and family members recall that she had been elected to the famous Daisy Chain at Vassar College, the informal honor society that recognized outstanding students.[2]

Her life after college had a picture-book quality. She married Thomas Mellon Evans, a Yale graduate who was the son of James Evans, described in Mellon family records as "a prosperous and respectable lawyer of an old and influential McKeesport family."[3] Thomas Evans became a banker, rising to become president of a small bank in his hometown of McKeesport, one of dozens of grimy factory towns on the Monongahela River, south of Pittsburgh. He and Martha nestled into a comfortable and secure spot on the lower slopes of the Iron City's formidable industrial aristocracy.

The Evans family was distantly connected to the Mellon clan, although their line had branched off the family tree a generation before the Mellons had become the titans of Pittsburgh. Martha Jarnagin Evans's mother-in-law, Rebecca Stotler Evans, was the daughter of Elinor Mellon Stotler, whose father had immigrated to western Pennsylvania in 1818. It was Elinor's older brother Thomas, known in later years as "Judge Mellon," who left the family farm for the law. Judge Mellon then parlayed his legal skills into a real estate and banking fortune that his sons Andrew, Richard, and James quickly nurtured into true dynastic wealth. Despite her more modest circumstances and her somewhat prickly and fretful temperament, Elinor Stotler remained close to her older brother, especially after her husband David Stotler's early death in 1848. It was her daughter Rebecca who later married James Evans and gave birth to the ambitious young banker who courted Martha Jarnagin.

Aunt Elinor's descendants did not rise so far as the Mellon sons did, but the newlywed Thomas and Martha Evans could claim membership in a small-town family that was respectable and relatively prosperous, though hardly wealthy. They lived in a pleasant home on Squirrel Hill, a neighborhood to the east of Pittsburgh's business district that also sheltered some of the city's wealthy barons.[4] It was there that their daughter Elinor, named for her great-grandmother, was born in February 1908. Two years later, on September 8, 1910, they had a son whom they named James, in honor of his grandfather. Martha's sister Mary Jarnagin Rodman lived with her young brood in nearby Oakmont, a pleasant town along the Allegheny River northeast of Pittsburgh. As Martha and Tom Evans began their married life, it seemed, as the narrator observed in the novel *Ragtime*, that thereafter "all the family's days would be warm and fair."

But when baby James Evans was barely toddling around on his short, chubby legs, his father fell ill with a rare pituitary gland disorder. In 1913, Martha Evans traveled with her ailing husband to Boston, where he was to undergo surgery. The young banker died on the operating table. According to family lore, the surgeon simply told the horrified widow, "I guess I cut too deep."[5]

The grief-stricken Martha Evans had returned to Pittsburgh a widow, her world suddenly transformed from one of promise and comfort to one of uncertainty and constraints. She sought ways to preserve whatever pieces of that world she could, and decided on one simple memorial to her beloved husband: she had her young son's name legally changed to honor his dead father. Baby James Evans was now Thomas Mellon Evans—so utterly had his world been changed by his father's death that not even his own identity had emerged unaltered. Martha Evans, little Elinor, and the newly named Tom moved from Squirrel Hill into a more modest home. Martha assiduously saved the insurance money her husband left her to provide for her children's education. She was determined to preserve the Ivy League dreams her husband had cherished: that his son would follow his father and grandfather to Yale, and that young Elinor would have the same education that Martha Jarnagin had enjoyed. Though by the standards of the day she was certainly not impoverished, her circumstances meant that she had to be very careful—too careful to squander money on her own health.

Somewhere in the smoky, polluted atmosphere of Pittsburgh, she had contracted a lung ailment, perhaps pneumonia, in an era when doctors could do little but encourage a healthier climate, skilled nursing care, and abundant rest. Such things were expensive, however, and Martha Evans refused to touch the children's college funds to pay for them. She grew sicker and weaker, and when young Tom was just eleven, she died. This emotional earthquake hit the children with even greater force than their father's unexpected death. Tom and his sister shuttled among their mother's concerned relatives in Tennessee for a few months before being taken in by his mother's sister Mary and her husband, Hugh Rodman.[6]

Hugh Rodman was a scientific entrepreneur, the son of a doctor who lived in Frankfort, Kentucky. Like Mr. and Mrs. Parker of Pasadena, he had been educated at the University of Michigan, emerging with an engineering degree. After working fretfully at a storage battery company in Philadelphia, he moved to Pittsburgh to work for Westinghouse, the emerging electrical giant.[7] There he met and married Mary Jarnagin, the sister of Martha Jarnagin Evans.

But because he wanted to pursue research that was of little interest to the company, Hugh Rodman soon grew dissatisfied with his work at Westinghouse. Around 1918, he struck off on his own, forming the Rodman Chemical Company to develop products for the steel industry. The small company, with about a hundred workers drawn from the city's Greek immigrant community, prospered enough to establish the Rodmans in a handsome but not lavish home on Thirteenth Street in Oakmont. They had three children, Hugh Junior, Mary, and Sayre. Mrs. Rodman had occasional cleaning help, but no live-in household servants. Still, it was by all accounts a happy family, with a preoccupied father and a busy, bustling mother. Baby Sayre was just an infant when Tom and Elinor came to live in the Rodman home, and he later said he always thought of them as "almost brother and sister."

If Hugh Rodman seemed remote and absent-minded as a father, far more at home tinkering in his laboratory than playing with the youngsters, Mrs. Rodman was a kindly, loving, and painstaking lady. She no doubt tried hard to fill the craters of lonely pain that had been carved into young Tom's heart by the loss of his parents. But already, this sturdy little man seemed unwilling, indeed unable to trust any piece of life he couldn't personally hold in his own tenacious grip. A smooth shell had enveloped him by his early teens. He was well-mannered, of course, and very, very smart. But he was difficult to read. One moment, he would be joking and laughing, and the next he would seem shy and distant. He was that paradox, a lively and sociable man with few truly close friends. And even the closest of his childhood friends agreed that he seemed to have never truly opened his heart to anyone.[8]

But in Paris in 1931, Mrs. Parker's warmth and sunny California outlook seemed to touch something in the cool, competent young man. And Tom Evans was clearly fascinated by his glimpses of family life among the Parkers from Pasadena, so different from the one he knew from his upbringing in gritty, granite-plain Pittsburgh. Mrs. Parker was comfortably familiar, but her two beautiful, high-spirited daughters were distinctly exotic. The hospital patient was Suzanne, called Dulce, the Spanish word for "sweet"; her sister was the tall, reed-slim blonde Elizabeth, her mother's namesake. Known as

Betty, she had a deep throaty laugh, as if all of life were a wonderful joke. They were like the rare birds that the dapper Mr. Parker collected in the elegant aviary behind their Pasadena home. "I like birds because the male is more beautifully dressed than the female," Edward Parker would say as he showed visitors through the beautiful habitat.[9] His daughters adored him, and giggled at his sly references to their own gorgeous plumage. Their aviary was the largely unspoiled world of southern California, with its orange-scented dawns and golden beaches. The family took its vacations in Hawaii, a Pacific paradise that made their own home in Eden seem nondescript. Both Tom Evans and John Foster were enchanted by the Parker girls, and when they learned that the family was departing for home on the same day—miraculously, on the same ship—the prospect of ending their golden European summer brightened considerably.

On the passage over from New York, Evans and Foster had met some young friends who had landed jobs with the Holland America line. Now, Tom Evans sought them out and wheedled first-class passage on the *Statendam* for Foster, who was far too weak to handle the bunks, steep gangways, and coarser meals of third class. As the boat train lurched into motion on the way to Le Havre, the wisdom of that decision became apparent. Tom Evans could not have failed to notice that the relatively short walk from the cab to the train had worn John Foster out. Tom recalled that Mrs. Parker had rented a wheelchair to ease her ailing daughter's passage from the railway platform to the first-class decks of the *Statendam*. Perhaps they would allow him to use it after they were aboard?[10]

Leaving the weary Foster in his seat, Evans went in search of the Parkers. When he found their compartment, Dulce was stretched out across one bank of seats, with Betty and her mother sitting opposite. The lack of a seat did not deter him. He simply sat on the floor at Betty's feet and began to talk intensely and, it seemed to the casual young teenager, endlessly. Holding an ice pack on her abdomen to calm her own upset intestines, Betty listened politely and made a few appropriate responses to the attractive young man. As Dulce tried to sleep and Mrs. Parker eyed him warily, Tom beamed up at Betty and talked on—perhaps about his adventures, his plans, his grandmother who lived not far from Pasadena. Finally he rose, said his farewells, and left the compartment—only to return a few moments later with a sheepish grin. He'd completely forgotten the reason he had sought out the Parkers' compartment in the first place, he said. Could he borrow Dulce's wheelchair after they had boarded the ship, so that he could wheel Foster aboard? Mrs. Parker instantly agreed, and Evans once again left, leaving Betty and her mother shaking their heads at the odd behavior of this energetic young man from Pittsburgh.[11]

Le Havre was an old, bustling port on the northern banks of the estuary where the Seine meets the English Channel. At the docks, the magnificent *Statendam* towered above the boarding crowd. It was the third Holland America liner to bear that name. Just two years old, the ship was a throwback to the elegant Edwardian era of ocean travel, with two masts and three massive smokestacks angled rakishly toward the stern. The ship's snowy white superstructure rose like a wedding cake above her dark shiny hull, so immense that the gathering passengers seemed like ants invading a rowboat. Evans got his friend aboard and settled him into his comfortable first-class stateroom, set amid luxurious public rooms modeled after a French château. Then he went down several hatchways to search out his own bunk in third class—which had been rechristened "tourist class" after American limits on immigration reduced the demand for cheap steerage fares.[12] It would be an unusual trip, separated from his childhood friend and his new acquaintances by the formidable presence of the first-class stewards. But Evans was not daunted. Once each day, he climbed up to first-class to help Foster change the dressings on his surgical incision.

"Did the steward give you any trouble?" Foster asked, as he admitted his friend to his stateroom.

"No," Evans answered with a laugh. "I just told him I was your valet." The two friends broke into laughter, and immediately began to make plans for Foster to smuggle Evans in for lunch. The Parker girls were delighted to join in the conspiracy, and Mrs. Parker displayed no surprise when her luncheon party was expanded to include the intruder from steerage.

Tom Evans seemed utterly at ease amid the mirrors and gilt-edged paneling of the dining rooms and opulent cut-velvet upholstery of the spacious lounges. His childhood life in Pittsburgh had already prepared him for the awkward role of penny-pinching tourist in a world of glittering wealth, a world where his own status was ambiguous and his welcome was unpredictable. He had met exactly the same circumstances in the world of the magnificent Mellons.

He spent most of his young years among boys whose lives were comfortable but hardly ostentatious. After going to live with the Rodmans, Tom had been enrolled at the Shady Side Academy, a private boys' preparatory school. Shady Side had educated some of the heirs to the smaller industrial fortunes in Pittsburgh, although most of the wealthy Mellons attended more prestigious private boarding schools in the East.

It was at Shady Side that "Buddy" Evans, as he was known there, had first met Johnny Foster. In 1921, when the eleven-year-old Evans had transferred to the school, the twelve-year-old Foster was already established a grade ahead of him. The following year, the school left the Pittsburgh neighborhood that had given it its name and moved to a new campus in Fox Chapel, across the Allegheny River to the north. There, Tom and John had adjoining cubicles in a top-floor dormitory suite at Morewood House, a Georgian-style red brick building which housed about forty boys of all ages. Foster's mother was a friend of Mary Rodman, and she had asked her son to look out for the newly orphaned Evans. The two boys traded weekend visits, set up a weekly poker game, and met each other at the family dinner parties and weekend gatherings that made up their social life. They shared a passion for the tinny, rattle-riddled cars of the day, and Tom good-naturedly joined in Foster's shooting and fishing expeditions.

If Foster and his other classmates had more spending money than he did, Tom Evans nevertheless seemed to fit easily into campus life. He had been "the youngster" of his graduating class in 1927.[13] As a sophomore, he had performed so well on his English College Board examination that he had skipped his junior year and caught up with Foster's class. He worked on the yearbook as assistant business manager and helped out on the student newspaper. The yearbook's anonymous authors joked that he had won the presidency of the debating group, the Forum, in the winter term of 1927 because "he dared once upon a time to talk against compulsory chapel." But although the yearbook noted that "no one can change Tom's mind once he has made it up," he was clearly a likable young man. The literary quote attached to his full-page profile was "A little nonsense, now and then, is relished by the wisest men," and the daily calendar for his senior year gleefully reported on his malodorous adventures in chemistry class. Describing Tom, some prescient classmate observed: "In contrast to Tom's mildness and cheerfulness, for which he is well-known, there are his quiet persistence and his never-failing astuteness at bargaining. There is a story that he bought(?) a $90 dollar Ford for $25 and his 10-year old 'racer.' If you'd ever seen his 'racer,' you'll just begin to realize what a businessman Tom is."[14]

But far beyond the simple, comfortable world of John Foster and Shady Side, Tom Evans had another close childhood friend: Larry Mellon, the youngest child of William Larimer Mellon, the formidable chairman of the Gulf Oil Corporation and one of the reigning princes of the Mellon empire. From the first, theirs had been a complicated, almost inexplicable friendship. But it was a connection that would change Tom Evans's life.

During the first two decades of the century, William L. Mellon—known among the older members of the family as Will—had become one of the most powerful Mellons of his generation. His father was James Ross Mellon, Andrew Mellon's older brother and a son of Judge Mellon, the dynasty's founder and the brother of Tom Evans's great-grandmother.

William Larimer Mellon had been Judge Mellon's first grandchild, and he became a lifelong favorite of the eccentric patriarch. By one account, Judge Mellon gave his pet grandson $20,000 when he reached age twenty-one and was no doubt delighted when the young man invested that stake briefly but profitably in the infant oil business. Tough and smart but earthy and unpolished—one writer thought he resembled an affable bloodhound; another recalled his "organ-grinder mustache"[15]—Will Mellon was an aggressive and plain-spoken executive, and even the family's severest critics concede that he, like his uncles, was an excellent judge of human character.

His early experience in the oil business in western Pennsylvania gave evidence of his shrewd energy in action. In the early 1890s, with financial backing from his uncles, he had gone from town to town buying up exploration rights and drilling leases in solitary sidewalk negotiations or in tough haggling over warm beers in local taverns. Soon, he had assembled a field of producing wells. When the giant Standard Oil, controlled by John D. Rockefeller, used its near-monopoly power over the railroads to prevent the Mellons from getting their oil to eastern markets profitably, Will Mellon had defiantly overseen the building of a 271-mile pipeline to carry the family oil from western Pennsylvania to a shipping facility on the Delaware Bay.[16] By 1885, Standard Oil had bought out the Mellons, giving the family a $2.5 million profit on young Will's prospering oil and pipeline business. Still only twenty-seven, Will Mellon then settled into an office at the family bank to oversee the family's interests in Pittsburgh's booming streetcar system.

Along the way, he had met the girl of his dreams, Mary Taylor, known to all as May. They married and began a family. May devoted herself to her children's care, assisted by a small troop of governesses and nursemaids, while Will pursued his all-consuming passion for business.

Given his background, it was not surprising that Will's uncles turned to him in 1902 when a problem arose with some Texas oil wells in which they had a substantial investment. They asked him to go to Texas to investigate, a trip that set him on the path that led to the formation of the Gulf Oil Corporation, one of the five major corporations that formed the Mellon empire.[17]

Unlike Andrew Mellon and his brother Richard Beatty Mellon, who both scrupulously avoided interfering directly with company operations, Will Mellon had a real gift for managing men. He quickly realized that the men his uncles had backed in the Texas oil venture were overwhelmed by the demands of the business. In 1907, on his advice, his uncles organized a stockholders' committee and successfully voted to reorganize the company, over the objections of its original top executives.[18] The Mellon-led committee put the reorganized company into the hands of Will Mellon, then in his mid-thirties, and he assembled an able team that built the young Gulf into a major competitor in the emerging national oil industry. By 1931, he was chairman of an enterprise that was producing, refining, and marketing oil from wells in Texas, Louisiana, Oklahoma, Mexico, and Venezuela. Besides running the vast Gulf operation and serving on dozens of family-controlled bank and corporate boards, he also was the steward of the family's political power, serving as chairman of the powerful state Republican Party. If Andrew Mellon, as some historians assert, was the most brilliant businessman America had produced up to his time, then Will Mellon was certainly his most successful apprentice.

It is not clear why such a busy and influential executive, already in his fifties when Tom Evans was orphaned, took such an interest in the young man. John Foster thought that the elder Mellon simply felt a duty to a needy and fatherless boy who was a relative, albeit an extremely distant one. There is some support in the Mellon family history for a close connection between the elder Mellons and Tom Evans's family. Old Judge Mellon's memoirs report that, after a beloved older brother died in 1862, the seven-year-old Andrew Mellon grew lonely in his parents' grief-darkened home and was sent to spend several winters with his widowed Aunt Elinor, who was Tom's great-grandmother.[19] Thus, Andrew Mellon would have been a childhood playmate of Tom's grandmother, Rebecca Stotler Evans, who was still living when Tom was orphaned. This small connection may support Foster's theory that simple family feeling prompted Will Mellon's attention to young Tom. "I think he just figured, 'Here was a Mellon, an orphaned boy without any money,' and he looked out for him."[20] But there may have been something more to it.

Mellon had four children of his own, and by Victorian standards, he was a remarkably involved family man. As one historian put it, "He had a knack for fathering."[21] He had married for love, and his wife May was remembered by her children as a mild, cultivated, and sweetly musical woman with simple, intelligent tastes that were not altered by her husband's increasing wealth and power. Unlike his well-tutored wife, Will Mellon had only a rudimentary education and retained a rustic social style born of his early years scouting for leases in the small boom towns of the early oil belt.[22] Together, Will and May Mellon established themselves and their children on a sprawling scale at Ben Elm, their comfortable estate on Squirrel Hill, and at their summer home on Lake Muskoka in the Ontario lake district north of Toronto.

Will Mellon's daughters, Rachel and Margaret, who was known as

Peggy, were pretty and vivacious. But his sons were perhaps a puzzle to him. The elder boy, Matthew, was an intelligent, cynical young man who ignored the family's business interests entirely and pursued an academic career at a German university, ultimately marrying a young German woman. Young William Larimer Mellon Jr., known as Larry, was the "after-thought" of the family, nearly ten years younger than his nearest sibling, Peggy. Larry remembered a quieter and lonelier life at Ben Elm, with a mother who was frequently ill and sometimes hospitalized, leaving him in the care of servants. A French tutor cultivated his innate gift for foreign languages, and he had inherited his mother's talent for music. But as a boy, Larry Mellon took little interest in the business machinery that supported his privileged existence—machinery that so clearly fascinated his father and his uncles. Indeed, by his own admission, he was ill at ease in the world into which he was born. "There were times when I felt ashamed to be from a family that was known only for wealth. I felt more at home with chambermaids than with people in my own group," he told a biographer years later.[23] To another writer, he posed the question: "What actually would give a child the cockeyed notion that the servants were real people, but the people who came to call on Sunday were stuffed shirts, that people who pulled up to the East Liberty Presbyterian Church on Sunday in Rolls-Royces didn't have their feet on the ground?"[24]

Did W. L. Mellon see in the bright and hard-working young Evans an appetite for business combat, a hunger for financial achievement, that he missed in his own sons? Or did he hope that something of Evans's appetites would somehow be communicated to Larry, who was so quietly contemptuous of his father's business achievements and associates? Whatever the reason, Will Mellon invited Evans to join Larry for regular weekend visits to the Pittsburgh mansion on Forbes Road and for longer summer visits to Lake Muskoka.

The two boys were only two months apart in age and, in hindsight, there seems to be an almost Dickensian quality to the arrangement: the modest but wellborn distant relative recruited to serve as a steady and practical influence on a discontented and unpredictable young heir. It was not always a comfortable arrangement for young Tom. Years later, Larry's older sister Peggy would recall teasing the young man mercilessly. "Tommy was very shy and very thin, and his head looked too big for his body. We liked to make fun of Tommy, he didn't look too bright." But she also recalled that her father invariably defended the young visitor, saying "He's got ability, he'll go beyond all of you."[25]

Despite that awkward beginning—and despite the obvious differences in their temperaments—Tom Evans and Larry Mellon became real friends.

They shared a caustic wit and perhaps an unspoken loneliness for the mothering that death and illness had denied both of them. In any case, their relationship survived Larry's departure from Pittsburgh each fall, when he returned to the Choate Academy while Tom remained at Shady Side. It was a friendship across a great economic gulf, of course. Larry Mellon was born to comfort and splendor, and "Buddy" Evans merely visited that world when invited, returning to the stolid middle-class Rodman home after each foray. But Larry Mellon scorned the pretensions of his world, and perhaps that was what drew him to the young Evans, who was cobbling together a life from the shattered pieces of his childhood. Late in life, Larry Mellon told his biographer that he "came to despise that jaded group of remittance people [in Pittsburgh] who lived on trust accounts and did little else. It was my feeling that a man should try to do something on his own. He could be a professional baseball player or a carpenter. It didn't matter what, just so long as a man was using his own talents."[26]

Tom Evans was "using his own talents" and he somehow made himself welcome in the Mellon empire—or, at least, in the duchy controlled by the unpretentious Will Mellon. Some Mellon family members would later brand Evans an outright pretender, insisting to one family historian that he wasn't a real Mellon relative at all but had simply been endowed with that potent middle name by a father who admired the famous family.[27] This ignores the geneological evidence, of course, but perhaps it underscores the young man's achievement in obtaining even temporary admittance to such jealously guarded gates. Once inside, Tom Evans—so smart, so fiercely observant from the emotional safety of his inner fortress—was ideally situated to study the social manners of that world and absorb its values.

It would not be surprising if the young man built his lifelong ideas about how the very rich behaved from his forays into Mellon society in Pittsburgh during the prosperous years between World War I and the stock market crash in 1929. What did he see? Stylish European travel each summer and expensive and cultivated hobbies like art-collecting and horse-breeding. Andrew Mellon, lonely and cold, had already begun to fill his ugly Gothic mansion in Pittsburgh with the splendid artwork that would ultimately become the endowment of the National Gallery in Washington, D.C. Like many in the family, Tom's friend Larry Mellon was an accomplished horseman and Andrew Mellon's son Paul, just three years older than Tom Evans, was developing an avid interest in raising thoroughbred racehorses. Larry Mellon's great-uncle Richard B. Mellon, Andrew's partner in business, had a racecourse and stables at Rolling Rock, a vast forested estate near Ligonier that he had developed into a private country club for the Mellons and their friends. Tom Evans was sometimes a guest there, with Larry Mellon; once or twice Johnny Foster was included in their party. It was commonplace in the Mellon family to escape the Pittsburgh smog at farmlike retreats in Ligonier and Sewickley, each several dozen miles west of the city, and to take extended trips to the cool, clean air of Canada each summer.

The young Evans might also have observed among the Mellons a serene, almost smug contempt for the opinions of the outside world. Andrew Mellon had a positive abhorence of the public, cringing at the approach of even a sidewalk newsboy. His only confidant was his brother Richard, his partner at the bank and in countless business ventures. Secure in the superiority of his own views, he seemed to care nothing for how his various business or political decisions would be viewed by the general population. In defiance of middle-class values, he and his English-born wife had divorced after waging a bitter public battle for custody of young Paul and his older sister. Will and May Mellon were more happily matched, and May Mellon carefully avoided any interference in her husband's business life. But in a sort of reverse snobbery, they both blithely refused to engage in the formal entertaining and ostentatious display of fashion and jewelry that was enjoyed by their wealthy friends and expected of others in the Mellon circle. Society's rules, society's expectations—these simply did not seem to exist for the Mellons.

What did exist, at least for Will Mellon and his uncles Andrew and Richard, was a complete and lifelong absorption in the fascinating process of building new businesses. Business was the preferred topic of conversation at every family gathering they attended. In a *Fortune* magazine profile of the family in 1967,[28] Richard B. Mellon's son recalled that his uncle Andrew regularly visited his father on Sunday mornings to talk business before church, and would frequently bring top executives of the family corporations to dinner. "I would be invited to sit and listen to their talk, which almost always was concerned with business," he recalled. Larry Mellon, too, recalled less cheerfully how business seemed to form the four corners of his family life. His mother, he once observed, had always found the Mellons "very absorbed in business, a totally different set of values" from those she had been taught among her own more broadly educated and cultivated family.[29] Will Mellon simply adored the daily drama of business life—and Tom Evans simply adored Will Mellon.

His frequent excursions into the world of Mellon-sized wealth had prepared him well for his stealthy visits to the elegant first-class quarters of the opulent new *Statendam*, where there was a lounge "extending through two decks, paneled with exquisitely carved oak embellishments and hung with Gobelin tapestries and period paintings."[30] And the playful, irreverent attitude of Betty Parker certainly helped make him feel welcome. Late one afternoon, she and John Foster were waiting in the first-class elevator lobby. Foster was wearing his best suit with a high starched collar holding his tie, and Betty was a vision in white satin, her silky blond hair gleaming in the chandelier light. Suddenly, the elevator door opened to reveal Tom Evans, clad in red Bermuda shorts and his white knit undershirt, with garters holding up his socks. He had taken the wrong elevator at the wrong moment. But before he could even blush, Betty had clapped her hands with glee and laughed as if his appearance was a deliberate joke staged for her personal delight. The friends waved as the mystified elevator attendant pulled the door shut.[31]

The weather remained clear and fine, and most afternoons found Betty and John nestled in neighboring deck chairs, sipping bouillon brought by solicitous stewards and sharing the shipboard conversations of people who, as Foster later recalled, never expected to see one another again. But Tom Evans intended to see the Parkers again—he refused to let them just drift out of his life. His ancient Mellon grandmother lived in the Los Angeles area. There would be occasions to visit, he explained. Could he come and pay his respects to the Parkers when next he was out West? Mrs. Parker was gracious—the two boys were always welcome. The teenaged Betty smiled happily; the two young Ivy League graduates seemed like men of the world, and she was flattered at their apparently platonic attention. Addresses were exchanged, and the happy party said their farewells in New York, where John Foster's mother was waiting to take him home.

Tom Evans made his own way from New York City to Pittsburgh, each mile along the train tracks pushing him closer to his future. Although he might have noticed the scenes of deepening hardship along his route—idle factories, anxious unemployed men on city street corners, Pennsylvania farmland looking ragged and unkempt—he had no fears about finding work. His friend Larry Mellon's father had promised him a job at the Gulf Oil Corporation. To be sure, his post was a modest one: a spot in the statistical department, later known as market research, where he would work side-by-side with his friend Larry. But it was his first job, at a company captained by his hero W. L. Mellon, and he no doubt faced it with all the optimism his scarred and isolated heart could hold. At Yale, he had been an excellent but hard-working student, pursuing his economics major with energy but growing a bit impatient with the theoretical tone of his studies. Now, he was ready to put theory into practice, and he was confident that working in W. L. Mellon's world would give him the chance to do that.

His new employer was known in Pittsburgh simply as "the Gulf," already a local institution although it was only a few years older than Evans himself. As Pittsburgh and the nation sank into the trough of the depression, Gulf seemed to be defying the bad news, building new storage tanks and a pipeline to connect its Oklahoma oil fields to refineries being built in Cincinnati and Pittsburgh. Its assets—oil wells, pipelines, and refineries around the country—had more than doubled in the previous decade and were now worth nearly a half-billion dollars. In Pittsburgh, builders were putting the finishing touches on Gulf's new headquarters building, a powerful soaring ziggurat on a newly broadened stretch of Grant Street, which Mellon money had transformed into the heart of Pittsburgh's business district.

As Tom Evans approached the old Gulf offices under a bridge spanning an industrial hollow, he could see, through the smog generated by thousands of smokestacks, monuments to the power of the Mellons—banks, hotels, corporate office buildings, clanging factories. Unseen, but far more potent, were the mortgages, the corporate directorships, the political campaign contributions, and the bank credit decisions that gave such enormous muscle to the Mellon wealth. And Tom, fresh out of college, was about to take his small place in that vast money-making machinery. Unlike most junior trainees, however, he would occasionally be able to discuss Gulf's business with the company chairman, over lunch at Ben Elm or during vacation visits to Lake Muskoka.

His relationship with this uncomplicated capitalist had already exposed him to the Mellon family's unsentimental business principles, rooted firmly in the peculiar experiences of the late nineteenth century. They were the views of men that history would later brand as "robber barons." But they were the views that shaped and ruled the entrepreneurial world in Pittsburgh, and in much of America, in the years when the alert Tom Evans was coming of age and dreaming of a career in business.

Much has been written about the founding of the Mellon empire, but each account was colored by the attitudes about wealth and business that prevailed at the time.[32] The facts are simple: the story began on a family farm outside Pittsburgh, where Thomas Mellon's father had settled after emigrating from Ireland. Thomas Mellon moved into the city in 1832 to study law. He was a frugal and humorless young man, who seemed almost obsessively determined to be wealthy. As he built his law practice, he invested every spare nickel in mortgages and liens, and his fortune grew. Enriched by the prosperity that accompanied the Civil War, he opened the T. Mellon and Sons Bank in 1870. In 1880, he turned a solid, profitable institution over to his son Andrew, a solemn young bachelor who lived with his parents. Andrew had only a patchwork education and no apparent ambitions or interests beyond entering the family business. Over the next two decades, by making loans and well-placed investments in burgeoning new industries, Andrew Mellon and his brother Richard transformed the family bank into a corporate portfolio of almost unimaginable wealth.

There was a dark side to the construction of this fortune. The muckrakers of the Depression era saw the Mellons as a greedy and ambitious family willing to seize on someone else's discovery—the famed Spindletop oil field, the patented process for making aluminum, the pioneering coke ovens developed in Germany—and manipulate it into a monopoly that could milk wealth from the rest of American industry. There were other bones of contention dug up from the muck: antitrust violations that allowed the Mellons to preserve their aluminum monopoly, special tax breaks obtained through the use of political influence, sharp practices used to obtain a robust flow of oil for the Mellon pipeline or cheap energy for the Mellon aluminum mills.

Defenders of the Mellons saw the family in a different light, of course. One political supporter, Republican Senator Philander Knox of Pennsylvania, offered this assessment of Andrew Mellon in 1921, as part of his campaign to persuade President Warren G. Harding to add the Pittsburgh banker to the Cabinet: "His is one of a few cases where his wealth is an accurate measure of his ability. He has never financially debauched any enterprise with which he has been concerned . . . With marvelous vision and imagination he has spent his life developing new fields for American energy and opportunity and in my deliberate judgment he is the greatest constructive economist of his generation."[33]

Another view of this family's values emerged in the early 1950s, when Stewart H. Holbrook reflected on the Mellons' methods in his book *The Age of the Moguls:* "They liked to find a man both honest and capable who had started a business and was in need of capital. They gave him the money—if he passed their thoroughly competent investigation. They took shares in the business and left the man to run it as he would, except that when and if he got into difficulties, the Mellons were ready to offer advice, and possibly more than advice."[34] The advice, or whatever exceeded advice, would almost certainly be accepted simply because the Mellons typically would demand all but a sliver of the honest and capable man's company in exchange for their financial support. It was, after all, their capital that had been wagered to turn the entrepreneur's dream into profit. So it was only fair to them, as shareholders, that most of those profits should flow into their own pockets.

But perhaps the most balanced perspective on the business practices at the turn of the last century can be drawn from Frederick Lewis Allen's classic, *The Lords of Creation*. Men like Andrew Mellon and his nephew, William Larimer Mellon, had come of age at a time when American enterprise was outgrowing its citizens' simple faith in free competition, individualism, and self-reliance. Unrestrained competition among the railroads in the 1880s, Allen pointed out, had been chaotic and utterly ruinous. If the legitimate goal of business was to maximize profits, some limitation on such costly competition had to be found—and it was, in the form of trusts and other business combinations that ultimately took the orderly shape of monopolies. Moreover, as railroads knitted the country together, America was moving toward a national economy, and business had to develop a national reach as well. As historian Olivier Zunz explains, "Large business organizations in the late nineteenth century stitched regional networks together to create a national market" but in the process they reshaped the smaller local marketplaces that were so familiar to small-town Americans. "The towns that composed the industrial belt of the East and expanding Midwest . . . experienced an extraordinary rate of population turnover and exchange. Each place became more readily identified as part of a network of places and relied increasingly on the network's existence for its life."[35] Local merchants no longer dominated their consumer markets. National manufacturers were reaching into those markets with brand-name products and national distribution patterns. A growing middle class whose members were willing to work for a paycheck began to branch off from the earlier middle class, comprised largely of small-town merchants, manufacturers, and professionals such as lawyers, ministers, doctors, and educators. A new science of business was emerging, and corporations grew up along hierarchical, bureaucratic lines. "Early in the twentieth century," Zunz writes, "keen observers contended that corporate capitalism had split the educated middle class into two groups—the independent entrepreneurs and the salaried professionals."[36] The men that Tom Evans admired—men like his mentor Will Mellon and his surrogate father Hugh Rodman—stood firmly and proudly in the former group; their views of the salaried classes ranged from benign paternalism to outright contempt.

The salaried professionals managed the wage-earning laborers, who were seen by managers and entrepreneurs alike as little more than another raw material, like oil or rubber. Leading businessmen at the turn of the century had no tolerance for organized labor, and their views were shared by many middle-class Americans, nowhere more staunchly than in Pittsburgh. There, steelworkers recruited from the poverty of Eastern Europe worked twelve-hour days, seven days a week, in mills that were dirty and dangerous. Wages were low, living conditions were bleak, and injuries were common. Unions were firmly resisted, and union organizers were sometimes dangerously unwelcome. Strikes were quickly and brutally sup-pressed, most notably the disastrous strike in the summer of 1892 by Carnegie Steel Company workers in Homestead, Pennsylvania. Their organizing effort failed, in part because of class and ethnic divisions among the workers and in part because of the raw force of the steel industry's pri-vate guards. The defeat of the Homestead strikers reflected forces that would effectively eliminate organized industrial labor as a meaningful fac-tor in the Pittsburgh region's economy for more than three decades.

As a result, a young middle-class man like Tom Evans would almost cer-tainly have opposed unions on principle. "Most of the people we knew expected their friends to take a dim view of organized labor, much as a preacher's colleagues are expected to take a dim view of Satan," one cousin said. "It never occurred to me, as a young man, that any respectable people thought otherwise, and Tom probably grew up the same way."[37]

Even the simple rights of citizenship were affected by the power of the industrial rulers. The Mellons and other business owners throughout the region dominated the local politics in virtually every factory town, and thus controlled the local court system and the police. Workers were expected to vote the company ticket; independent political activism was as dangerous to a working man's tenure as unionism. The Mellons' politi-cal power stretched across Pennsylvania. And since 1922, that influence had been wielded personally by Tom Evans's mentor, Will Mellon. In the cynical backroom deals that were routine in those days, he helped select senators, governors, and mayors who would be protective of the family's financial and industrial interests. Tom Evans once told a historian of an occasion when a telephone call came in for Will Mellon while Evans was visiting with Larry Mellon at Lake Muskoka in Canada; hanging up, the senior Mellon explained that the caller was the governor of Pennsylvania. "He has to make a speech and wants to know what to say," he told them.[38]

To one historian, the Pittsburgh that bred Tom Evans was "synonymous with the spectacular advance of American industry, and the byproducts: labor unrest, poverty, assimilation of a heterogeneous immigrant working force, and disruption of community cohesion."[39] The editor of the remark-able *Pittsburgh Survey*, a sweeping assessment of the civic and economic life of the region begun in 1907, saw the city as a paradigm for the industrializ-ing nation. It "is not merely a scapegoat city," he wrote. "It is the capital of a district representative of untrammeled industrial development, but of a district which, for richer, for poorer, in sickness and in health, for vigor, waste and optimism, is rampantly American."[40]

Life in the steel industry in Pittsburgh had become so harsh by the early 1900s that an early sociologist, writing the year before Tom Evans was born, felt he needed to explain why the workers had remained so passive. "The men believed in the existence of corporation secret service departments, whose agents were 'working shoulder to shoulder at the rolls or furnaces with honest workmen, ready to record any "disloyal" utterances.' "[41] Conditions were little different in the other basic industries that dominated the unusually lopsided Pittsburgh economy. Mellon-owned aluminum mills and bauxite mines were the scenes of numerous violent, largely unsuccessful labor actions in the second decade of the century, when Tom Evans was a child. Participants were blacklisted, strike breakers were recruited among southern blacks or Mexicans, and the workers' efforts to improve their conditions almost always failed.

The pattern of labor relations was very similar at Gulf under Will Mellon's leadership. One Depression-era muckraker believed that only the demand for American oil during World War I had prompted the company to settle a skilled mechanics' strike in 1917 by recognizing the workers' union. "But this meddling came to naught in the depression of 1920 and the unions were no more. . . . By 1925 hardly a vestige of unionism was left in any Mellon industry, save coal and construction. In a broader sense that was also true of American industry as a whole."[42]

By the late 1920s, the miners' union had come under attack by the mine owners, who included the Pittsburgh Coal Company, in which the Mellon brothers had a substantial stake. The battles were long and bloody, with casualties continuing into the early years of the Depression. In 1931, as Tom Evans was reporting for work at Gulf, radical union leaders were organizing a strike in the coal industry in western Pennsylvania. By that winter, a particularly severe one, hundreds of strikers would be evicted from their company-owned houses and would live in tents scattered across the acid-scoured landscape. The strike was resisted "with the barbarity usual to such incidents in the Pittsburgh district," muckraker Harvey O'Connor wrote.[43] Even less polemical historians agreed that the captains of Pittsburgh industry were unusually harsh in their militant opposition to union organizing efforts.

Low-level Gulf workers were struggling even before the depression hit. Said O'Connor: "At the Port Arthur refinery, largest in the world . . . Mexicans and Negroes did the dirty work at rates averaging around 25 cents an hour in good times. Their families lived in company shacks renting for $7 a month: two rooms, a kerosene stove, and water at central wash sheds. In the field the seven-day week was common."[44] But even though labor was cheap, Gulf had laid off an estimated 5,000 workers by 1930, as hard times began to squeeze.

One may question the fairness of O'Connor's condemnation of business leaders of an earlier age for attitudes that were deeply embedded and largely unquestioned in the culture of their day. But what is evident, apart from moral judgments, is that the balance of power between labor and owners had been so profoundly skewed for so long that Pittsburgh's industrial leaders simply could not imagine any other way of life. As one historian observed, "The destruction of unionism, company political influence, and ethnic fragmentation produced an enlightened despotism, at best, and a ruthless suppression of dissent, at worst." He continued, "In the absence of any significant countervailing power, the business leadership was free to shape the life of the region. This had led, by the early twentieth century, to the mutilation and pollution of the physical environment, and to a low priority for housing, health, and social welfare institutions."[45]

Visitors to Pittsburgh during the years that Tom Evans was growing up there were regularly appalled by the sheer ugliness of the place. "It looked like hell, literally," wrote Lincoln Steffens.[46] To be sure, there were some grand monuments to the local wealth, among them H. H. Richardson's magnificent Allegheny County Courthouse. And the intricately folded hills sliced by broad rivers had once been a beautiful cradle for the growing city. But the soft coal that fueled the regional economy was a dirty fuel, producing tons of black soot that had settled on the city year in and year out. White houses turned gray; women wore veils to keep the grit off their skin, and professional men went through two white shirts a day. Children climbed trees whose bark, furry with soot, blackened their hands and knees. Window curtains, open to the gritty breezes, had to be washed and ironed weekly. The rivers that had carved the magnificent valleys of the area were little more than industrial sewers plied by oily barges. Even trees and grass ultimately were blighted by the filthy, acidic air and the sour wastes that seeped into the soil. Well into the 1930s, it was not unusual for Pittsburgh's street lamps to be lighted at midday to lift the grim twilight that the hovering ceiling of soot and fog created. Recalling the widespread pollution of that era, John Foster spoke for countless comfortable Pittsburghers of his vintage when he said, "I never minded it. To me, it meant the mills were running, and that meant prosperity." A writer in *Harper's Monthly Magazine* in 1930 captured his own reaction to Tom Evans's hometown with his title: "Is Pittsburgh Civilized?" He concluded, "Pittsburgh has the wealth to buy a high degree of civilization. It remains, on the whole, barbaric."[47]

The overarching cultural value was ceaseless, productive work; everything else—art, learning, the stimulating conversation of intellectual life—was just a frill, a luxury for the idle. The bleak and blighted life faced by most working-class citizens of the region was not seriously questioned by Will Mellon and the other proud citizens who owned or financed the mills and mines and factories that were literally poisoning the world in which they and their families lived. And yet these men all considered themselves to be good, industrious, God-fearing people who were living lives of great accomplishment. As Frederick Lewis Allen saw it, their peculiar religion was woven from more than just the simple strands of Christian teachings. "There was the Benjamin Franklin philosophy of frugality. There was the Puritan philosophy of sobriety, continence, and Sabbath observance. There was the laissez-faire tradition of business competition as a hard-fought battle without fear or favor."[48] There was, too, the widespread belief that one's private affairs were nobody's business, even if those affairs affected the lives of thousands of workers or consumers or citizens. "The belief had almost inevitably grown up that government interference into economic operations was the beginning of tyranny," Allen explained. "The law of supply and demand offered all the regulation which an American would tolerate."[49]

Allen's final conclusion about what motivated these business titans cannot be improved upon: "Through the story of these men's adventures and exploits there runs the thrill of conflict, of immense tasks boldly accomplished and emergencies boldly met, of a continent subdued to the needs of industry; yet . . . the dollar is omnipresent, and its smell pervades every episode."[50]

This was certainly true of the founder of the Mellon dynasty. Judge Thomas Mellon was "a cultivated man, endowed with a formidable intellect and a will as hard as the finest Pittsburgh steel," a later historian noted. "His fault was to overvalue money and so in the end he failed himself. But he was a genius all the same . . . a man who set for his ambition the singular goal of raising a family of millionaire businessmen and brought it off."[51]

He did rather more than that. He founded a dynasty that, almost within his own lifetime, had become America's richest family, seemingly untouched by the economic fears that haunted America in that anxious autumn of 1931. As Tom Evans reported for his first day of work at Gulf, his boss's uncle, the gray and feeble-looking Andrew Mellon, was ruling the nation's finances, as he had for a decade, as Secretary of the Treasury. He had resigned from more than fifty corporate boards to take the Cabinet post first offered to him by President Harding in 1921. At that time, the assets under his family's control were estimated to be worth more than $2 billion. The publicity-shy Mellons were known as bankers, where they were known at all. But the family also held a patent-based monopoly on the increasingly important American aluminum industry. They controlled gas companies, railroad car companies, chemical companies, electrical utilities. As one Depression-era biographer noted, "The Mellons were masters of Pittsburgh. Substantial businessmen professed to believe that they could be ruined by the Mellons' displeasure."[52]

The slice of Mellon interests that Will Mellon personally oversaw had grown to immense size by the end of the 1920s. Gulf Oil, worth $272 million in 1921, was estimated to be worth nearly $800 million by 1928. By then, the enterprise was the "mightiest of Mellon corporations," O'Connor observed.[53] Indeed, he calculated that if the Mellons had been stripped of all their assets except their ownership of Gulf, they still would have been among the richest dozen people in the nation. With 5,400 wells in production, Gulf was pumping out 65 million barrels of oil a day by 1931. Added to that were thousands of miles of pipelines, dozens of tankers, and 3,000 company-owned service stations all across the country.

From the public's perception, not even the deepening recession settling across the continent in 1931 seemed to affect this marvelous money machine. "In good times their profits would be gigantic—Gulf's ran to $44,500,000 in 1929—and in hard times they could call on their enormous reserves to buy out distressed properties for a song," O'Connor explained in confident hindsight.[54]

But O'Connor's confidence in the Gulf was uninformed. In reality, on the day Tom Evans showed up for work in the fall of 1931, the corporation—and the entire Mellon family—were beginning to feel the first pangs of real economic anxiety.

The cause of the Mellon family's growing concern was a peculiar debt the Gulf Oil Corporation had incurred in the earliest months of the Depression. In June 1930, the company had gone to the bond market to borrow $60 million to build a pipeline to carry its petroleum from the southern oil fields to refineries in Ohio. In the unsettled market conditions after the Crash of 1929, money was expensive to borrow unless investors were given some collateral to reassure them. The collateral in this case was a "sinking fund," into which was deposited a portfolio of securities owned by the three wealthiest Mellons—Andrew, his brother Richard, and their nephew W. L. Mellon. The three Mellons collectively pledged to bondholders that they would maintain sufficient securities in the sinking fund to cover 130 percent of the face value of the bonds, or about $78 million. When the bonds were issued, this collateral arrangement seemed sensible—when would those three Mellons ever lack for $78 million? But as the stock market continued to cut a long, deep gouge in the nation's wealth in 1931, the pledged securities shrank to a fraction of their 1930 values. Additional stocks had to be added to the sinking fund to avoid a default on the Gulf bonds.[55]

The shrinking stock market, of course, was just one symptom of the profound economic illness that had gripped the nation—and that would soon hit Gulf. The declining economy meant less consumption of oil, and yet taxes on gasoline and other oil products were increasing as local governments struggled to raise money for basic services and expanded relief efforts. Through the 1920s, oil had gushed out of the Texas and Louisiana rigs with a careless abundance. Tanks had to be built to hold it, pipelines had to be built to carry it, and refineries had to be expanded to process it. But in 1931, the state of Texas imposed mandatory conservation measures on the oil industry, requiring Gulf to cut its output. The flood of oil to the expensive new refineries shrank to a trickle. A Gulf company history quoted Will Mellon's assessment of the damage: "The expense of maintaining and operating properties was not reduced by the restrictions upon production," he said.[56]

Then, with demand already weak, an ocean of new, high-quality oil was discovered in east Texas. To stay competitive, Gulf had to move into the new east Texas fields, spending money at a time when the price of crude oil was dropping precipitously. Indeed, in 1931, Gulf faced an unendurable paradox: it was selling more gasoline than ever before, but was actually losing money in the process. At the same time, the amount of cash it needed to service its debt had nearly doubled, in part because of those troublesome pipeline bonds.

Thus, the situation inside the fabled corporation as Tom Evans began his working career there was as bleak as it had ever been. As a Gulf corporate history put it, "in 1931, the roof fell in on Gulf."[57]

CHAPTER TWO

A POCKETFUL OF DREAMS

The roof had already fallen in for much of Pittsburgh. With its one-note economy, the city was especially vulnerable to the Depression's impact on basic industries. Most of its citizens worked in factories or mining operations and were already struggling to make ends meet, with no savings and few skills beyond those demanded by their foremen. As tenants of company-owned housing, many of them did not even have a roof over their heads when the mills shut down.

The city's suffering outstripped the traditional charitable impulses of its prosperous elite. Some citizens looked for inspiration to Philadelphia, where a partner in Drexel and Company, affiliated with the famed House of Morgan, had organized a drive in November 1930 that had raised $7 million to support charitable relief organizations. By the fall of 1931, the money was gone but the needs were as severe as ever. In Pittsburgh, voluntary relief efforts were even less successful. In late 1930, business leaders there set up "the Pittsburgh Plan," a voluntary fund to which companies were urged to donate the equivalent of one day's payroll. Those still employed were urged to chip in a day's pay—a substantial sacrifice—and other voluntary donations were sought. The fund, which raised just $2 million, was to be used to pay unemployed workers to maintain parks and other public facilities, which was considered far healthier for their character than a demeaning dole.[1]

But by late 1931, as Tom Evans settled into his duties at Gulf, the Pittsburgh Plan was exhausted. Companies could no longer afford to contribute, although the need was growing daily. Efforts to augment the fund with donations from the city's wealthiest citizens faltered, despite Andrew Mellon's kick-off appeal: "It is an opportunity for service such as may not come to us again in our lifetime," he said. "The men and women who temporarily find themselves in difficulties . . . are not strangers but our own people who work in our shops and in our industries."[2] He and his brother Richard announced gifts to the fund of $300,000, and Will Mellon gave $40,000. But for many in Pittsburgh, unaware of the increasing problems the family was facing, the Mellons' donations seemed far too small compared to their fabled wealth.[3] When other wealthy donors were even less generous, critics somewhat unfairly blamed the Mellons for setting a poor example. "An editorial commented on the coldness of certain rich men," the critical Harvey O'Connor wrote.[4]

To inspire greater generosity, the Mellon family announced that it would match gifts of up to $750,000 if others in the city could raise that amount. When the gifts still did not materialize, the Mellons gave their matching gift anyway. But it was nowhere near enough, as more families sought help. John Foster, who was in law school that bitter winter, recalled that on visits home he would pass half a dozen out-of-work people in each downtown block, all trying to sell a few gadgets to raise money.

In late 1931, the Bank of Pittsburgh failed. According to Harvey O'Connor, Will Mellon and his uncle Richard Mellon had favored a rescue plan organized among other Pittsburgh bankers, but Andrew Mellon had rejected the deal on the principle that propping up unhealthy banks was foolhardy. "Within the month a score of smaller banks closed their doors. Tens of thousands of Pittsburghers, most of them workers and small-business people, found their savings and reserve funds tied up in the bitterest winter in the city's memory," O'Connor wrote.[5] But banks were failing all across the state, all across the nation. The Mellons could not have saved them all.

They could not even save their own employees. The lucky ones were working short weeks; the unlucky had no work at all. Thus, by the standards of most middle-class people in Pittsburgh in that winter of 1931, Tom Evans was certainly among the lucky; among the laboring classes, he probably looked rich. He had an Ivy League education. He had a place to live, even if it was only a small dingy apartment on an ugly uphill street. He had a car, even if it was one he had patched together. He had a job, even if it was some lowly assignment in the market research department at Gulf. And he had a lovely young college girl waiting to see him on his increasingly frequent visits to his grandmother in California. And best of all, for an ambitious young man, he occasionally had the ear of Will Mellon, the chairman of the company, at a time when the company was experiencing the most remarkable overhaul in its history. It was a time, Evans said later, that made the economic and business theories he'd studied so ardently at Yale come alive, each morning. The possibilities of life took root in his imagination and began to grow.

Will Mellon decided at the age of seventy-two that he wanted to lessen his workload and spend more time on his immense yacht. He recruited Colonel James Frank Drake to take on the presidency of Gulf. Drake was the obvious choice. As Mellon biographer Burton Hersh put it, Drake "had a well-organized, methodical mind. Will Mellon was a wildcatter, and Andrew Mellon had always understood that Will needed someone to be the bean-counter."[6] Drake was far more than that. He was a graduate of Dartmouth College and had a degree from the college's Amos Tuck School of Administration and Finance. After serving in the Army Ordnance Service in World War I, he had joined Gulf as a personal assistant to Will Mellon. He had overseen the enormous task of preparing the oil company's first depletion schedules, required by the federal government. When Andrew Mellon went to Washington as Treasury Secretary, Drake went with him as "an unofficial, trouble-shooting assistant," according to a Gulf corporate history.[7] There, he was trusted with some of the Secretary's most sensitive assignments, including evaluating various candidates for the politically sensitive job of Commissioner of Internal Revenue. An intuitive and gifted manager, Drake later worked for the Mellons at the Standard Steel Car Company, and after it was sold to the Pullman Company, he became chairman of the combined companies.[8]

Drake himself recalled, years later, the bleak mood he found when he arrived at Gulf that spring, just months before Tom Evans arrived. "Can you imagine a worse time? Even the Gulf company was losing money, they were cutting off their dividends. That is the baptism I got."[9] It was a baptism of fire for the company, too. Payrolls were slashed, entire departments were overhauled. Drake believed firmly in decentralization, and he quickly reorganized the sprawling operation that Will Mellon had created. Oil production, transportation, refining, and marketing, where Evans worked, were all put in separate departments each with its own accounting system, bolstered by the modernized accounting methods that Drake insisted on. There were layoffs, as excessive overhead was reduced. "What Drake did was to infuse order," the corporate history noted. "Under him the company became more closely knit, more aggressive in its pursuit of earnings and more careful in its spending."[10] These were lessons that Tom Evans would follow closely.

Scholars who have studied the company agree that while its financial fortunes may have been uncertain on the day Tom Evans arrived for work, it was in the hands of two of corporate America's most talented executives—each with distinctive skills, but each outstanding. Will Mellon was a visionary, an acute judge of human potential and a father figure who inspired respect, affection, and intense loyalty from those he recruited. Drake, while perhaps less loved, was a superb general who could marshal all the muscle and money of the corporation and get it marching efficiently in a profitable direction. As Tom Evans made himself useful, eventually serving Will Mellon in the same jack-of-all-trades role that Drake had originally filled, he was actually participating in a daily tutorial in the profitable art of turning a troubled but promising business around. And he loved every minute of it.

It was, in fact, his whole life. John Foster, who had finished law school and returned to Pittsburgh, lived just a few blocks away from his childhood friend. He remembers that when others in their group were heading out to a movie or some other entertainment in the evening after work, Tom Evans would stay home hunched over books, brought home from the office, that contained the balance sheets of various publicly traded companies. "He would spend the evenings going through those books, looking for promising companies. He would be so excited when he would find one that he could buy for less than its assets were worth in liquidation." He found such companies by calculating their "net quick assets," which is the term accountants use for the value of a company's cash and other liquid assets minus any outstanding debt. His friends teased him about his obsession and gave him a nickname: "Net Quick" Evans, after the tool he relied on to find his imaginary takeover targets.

Of course, such takeovers were just dreams. Tom Evans made about $25 a week and was so careful with his pennies that he patronized a dry cleaner who gave him a 25 percent discount for returning the hanger with his dirty suits.[11] The stock market crash and the ensuing depression had made penny-pinchers not only out of young clerks but also out of bank loan officers. Those who had survived the Crash without ruin, suicide, or prison were unlikely to risk lending to a twenty-one-year-old dreamer who wanted to buy some undervalued company that he believed could be liquidated at a profit.

But that didn't deter Evans from doing his dream shopping. It filled the empty evenings at home between visits to California. Usually his long courtship of Betty Parker was disguised as dutiful visits to his grandmother, Rebecca Stotler Evans, whom he knew as "Gangie." But occasionally, business would take him to the West Coast. Once he and Larry Mellon spent several days in Los Angeles looking for new locations for Gulf filling stations. Laughing and soaking up the scented, soot-free sunshine, Tom and

Larry drove Betty to several promising intersections and asked her to help them count the passing vehicles. As the outing suggests, there was more camaraderie than romance in Betty's early relationship with her regular Pittsburgh visitors. Tom and John Foster were simply her best friends, she later recalled.

John Foster also found a few excuses to stay at the beautiful Parker home in Pasadena, including the 1932 Olympics in Los Angeles. But soon, his heart had wandered elsewhere, to a young Sewickley neighbor, and Tom's intentions toward Betty had become clearer. Their courtship continued under the California sun, with occasional mornings spent swimming in the surf near the Parker family beach house. The zest for life and the easy laughter were still there—"Tom had a wonderful sense of humor," Betty recalled—but the two young friends were growing up. One Easter, Betty was visiting New York City with her father while Tom was also in the city on business. As they walked arm in arm across the newly built George Washington Bridge, Tom asked Betty to marry him. Startled, she turned to look at him—and realized she loved him. "I'll have to ask my father," she answered him, with an uncharacteristic shyness.[12] Her father said yes, and on June 26, 1935, shortly after her college graduation, Elizabeth Parker became the wife of Thomas Mellon Evans. Larry Mellon, an impressive link to the Mellons of legend, was the best man. John Foster and his wife, Ann, newly married themselves, came out on the train so that John could serve as one of the ushers.

Tom and Betty Evans spent their honeymoon in Hawaii, a largely unspoiled paradise where Betty had vacationed since childhood. They returned by ship to Los Angeles and boarded the train for the long trip to Pittsburgh. The dirty, factory-ringed city was nothing like her southern California home, but Betty approached her new life with the happiness of most new brides. From the train station, Tom took her to the tiny upstairs apartment, next to a grocery store, that had been his bachelor home. "I had never seen such a mess," she recalled with a laugh. There was a scratchy horsehair sofa, and two ugly iron beds with straw mattresses—and a small gin-still in the bathtub. Also in residence was the elderly black man who had served the Evans family in earlier prosperous years and who stayed on with Tom in lieu of a pension.

Slowly, Betty adjusted—although she later recalled her early years in Pittsburgh as a time when she was "perplexed and troubled by black smog in the air and lack of sunshine."[13] She gratefully received gentle guidance from kindly May Mellon and from John Foster's mother. Behind the wheel, she learned her way around Pittsburgh, dropping her husband off at the towering new Gulf Building each morning and picking him up again after work. The couple had found a home—staying in Tom's bachelor quarters was unthinkable—and Betty learned the rituals of Pittsburgh housekeeping. At Tom's insistence, she hired a cook, a pleasant black woman named Mimi Bradshaw. Together on stepladders, the two women would massage the wallpaper with the gummy, absorbent dough that the city's homemakers used to lift the latest accumulation of soot from the papered surfaces. She hung sheer curtains at the windows, which had to be kept open to the dirty breezes in the hot summer months. And she took the curtains down and washed them each week, marveling in disgust at the soapy gray water that drained away. She made new friends, grateful that Ann Foster was just around the corner from her new home on the top of Negley Hill. Some women in her circle were soon sporting maternity smocks. But not Elizabeth: Tom had extracted a solemn promise that she would not get pregnant for two years, to give them a chance to accumulate some small savings before the expenses of a child bit into their budget.[14]

On alternate Sundays, they would drive east up the Allegheny River to Oakmont for dinner with the Rodmans, who seemed to Elizabeth to approach life with a needlessly severe frugality. In a clearly autobiographical short story written decades later, she observed that her young heroine "had never seen such people—people who always seemed to find things difficult."[15] The aunt in the story, a soft gray woman, was afflicted with ill-fitting dentures, asthma, and bursitis. The young bride was painfully intimidated by the older woman's habit of quizzing her about her homemaking skills: Do you know how to make vegetable soup? How to force forsythia? How to use philodendron? She didn't yet know what philodendron was, and grew tired of constantly confessing her ignorance. But her inherent delight in the absurd rescued her from "this stuffy southern formality with its stilted way of conversing." She giggled inside over the way her host and hostess, who did not serve cocktails or wine, passed pitchers of bourbon and rum to pour over the ice cream and cake. "Dessert took forever because everyone accepted a second helping of ice cream and cake—which was, of course, inedible without rum or bourbon."[16]

Young Sayre Rodman, a teenager when Tom Evans introduced his new bride to the Rodmans, recalled finding her quite exotic—the first "California girl" he had ever met. Despite the strange stuffiness, Tom's young wife tried to approach the Rodman family with the same casual, vivacious energy she brought to the rest of life, but in that reserved, middle-class household her charm seemed too flighty, insufficiently solid. She, like May Mellon before her, was deeply shocked to discover how much of Pittsburgh small talk revolved around money—making it, saving it, investing it, counting it, and somehow keeping score by it.

And money was a touchy subject between Tom and Betty. When they married, Tom was still laboring in the marketing department at Gulf. Wealthier friends were gravitating to the pleasant suburbs west of the city, but Tom admonished Betty, "We can't afford to move out there." When she pressed him, he retaliated with questions that shocked her. "Well, where is your money? All my friends' wives have money of their own. Why don't you?"[17] She had, indeed, grown up with far more luxury than Tom had experienced at the Rodman home. But her father earned their wealth. She had no ancestral trust fund to take with her as a dowry. Sheepishly, she approached her family for an allowance. The request startled her parents, but they agreed to provide her with thirty dollars a month, which provided a few comforts. But she pressed her husband, in turn, to go to his boss, Colonel Drake, and demand more money. "I even specified the amount," she recalled later with a laugh. He resisted for a time—hating to acknowledge his subservient position, perhaps, or just unwilling to make demands when his grip on the Mellon world was so tenuous. But finally he agreed to confront the colonel. "He came home and was just jubilant," she added. "He'd gotten it!"

Tom relished his work in a way that simply baffled his boyhood friend Larry Mellon. "Once I got the idea that dollars were foolish, the people that were chasing them seemed foolish," Larry Mellon once said.[18] And Tom Evans was certainly determined to chase down some dollars. By the summer of 1935, after serving as best man at Tom and Betty's wedding, Larry Mellon had finally reached the breaking point in his boredom with business life. Married and the father of a young son, he had tried to settle down to the life that his wife and his family expected him to live. But it was no good—he was not cut out for an office job, he told his father. And he hated being cooped up in gritty Pittsburgh. He wanted to be a rancher out West. Seeing his determination, Will Mellon let him go—after telling his youngest child that "I ought to have my head examined," as Larry Mellon recalled later.[19] His departure from Pittsburgh, and his subsequent divorce, moved him somewhat to the edge of Tom Evans's life. They visited whenever possible, but they talked of old times, not of their current pursuits. As Tom Evans struggled for all he was worth to enter the world that Larry Mellon had struggled so stubbornly to escape, only their shared childhood experiences held them together.

Gradually, Tom Evans became a sort of confidential troubleshooter for Will Mellon, keeping him informed about activities in the company during the older man's increasingly extended vacations aboard his massive motor yacht, the *Vagabondia*. That put Evans in close contact with Colonel Drake as he implemented his ideas about decentralizing Gulf's operations and beefing up its accounting controls. These were invaluable times for Tom Evans, experiences that more than made up for the long hours and late nights.

In 1937, the couple celebrated their second anniversary, and Betty, freed from her promise, almost immediately became pregnant. They moved to a larger home, where their first child, Thomas Mellon Evans Jr., was born in March 1938. But as Betty prepared the nursery, Tom was dreaming of a very different addition to the family: a new company, one of his very own.

Tom Evans always said that it was his mentor, the Gulf chairman, who first mentioned to him the possibilities posed by the plight of another Pittsburgh company struggling to survive the Depression. The H. K. Porter Company had been founded right after the Civil War by a young entrepreneur named Henry Kirke Porter. Porter had studied for the ministry before enlisting to serve with the Massachusetts Volunteers in the Civil War. After the war, he was preparing to enter the ministry when his father gave him $20,000 to develop a business. The company he built made steam-powered switching locomotives, the small engines used to haul raw materials and heavy finished products around factories, coal mines, and steel mills. At the time Tom was born, the Porter Company employed more than a hundred workers and was worth nearly $1 million. A decade later, in 1920, its value had more than doubled and it was the largest manufacturer of these specialized steam engines in the world, turning out 600 locomotives a year.[20]

But as the Jazz Age hustled toward oblivion, Porter stalled and began to slip: its customers were turning to locomotives powered by electricity or diesel fuel, and the managers who had taken over after the founder's death in 1921 had failed to keep up with the changing technology. When the Depression hit, it was more than the Porter balance sheet could bear and the company was forced to seek the protection of the bankruptcy courts. Its principal creditors were investors who had purchased its bonds over the years, and who were not being paid the regular interest they were owed. These bonds were tucked into trust funds and safe deposit boxes all over Pittsburgh, silently shrinking in value until they were worth barely a tenth of what the original bondholders had paid for them.

Meanwhile, Tom Evans was chafing to do something bigger than his duties at the Gulf allowed. The mild-mannered reputation he had earned at Shady Side was becoming frayed as he grew blunt and impatient with the bureaucratic diplomacy of corporate life. Will Mellon, ever the keen judge of men, called him in one day for a chat.

It was clear by his early twenties that Tom Evans would never charm his way up the corporate ladder. Yet he was very smart, hard-working, and almost frighteningly ambitious. Will Mellon had just the prescription: "Tom, you don't want to make a future working as a vice president at Gulf. This Porter company is in trouble, and you could take it over."[21] The idea was audacious, but intriguing. And W. L. Mellon wasn't pushing Evans out the door, only opening it so that Evans could see other possibilities. "W. L. said he'd always have a desk for me," Evans later recalled. "I appreciated that. Unfortunately, the only one that appealed to me was his, and it was already occupied."[22]

Indeed, after doing his usual stint of rigorous study and analysis, Evans was certain that he *could* take control of the Porter company. But first he had to scrape together enough money to do so. Although credit was somewhat more available than it had been in the early 1930s, his dreams still outstripped his status: a twenty-four-year-old junior executive at Gulf.

Then, as he was trying to figure out how to finance his ambitious takeover plan, inspiration came in the mail, enclosed between the covers of *Fortune* magazine. The hefty, beautiful publication had been born in February 1930 out of Henry Luce's conviction that "the great businessmen were the new supermen of civilization."[23] It was a philosophy that appealed deeply to Tom Evans, who was an avid and regular reader. As he thumbed through the September 1935 issue he noticed an intriguing profile of Floyd Odlum, who had become a multimillionaire almost overnight by investing in the undervalued shares of twenty-two investment trusts decimated by the 1929 crash.[24] The trusts, today known as closed-end mutual funds, were trading in that crash-scarred marketplace at prices that were substantially less than the value of the securities they owned. Odlum's rags-to-riches story was built on a simple strategy of quietly stalking undervalued companies and sprucing them up enough to make a profit. With delight, Odlum told *Fortune*: "You know, three times I have had the pleasure of getting control of a company before the directors had any idea I was doing it." Like Evans, Odlum had his mentor, a wealthy businessman named Sidney Z. Mitchell. Mitchell invited Odlum to share in the purchase of some securities offered to Mitchell at rock-bottom prices by the underwriters. Lacking cash, Odlum had to raise money quickly to take advantage of the offer, and he came up with an inspired device. He and a friend made a deal: promising to split any profits he made, Odlum borrowed some securities that the friend owned, presented them to a bank as collateral for a loan, and used the loan proceeds to buy the bargain-priced shares. The deal ended badly for Odlum, because the "bargain" shares declined in value.

But the way he financed their purchase—that was an idea Evans could use. The more he considered it, the more plausible it seemed. But where could he borrow the collateral he would need to get a loan?

He approached Will Mellon with the article, and suggested that Mellon play the role of Odlum's friend by lending him some shares of stock that Evans could use to obtain a bank loan. Obviously he could not use the loan to buy the Porter bonds—that would be too much of a gamble, since it would take years to restore value to the ailing company. Instead, he planned to invest the loan proceeds in something safer and then cash out at a profit and use the cash to buy up the Porter bonds. He offered to pay 3 percent interest on the value of any shares that he borrowed, expecting to cover that expense out of his profits on the deal. His mentor, always fascinated by intricate financial arrangements and confident of Evans's ability, agreed to help finance his plan, but only on the condition that Evans limit his stock-market speculation to the purchase of Gulf shares. Evans agreed—what else could he do? To avoid any hint of favoritism, Will Mellon arranged for Evans to approach a New York bank for a $50,000 loan, rather than sending him across the street to the family-controlled Mellon Bank in Pittsburgh.[25] Fortunately, Evans's experiment did not end as Odlum's had. The stock market was strong in 1935 and 1936, and Colonel Drake's decentralization and streamlining of the sprawling Gulf empire was beginning to bear fruit. The company had finally won the right to explore for oil in Kuwait, on the Persian Gulf. In 1936, the company saw its revenues increase 20 percent, and shareholders were granted a 100 percent stock dividend, worth more than $113 million. Gulf's stock soared. And new shareholder Tom Evans soon had the small war chest he needed to wage his first battle for control of an American company.

It was an audacious ambition, one that almost seemed to have been plucked from the mothballs of the early Mellon years, when the aluminum trust and the infant Gulf operations were being forged. But as he prepared to enter the corporate battlefield, Evans had more to inspire him than his mentor's exciting boyhood reminiscences. He had the fresh newspaper headlines out of New York detailing an upheaval that was shaking the elder statesmen on Wall Street. The eye of the storm was a tiny Texan named Robert R. Young, just turned forty, who in 1938 was waging a startling proxy fight for control of the coveted Chesapeake and Ohio Railroad. Young's story was bound to have captured Tom Evans's imagination, for the two men had much in common. A restless, diminutive man, Young had been raised in the Texas panhandle. Like Evans, Young had experienced early tragedy. His mother died when he was about eleven years old. His stern, old-fashioned father, a small town banker like Evans's, initially tried unsuccessfully to put his unruly son in an orphanage. Failing that, he exiled his son to military school and then to college. That did not tame Young either, although like Evans at Yale he was an outstanding student. Young dropped out of the University of Virginia after spending more time gambling than studying. Energetic and attractive, Young had copper hair, a puckish grin, and a rustic wit. In style and appearance, he strongly resembled a later Texas entrepreneur, H. Ross Perot. But Young's bright Huck Finn image masked a lifelong tendency to brood. He dabbled in poetry and collected art more seriously—his wife, Anita, was the sister of artist Georgia O'Keeffe. But he was also a man who could hold a grudge.[26]

Like Evans at Gulf, Young too had tried the corporate road to success: four years at Du Pont, two quick job changes, then five years at General Motors.[27] His early mentor was the famed financier John J. Raskob, chairman of the General Motors finance committee and the man who conceived and built the Empire State Building. Young always said he made his first million by betting against the market, and against his ever-bullish mentor, on the eve of the 1929 crash.[28] Around 1932, at the age of thirty-four, he formed his own brokerage and investment firm with a partner from the finance office of General Motors and acquired a seat on the New York Stock Exchange.

And like Evans, Young was fascinated by the search for corporate diamonds in the dust; he specialized in buying up the seemingly worthless securities of companies that could be refurbished into profitability. Business was tough at first, but as the market began to recover in 1933 and 1934, Young began to prosper. He and a group of his wealthy clients, including top executives still at General Motors, gradually built up a substantial stake in the Alleghany Corporation, a famous name from the 1920s which controlled thousands of miles of railroads, including the Chesapeake and Ohio.

As early as 1932, Young had approached the company to request a seat on its board. He was told to go see James Swan, a C&O director and president of the Guaranty Trust Company, the railroad's bank. The bank was the trustee of a substantial issue of Alleghany bonds that were secured, in part, by Alleghany's controlling block of C&O shares. When Young made his case to Swan for a seat on the board, the banker rebuffed him and the Texan was stung by the icy response.[29] In April 1937, as Evans was growing increasingly itchy to leave Gulf, newspapers announced that a syndicate that included Young's rich General Motors clients had expanded their holdings into a controlling stake in Alleghany. While most of the money came from the auto executives, Young had another key backer in the deal, Allan P. Kirby. Kirby, who lived in Wilkes-Barre, Pennsylvania, was the heir of a cofounder of the Woolworth chain of dime stores. But Kirby had no appetite for publicity and was content to let Young take center stage, which suited Young perfectly. His unpredictable leadership soon unsettled the General Motors clients, however, and they pulled out. Young and Kirby pressed ahead and took control of the troubled corporation, a debt-heavy holding company with as many layers as a Russian doll.[30]

The company had originally been financed by the House of Morgan. Soon after Young and Kirby took control, Young was summoned to a meeting with Thomas W. Lamont, the senior partner at Morgan. Young arrived at the austere Morgan headquarters at 23 Wall Street, opposite the New York Stock Exchange in downtown Manhattan, and was ushered into Lamont's presence. The meeting did not go well: the prickly Texan was offended by the patrician Lamont's stated expectation that Young would defer to Morgan's advice as he developed his business plan for the troubled Alleghany holding company. Bankers rubbed Young the wrong way, whether the banker in question was a Morgan in Manhattan or a father in Texas. "So intense was his resentment that he often referred to this meeting as a turning point in his life," Young's biographer noted. "He said later that Lamont made him feel 'just like a country boy,' that he 'literally put me on the carpet, spanked me and raked me over the coals for having the temerity to be developing a . . . plan without discussing it with Morgan's.' "[31]

Perhaps the root of Young's anger was his awareness that the bankers truly did hold all the trump cards. They had insisted on a protective clause in Alleghany's bonds: every dollar's worth of bonds must be backed by $1.50 worth of the company's stockholdings. (It was the same sort of provision that had been added to the fine print on the Union Gulf bonds of 1929, the ones that had caused such anxiety within the Mellon family in the bear market of 1931–32.) If the value of the collateral securing the Alleghany bonds fell below the required level, the Guaranty Trust "had the right to assume receiver-like control of the collateral, with the power to impound all income and exercise all voting rights—in other words, the right to take over control of the C&O from Alleghany."[32]

When the stock market suffered a severe slump in 1937, the bank's collateral did shrink below the legal threshold, and Guaranty Trust showed no sign of overlooking that fact. Boxed into a corner, Young fell into a deep, sudden depression that disabled him for several months. Not until March 1938, shortly before Alleghany's annual shareholders meeting, did he get back into the fight, formally demanding that Guaranty Trust give him the power to vote the collateral shares for his slate of three directors. The bank refused, intending to elect three directors of its own choosing. Young went to court, and the legal skirmishing locked up the disputed block of stock.

That shifted the balance of power in the board election to the company's other public shareholders. Who would they support in the fight, the bantam-weight Texan or the big-city bankers and their Wall Street allies?

"Young was now in his first proxy fight, and many of the techniques which he developed were to re-appear in the future, refined and sharpened," his biographer noted. "He started a campaign to win over the support of the small stockholders . . . Aware of the anti-Wall Street bias of the 1930s, Young never lost an opportunity to point out the role of top representatives of the Wall Street bankers in the C&O."[33]

Young's antiestablishment and highly confrontational methods shocked traditional business leaders on Wall Street—indeed, in boardrooms across the country. Tom Evans could not have missed the publicity generated by newspapers largely sympathetic to Young's "tilt with Wall Street." The outcome looked to the fascinated public like a draw: Young had collected proxies representing 41 percent of the common stock, but his opponents controlled enough stock to prevent a quorum and thus block the annual meeting. The impasse was resolved by a compromise that expanded the board enough to seat both rival slates of candidates. It could not be said that David had defeated Goliath, but neither had David been defeated himself—thanks to his ability to rally small stockholders to his cause.

But in Pittsburgh, Porter's stockholders were of no help to Tom Evans. He had looked at the Porter balance sheet too closely to believe that those shareholders still had any meaningful stake in the decrepit company. Evans knew that a company that cannot pay its bills belongs in reality to its creditors, not to its shareholders. And the most powerful Porter creditors were its bondholders. Evans saw that the more Porter bonds he owned, the more leverage he would have in the inevitable negotiations over the unpaid debts. So his strategy was to find those shrinking bonds that Pittsburgh investors had tucked away and to offer the owners ten to twenty cents on the dollar for them.

Corporations with publicly traded stock typically maintain lists of their shareholders. But then, as now, bondholders were far more difficult to locate. The Porter bonds did not trade publicly in any volume. Local Pittsburgh brokers might remember who had bought them, but Evans was no doubt reluctant to tip his hand so early for fear it would drive up the price of the bonds. How to find the scattered bonds? His friend John Foster rode to the rescue, at last repaying the favors of Paris. After working as a bank examiner in the early years of the Depression, Foster had landed a job as a trust officer at the Colonial Trust Company in Pittsburgh. He learned that one of the trust funds in the bank's care owned a big block of Porter bonds. On Evans's behalf, he approached the trust officer who controlled that account to see if he would be willing to sell the bonds for cash. The offer Foster outlined seemed reasonable, since the bonds were paying no interest and the company's prospects looked dim. The deal was struck, and Tom Evans was able to acquire a hundred Porter bonds, with a face value of $100,000, for just $10,000.[34] He was on his way.

Porter's creditors had been patient with the ailing company, hoping that it would recover as the Depression lifted. But by 1937, patience had worn thin. That year, by virtue of his substantial bond holdings, Tom Evans was named one of the trustees who would oversee the company's operations on behalf of creditors. It was the first time many Pittsburgh businessmen realized what a substantial investor young Evans had become. In 1939, when the company's creditors finally resolved Porter's bankruptcy, the bondholders were transformed into stockholders, taking new shares of stock in lieu of the money owed to them as bondholders. And Evans owned enough bonds—and thus enough of the new stock—to demand the presidency of the company. The board of directors granted his wish in March 1939. He was twenty-eight years old. And he would never work for anybody but himself again.

CHAPTER THREE

A MILLION-DOLLAR BABY

By the time Evans took control in 1939, Porter had only about forty employees and its order book was slim, with barely $10,000 in repair parts sold. It had not paid its property taxes in more than five years. There was only $28,000 in the till. It was as close to death as a company can get and still survive.

Tom Evans, full of energy and youthful confidence, was determined that it would survive. He scoured the company's balance sheets for assets that could be turned into cash, immediately focusing on the company office building opposite the factory on Harrison Street at Forty-ninth Street, in an industrial neighborhood north of Pittsburgh's downtown district. To the astonishment of the company's secretaries and junior executives, he promptly moved them into unused space in the factory across the street and sold the building. He pressed the salesmen for fresh sales and cheered in relief when the beleaguered Russian government placed an unexpected order for locomotives.[1] He found some vacant company land, some scrap materials and other unused equipment, and he sold them all. The company was inching into the black—at least enough so that it could get a $25,000 loan from the Union Trust Company, part of the Mellon banking empire. Evans plowed the loan into spirited efforts to expand the company's product lines. "You can't live on locomotives, because they never seem to wear out," he said later.[2] And Porter's mainstay product was a highly specialized form of train engine—"a fireless locomotive that ran on stored steam."[3] At first, he tried to shift the company's manufacturing muscle to produce equipment for the chemical, food, and oil industries. But his efforts were sometimes comically unsuccessful. "I can recall the time we tried to develop a new type of hydraulic locomotive," he told an audience years later.[4] "It would run backward but not forward. Another time, when we were manufacturing special orders of process equipment, we took an order for a specially designed large pressure vessel for an oil refinery. When it was built, we found it was too big to get out of the door of our plant." He found humor in these adventures when he looked back on them, but they had been infuriating at the time. Evans was driving the company hard, and driving himself even harder.

Although Evans was the president of Porter, he was not its only shareholder. Other bondholders-turned-investors sat on his board, and they were growing increasingly concerned about his stewardship of the company. Perhaps his brusque, take-charge manner irritated the older, more conservative directors. He was, after all, young enough to be their son and was anything but deferential. Shortly after he'd gotten the Union Trust loan, some of the directors tried to kick him out as president. Alone, he didn't control quite enough of the Porter stock to keep them from doing so. Fortunately, his Mellon-controlled bankers stood behind him, telling the disgruntled directors that the bank's $25,000 loan was based on the assumption that Tom Evans would remain in charge. If they kicked him out, the bank told the directors, the loan would fall due immediately, and the company did not have the money to repay it. The directors backed down, and Evans had some breathing room.[5]

He took the lesson of the boardroom rebellion to heart—though not by softening his manner or treating directors and executives more courteously. Instead, with every penny he could scrape together, he bought additional shares of Porter's stock. Soon his grip on the company was strong enough to defy any criticism. Now he was truly working for himself—that is, Evans the chief executive was working for Evans the chief stockholder. This felt right, safe, comfortable. This matched the business world he'd memorized among the Mellons, and it seemed to fit into his view of himself as perfectly as the keystone in an arch.

As American industry began to arm Hitler's opponents in Europe, Porter began to sit up in its sickbed. There was tremendous demand for firepower, and American industry went into overdrive to produce bombs and shells for the allied forces. Suddenly, Porter's lowly fireless locomotive was in intense demand. After all, one cannot have a locomotive belching sparks and cinders in a munitions plant.[6] The locomotive orders turned Evans's attention to the munitions industry, and looking around, he found an idle factory in nearby Blairsville. Somehow, Evans patched together a credible bid for a contract to manufacture naval artillery shells, using equipment furnished by the Navy, at a price that undercut the much larger companies who thought of government contracts as their natural right. The move rankled the Pittsburgh establishment, which had long experience in harvesting the profits of war. But it bolstered Porter's health, and that was all Tom Evans cared about.

He continued to look for war-connected businesses, and found the Quimby Pump Company, with factories in Newark and New Brunswick, New Jersey. Then he diversified into oil and gas, investing in wells in Ohio, Pennsylvania, and Kansas. In 1940, Porter's sales were double what they had been in 1939. In 1941, sales tripled over the prior year. By the time the United States entered the conflict, the Porter company was ambulatory and even had a small bank account. It was fashionable among the Pittsburgh trust-fund crowd to idealize military glory. But Evans, who was exempt from military duty because of his role in the munitions industry, often said privately that war was the most idiotic activity on earth. He found glory enough running his baby business empire, although he later recalled that he "worked all the time, around the clock."

His preoccupation increased the strain on his marriage, revealing with sharper clarity how terribly mismatched he and Betty were. When they were courting, Betty Parker seemed at home in the world of wealth in a way that eluded Tom Evans. Her doting father was rich and intelligent, her mother was gracious and warm, and her parents seemed quite happily married. She had been loved and pampered since birth.[7] By the time of her marriage, Betty was accustomed to a life in which summer brought first-class passage to Europe, where she and her sister shopped, saw the cultural sights, and flirted with equally wealthy young men from home. Her childhood bore no resemblance to the bleak tragedy that Tom Evans had experienced—the death of his father and the loss of all financial security, the tragic loss of his self-sacrificing mother, his awkward adoption by the Rodmans.

There is no doubt he had been deeply wounded by these events. Betty remembered the occasion when, as a young bride, she found her husband weeping in his dressing room one winter day. Shocked out of her usual off-handedness—she had never before seen a man cry—she asked what was wrong. Trying to compose himself, Tom explained simply that he had been thinking about his mother. Perhaps it was around the anniversary of her death, or perhaps something else had brought her forcefully to mind. But he shared with his young wife his personal version of his mother's fate: how she had lived frugally so that she could set aside all her husband's insurance money to provide a good education for Tom and his sister, and then had fallen ill with pneumonia. The doctor had told her, Tom explained, that she needed skilled nursing care to recover, but she had refused to touch her children's college fund. And so she had died, leaving a hole in her young son's heart that no amount of money could fill.[8]

With his emotional hunger and deep sense of obligation to the Rodmans, it perhaps was inevitable that he would absorb his uncle's single-minded work habits and his aunt's frugal, almost fearful view of life and its hazards. Betty's carefree, free-spending world fascinated and attracted him, but it did not seem to her that he could embrace it. He had stood too long as an outside observer of wealth, through his long friendship with Larry Mellon. And his rich friend's turbulent and often unhappy life had perhaps taught him that his own values—Rodman values—were best. Careful budgets, hard work, with money set aside for a rainy day, that was how to get ahead.

From the first, Evans had baffled Betty with his mixed signals about spending money—encouraging her to live in a fashion suitable to his ambition, but then flaring into outrage at the expense involved. Even as he had shocked her parents by suggesting that she arrange a personal allowance from them, he had insisted that she hire a cook rather than busy herself in the kitchen as she was eager to do.

She later recounted, in a transparently autobiographical short story, her experience of shopping on Madison Avenue in New York for a custom-made silk brocade evening jacket. It was after the war when Porter was prospering. Over cocktails, she had told Tom that she planned to have her local Pittsburgh dressmaker provide a black velvet skirt for the ensemble because the Madison Avenue shop was so expensive. He protested that the New York shop should do the whole thing, but then he asked how much the jacket had cost. "He was horrified at the price and asked if I could get out of it. 'No, because the brocade has probably been cut; and besides, I put down a deposit of half the cost.' He was one who did not believe in paying for anything until it was finished, and was incredulous that I had made a deposit. He gave up. 'Have them make the whole thing,' he said."[9]

As the Porter empire grew during the war years, the Evans family grew as well. In January 1942, Betty Evans gave birth to a second son, whom she named Edward Parker Evans, after her father, and whom she called Ned. Evans began to buy ever more luxurious homes in the elegant locations that were seasonally populated by people like the Parkers, and even the Mellons. In the next few years, he bought a thirty-five-acre farm in Lingonier, near the Mellons' pleasure outpost at Rolling Rock. He bought a retreat on exclusive Fisher's Island off the Connecticut coast. He rented an apartment suite at the Waldorf-Astoria in New York City. Betty insisted later she had never wanted all of those homes—she was content in the fourteen-room Sewickley home they had acquired at the end of the war, and preferred to spend her vacations with her little boys at the Parker family beach house in Malibu. But Evans was acquiring his homes as he acquired new companies, reaping the bargains that were still left from the Depression. The homes helped him build his business, he insisted. They were investments.

But once the various households were established, he complained endlessly about how expensive they were to operate, how inept Betty was as a homemaker. Groceries had to be brought by boat to Fisher's Island, after all. They were bound to cost more than her weekly orders from the Select Food Market in Sewickley. Her life, it seemed, had become a long, dull argument about what he termed her extravagance and what she felt was his stinginess. She could not forget the genteel penny-pinching she had experienced in the Rodman home as a young bride. Was that the only approach to living that her husband understood?

But whatever sorrows began to grow in Betty's life, Tom Evans remembered these years as a time when he learned, firsthand, how factories operate. His apprenticeship at Gulf had confined him to the executive suite. At Porter, he was learning a manufacturing business from the inside out. But the more he learned, the more he realized that Porter could not ride into the postwar future on the strength of its small-scale steam locomotives. It still needed to diversify. He had used about $600,000 in after-tax profits that Porter had generated in the first three years of the war to buy the Quimby operation and another small company that made steel castings. But neither acquisition seemed to have the postwar staying power that Evans wanted, and he soon sold them.[10]

In 1944, amid a wartime boom of astonishing vigor, his third son, Robert Sheldon Evans, was born. With Porter's pocketbook plump with profits, Tom Evans began to dream of expanding his corporate family too. The company he picked out was the Mount Vernon Car Manufacturing Company, which was on the block for $2.7 million. The company was owned by a family trust, and Evans heard that the heirs wanted out.[11] The company, with about $10 million in assets, was an important fixture of Mount Vernon, Illinois, a small town about 115 miles due east of St. Louis. Its primary business was the manufacture of railcars, a business valued at about $2.5 million. But besides that, there was an attractive subsidiary, J. P. Devine, which made processing equipment for chemical plants. Best of all, there was the corporate bank account, which contained $3.5 million in cash. The rail car business seemed sturdy enough, the processing equipment subsidiary would give Evans the diversification he was seeking, and the cash would more than cover the cost of buying the company. If he could someday sell off the railcar division for something close to its value, he would wind up with a profit of more than $3 million in cash and an attractive new business to add to Porter's portfolio. To him, the deal made perfect sense.

Indeed, it seems so sensible in hindsight that later observers could only wonder why few but Evans saw the beauty of it. Here was a company being offered for sale for less than the cash in its pocket! All a fellow had to do was borrow the purchase price, buy the company, and use the company's own cash to pay off the loan—it was like getting the company for free. Why wasn't everyone lining up to bid against him? The answer lies partly in the psychological baggage that American industry carried out of the Depression. Despite the almost unprecedented prosperity brought by government wartime contracts, many American business leaders believed that the nation would slide promptly back into a depression the moment the war was over. A gamble on the scale that Evans was prepared to take was simply unthinkable for most of them. The engine for the deal, after all, was debt. And going into debt to finance a speculative venture—well, wasn't that what the 1920s had been about? And didn't it end very badly?

When Evans looked around at the American business landscape in the last days of the war, he saw dozens of cash-rich companies, fattened by their lush wartime profits, whose stocks were trading for a small fraction of what the companies were actually worth. Most of his contemporaries, and virtually all of his elders, saw a very different scene. To them, the corporate landscape was littered with former casualties of the Depression that had been rescued by a temporary wartime windfall, one that might well have to sustain them through seven more lean years.

And what his conservative Pittsburgh neighbors saw when they looked at Thomas Mellon Evans in 1944 was a brash young man with an exotic and expensive wife and a growing family to support on the uncertain profits of a company that was barely four years out of bankruptcy. For him to incur a huge debt to acquire a company fully three times the size of his own—well, it seemed rash, hasty, and shamelessly ambitious. Their raised eyebrows did not worry Evans. His only worry was where to get the cash to do the deal. He could not rely on Will Mellon this time, he knew; the old man had helped him realize his dream of going into business for himself and was now largely retired. This time, it was up to Evans alone.

While he looked around for a way to finance his first major acquisition, Evans held off other possible bidders by using $30,000 from Porter's cash box to buy an option on the Mount Vernon company. Filled with restless energy and the certainty that he was right, he approached a number of the large rail-car manufacturing companies—the industry was dominated by a "Big Four," which included the Mellon-dominated Pullman Company[12]— with a revolutionary proposal. He wanted to sell them something he did not yet own, Mount Vernon's railcar division, and use the money they put up to actually buy the company, with the two transactions taking place more or less simultaneously. He raised more eyebrows around Pittsburgh, but could not raise the cash he needed. As the deadline on his purchase option neared, it began to look as if Porter's $30,000 had been washed down the rat hole of its young president's ambitions. Older, wiser business-men in Pittsburgh nodded knowingly over their coffee cups at the Duquesne Club. Tom Evans was a young man in a hurry, they agreed, and haste makes waste.

Evans didn't waste any more time in Pittsburgh. He went to New York and found a commercial lender who was willing to stake him to enough money to buy Mount Vernon, albeit at a very high interest rate. On the day the option was to expire, Evans traveled from Pittsburgh to Mount Vernon and presented his check for $2.7 million. The company, three times the size of his own, was now his. *Fortune* magazine later described what hap-pened next: "After the closing Evans held an organizational meeting [and] stated crisply that a young man in Mount Vernon's treasury department would become treasurer. An elderly Mount Vernon lawyer . . . said, 'That's quite a young man for that position. He's only thirty-eight.' The [lender's] representative said, 'Well, the guy who just bought Mount Vernon and gave him the job is exactly thirty-three.' "[13]

Two weeks after the deal closed, Evans and his old friend John Foster, now a labor relations executive, met for lunch in Washington, a frequent destination for businessmen involved in the war effort.

"Be sure to check *Time* magazine tomorrow," Evans said proudly. "It'll have my picture in it." In fact, some New York friends were gathering at Tom's apartment at the Waldorf the next evening to celebrate the event. Why didn't John detour through New York on his way home and join in the fun?

Foster couldn't make the party, but he grabbed the first copy of *Time* he saw the next day to check out his friend's first taste of national publicity, a short and extremely complimentary feature in the "Business and Finance" section of the formidable magazine's March 27, 1944, issue. Wrapping around a photograph that showed Evans's still elegant but now slightly puffy features, the story was called "Young Tom Evans." American rail-roads had been "on a buying spree," ordering 1,800 rail cars in just three days in mid-March, it noted. "But the big surprise," *Time* continued, "was that the bulk of the orders went not to the moss-backed mastodons which have dominated the field for a generation, but to a young outsider, the bustling Mount Vernon Car Manufacturing Company of Mount Vernon, Illinois. This was no surprise to Mount Vernon's new boss, Thomas Mellon Evans. Tom Evans, just turned thirty-three, slick-haired, aggressive, plunked himself into the president's chair a fortnight ago and calmly announced that he was out to carve himself a rich slice of the rail car business. . . . His $3 million order from the Southern Railway for 1,000 freight cars was proof he meant business." The acquisition was likely to push Porter's revenues to around $35 million, with profits of about $1 million, the article predicted. "But Tom Evans looks to the postwar world to provide the real windfall," it concluded. "He sees no reason why there should not be a market for a hundred thousand cars a year for at least five years. And with his sleeves already rolled for battle, he confidently predicted: 'Our share is 10 percent but we'll get more.' "

In 1945, as the war ended, Betty Evans became concerned about her infant son Robert Sheldon Evans, a frail infant prone to lung infections. He needed warmer, cleaner air than a Pittsburgh winter could provide. Tom and Betty decided she should take the baby and his older brothers, Tommy and Ned, to Sea Island, the classic golf resort on the southern coast of Georgia. A place was found and Betty began making friends among the other wealthy families escaping the northern winters. But Tom found himself working harder than ever.

The effect of the Mount Vernon transaction on Porter was dramatic. Overnight, the modest company had been transformed into a substantial conglomerate with access to the capital markets. Never again would Tom Evans have to scrape around the downtown byways of New York City to find the money he needed to do a deal. John Foster recalls meeting Tom Evans for lunch at the Harvard-Yale-Princeton Club in downtown Pittsburgh one day in 1945. Settling in across the table, Evans could not contain his delight as he asked, "Ever see a check for a million dollars?" Like a magician reaching into a top hat, Evans reached into his jacket's inner pocket and pulled out a check from a local brokerage firm that had handled the sale of some Porter preferred stock. And that was just the first installment. By selling more preferred shares, Porter was able to raise $2.5 million, and Evans planned to use the money to streamline the company. In 1946, perhaps sensing the sickness that was affecting the American railroads, he found a buyer for Mount Vernon's railcar manufacturing facilities, and tucked another $2.5 million into Porter's bank account. His gamble on the acquisition had paid off, but Porter was still not operating on all cylinders—even if Tom Evans was.

The problem was that Evans was a finance guy. A corporate balance sheet was more fascinating to him than a best-selling novel—or a touchy union problem on his factory floor. Tracking down the financing for a deal like the Mount Vernon purchase was far more fun than hunting pheasant in the golden fields of the Rolling Rock Club. He had found what he loved to do: find promising companies and buy them cheap. But he needed someone to run them, to trim away fat and produce a lean, profitable operation. In 1946, he approached Clarence R. Dobson, who was the chief industrial engineer at the Jones and Laughlin steel company in Pittsburgh, one of the giants in the industry.

It was a remarkably self-assured choice for such a young man. Dobson was considerably older than Evans, a thick-skinned, twenty-year veteran of a tough business. He knew everyone who mattered in the industrial aristocracy of Pittsburgh—indeed, he might have been one of those skeptics frowning over their coffee cups when Evans was struggling to finance the Mount Vernon purchase. Dobson "didn't particularly want to become Porter's vice president in charge of operations because of Evans' reputation in Pittsburgh," *Fortune* magazine later explained. "Evans was considered an opportunist, who also had sinned by making too much money too fast." Besides, Dobson didn't think Porter's seven manufacturing plants and odd assortment of businesses looked particularly promising, despite the cash in hand. "These factors made Dobson reluctant to leave the best job he'd ever had."[14]

But Evans courted him with all the charm he could muster—a considerable amount, for the shy young student had grown more self-confident with his early success. But he didn't rely only on his wit. He assembled a substantial salary and bonus package to tempt the senior executive, and he graciously agreed to be guided by Dobson in reorganizing the "hodgepodge of companies" that he had assembled.[15] Eventually, in October 1946, Dobson agreed, startling his colleagues at the Duquesne Club by becoming vice president of operations for H. K. Porter.

He had his work cut out for him. The nation was awkwardly converting to a peacetime economy in a political environment that was still deeply divided over the appropriate role of government. President Truman had outlined an ambitious plan to Congress in September 1945, one that reiterated the values of the New Deal that had been so hated in conservative business circles. He called for unemployment insurance, tax reform, an increase in the minimum wage, and federal aid to housing. He also asked Congress to extend for another year the wartime laws that gave Washington considerable control over business pricing and resource allocation decisions.[16] The abrupt cancellation of wartime defense contracts—"$15 billion in less than a month," by one account[17]—led to widespread layoffs in the industries that had prospered so richly during the war. Economists and government planners were worried that when 12 million military personnel were demobilized, unemployment would return to the appalling levels of the great Depression.

But there was no possibility of demobilizing more slowly, to allow the domestic economy to absorb the troops gradually, because the war-weary nation simply would not stand for it. Truman faced an enormous array of discontent. There were not enough homes or apartments for the new families that the former soldiers were forming. Consumers were tired of patching up their rusting cars and their winter coats, and were hungry for real butter and steak. But consumer goods were still scarce.

And the American labor movement, which had shrunk to irrelevancy in Pittsburgh and most other industrial areas in the 1920s, had been reborn. Union membership rolls had increased 150 percent during the 1930s, and the war had brought even greater gains. By 1945, there were nearly 15 million union members, representing more than a third of the nonfarm work force. With growing numbers came greater courage and greater militancy. Unions had led a record number of work stoppages in 1944. The postwar layoffs not only put union members out of work, they also reduced overtime work and produced smaller paychecks for those still on the job. By late 1945, unions everywhere were demanding wages that would compensate them for the loss in purchasing power they had experienced during the wartime inflation.

Pittsburgh, where Dobson was trying to wrestle H. K. Porter into shape, was especially hard hit. "A strike of 3,500 electric company workers in Pittsburgh threw an additional 100,000 out of work," one historian noted. "The city's trolleys came to a halt, the street lights went out, and office buildings shut down for fear of elevator failure."[18] Business leaders in industrial cities like Pittsburgh were outraged at the demands of "Big Labor," and dug in their heels, despite the richness of their wartime profits. As the President wrote his mother during that difficult fall, "The Congress are balking, labor has gone crazy and management isn't far from insane in selfishness."[19]

Part of this unrest, obviously, was simply an understandable desire to return to business as usual, to be rid of the patriotic drama of wartime and to pick up the pieces of a simple, family-centered life again. But other forces were at work, less obvious to the average American. The nation had entered the Depression as a land in which almost every medium-sized city still had its hometown industries, factories that were owned by local families, run by local managers, and served by local lawyers, bankers, and accountants. The factory payroll and purchases fueled the local economy, and the factory's distribution needs shaped the local highways and railroad spurs. The owners formed the civic elite, the managers and professionals formed the local middle class, and the factory workers and secretaries and janitors and security guards formed the community's working class. It was a world in which corporate power had a familiar face, one that could be seen smiling graciously at the local Symphony Hall or nodding proudly at the high school graduation ceremony. In larger cities like Pittsburgh, St. Louis, and Cleveland, the locally controlled industries were bigger, richer, and more numerous, of course. But the same pattern of familiar power and accessible ownership obtained. Industry was rooted in the community as firmly as the school system, and in the minds of most citizens, it had a similar stake in the community's welfare.

But in reality the boundaries of the hometown economy had been quietly dissolving for decades. The giant trusts assembled by the entrepreneurial titans of the late nineteenth century had made national industries of steel, sugar, copper, and a host of other primary materials. The Depression left many local industries weakened, and they lost markets to stronger and larger firms elsewhere. Workers migrated to larger cities, where a longer menu of industrial opportunities awaited them. Mobilization for the Second World War shoved those industries into overdrive, pulling even more workers into jobs far from home. The wealth the war generated among the owners of industry, like Tom Evans, allowed the more adventurous of them to look beyond the ridges of their home horizon.

Mount Vernon, Illinois, near a small lake in the gently dimpled landscape of southern Illinois, was a long way from Pittsburgh. But in a drama growing increasingly common, an ambitious outsider, Tom Evans, had reached into that community and grabbed a piece of the local economy to serve his own ends. Power—over the company's payrolls, its property, its purchasing, its people—was no longer wielded by some wealthy citizen with a stake in the local culture. It was in the hands of some ambitious young man in a big muscular city in the midst of the Allegheny Mountains, a man no one in Mount Vernon had ever met before, or even heard of. As suddenly as he had purchased the company in 1944, Evans sold off its core business in 1946. Another new face owned the heart of the small town's economy. The anxiety that this shifting pattern of ownership created was no more than a wisp on the air as the war ended. But it would grow.

And it was felt not only by factory workers but by Americans on many of the middle rungs of the social ladder. America's attitude toward the men who dominated its industrial landscape was in flux. Thirty years earlier the "trusts" that monopolized major industries had been attacked and vilified. The 1929 crash added Wall Street to the public's rogues gallery, and the layoffs and plant closings of the Depression further stained the public image of big business. World War II seemed at first to have changed all that. Jobs were plentiful and business and unions were joined in patriotic cooperation. Hostility toward the corporate world began to diminish.[20] Moreover, American industry was responding to the demands of the war with an almost super-human speed, generating a flush of patriotic pride in the country's "can do" industrial spirit. But the economic upheaval and labor unrest that followed the outbreak of peace put business back on the defensive. As major industries resisted the demands of labor, the workers' hostility toward big business grew. The rest of the nation felt trapped in some new combat zone. "These battles apparently forced many other Americans to worry about their own stakes in the conflict between big unions and big business," one author noted. "The result was a new phase of increased hostility toward the giant firm."[21]

Americans were grudgingly learning to live in a world of big business but they were clearly ambivalent about it. They wanted the comforts that industry could provide, but they were increasingly worried about the power that industry possessed. The New Deal had seemed a counter-weight to that power, but Roosevelt was gone and Truman was an enigma to most Americans. Big labor unions could hold their own against such power, but labor unrest was too much like wartime, with its dramatic rhetoric and its confrontation and its last-minute deadlines. Politically, there was a growing reaction to the liberalism of the Roosevelt years, and a conservative chorus began to dream openly of returning America to the kind of unfettered capitalism that the Mellons and other great business barons of the nineteenth and early twentieth century had enjoyed. Economically, with the relaxation of wartime economic controls, prices were rising and people were starting to worry about stretching the household budget a few extra inches each week. In business circles, theorists were looking for a more benevolent version of the past, something they called "welfare capitalism." Their utopia was a paternalistic world in which "industry itself . . . should protect the welfare of its employees to such an extent that social legislation, and perhaps unions, would lose their appeal."[22]

As these adjustments in attitudes took root in the growing American anxiety about Big Business, the corporate leader began to portray himself as a sort of statesman of the boardroom. Following in his wake were ambitious young corporate animals, who took a spot in one of the small offices of middle management, hoping to find a small slice of anonymous security. Fitting in, increasingly, was what mattered for both the leader and the led.

And Tom Evans simply could not fit in with this bureaucratic, nearly military vision of professional management. He could not curb his tongue, or find the diplomatic way to deliver bad news. He was in too much of a hurry to worry about his employees' feelings, and too busy building his acquisition war chest to worry about the frills that "welfare capitalism" required. Old-fashioned "shareholder capitalism" was his philosophy, and he clung to it with all the self-interested passion of a substantial shareholder.

His own shareholders were far less confident about Evans. As he and Clarence Dobson struggled to wrestle Porter into profitable shape in 1946, the company stock began to slide. The sale of the Mount Vernon railcar division brought in some cash but cut ongoing revenues. At the end of the year, the company got a bonanza order from the Consolidated Railways of Columbia: fifteen steam locomotives, with a price tag of more than $1 million.[23] But such orders were harder to come by. With Dobson cracking the whip, none of the ill-sorted divisions at Porter were actually losing money, but pretax profits were only about 2 percent of revenues. As Porter's stock price shrank from the mid-teens down to the low single digits, Evans realized that the company he was running fitted his basic formula for the kind of company he was always looking for in his handbook of corporate financial statements. It had promise and, of course, a very smart management team. But its shares were trading for less than the per-share value of the company. "Net Quick" Evans knew a bargain when he saw one, even if his own investors didn't. He decided to use some of the company's cash to buy Porter's own stock back from the public. The company erased the repurchased shares from its ledger, a step that had the happy effect of gradually increasing the ownership percentage of the remaining shareholders. Without buying a single share with his own money, Evans eventually increased his personal stake in the company substantially, to more than 77 percent.

He began to be noticed in Pittsburgh, which had been slow to acknowledge the applause that Henry Luce's publication had already given the young Evans. In late September 1946, he got a telephone call from a journalist at the *Pittsburgh Sun-Telegraph*. The paper had been running a series of profiles of the "new men" who were "taking their places behind the executive desks of the great companies" in town, and wanted to include him in the series. Evans quickly agreed. Shortly thereafter, he ushered the reporter into his office in the Oliver Building. The man was struck by the easy manner of this "stocky, easy-to-meet Pittsburgher" whom some people called a "financial genius." Evans, who had just marked his thirty-sixth birthday, wasn't stuffy like the older executives the reporter often met. As they talked, Evans often laughed and swung back in his swivel chair, propping his feet up on his desk. "And it's a desk of ordinary size of ordinary walnut," the reporter noted. "This man is without pretense himself and pretense amuses him."

The journalist was clearly fascinated by his youth. Although Evans was only thirty-six, he wrote, "already his business accomplishments have all the earmarks—and financial stability—usually associated with age and long experience." The thumbnail biography Evans provided to the reporter emphasized his parochial correctness: his Shady Side Academy education, his study at Yale, his connection with Gulf. But he also boasted of having speculated in the stock market "at a time when most men thought the stock market was poison." And he clearly relished his recent success in selling the Mount Vernon railcar operation at "a juicy profit." He was having fun, he told the reporter, and his zest for his life as chief executive could be read between every line, and could be seen on his face in the otherwise unflattering photograph the newspaper's photographer snapped in the office. His uneven hairline was creeping up his forehead, he had a faint five o'clock shadow, and well-fed jowls had replaced his once-square chin. But the searchlight eyes shone with pure joy.

Of course, as he discussed his travels to various Porter divisions around the country, he emphasized that his "real reward each day" was his home life with Mrs. Evans and the "three sturdy boys" who had just moved into a new spacious home in suburban Sewickley. In reality, Mrs. Evans and the three sturdy boys saw very little of him. To Betty Evans, it seemed that the beaming young man who had sat at her feet on the boat train from Paris just fifteen years ago had vanished entirely. There had always been small selfish quirks. Like refusing to give her directions around Pittsburgh when she was a new bride, and that frustrating two-year moratorium on having the children she so keenly wanted. Or his insistence on taking the lower berth when they traveled by train, leaving her to make the awkward climb into the upper one.

One of her most introspective short stories, "A Pregnant Experience," gave a sense of the early fault lines in their relationship. Set sometime between 1943 and 1945, it begins with a young couple making their way to a party at the home of friends one snowy evening. "Most of our close friends had arrived. Twelve for dinner tonight, David told us. I was the only pregnant lady." The liquor flowed through the dinner, and afterward some couples danced to Big Band music on the phonograph. As Tommy Dorsey and Artie Shaw filled the crowded rooms, the narrator grew tired, with that special weariness that growing a baby produces. At 11 P.M., she asked her husband if they could go home. "No, not yet. Must finish my drink— it's much too early." An hour later, she found him dancing with his hostess around the dining room table and asked again if they could go home. "He ended the dance by tossing Gretchen into the air and saying 'no' to me simultaneously, even managing to place a kiss on her as she landed. Getting my coat, I sneaked out the front door unnoticed to the car. The keys were in it, so I started the car and drove off. The drive seemed endless. I was mad and unhappy but kept going on the icy, dark, and lonely roads."[24]

But she arrived home without her house keys, and the doorbell did not rouse the nursemaid on the second floor. "Can you picture me standing in the cold, great with child, on the outside wanting in?"

Suddenly, she was startled by a tall man who had stopped nearby and was making strange, incomprehensible sounds. Her heart pounding, she froze until she suddenly realized that he had a speech impediment of some sort. With halting syllables, he explained that he was a night watchman from a nearby street. He had seen her predicament and was trying to help. He gathered pebbles from the yard and together they threw the small stones at the window of the nurse's room at the rear of house, finally awakening her. As the nurse opened the front door, the young wife thanked her rescuer, "who had no doubt saved me from freezing solid. He gave a lopsided smile saying, 'Glad a ca elp.' . . . My husband? You are clamoring to know? Someone brought him home in the dawn's early light. He didn't feel so good that morning."[25] Was there a moral to the tale? she had asked when she began the story. She did not provide one. But was it perhaps that the lowly, inarticulate watchman had shown more gallant regard for her safety and comfort than her smart, ambitious husband had?

CHAPTER FOUR

THE NEW MEN

H is purchase of the Mount Vernon railcar company and his other wartime mergers put Tom Evans on the cutting edge of a changing philosophy of American business that was emerging from the wreckage of the Depression and the crucible of war. It looks like a trend only in hindsight; at the time, Evans simply seemed to be another of the young postwar mavericks whose methods and appetites baffled and angered their elders.

They were oddballs, ambitious young misfits unwilling to climb the traditional corporate ladders, unwilling to settle into the safe, secure professional jobs that upper-class fathers desired for their offspring. There was an acquisitive gleam in their eye, an appetite for business combat that would have been far more familiar to old Judge Mellon and his sons than it was to the anxious Establishment survivors of the Depression and the global warfare that followed.

As the war ended, some of these hungry misfits had followed the trailblazer Robert Young into the nation's troubled railroad industry, which was hedged about with a tangle of government regulation and controlled by largely passive, conservative investors. Railroad stocks, the playground of the stock market buccaneers of the nineteenth century, had matured by the late 1920s into the sort of investment likely to be tucked into a widow's trust account, or an orphan's college fund. But the Crash and subsequent Depression masked the substantial damage that changing transportation patterns and business habits were doing to the nation's railroads. Convinced that the railroads would resume their central role in the industrial economy once the Depression lifted, some ambitious mavericks thought railroad stocks looked cheap in the late 1940s. In 1945, Robert Young began nibbling up shares of the New York Central Railroad, whose Manhattan terminus was housed in the elegant Grand Central Station. Serving the nation's financial capital, the New York Central was the queen of railroads and the station was her palace. Some old timers still called it "the Vanderbilt line."[1] The possibility that it would fall into the hands of the antiestablishment Young, the man who had made a name for himself vilifying the Morgan interests, made big news on Wall Street.

By 1947, Young's friend Patrick B. McGinnis, a railroad bond analyst turned Wall Street investor, was waging a fight for control of the Norfolk Southern Railway. McGinnis, a bluff Irishman, was the son of a former workman on the Vanderbilt line. The younger McGinnis had scrambled his way up to Wall Street from an unpromising series of small-town jobs and part-time scholarship studies. By 1931, more than half of the $12 billion in railroad bonds that he monitored were in default, and could be picked up for pennies. McGinnis made himself an expert on the hidden values and pitfalls of these suddenly speculative securities. During the 1930s, he was occasionally called to testify when the Interstate Commerce Commission held hearings on some bankrupt railroad. By 1938, his Wall Street firm had literally written the book on bankrupt railroads, collecting a mountain of financial data into a catalog to guide other speculators. As he became richer, he kept looking for the right opportunity to try his hand at a takeover. Sometime around 1946, he found the Norfolk Southern Railway, which consisted of "some 700 miles of tracks carrying sand and gravel, coal, and a miscellany of manufactured goods mostly through North Carolina."[2] As an expert witness, McGinnis had become friendly with the rich attorney who was the receiver for the bankrupt railroad. He and the receiver together acquired enough shares to give them control, but then the attorney died suddenly. McGinnis had to quickly find other investors to join him in the deal. Finally in 1947 McGinnis was elected chairman of the board, to the consternation of the railroad establishment, which considered McGinnis an opportunist on the same order as his close friend, Robert Young.

A few years later, Ben W. Heineman, a brilliantly talented lawyer in Chicago, was successfully representing dissident shareholders demanding a better dividend from the Chicago Great Western Railroad. Heineman had been raised in Wausau, Wisconsin, where his grandfather had started a successful lumber business in the mid-1800s. Heineman's father, prominent in state Republican circles, suffered substantial losses in the brutal stock market that followed the 1929 crash, and took his own life in 1930, the year his only son graduated from high school.[3] Young Ben, an extraordinary student despite being blind in one eye, went on to the University of Michigan and Northwestern University Law School, where he graduated near the top of his class. He joined a large Chicago law firm where he worked until America was drawn into the war. After distinguished service with the Office of Price Administration and the State Department, where he helped to draft the first lend-lease agreement with France, he returned to Chicago in 1944 and set up his own firm with a former colleague, specializing in corporation law.[4] His scholarly and yet practical grasp of the state laws that governed business made him a man to watch, a man who could be useful in a corporate battle. By the time he won the long-shot dividend case, a sense of siege was descending upon railroad boardrooms across the country.

But these railroad skirmishes were waged amid a thicket of red tape; indeed, many national lines were virtual wards of Uncle Sam, who had adopted them to keep the wartime machinery running. Easier hunting could be found beyond the rail yards in industries that would profit from the coming of peace. It was to this field that the most unsettling of the new financial mavericks gravitated.

If Tom Evans had returned to the Yale Bowl in New Haven to see his alma mater lose miserably to the University of Georgia Bulldogs in the fall of 1931, he might have noticed No. 26 on the Georgia team, a tall, darkly handsome sophomore named Louis E. Wolfson. The young man tackled his Ivy League opponent, Yale's fabled Albie Booth, with such ruthless energy that he injured his own left shoulder stopping the kickoff run that opened the second half.[5] Lou Wolfson had been born on January 28, 1912, the son of Morris Wolfson, an enterprising Russian Jew who had first settled in St. Louis and later moved his wife and eight children to Jacksonville, Florida, where he went into the salvage business—the "junk business," as some called it.[6] The elder Wolfson, though uneducated and nearly illiterate, was successful enough in the scrap business to send many of his sons to college. Lou Wolfson was an indifferent student at Georgia, and only the dream of becoming a professional football player sustained him through the tedium of class work. When his injured shoulder did not heal properly, he gave up on college and returned home in 1932.

Movie-star looks and somewhat humorless intensity aside, Wolfson had clearly inherited his father's entrepreneurial gift: soon after leaving school, he scraped together enough borrowed money to form a small construction supply company, the Florida Pipe and Supply Company, which he initially owned with his father and his older brother Sam.[7] The business, which his other brothers joined as partners, was prospering even before the outbreak of World War II brought plans for new airfields and other defense projects to central Florida.

Several of his brothers enlisted, but Wolfson was turned down for military service because of his shoulder injury and a bad kidney. "His civilian status embarrassed him greatly," one writer noted. "Sometimes, in a railroad station, he would see a forlorn-looking soldier saying good-bye to his wife. He would slip a hundred-dollar bill in an envelope and send a porter to give it to the startled couple."[8]

As Evans was struggling to restore the health of H. K. Porter, Wolfson and his brothers were getting rich from the family business, whose government contracts were bringing in more than $4.5 million in revenues a year. After the Allied victory in Europe, with peace on the horizon, Wolfson began shopping for potential war-surplus facilities that he could buy cheap, spruce up, and liquidate for a profit. He found his bargain in 1946 when the St. John's River Shipbuilding Company, a government-owned shipyard in Jacksonville, was on the block. The transaction revealed the intense, almost reckless energy that Wolfson brought to the game of business, which he played as passionately and aggressively as he had once played football. The Federal Maritime Commission, which conducted the St. John's River auction, initially required that any successful bidder would have to operate the yard, not merely dismantle it. But the first round of bidding was thrown out because the sale had not been properly advertised. Wolfson won the second round of bidding, with a last-minute bid that almost matched the commission's confidential appraisal of the yard. Then he promptly began dismantling the shipyard; somehow, the requirement for continued operation had been dropped in the second round of bidding, and Wolfson's rivals had failed to notice the change. The deal was extraordinarily profitable for Wolfson and his partners, passionately loyal admirers who came to be known as the Wolfson Group. But the circumstances of his success were so clouded with allegations of political arm-twisting and possible bribery that the deal became the subject of a congressional investigation in 1947 and a grand jury investigation in 1952. None of the vague allegations was ever brought home to Wolfson, but the episode contributed to the financial Establishment's growing mistrust of him and of all the hungry, aggressive young troublemakers like him who seemed to be grabbing so much, so fast.[9]

And Wolfson was just getting started. In 1947, with the wealth he extracted from his lucky shipyard venture, he began to diversify. He bought a chain of theaters serving black neighborhoods in that still-segregated era, and he quickly tripled his investment in Monogram Pictures, which had a big hit with *The Babe Ruth Story*. At a second Florida shipyard, in

Tampa, he built freighters for the French government and dredging ships for the Dutch, reaping additional millions in profits, and then liquidated that shipyard as well.[10] Then, in 1949, came the deals that honed his combat skills and intensified political rage over his business tactics: the takeover of Merritt-Chapman and Scott, a well-known construction and marine-salvage company in Manhattan, and the purchase of Capital Transit Company, the mass transit company serving Washington, D.C.

Capital Transit was put up for sale because the North American Company, a huge public-utility holding company, was required by the New Deal's Public Utilities Holding Company Act to divest itself of its 45 percent stake in the transit company. Thanks to a surplus stored up over the years, the transit company had more than $5 million in cash in its coffers— but at then-current stock prices, control of the company could be had for less than $2 million. Capital Transit was a substantial company, worth nearly $30 million and operating nearly 1,000 buses and 500 streetcars in the nation's capital. The company's board of directors "was composed of some of the most prominent Washington business and financial leaders. The management of the company was vested in the hands of an outstanding group of career transit officials . . . It became one of the outstanding transit companies in the United States and was a source of considerable pride in the community."[11]

But in the new world of the postwar economy, Capital Transit was a sitting duck. It was a public utility, and in the view of the stock market, public utility stocks were low-risk investments that were supposed to pay substantial, regular dividends—that was the investor's compensation for giving up the high-powered growth and rising stock prices that less-regulated industries offered. Capital Transit, however, paid a fairly stingy dividend, which "tended to depress the market value of its stock to an abnormally low level."[12] At the same time, the company was building up a substantial cash reserve, a practice that "was undoubtedly a wise one in view of the fact that nationally mass transit was and is a declining industry faced with serious economic and competitive problems."[13] But however wise management may have been about mass transit, it was extremely naive about the changes that were sweeping the marketplace with the advent of men like Robert Young, Tom Evans, and Lou Wolfson. The policy of paying small, stock-depressing dividends while building up cash in the company coffers was guaranteed to put Capital Transit on the radar screen of any enterprising financier looking for cash-rich companies whose stock could be purchased for less than the money in the company's bank accounts.

In management's defense, there were not many such bargain-hunters around, even by 1949. There certainly were none on the Capital Transit board, which had only briefly explored the possibility of using some of the company's own cash to purchase North American's shares of Capital's stock, which could then be canceled. Even after their lawyers assured them that the purchase would be legal, the prominent directors did nothing. Nor did anyone step forward from the Washington financial community to pluck this ripe plum from the tree. Indeed, a congressional subcommittee later tackled the question of "why some local financial group did not purchase the Capital Transit Company stock owned by North American." It concluded that the explanation lay in "the conservatism of the local financial community, a belief that the company was not an attractive long-range investment, and, perhaps, sheer lethargy."[14]

One exception to that assessment was Grady Gore, a local real estate broker who already owned some Capital Transit stock. But Gore was in the frustrating position of being able to see an opportunity that he didn't have the money to grasp. He had been among those urging the board to consider the stock-repurchase plan. When that failed, he tried to purchase some of the stock held by North American himself. But the holding company insisted on selling the stock in a single block, which no doubt made the block more attractive to someone interested in taking control of the company but which also put it beyond Gore's means.

In the early spring of 1949, Gore stumbled across just the sort of risk-taking person he had been looking for. One of the guests at a dinner party at his Washington home was Walter C. Troutman, a former football captain at the University of Georgia and a friend of Lou Wolfson. Gore casually complained to Troutman about the stubborn refusal of the capital's leading businessmen to see the opportunity that sat on their doorstep.[15] Troutman promptly telephoned Wolfson in Jacksonville, who sent an aide north on the next train. The situation was as Gore had described it, and Wolfson and his brothers and associates soon offered $20 a share, or just over $2 million, to acquire North American's interest in Capital Transit.[16] Other purchases made quietly in the open market gave the Wolfson group a 51 percent controlling stake by early June 1949.

With any other company, that would have been that. But Capital Transit was a congressionally chartered public utility owned by a regulated holding company. North American could not sell it without the permission of the Securities and Exchange Commission, and Wolfson could not buy it without the permission of the Interstate Commerce Commission. Both agencies held hearings on the transaction in the summer of 1949. And both hearings produced fierce opposition to Wolfson. At the SEC hearing on June 28, the protests came from other shareholders, led by two prominent local business leaders. Shocked out of their "lethargy," they urged the commission to give them time to organize a local group to purchase the company. They simultaneously pleaded with the company board to reconsider the rejected idea of purchasing and canceling the stock. But the minority shareholders missed their best opportunity to block Wolfson by failing to fight him at the hearings held before an Interstate Commerce Commission examiner, Vernon Baker, on July 22, 1949. Baker was clearly already skeptical of the Wolfson group, which had claimed in its ICC application that the members of the group were all "individuals" who would vote their shares independently.[17] Baker found that a trifle unlikely, given what he knew about Wolfson's loyal associates.

On August 11, Baker submitted a draft report to the ICC strongly urging that Wolfson's bid be rejected. Wolfson and his associates were not local residents, as Capital Transit's congressional charter envisioned, Baker noted. Moreover, the Wolfson group had no experience in the public transportation business and had "failed to establish that the proposed transaction would be consistent with the public interest."[18] The record before Baker included the full story of Wolfson's acquisition and subsequent liquidation of the St. John's River and Tampa shipyards, the embarrassing congressional investigation of the St. John's River transaction, and the unproductive federal grand jury examination of that deal. "These matters should have raised such questions about the suitability of the Wolfson group as purchaser of controlling interest in the Capital Transit Company as at least to have made it incumbent on the ICC to have investigated such suitability further," a congressional panel later determined.[19]

But Wolfson's lawyers filed an opposing report, and Baker's recommendations were ultimately rejected by the ICC, which noted that there had been no public opposition at the hearing before Baker. The SEC had already given its approval. With the ICC's action on September 2, the Wolfson group finally took control of Capital Transit. Later that year, the board of directors voted to tap the hoarded surplus by quadrupling the bus company's dividend to its shareholders, the first in a series of annual dividend enrichments.

Grady Gore was well compensated for his efforts, making roughly $75,000 on the deal.[20] The veteran senior managers and the conservative directors at Capital Transit did not fare so well, despite assurances to the contrary that regulators had received from the Wolfson group. Doran S. Weinstein, a balding and bespectacled young man in his early thirties who had worked for Wolfson since 1940, had testified before the ICC that the group did not plan to actively participate in the management of the transit company. "Our only interest in that respect is to protect our investment," Weinstein said. The same message was delivered to the SEC by J. A. B. Broadwater, a hawk-faced former Tampa Shipbuilding executive in his early fifties whom Wolfson had retained when he liquidated the shipyard. "We have no plans at all about disrupting the present management," Broadwater testified. "We consider it would be very unwise."[21] Nevertheless, within twenty months of taking control, Wolfson had replaced almost all of senior management with his own men. Situations change, he shrugged when questioned about the moves. Broadwater became president, and Weinstein became assistant to the president and secretary. The board of directors similarly reflected Wolfson's control; only two members were longtime Washington residents.

These steps raised eyebrows in Washington, and official Washington nursed a simmering hostility toward Wolfson that lasted for years. But in Wolfson's view, a company's riches belonged, first and foremost, to its shareholders. "I'll protect the stockholders within the limits of the law in spite of everything—including Congress," he later told the *Washington Star.*[22]

Controversial as it was, Wolfson's acquisition of Capital Transit was a straightforward stock purchase. Such deals had been routine for decades, and only Wolfson's previous record and his subsequent distribution of the company's cash to its shareholders made the transaction noteworthy. His takeover of Merritt-Chapman and Scott was different—it was a proxy fight, one of the earliest of the postwar period. By waging it the same year he was attracting so much unflattering attention in Washington, Wolfson seems to have done the public image of the proxy-fighter little good. The angry accusation that he was "milking" Capital Transit inevitably suggested that this was his universal business strategy, although like Tom Evans he was principally trying to build an empire, not liquidate one.

Merritt-Chapman, an engineering and construction company based in Manhattan, was listed on the New York Stock Exchange and was considered a blue-chip investment. But to some of its aggressive young stockholders, its management seemed stodgy and internally divided. The dissidents were led by three executives of Hirsch and Company, a New York brokerage firm whose customers owned a considerable number of Merritt-Chapman shares.[23] As their plans took shape, representatives of the shareholder group called on Senator Claude Pepper of Florida. By one account, they asked him to suggest someone from the South who might be willing to serve on their slate of candidates for the board of directors.[24] Another story held that they hoped the senator could suggest "some young and vigorous man they could put in as president."[25] A third version reported that the dissidents were looking for someone with money who would join their fight.[26]

By all accounts, the senator responded promptly by pointing to a photograph of the handsome young Lou Wolfson hanging on his office wall, and saying, "Him."

In the most complete account available from the time, Wolfson recalled that the Hirsch group asked him to be president of Merritt-Chapman if they were successful, and he declined because he preferred to be his own boss. "The offer set him thinking, though, and back home he sat up all one night, studying [the company's] financial statements. Soon it was clear to him that the company did offer tremendous possibilities, once the factional strife was ended. The next morning he and his brothers started buying Merritt-Chapman stock."[27] They accumulated more than 35 percent of the outstanding shares, and joined with the Hirsch group to fight for control of the company. It was Wolfson's first proxy fight, and he afterward insisted that he got into it only because the Hirsch group had assured him that such a fight could be avoided. And it was a difficult scuffle, with the SEC entering the fray as a "friend of the court" to question some of the tactics involved on both sides. In any case, when the dust settled, the insurgents held thirteen of the twenty-one seats on the company's board of directors. Once again, dividends were substantially increased. But by 1951, Wolfson had grown frustrated with the lack of progress at the company, and staged his own boardroom coup. "There seemed to be no leadership. I injected myself more and more, and came out as chief executive," he recalled later. "Merritt was ripe for someone to come out as a leader."[28] He was determined that the company's stockholders would profit—indeed, he vowed that if the company ever had to suspend its dividends, he would not collect his annual salary either.

Those were exactly the priorities that maverick investor Charlie Green insisted on. Like Wolfson, he was the son of hardworking Jewish immigrants. Green was born in February 1908, just a year after his Polish-born parents had immigrated to New York City from their adopted home in Russia. His father was a tailor, and Charles's childhood was short and scrappy. He was one of seven children, living in a working-class neighborhood near New York's old Madison Square Garden, at Madison Avenue and Twentysixth Street. As a child, he peddled newspapers and ran errands for a ribbon factory to bring in extra money for the large family. He attended city schools, and at age ten, found a safe haven by helping to organize the Madison Square Boys Club. Somewhere along the way, he discovered the magic of the stock market, and by the time he was twenty-one, "he had saved up enough to lose over $10,000 in the 1929 crash," according to one report.[29] He worked as a coffee salesman, and then sold furnaces and heating supplies while studying business administration at night. Eventually he got a job as a salesman for the Gillette Safety Razor Company, based in Boston. Stocky, loud, and fun-loving, with a wide smile and elfin ears, Green was a success in sales—but he chafed at working for other people, and he was anything but smooth. As one writer who knew him observed, "Green was typical of scrappers of his class: rugged, pugnacious, resourceful, willing to charge in with fists flying, and virtually impossible to KO. He moved too fast."[30]

In 1934, when he was just twenty-six, he set out on his own. He formed the Green Sales Company in New York City, which initially specialized in razor blades, and then expanded into "drugs, sundries and electric appliances."[31] He found a profitable niche, wholesaling goods to military post exchanges, the subsidized "general stores" that served the residents of military bases.[32] In 1938, his former employer, Gillette, went to court to try to block him from selling razor blades at discount prices. Green fought back and won, although his business gradually began to focus more on appliances.[33] Peacetime brought with it a desperate consumer hunger for his products. Green prospered, and put every spare penny into the recovering stock market.

He had little formal training in financial analysis, beyond the practical education of running his own business, but he had an instinct for balance sheets. "Breed the talents of the hard sell to intuitive financial skill, and you have a formidable offspring. This was Charlie Green, a new breed," one writer of that day observed.[34] And he took his investments seriously, viewing his role with a breathtaking simplicity that challenged the emerging postwar dominance of professional corporate managers and the traditional passivity of pension funds, trust officers, and mutual funds. "I look at it this way: I own stock, I'm a partner," he once explained. "If I'm a partner, I've got the right to have a say in how they run the company, haven't I? If I'm a partner, I like to have my other partners listen to what I've got to say about how the company's run. If owning stock doesn't make me a partner, then all that stuff they hand out about how if you own shares you're a partner in American business is a lot of baloney."[35]

By 1948, at the age of forty-one, Green had become a substantial stockholder in the Twin City Rapid Transit Company, a $40 million holding company which provided bus and streetcar service to Minneapolis and St. Paul.[36] The sixty-year-old company was slow and stodgy. It was overseen by a board heavy with civic luminaries who owned little if any stock and who treated their board duties as "their hobby—as toy electric railroads are for other men," one bitter writer noted.[37] The cash surplus that the system reaped during the war, when gas rationing pulled many commuters out of their cars and onto the streetcars and buses, had been used to reduce the company's debt. Only one dollar in dividends had been paid in twenty years, during which the company's stock had fallen from more than $100 a share to barely $10. Charlie Green, that Twin City "partner" back in New York, grew irritable. He traveled to Minneapolis to meet with "his" company's president, D. J. Strouse, but the meeting ended in a shouting match. Strouse was not interested in Green's views on how the streetcar system should be run. Green returned to New York and, with the help of a Detroit attorney named Bingham D. Eblen, he waged his first proxy fight, aimed at the annual shareholders meeting in March 1949. Green and Eblen drafted James A. Gibb, one of Eblen's law clients and a man with some transportation industry experience, to join their campaign for three of the nine seats on the board of directors. It was an ugly campaign, with Green falsely accusing Strouse of some unspecified misbehavior involving the company's purchasing program, and Strouse unfairly denouncing Green as an unqualified opportunist. Green's team did not win but it attracted enough support that Strouse held out an olive branch: when two company directors resigned two months later, in early summer 1949, Eblen and Gibb were offered seats on the board.[38]

The transit company's finances continued to deteriorate, however, and Green and Eblen continued to campaign for additional support among shareholders, demanding a change in management and greater representation on the board.[39] Green found that, under Minnesota law, he already owned enough stock to force a special meeting of company stockholders, and a meeting was called for mid-December. What happened in advance of that meeting was to embroil Green in controversy for years—and add considerably to the Establishment's distaste for the concept of "proxy fighting."

Green testified at subsequent investigations of his tenure at Twin City Rapid Transit that his search for shareholder support led him to a stockbroker who, in turn, introduced him to a fellow shareholder, Isadore Blumenthal, a Minneapolis nightclub owner. Unfortunately, Blumenthal was also known as Kid Cann, under which alias he had an extensive record of arrests, including one for allegedly murdering a crusading newspaper editor in 1935. He was never found guilty, except for a few convictions for liquor violations during Prohibition. But his subsequent rise from ex-bootlegger to the millionaire owner of the Club Carnival nightclub had been characterized by remarkably polite treatment from Minneapolis law-enforcement officials, who did not stand particularly tall in the ranks of vigorous urban crime-fighters in that day. A top police detective once accused the local press of "persecuting" the enterprising businessman, who the detective said "runs a very clean place now." One local editor pointed out that Blumenthal's past convictions for liquor violations made it illegal for him to run any sort of establishment that had a liquor license, however cleanly he did so. The detective promptly claimed he had been misquoted. Suffice it to say, Green may have been the only man in Minneapolis who did not realize that his new ally in the Twin City fight was a man likely to be described by newspaper reporters as "a gangster" and "a notorious rackets boss." He naively took Blumenthal's advice and hired a well-connected Minneapolis lawyer named Fred A. Ossanna to assist in his proxy fight.[40]

By November 1949, he had gathered so much support from large stockholders that Strouse and his backers on the Twin City board gave up the fight and resigned. Green became president of the company, and his ally Bingham Eblen became chairman of the board. Jim Gibb was put in charge of operations, and the locally powerful Fred Ossanna—who came highly recommended by Isadore "Kid Cann" Blumenthal—was installed as general counsel. "His annual retainer was $24,000, with the further stipulation that he would be paid $300 a day for any time actually spent on company business."[41]

Ready to take charge, Green sold his new home in New York's Westchester suburbs. His wife and three small children settled into a home in Florida, while Green prepared to brave the Minnesota winter in a redecorated apartment in the Calvin Beach Hotel in Minneapolis.[42] But his support in the Twin Cities quickly eroded as the local press condemned Green's "gangster" allies and his clumsy cost-cutting in pursuit of a dividend-generating profit. "Green seemed determined to show the Minnesotans how a big-time operator from New York did things, for he at once began throwing his weight around . . . with a lack of diplomacy that, as later brought out in testimony, astounded even his own associates," one magazine complained.[43] Trying to put the transit line on a profitable footing for its shareholders, Green demanded a fare increase, cut employment by nearly 25 percent, and eliminated or reduced some unprofitable routes—arguably necessary steps, given the fiscal distress the company was experiencing, but steps which made him extremely unpopular in Minneapolis and St. Paul. State transportation officials went to court to block him from further reductions in service.[44] By that point, the new management of Twin City had "split into two camps; one headed by Green himself, the other by none other than Ossanna, who knew the local ground rules better than Green could have imagined."[45]

The boardroom bickering generated another proxy fight between the two factions, which was to climax at a shareholder meeting scheduled for December 1950. The battle was exceptionally muddy, and some of the mud stuck. In November 1950, Green testified before the Minnesota Rail-road and Warehouse Commission, accusing Ossanna of proposing that the company raise a $20,000 slush fund to bribe city officials in Minneapolis. An investigator for the powerful United States Senate crime investigating committee—the famous "rackets committee"—sat in on the hearings, but insisted that his interest was purely informational.[46] Green also told a local grand jury that Ossanna had proposed that the company build the slush fund with kickbacks from a local fuel supplier who sold fuel to the company at inflated prices. Ossanna was indicted just two weeks before the shareholder meeting, although the indictment was later dropped. Ossanna retaliated with a blistering recital of how Charlie Green abused his company expense account. Green had charged the company $10,517.20 for his move from New York to Minneapolis and for "fitting, decorating and furnishing" his hotel apartment—including bills for wallpaper ($603.50) and new carpets and drapes ($597.47).[47]

When the shareholder meeting convened on December 18, 1950, it opened with an incident that became part of the early 1950s folklore about proxy fights. As Charlie Green entered the boardroom at Twin City, four off-duty detectives of the Minneapolis police force, hired by Ossanna, stopped him and ordered him to hand over a nickel-plated pistol that he was carrying. Green had a license for the gun and was carrying it legally in self-defense. But he was disarmed, nevertheless, and the incident was widely and gleefully reported by his adversaries. Green then got an injunction delaying the meeting until February 26, 1951. But his maneuvering simply postponed the inevitable and he lost to the local powerhouse. He sold his stock—allegedly to people fronting for local crime bosses, *Collier's* magazine later charged—and he left Twin City Rapid Transit to Fred Ossanna's management. He had no idea who the actual buyers of his shares were, and probably didn't care; he made a nice $100,000 profit on his $300,000 investment, and he had escaped Minneapolis in good health.[48] It was an invaluable education for this scrappy proxy fighter, but it came at the price of headlines that would deepen the public's mistrust of those who fought for shareholder control of America's companies.

By early 1951, as Green was being shoved out of Twin Cities, he was already doing the groundwork for his next proxy fight, a battle for control of United Cigar–Whelan Stores Corporation, a national chain of 1,300 drugstores and cigar shops based in New York City. While he had been out of his element in the midwestern mass-transit business, Green had been both a stockholder and a wholesale supplier to the New York chain for many years and "he knew the cigar-store and soda-fountain business inside and out."[49] In June 1951, just a month after the company's annual shareholder meeting, he mailed a letter to United Cigar stockholders urging them to support his call for a special meeting to elect a new board of directors for the company. Disclosing that he controlled more than 57,000 shares of the company's common stock, Green gave a withering account of management's performance. Beginning in 1946, "profits have dropped in every single year and receded below the 1942 level in 1950," he wrote.[50] But during that same period, top executives and directors had received more than $1.6 million in salaries and bonuses, "while common shareholders have received no dividends." If there was enough spare cash in the company strong-box to finance an expensive private airplane for the executives, he continued relentlessly, why wasn't there enough to pay dividends?

Walter B. Baumhogger, president of United Cigar–Whelan Stores, had known for some time that Charlie Green had been preparing for a fight. Baumhogger tried to defeat Green by revising the company bylaws to raise the percentage of shareholder support required to call a special meeting. And he dredged up all the recent unpleasantness from Minneapolis, including the charges of expense-account abuse and the public outrage and internal strife. But despite Baumhogger's efforts, Green soon gathered enough support to require the company to convene a special meeting in September of 1951.

In a letter to shareholders announcing that meeting, Baumhogger tried to appeal to their sense of fairness. When his management team had taken over in 1938, he wrote, the common stock had no book value and the company was carrying a capital deficit of $1 million. At the end of 1950, he continued, the company had a book value of nearly $12 million. And the tide was clearly turning, he argued. "For the nine months ended March 31, 1951, our earnings, after taxes, were approximately 94 percent greater than those for the nine months ended March 31, 1950."[51] It was a record to be proud of, although of course management was determined not to rest on its past achievements. Only in talking about his adversary did Baumhogger lose his cool, statesmanlike grip. He continued to offer additional details of the Twin City proxy fights, and called Green a "proxyteer," one of the first uses of what would soon become a common epithet. He suggested that some of Green's candidates for the board—a real estate developer, a coffee merchant, a leather goods supplier—were all simply interested in enriching themselves by doing increased business with United Cigar–Whelan Stores.[52] "Mr. Charles Green comes along," Baumhogger wrote to shareholders, "and tells you stockholders in effect that he, his family and his friends have been buying stock in this company. Therefore, because of that, and the other charges he has made, he asks you to help him throw us out and give him control of the company. Of course, Mr. Green has never had any chain store operation experience in his entire life—but that has nothing to do with it." It wasn't particularly articulate, but it caught management's mood.

As interesting as what management said about Green was what it did not say. On the eve of the shareholder meeting, a scathing *Collier's* magazine article about the Twin City Rapid Transit proxy fights hit the stands, under the sizzling headline "How Mobsters Grabbed a City's Transit Line." An accompanying illustration showed a giant tarantula with its barbed legs clutching a collection of city street cars and buses. "The article was so unflattering to Green that the Baumhogger management deemed it worthy of circulation among the stockholders," one chronicle later reported. The Securities and Exchange Commission, however, "declined to permit the management to include the article in its proxy material, so dubious were the statements in the story."[53] Indeed, Green would later sue *Collier's* for libel and win an out-of-court settlement reportedly worth $20,000. As part of that settlement, the magazine published a "corrective statement" in January 1954, expressing its regret over its portrayal of Green as a fast-buck operator and describing him instead as "a substantial stockholder of long-standing" who "enjoyed a good reputation in his business and home communities." The magazine also insisted that it had not intended to imply "that Green, who had substantial interests in many large corporations, was either a gangster or linked up with gangsters, or that he at any time illegally carried weapons. The facts are to the contrary."[54] But that retraction would come years too late to help Green in his battle with Baumhogger.

On September 25, some three hundred shareholders of United Cigar streamed into the Art Deco auditorium of Manhattan's elegant Chanin Building, on East Forty-second Street near Grand Central Station. Baumhogger, whom the board had elected as chairman specifically so he could preside over the crucial session, defended management's record. He stressed that the company had built up an ample supply of cash and had expanded its inventory before prices had been pushed up by postwar inflation. "If the chain drug business continues as at present," he predicted, the company would prosper.[55]

Green took the floor. He was fed up after "thirteen years of getting promises" instead of dividends, he said. Some stockholders loyal to management rose to argue with him, only to meet arguments in turn from those who supported him.[56] As tempers escalated, Green accused an outraged Baumhogger of lying about the company's financial situation. The stormy meeting dragged on for more than two hours, broke for lunch, and reconvened for another two tempestuous hours in the afternoon. Green told the audience that his group had mustered more than a million shares to vote against the present management. But there were 2.3 million shares outstanding, and at a special meeting, management could be removed only with the approval of a majority of all outstanding stock—or a minimum of 1.15 million shares. Late in the afternoon, Baumhogger finally announced that the media-mobbed session would be adjourned to permit the proxies to be counted.

The meeting did not reconvene until October 8. By that point, Baumhogger and his management team knew that Green had won 1,010,711 of the 1.6 million votes cast at the meeting, while the management slate had received less than 600,000 votes. Under the bylaws, Green's tally was not enough to win the fight at a special meeting but it would be enough at a regular shareholder meeting, scheduled for the following spring. That was enough to frighten management into a compromise with Green— it was those negotiations that had delayed the resumption of the meeting. When seventy-five shareholders finally reassembled at the Barbizon-Plaza Hotel, Baumhogger had passed the gavel to B. A. Tompkins, a senior vice president of the Bankers Trust Company and a member of the board's executive committee. With neither Baumhogger nor Green in the room, Tompkins told the audience that the company's management recognized that a substantial number of stockholders wanted a change. Indeed, Tompkins conceded that if shareholders at the next annual meeting in May gave Green the same degree of support he had gotten at the special meeting, he would win his battle. "Under all the circumstances, the directors feel that appropriate recognition should be given the stock represented by Mr. Green and his associates," Tompkins said. "Consequently, discussions have been held looking toward the reconstitution of the Board of Directors so as to give Mr. Green and his associates substantial representation."

One of Green's loyalists got the last word. Leo Burtisch, Green's candidate for president of the company, read a statement from Green indicating that his group was ready to cooperate. However, he added, Green expected not just "substantial representation" but a clear majority of the seats on the board. A week later, the company announced that 7 of its 12 directors had resigned to permit the election of Green and 6 of his allies. Baumhogger and Tompkins remained on the board, and Tompkins was named chairman, although no one expected him to hold the position for long. Leo Burtisch was selected as executive vice president and general manager. And Charlie Green was named chairman of the executive committee. The changes were reported in a tiny story in the *New York Times* on October 17, 1951. But that represented an enormous victory for the scrappy former Gillette razor salesman. He had waged a proxy fight that was played out on

Wall Street's doorstep, in the heart of New York City, involving a company that was a familiar presence in communities all across the country. And despite all the mud-slinging and raucous taunts about "proxyteers," he had won.

In 1948, another swashbuckler of the boardroom arrived on the scene. Leopold D. Silberstein, short and broad-shouldered with a marked resemblance to Lou Costello of the famous Abbott and Costello comedy team, was a well-to-do Jewish refugee from Nazi Germany. Born in Berlin in 1904, Silberstein enjoyed a childhood of middle-class comfort. His father had a modest import-export business, but young Silberstein set his sights on a financial career. He majored in economics at Berlin University, graduating in 1924. According to one account, he started out working for the Berlin Stock Exchange.[57] At some point, he was hired as a bookkeeper for the Berlin firm of V. Goldschmidt, Rothschild and Company, whose partners had once included a member of the famous banking family. In 1930, he joined Bechol and Company, another Berlin investment bank. Despite the Depression-era convulsions in the German banking system, he built a modest fortune.

But no amount of money could protect Silberstein and his family from the perils of Hitler. Seeing the threat as clearly as if it were printed on the stock ticker, he moved his wife and two children to Amsterdam in the summer of 1933, after pleading in vain for his parents to join him there.[58] In his new home, he found financial work at Louis Korijn and Company, a Dutch investment house specializing in European and American securities and American commodities. He was clearly a man of some substance. In September 1934, he and G. L. Korijn, a partner in the Dutch firm, sailed to the United States on the Holland-America line's popular *Statendam* and were interviewed by one of the journalists who routinely sought out newsworthy figures arriving on the luxury liners from Europe. His comments, made in excellent but heavily accented English, captured both his eloquence and his deft humor: "For more than two years," he said, "I have followed with interest the energetic efforts of your government to help this country through the most terrible crisis the world has ever seen. Although we Europeans do not always understand the measures adopted by your government, we all hope that the methods will succeed and bring a new air of prosperity to the United States, for the benefit of the whole world."[59]

Seven years later, in May 1940, Silberstein's safe haven in Amsterdam was invaded by German troops. Two days after the Germans marched in, he loaded his family and whatever cash he could raise quickly into a small boat and steered for England. British authorities, wary of spies among the waves of refugees seeking asylum, allowed his wife and two children to stay, but ordered Silberstein himself to be interned elsewhere in the Common-wealth. He was shipped to Australia, where authorities offered to release him if he enlisted in a British construction battalion. He declined, and began an amazing odyssey along the fringes of world war. Citing his service in the Dutch militia, he was able to travel on Dutch papers to Shanghai in early 1941, where the international enclave remained open although the native city was already in Japanese hands. He operated profitably there, investing in local real estate with cash that he had wisely placed in banks in neutral Portugal while he was working in Holland. Tapping those sequestered funds required the help of the local Portuguese consul, who supposedly helped Silberstein get the money in exchange for a share of the profits, according to one fairly hostile account. The friendly consul also arranged citizenship for Silberstein and gave him a consulate job, which conferred precious diplomatic immunity on him in those perilous days. When the Japanese abruptly invaded the international settlement on the day after Pearl Harbor, Silberstein was named to the Neutral Portuguese Commission that arranged prisoner exchanges.[60]

In 1943, when his protective consul was called home to explain the lib-erality with which he dispensed Portuguese passports, Silberstein was also able to leave Shanghai. He parted from his patron at the Portuguese colony of Goa, south of Bombay on the western coast of India, where he finally got permission from British authorities to return to London after he shared his knowledge about the Shanghai situation with their military intelligence officers. Back in Britain at last, he was reunited with his wife, Tilly, and his two children, Elizabeth and Charles.[61] He invested in a British leather processor, on whose board he served, but he was determined to leave Europe behind the moment peace made that possible.

On September 30, 1948, after fifteen years of flight and fear, Leopold Silberstein and his family arrived in America. Compared to other wartime refugees, of course, he was extremely lucky. He had investment skill, a sub-stantial nest egg, a command of the language, and a number of contacts on Wall Street that dated from his Amsterdam years. He formed a brokerage house, Uno Equities, which did a good but unpretentious business in small, over-the-counter securities and in what were starting to be called "special situations." These were opportunities to invest in companies that had fallen on hard times. Their shares could be had for very little money, and powerful shareholders could reasonably hope to improve the situation enough to make a profit. Robert R. Young had built his Wall Street fortune by speculating in just such situations, and Evans had followed the same route in taking over H. K. Porter.

In 1950, Silberstein saw a situation that looked particularly special: a struggling mining company called Pennsylvania Coal and Coke Corporation. One business writer called it "the sickest of companies in an industry crying for help." Once a major producer of soft coal, with operations centered on the region between Altoona and Pittsburgh, it had a formidable history and a distinguished board of directors. But by 1950, it had only about $4 million in assets and was losing more than $100,000 a year on sales of less than $6 million. Silberstein and some of his loyal clients began buying the company's stock. There were 148,000 shares outstanding, and by the spring of 1951, he and his friends had quietly accumulated 75,000 of them. Their controlling stake had cost about $750,000.

When the company's unsuspecting management convened the annual shareholders meeting on April 3, 1951, Silberstein and his backers were in the audience. Silberstein, dressed with a European elegance, rose to propose a slate of directors to replace the existing board and to explain in his accented English that his group had just enough votes to elect it. "The coup came as a complete surprise to most of the officers," one journalist noted. "A new board of directors was elected, most of them Silberstein men, and as one of the former directors put it: 'When Silberstein went in, we went out.' "[62] It was one of the first "surprise raids" of the postwar proxy skirmishes and it added a new nightmare to the troubled sleep of top corporate managers who heard about it. Who was secretly buying up their shares? To what purpose? So long as those purchases were made in "street name"—that is, in nominee accounts legally maintained by the brokers handling the transactions for their customers—it was impossible to know whether a company's shares were in friendly or hostile hands. The managerial establishment's hostility toward corporate raiders ratcheted up another notch.

Silberstein took a hands-on interest in his new business. He was able to borrow $2 million to install modern mining equipment. Within less than a year, the company's workforce had been cut to a fourth of its former size, without any reduction in the tonnage of coal it produced, a feat which did little to allay the anger of the workers who had lost their jobs. But growth would add more jobs, Silberstein argued. And by the end of 1951, he had restored the company to profitability. That done, he borrowed additional money to purchase three government-surplus cargo ships to carry his coal, and he began looking around for natural gas properties to acquire, recognizing that coal was facing stiff competition from other fuels. He was starting small, to be sure, but his vision was clear: he would build his little coal company into the financial empire he had envisioned as a youth in pre-Nazi Berlin, before Hitler had stolen his dreams.

He was aided in his effort by a recovering economy, which was also producing better profits at H. K. Porter, in nearby Pittsburgh. With a stronger market, Tom Evans finally had to keep his promise to Clarence Dobson and start to sell some of the weaker divisions he had accumulated in his first few years as chief executive. That meant more travel, more time away from home. But Evans was as successful selling companies as he had been buying them, eventually reaping more than $4.3 million in profits from the motley assortment. He collected something else in the process, however: a growing reputation as a "liquidator." This was not the image he wanted. It smacked of the corporate junkyard in the eyes of a public already growing suspicious of the antics of men like Louis Wolfson and Charlie Green. And it deterred the family owners of the small companies on his shopping list from doing business with him. Their reluctance reflected a growing anxiety about the changes that were sweeping through American business— indeed, through all of American life.

The nation was deeply divided over the path it should follow into its postwar future. Business leaders strongly supported a dismantling of the New Deal, but were less willing to give up the federal controls on wages that helped rein in the power of the robust unions that had emerged from the Depression and the war. The unions, on the other hand, argued that corporations could easily afford to increase wages without increasing prices to the consumer, a proposition that business leaders insisted was unrealistic. Nobody wanted more inflation, but no one wanted lower profits or lower wages either. The impasse was frustrating, and the arguments were fierce.

On April Fools' Day of 1946, 400,000 miners walked off the job. The effect on the economy was devastating. It "slowed, faltered, wobbled toward a dead stop. Within a month, freight loadings dropped 75 percent and steel plants were beginning to bank their fires. A fury of anti-labor feeling swept the country bursting into denunciations on the floors of Congress."[63] The strike lasted for forty days, a biblical plague that was felt especially hard in Pittsburgh, the heart of the steel industry. The unpaid wages reduced retail sales. Even grocery store clerks were worried.

President Truman finally brokered a settlement with the miners—and was promptly challenged by a rail strike. Citing the danger to the nation's economy, Truman threatened to nationalize the railroads and draft the striking workers into the armed forces, a shocking move by Roosevelt's political heir. The strike was settled moments after Truman began the address to Congress in which he planned to ask for the emergency power to carry out his threat.

The crisis was averted, but its impact on the American spirit was felt. The economy simply did not seem to be working. Every time consumers turned around, prices were higher—for movie theaters, for subways and buses, for newspapers.[64] Vacant apartments could not be found; scattered food shortages infuriated shoppers. Well-to-do customers like Betty Evans in suburban Sewickley could tip handsomely enough to get the occasional veal chop or chuck steak from the Select Food Market there. Less prosperous shoppers were lucky to get frankfurters. Tom Evans, who loved automobiles, was finally rich enough to afford a shiny new version of whatever he fancied. But new cars were almost impossible to find, even for people willing to pass a few handsome bills under the table to the car dealer. Americans who, just a year earlier, had been unified in the effort to defeat the nation's enemies started resenting the fellow citizens who stood ahead of them in line. Lip service was still paid to liberal ideals, but liberal ideas did not seem to be able to deliver the peaceful prosperity the whole nation longed for. Tempers grew short, and "in every section of the United States, on all levels of society, the ill-tempered, the mean, the vicious in human beings pushed to the fore," one historian of the period noted. "These were the months when justices of the Supreme Court of the United States insulted each other in newspaper headlines and New England poultry farmers whined to their congressmen about grain being sent overseas to the starving." There were race riots in the North, lynchings in the South, attacks on Japanese-American veterans in the West, and snide anti-Semitism and overt racism everywhere.[65]

This sour atmosphere was inevitably felt in the corporate boardroom—indeed, the first skirmishes of the postwar proxy crusades began as early as 1946. One target was Bell Aircraft in Buffalo, New York. The company had been founded in 1935 by the charismatic Larry Bell, a visionary aviation pioneer who talked fondly of the days when "we used to go into the air without a single instrument, unless you counted your wrist watch."[66] It had become a defense-industry powerhouse and a highly visible part of the corporate landscape during World War II, producing fighter planes and bombers for the new Army Air Corps and experimenting with early helicopter technology. During the war, Bell had skimped on dividends, building up the surplus that Larry Bell planned to draw on when defense contracts became scarce. "At the end of 1945, consequently, Bell found itself with a huge cash reserve and practically no business."[67] Its working capital totaled $43 a share, but that share could be purchased for only $18.

By 1946, Bell's tempting condition had attracted the attention of two remarkable figures in Wall Street history. The first and most notable was Benjamin Graham, a legendary stock analyst who helped formulate the "value approach" to investing and who was a partner in the Graham-Newman Corporation, a "special-situation" investment partnership. The second was Jackson Martindell, an eloquent New York investment counselor with a remarkable gift for self-promotion. The dissident investors were able to recruit to their ranks the formidable Edward Stettinius, who had been Franklin Roosevelt's last secretary of state. The dissidents complained about the richness of management's compensation, but Larry Bell and his top executives feared that the rebel shareholders simply wanted to liquidate the company. Martindell denied the charge. "But Benjamin Graham says bluntly that his own objective was to make Bell set aside whatever was needed to develop its helicopter business—the only real project Graham saw for the company at the time—and disburse most of the remaining funds to the stockholders," *Fortune* later reported.[68]

Bell's management fought back. "We just kept telling the stockholders that a bunch of Wall Street sharpers wanted to take Larry Bell's company away from him," one executive explained,[69] revealing the blind spot that many Americans had about who actually owned a publicly traded company. When the proxy votes were counted, almost 40 percent of the shareholders had supported Graham and Martindell—not enough to win, but enough to scare Bell into finding friendlier hands to hold its stock. The Equity Corporation, a passive investment trust, bought up 35 percent of the stock, including shares owned by Martindell's group.

Before the dust had settled at Bell Aircraft, a group of substantial shareholders in International Telephone and Telegraph revolted against the founding management and demanded a change. This time, however, an open proxy fight was avoided when the smooth, soft-spoken J. Patrick Lannan, a gifted Chicago lawyer and one of the ITT directors, was able to broker a settlement in 1948.

These disputes drew a few worried glances from other business executives. Shareholders were still thought of as a docile group, content to collect whatever dividends were distributed and leave the business of the company to its professional managers, who typically owned very little stock but who were compensated generously for their time and effort. To be sure, the ITT rebels were an aristocratic lot, led by a substantial financier, Clendennin Ryan of Chicago. And Ben Graham was already a widely admired figure on Wall Street—a distinctly different breed from Robert Young and his early followers. But still, something was shifting ever so slightly in the relationship between the powerful managers and the titular owners of corporate America, the stockholders. It was worrisome to those discerning managers alert enough to notice it.

The sense of unease in boardroom America deepened in January 1948 when both Washington and Wall Street worked overtime to unravel "the Follansbee mystery." The story opened on Friday, January 9, with what seemed to be a legitimate bid to take control of the Follansbee Steel Corporation of Pittsburgh. The following Monday, two of the company's top executives denied any knowledge of the takeover attempt, but a New York attorney who claimed to represent the purchaser insisted the bid was legitimate.[70] State and federal securities regulators promptly launched an investigation and by the end of the week, had stumbled across a script that would have done justice to the Marx Brothers.

The takeover bid had been quickly traced to a man named A. Terry Fahye, whom newspapers breathlessly described as "a man with triple identity who was barred perpetually in 1939 from engaging in security dealings in New York."[71] The purported purchaser of Follansbee, Alan Adams Haye, was actually Fahye, according to New York Attorney General Nathaniel L. Goldstein. And Fahye was also known as Albert Bennett-Fay, a former broker who had been barred from the securities business by a New York State court in November 1939 for misrepresentations he allegedly made in selling shares of a company he controlled. Moreover, Goldstein said, Fahye had once employed Irving Wexler, alias "Waxey" Gordon, a Prohibition-era "beer baron" and racketeer. At the time he made his $9 million bid to purchase Follansbee, the attorney general said, Fahye had only $54.58 in the bank. He was charged with violating the previous court order barring him from the securities business. At his arraignment on January 30, 1948, he chatted voluably with reporters. He had never done anything illegal in his life, he insisted, and all his stock transactions in connection with the Follansbee bid had occurred out-of-state and were thus entirely legal. It was true that Irving Wexler had worked for him as a salesman since 1944, he said. But when he learned later that his salesman was actually "Waxey" Gordon, the beer bootlegger, he said, "you could have knocked me off the chair." And yes, he had used a couple of different names over the years, but that was "a common business practice."[72]

As for the Follansbee takeover, Fahye said the only thing that had gone wrong was that "premature publicity" had upset his plan to acquire options on a controlling block of Follansbee stock and then sell the company to some automobile manufacturer or other major steel user at a profit. While he did not himself have the millions of dollars that such a takeover would have required, that did not worry him much. As he had told a congressional investigating panel a few days earlier, there was always plenty of money looking to buy a steel mill, with postwar steel production lagging behind robust industry demand.[73] The state's charges against Fahye arising from the Folansbee deal were thrown out by a New York judicial panel later that spring. But the episode did nothing to reduce the mistrust and suspicion that had begun to settle on the daring young men who were seeking control of established industries in America's heartland.

These new arrivals on the business scene were young, hungry, aggressive men in their thirties and early forties—men like Thomas Mellon Evans, Louis Wolfson, Leopold Silberstein, and Charlie Green. They were cranking up the pace of business life, pushing for more, sooner, faster. They seemed to lack sufficient deference toward their elders, the conservative, careful, dignified executives who had steered their companies through panic, depression, and war. These young adventurers borrowed too much, saved too little, took too many risks, and didn't seem to care whom they offended in the process. They saw business as a fascinating game, not a sacred trust. They were determined, quite simply, to grab as big a piece of the American pie as they could.

That, at least, was how they looked to the American business establishment in the years immediately after World War II. The worried forty-eight-year-old protagonist of John O'Hara's novel *From the Terrace* acknowledged this cultural change as he debated his own post-military career. "Fifty doesn't look so old to somebody my age," he said, "but most people aren't my age. They are younger. And fifty looks pretty old to them." To his wife's assurances that most of the nation's really wealthy men would consider her husband a youngster, the clear-eyed hero responded, "No. Not most of them. Most of the men with money and making money, are my age and younger. That's why I'm wondering about taking a whole year out to loaf."[74]

For men like Evans, there was no question of taking time to loaf, to recover from the exhaustion of war and prepare for the new world left in its wake. They were on the move.

CHAPTER FIVE

ST. LOUIS BLUES

For Tom Evans, 1949 was the year that he began his lifelong shopping trip through corporate America. His official rationale was that H. K. Porter needed to diversify its product line "to take the place of the dying locomotive business."[1] And in his view, "one of the quickest, and probably the most economical way, was to add new products by the acquisition of good, going businesses."

His favorite place to look for potential acquisitions was among the slightly threadbare, dusty, and outdated family corporations that made up the social and economic bedrock of America's smaller cities. He especially liked companies that had been founded by the grandfather, or even the great-grandfather, of the current generation of stockholders. "More often than not, family-held corporations are ultra-conservative in their development and growth programs," he later said, his contempt barely hidden behind words tailored for a formal business audience. "They are too willing to accept the status quo. And, as all of us know, there are major tax problems involved with inheritance and diversification of investments."[2] In a more candid explanation for his acquisition choices, he once said he looked for a "family company run by a third-generation Yale man who spends his afternoons drinking martinis at the club."[3]

Besides, Evans had little competition in the bidding for these firms—most large corporations had no interest in the hand-to-hand negotiations that such family acquisitions required. It was a buyer's market, the kind Tom Evans liked best. And in 1949, he experimented widely in it. As he explained later, it was a time that taught him "that it is easier and often

Childhood tragedy may explain the somber gravity
of young Thomas Mellon Evan's senior portrait at
Shady Side Academy in 1927.

Thomas Mellon Evans, front, third from left, was active in student life at Shady Side, including the debating society.

Thomas Mellon Evans, rear, second from right, with some of his classmates at Shady Side in 1927.

Alfons B. Landa, a brilliant legal tactician
with rich social and political connections,
was both Tom Evans's ally and his adversary
in the early takeover wars.

Elizabeth Parker Evans was escorted
into court by her lawyer, John E.
Rose, at the beginning of her bitter
divorce battle with Thomas Mellon
Evans in the fall of 1952.
(The Pittsburgh Post-Gazette)

The corporate establishment seemed to shake when Robert R. Young, at right, defeated management (with a bit of help from Tom Evans) and took control of the New York Central Railroad in 1954. With Young as he marched into his new railroad's headquarters were Alfred E. Perlman, his new chief executive, and Lila Acheson Wallace, one of his new board members. *(New York Times Pictures)*

The flashbulbs were popping in New York in 1954 when "wonderboy financier" Louis Wolfson announced he would seek control of Montgomery Ward, a catalog retailing giant in Chicago.

Wolfson's appearance at Senate hearings on his strike-bound Capital Transit company in July 1955 drew so much press attention that capital police had to remove photographers from the hearing room. *(Corbis Images)*

Despite his soldier-of-fortune smile, raider Leopold D. Silberstein, right, was headed into a quagmire in March 1956 as he fought for control of Fairbanks Morse, an industrial conglomerate in Chicago. With him at the company's annual meeting were two legal advisers, Oscar Chapman (left), and Barnet Hode. *(Associated Press)*

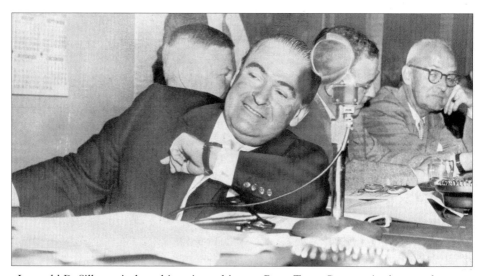

Leopold D. Silberstein kept his poise at his own Penn-Texas Corporation's annual meeting in May 1957, as he tried to fend off a "counter-insurgency" raid led by Alfons Landa.

With Landa's help, Thomas M. Evans moved into the chairman's seat of the Crane Company of Chicago in 1959, but some of his stormiest takeover fights were yet to come.

David Karr, a former aide to political columnist Drew Pearson and a target of Senator Joe McCarthy's suspicions, was one of the first press agents to specialize in proxy fights.

Thomas M. Evans, Jr., followed his father to Wall Street but carved out his own niche as a young trader *(Vincent James)*.

Past conflicts seemed forgotten as the Evans men gathered at a family birthday party in 1992. Tom Evans is seated; behind him, from left, are Edward P. Evans, Robert S. Evans, and Thomas Evans, Jr.

more practical to buy a company and broaden its research and product development program, than to try to start a concern from scratch."[4] It was also, obviously, a lot more fun for Tom Evans.

In July, he acquired the Jarecki Manufacturing Company, but it was a mixed bargain at best. The company owned fifteen oil-field supply stores, all of them unprofitable, but its core business was manufacturing industrial valves at a plant in Erie, Pennsylvania. Hoping that the faithful Dobson would be able to patch the company up—Dobson promptly moved the valve division from bleak Erie to better facilities in Tulsa, Oklahoma, leaving jobless workers in his wake—Evans continued to shop.

His eyes quickly lit on the seventy-year-old Quaker Rubber Corporation, occupying a site that stretched between the Delaware River and the Pennsylvania railroad tracks in Philadelphia. It was one of the most important manufacturers of industrial rubber products in the country. Its history dated to 1885; by the turn of the century, Quaker's products had become critical components of industrial conveyor belts, and its hoses were used for handling acids, chemicals, and all sorts of liquid raw materials. Like many family companies, Quaker treasured its history. Its workers flushed with pride when they spoke of their response to America's desperate need after the Japanese had bombed the American Pacific fleet at Pearl Harbor. Within hours, the Defense Department had called the company seeking to have all the fire hoses the workers could produce rushed to the Pacific to help fight the inferno raging along the waterfront. The men worked through the night turning out fresh hoses. The coiled hoses were piled on trucks, as military police on motorcycles gunned their engines impatiently. As soon as the trucks were loaded, they were escorted with sirens wailing to the airport south of the city. Military planes carried them west, and they arrived in Pearl Harbor in time for firemen to use them fighting the blaze spreading along the shore.

Quaker was a jewel, and Evans managed to buy it from its family shareholders for far less than the value of its assets. Dobson went to work modernizing the Philadelphia plant, earmarking $1.5 million for expansion and new equipment. And Evans kept shopping.

In 1950, he hit his stride—indeed, it seemed to his wife and family that he had given himself over completely to his business ambitions. By mid-October, he had acquired the Connors Steel Company, in Birmingham, Alabama, a region that was growing quickly with few local steel plants to serve it. It was the second southern steel company to be founded by George W. Connors Sr., who had helped form the Atlantic Steel Company in Atlanta at the turn of the century, but was determined to go into business for himself. In 1908, he moved to Alabama to start Connors Steel, whose first products were barrel hoops, metal straps to hold baled cotton, and light steel rails for the mining industry. The Connors family had much to be proud of: George Connors, one of the geniuses of the steel industry, was the man who discovered that steel rails could be rolled successfully on a continuous mill, and patented the process. But here, too, the energy of the founder had grown weak in subsequent generations. Connors had slackened its sales effort and persisted in manufacturing products, like those cotton bale ties, long after the market had become unprofitable. So Evans was able to buy the company at a bargain price and Dobson was able to transform it. Salesmen fanned out to all the principal southern cities. Unsuccessful products were scrapped, and within eight weeks of the purchase, Connors was launched on a $2 million modernization campaign.

By then, Tom Evans had purchased Delta-Star Electric Company in Chicago. It had been founded in 1908 by Herbert W. Young and Allen S. Pearl, two pioneers in the electrical industry. It, too, treasured its history. Its founders had helped electric power move outdoors by developing weatherproof switching equipment that could be mounted on rooftops or in power transmission yards. Before Delta-Star's innovation, electric generating stations were costly to build and required a great deal of indoor space. Afterward, as Evans once put it, "the outdoor substation [became] a familiar sight along our highways, on the outskirts of cities and towns, and close to many large manufacturing plants."[5] The builders of the massive new Hoover Dam turned to the company in 1935 to produce the largest disconnecting switches built up to that time, able to handle an unprecedented 286,000 volts of power. By the time Tom Evans arrived in December 1950, Delta-Star owned roughly 25 percent of the market for all the high-voltage switches sold to the electric-utility industry. But its family owners had grown a bit complacent, and Evans was once again able to buy the company for less than the value of the assets on its books.

With an industrial rubber company and one of the leading electrical equipment manufacturers added to the chemical company he already owned, he was well on his way to attaining the kind of diversity he felt Porter needed. Along the way, he purchased a few smaller companies and shed a few others, including a small steam pump manufacturer and H. K. Porter's locomotive business, the core of its original existence.

Porter's stock had begun to recover, but it still looked like a bargain to Tom Evans, so in the fall of 1950 Porter went into the marketplace to buy up more of its own stock, offering to buy 500,000 shares at $15 a share. Those who lacked faith in Evans's ability to turn the company around paid a substantial price: in December, Porter announced a dividend of $1 a share—compared with just 15 cents in per-share dividends the prior year. As the company's largest shareholder, Evans received the largest chunk of this dividend payment, of course.

In early 1951, when Leopold Silberstein was shaking the Pittsburgh establishment with his surprise takeover of Pennsylvania Coal and Coke, Tom Evans was continuing his own shopping spree. He purchased fourteen more oil-field supply stores from the Dresser Company, hoping that their revenues would bolster the still struggling stores he had acquired when he bought Jarecki in 1949. In September, he bought Buffalo Steel Company, expanding Porter's steel making capacity.

Evans was becoming a formidable figure in Pittsburgh—and a controversial one. Critics complained that he drove hard bargains, paying far less than he should have for the companies he bought. These criticisms, while not wholly fair, reveal the expectations of Evans's contemporaries. An established, even historic, family-owned company worth $100 a share should not, somehow, be purchased for half that—even if the sellers of the shares were happy to take the money. There was some suggestion that it was not fair, or honest, or at least gentlemanly to acquire such companies at such fire-sale prices. As a Pittsburgh journalist observed a few years later, some of the conservative businessmen in Evans's hometown "unquestionably felt his practice of gobbling up going concerns was not quite cricket."[6] Evans would have laughed at this analysis, just as Louis Wolfson would have bristled and Charlie Green would have grinned. As Wolfson observed a few years later, "I've broken up some clubhouses that were being run on stockholders' money, and I'll break up some more."[7]

But in some circles, Evans was also being branded a "liquidator." And this label did disturb him—indeed, it was quite unfair. Unlike Wolfson, Evans had really only liquidated his mistakes. Small companies he had acquired in the early forties, before he had quite found his way as a conglomerate-builder, were sold. Some others were shut down, their operations moved to more modern facilities or sold to companies that could make better use of them. Perhaps this looked like ruthless asset-stripping to the executives or small-town citizens affected by this weeding-out process. But Evans clearly was buying companies to build them up, not to liquidate them. His experience with Jarecki Manufacturing is a case in point. He was slow to liquidate even the money-losing oil stores that he acquired with the company, and threw good money after bad by acquiring additional stores to see if a larger operation could acquire some economies of scale that would make it profitable. And at Quaker and Delta-Star and Connors, a takeover by Evans was the prelude to long-overdue improvements in facilities and sales techniques-steps the family owners had not made. But somehow the "liquidator" label stuck, no matter how angrily Evans plucked at its corners.

Still, it did not slow him down. In 1952, he added yet another important industrial company to Porter's lineup with the purchase of the Watson-Stillman Company in Roselle, New Jersey. This antique gem had been founded in 1848 in a small factory building on the Lower East Side of New York. Through the Civil War and for a decade afterward it made steam engines, hydraulic jacks, lever punches, and metal shears—the high-technology industrial products of that era. In 1883, it was reorganized to specialize in the design and manufacture of even more advanced hydraulic equipment. Evans clearly relished the history of the old company—he later spoke of finding old advertisements for the company's early hydraulic presses that promised "an easy and rapid method of pressing oil from fish, cider from apples, and wine from grapes." Watson-Stillman equipment became part of the fanfare and hoopla of the Barnum and Bailey Circus on a Sunday afternoon in late March 1904, he continued, when men, elephants, horses, and camels tested their relative hauling strength by tugging on ropes attached to the company's hydraulic weighing cylinders. Newspapers had gleefully reported that a single elephant could pull 4,700 pounds, and a hundred men working together could pull 6,700 pounds.[8]

There was a more serious side to the company, of course. Watson-Stillman hydraulic jacks and other hydraulic equipment were used in the construction of the Queens-Midtown Tunnel under the East River in New York. The company built the largest injection-molding machine of that day, and designed and built a machine with a pulling power of 4 million pounds that was used to stretch slabs of aluminum plate, that golden goose of the Mellon family, into thin flexible sheets. It was just the kind of company that Tom Evans could love, with a stable of quality products essential to American industry. Let the rest of America focus on consumer gadgets and newfangled technology fads. Evans was from Pittsburgh, and he knew what made the heartland economy hum: factories and the whole intricate circulatory system of power lines, pipelines, and rail lines that connected those factories to their raw materials and their markets. It was an old-fashioned view of the economy, one that old W. L. Mellon would have fully comprehended. And with the American economy alone entirely unscathed by war, it was a vision on which an enterprising young man like Tom Evans could build a global empire.

As his mentor had predicted, Evans was surpassing the achievements of the privileged children who had teased him on his visits to Ben Elm—at least in terms of his money-making ability, which was how he probably kept score. The eldest of W. L. Mellon's offspring, Matthew Mellon, had been briefly infatuated by the Nazis in his adopted homeland and had enthusiastically defended Hitler's prewar policies in an essay for the *Pittsburgh Press*. "Being a property owner in Germany I regard Adolf Hitler as having saved my home from the Communist rabble that would have spread all over Europe had he not come into power in 1933," the young American-born professor wrote. But by 1938, at his father's insistence, he returned home with his wife and new baby boy and settled down to the life of an independent scholar and vagabond.[9] Life had taken an even more unlikely turn for Tom Evans's dear friend and best man, Larry Mellon. While Evans was nurturing Porter into a budding conglomerate in the late 1940s, Larry Mellon had been herding cattle on his western ranch, musing in the saddle over how to balance his inherited wealth against his deeply personal definition of his Christian duty. In 1947, he read about the work of Albert Schweitzer, the pioneering medical missionary to Africa, and fell under the spell of that remarkable man. With the courageous support of his second wife, Gwen, he went to medical school; Gwen became a laboratory technician. In the summer of 1952, as Evans closed in on the Watson-Stillman deal, Larry and Gwen Mellon were in Haiti, prospecting for a site for the charity hospital he was determined to build with his trust fund when he completed his medical residency.[10] The Mellon daughters had married, one to a conservative debt-wary businessman[11] and the other to the fun-loving and elegant heir of an aristocratic New York family, a dashing figure who had died in the war and left her a widow with small children.[12]

So it was Tom Evans who actually followed in W. L. Mellon's footsteps, and not only in business. In January 1952, Evans dabbled a bit in another realm his mentor had dominated: Pennsylvania state politics. Evans, an enthusiastic supporter of Senator Robert Taft of Ohio, entered the race for delegates to the 1952 Republican convention. The son of a president and himself a widely respected Yale man, Taft had been a rock-solid opponent of the New Deal, and he was revered in the American heartland for his plain-spoken support for the decent, family-centered virtues which "traditional America liked to believe belonged especially to its way of life."[13] He opposed American involvement in foreign affairs, and supported a rugged individualism over government intervention. "At the height of the furor over meat prices, reporters asked the senator for his solution and he replied: 'Eat less.' It was the purest Taftiana—in its magnificent tactlessness and its bedrock assumption that a real American solved his own problems."[14] The Republican State Committee in Pennsylvania had already decreed that all seventy of its delegates would go unpledged to the GOP nominating convention that summer in Chicago's International

Amphitheater. The deeply divided Republican Party had its Eisenhower enthusiasts and its dark McCarthyite fringe, but Evans made his loyalties clear—even his youngest son dutifully wore a Taft campaign button to school, defying all the young chests emblazoned with "I Like Ike."

But by January 1952, when Evans made his entrance into Pittsburgh political circles, his own "family values" were anything but Taftian. A decade of constant travel and "working around the clock" had taken its toll on his marriage. Elizabeth Parker Evans had never felt at home in the dirty, money-obsessed capital of Evans's business empire, and she and her husband had very different ideas about what money was for and how life should be lived. She had fretted that he seemed to prefer his business interests to the needs of his three young boys, who were such a golden part of her life. How could a father, hearing his young son happily crowing "Here comes me, Daddy, here comes me," remain impassive behind his newspaper? Her frequent visits to her family were accepted resentfully, and were sometimes abruptly cut short by what seemed like her husband's jealousy over the delight she took in the Parkers' relaxed and gracious California family life.[15] They seem to fight about everything.

Sometime that year, Betty and Tom Evans finally confronted the gulf that had opened between them during twelve years of marriage. He later claimed he had offered her a very generous separation allowance in hopes that the matter could be settled quietly. But she rejected his offer, perhaps because her lawyers advised her it was inadequate or perhaps simply because her trust in him was so entirely destroyed. In any case, in late October, she sued her husband for a "bed-and-board divorce," an unusual and now extinct arrangement that lawyers called "a Catholic divorce." It allowed an estranged couple to live apart, with court-ordered alimony and household support payments, but it did not actually dissolve the bonds of matrimony. Neither party would be free to remarry; indeed, if the couple began living together again, the "divorce" was automatically dissolved.[16]

Betty Evans's application for temporary alimony and support produced three-column headlines in the local papers and the flashbulbs did not stop popping until the entire heart-scarring story, all the old arguments about bills, all the ugly episodes of petty cruelty, had been aired before a fascinated Pittsburgh. There was little grist for gossip initially—just some raised eyebrows at her recital of the four luxurious homes, six automobiles, and a sea-going yacht that made up the Evans domain. Her grounds for separating from the man that reporters described as "one of Pittsburgh's more brilliant young industrialists," were described in the newspapers simply as "indignities."[17]

Possibly one of those indignities arose from Tom Evans's intensifying feelings for the wife of one of his wealthy neighbors at his winter home in Sea Island, Georgia. Josephine Schlotman Mitchell was the daughter of a wealthy Detroit banker and industrialist and the wife of a well-known sportsman, W. Ledyard "Ledge" Mitchell Jr. A newspaper photograph of Josephine Mitchell, then in her mid-thirties, showed a beautiful woman with thick gracefully arched eyebrows and wide-set eyes in a heart-shaped face crowned by glossy waves of dark hair. In 1935, the same year Evans had married Betty Parker, Josephine Schlotman—a celebrated debutante in her home city—had eloped with Mitchell. They were the parents of three young girls who had scampered with the Evans boys on the beach at Sea Island. The Mitchells and the Evanses had become fast friends, vacationing together in Europe and socializing frequently. For Betty, Tom's liaison with Josephine must have cut through those happy memories like a razor.[18]

If Tom Evans thought his separation from Betty Evans would be simple, he had not allowed for her profound sense of betrayal or for the intense dislike he had generated in the heart of his in-laws. His wife's father, Edward F. Parker, was one of the leading lawyers in southern California, and he made sure that his beautiful and intensely unhappy daughter was aggressively represented—coincidentally choosing a Pittsburgh legal team that included the brother-in-law of Evans's lifelong friend John Foster.[19] Edward Parker, elegantly dressed down to his shiny cane and almost regal in his anger, was at his daughter's side throughout most of the long gloomy November hearings at which her demands for alimony and household support were debated before the sternly disapproving Judge John J. Kennedy.

The courtroom battle kept the local newspapers riveted. Part of their fascination, of course, was the view the trial produced of life as it was lived in the handsome mansions of Squirrel Hill and Sewickley. In her initial appeal for separate living expenses, Betty Evans had asserted that her husband was worth $15 million and brought home about $500,000 a year— nearly $90 million and $3 million respectively in late-century dollars. These were simply staggering amounts of money at the time, when fewer than 30,000 people in the country owned $1 million or more in property[20] and when roughly 80 percent of the population earned less than $10,000 a year. Reporters carefully counted the number of rooms, bedrooms, baths, and garage spaces in the four homes the Evanses owned. In responding to the initial alimony demand, Evans denied he was as rich as his wife claimed—his "spendable" income in 1951 had been less than $71,000, he said, or about $410,000 in 1990's dollars.[21]

The couple did not even agree on the number of automobiles they owned. Was it six, as she said, or just four, as he insisted? Was the boat he owned the "sea-going yacht" his wife described, or a mere "sailboat with auxiliary power," as his lawyers insisted?[22] She spent $9,000 a year on new clothes, he complained, high-priced but soon obsolete outfits with silly and ridiculously expensive hats. "The trouble is she wears a dress once or twice, and then I see it worn by her sister, who has been her guest for some time," Tom Evans testified.[23] "I don't think I should furnish the sister's clothing." He owned forty-nine suits, she countered, and had the chauffeur deliver them back and forth to the cleaners. No doubt she had counted his suits, he retorted, "but they represent all the clothing I have purchased in ten years. I wear a suit until the moths get into it." Why couldn't she be like that? And the chauffeur took them to be cleaned because she had refused to, he added spitefully.[24]

For the typical Pittsburgh family, even Tom Evans's version of his life seemed a paradise. A mansion with six servants? Plus a chauffeur? Thousands of dollars worth of new dresses and suits each spring and fall? Tom and Betty Evans were members of every stylish club in the city, from the Duquesne Club to the Rolling Rock Hunt, that private enclave of the Mellons and their friends. And the parties! "We give one or two large parties a year, medium-sized parties with 24 to 30 people every couple of months and smaller affairs," Betty Evans had testified.[25] It was a life like the ones American saw played out in the movies, and Betty—slim and beautiful, with a perfect oval face and gleaming blond hair—could have been a movie star herself. Reporters described her outfits each day, and one noted that she had "armed herself with dark glasses as protection against photographers."[26] There was nothing glamorous about her increasingly stocky husband, except his self-made money and the speed of his ascent to millionaire status. He was a hometown boy, a graduate of Shady Side. Next to his exotic wife, he seemed down-to-earth and simple. He spoke the local language: "I was raised on the philosophy that one must save something out of his income," he testified. "Mrs. Evans didn't agree with that philosophy." His patience with her wasteful habits had reached the breaking point, he said, when he "found his dogs eating steak. That did it. I shut off her paying the bills and paid them myself." As for his money, he said, "I'd like to leave it to my children."[27]

The coverage of the trial reveals that neither the judge nor the male reporters had much sympathy for the beautiful Mrs. Evans, despite occasional observations that she appeared nervous and sometimes broke down in tears during her testimony. There were snide observations that she was "unable to recall how many dresses and pairs of shoes she owned. But she did remember one fur coat."[28] She couldn't remember details of her family budget, and once "had difficulty remembering exactly how many rooms there were in each of the four homes" in which she lived.[29] She had asked for $695 a month for the household food budget, a reporter noted, "but Mr. Evans replied he had been informed that $1 a meal per person is sufficient." In all, her lawyers sought $3,000 a month on her behalf; Evans offered less than $900 a month, expecting her to draw an equal amount from her own personal investments of about $100,000. The judge clearly gave more credence to Evans's estimates of the necessary household expenses. "After all," the judge said once, "he's the paymaster."[30] And there could be no mistaking the judge's disapproval of Mrs. Evans's demand that her angry husband should move out of the embattled family home. "I am not going to force any such thing. Both should be there with those two boys—it takes two to raise boys, both the father and mother are needed."[31] (Young Tom Junior was away in boarding school, leaving Ned and Shel at home.)

These were just preliminary insults, though, compared to the arguments Tom Evans's attorneys made at the close of "one of the most bitterly fought temporary alimony suits in the history of the court."[32] The courthouse journalist covered Mrs. Evans's demands in a few dismissive paragraphs, and devoted the remainder of his lengthy story to the husband's case. Evans had shown that he could not afford to pay what his wife demanded on top of providing for his boys' education and maintaining his other homes, which he said were important to his business. "During his testimony Mr. Evans pointed out that dissension and breakup of the family was caused by his wife's 'extravagance' and attempts to 'undermine my authority' in the home." Then Mahlon E. Lewis, Evans's lawyer, really began punching, painting a portrait of the elegant blond California-bred mother as only a true Pittsburgher could see her.

"It is apparent that Mrs. Evans has received some very bad advice," he began. "Whether that advice came from her father, Mr. Parker, who is a California lawyer, or from her own attorneys, I have no way of knowing. Mrs. Evans says she does not understand these things. I say to Mrs. Evans the time has come when she must understand them." He continued, "Her whole attitude evidences a great lack of maturity, at least insofar as it pertains to her relationship with her husband. Sometime in the course of her life, Mrs. Evans must learn to be less extravagant, less careless of her money. She must learn to live within the budget; she must learn that money does not come from a bottomless well that she can dip into at her whim." He turned to the judge and insisted, "with all the sincerity at my command," that the judge would be doing Mrs. Evans a great service by limiting her alimony to "not more than the law would allow under the applied formula in such cases." That formula would dictate alimony from Evans of $831.29, in addition to the free use of her husband's furnished home in Sewickley and his support of their three children. "Such an award will enable her to live in far greater luxury than all but a very few favored people in this world," Lewis concluded.[33]

Judge John J. Kennedy issued his decision a few weeks later. He granted Mrs. Evans $1,150 a month in alimony, more than the formula would have dictated but far less than she had sought. The amount was granted on the condition that her personal income, derived from stocks and bonds in companies that her estranged husband controlled, would not fall below $1,000 a month. The courthouse reporter declared this "a victory for Mr. Evans in the bitterly fought case." But within a few months, Mrs. Evans was back in court demanding an absolute divorce decree, and her husband did not oppose her. Finally, she was able to answer the awful lecture she had been given during the alimony hearings. On the stand, "twisting her handkerchief into knots," the beautiful Mrs. Evans—nervous and almost too thin, but still elegantly dressed, right down to one of the stylish hats she so adored—talked about the life of careless insults and verbal abuse she had experienced.

She told of an incident that foreshadowed the short story she wrote decades later, although in that later version she had left out the angry, hurtful arguments. She and Tom went to a party on a rainy night, she testified, but she became ill and asked to be taken home. On the way home, they quarreled and he abruptly stopped the car and told her to get out.[34] She walked home in the rain, she said. He had become a tyrant of the breakfast table, pounding the table and shouting at the boys. He even seemed resentful of Joan, her beloved golden retriever.

But the real hostilities in the mismatched marriage were rooted in her husband's absolute obsession with building his industrial empire. "He had more concern for his business than he did for me," she testified tearfully.[35] Her story poignantly portrayed the pain of being reduced to an ornament, a trophy her husband displayed for visiting executives or mentioned to inquiring journalists—the lovely, stylish wife and the three sturdy boys. Behind that happy facade, she said, was a man who had told friends behind her back that he no longer cared for her and found it impossible to live with her. When she confronted him and asked if he had made such statements, she said, he conceded he had. "During this time I was as good a wife to him as I could be, and I did not deserve that treatment," she said.[36]

Betty's mother, the good-hearted, patient woman who had welcomed the young Tom Evans into the *Statendam*'s first-class lounges and restaurants more than twenty years earlier, took the stand in her daughter's defense. Her daughter, she said, had become so unhappy in her home life that she had lost weight and required a physician's care. "She had always been a very healthy young woman previously," Mrs. Parker said. Her nerves had been tested even further when she had surprised an intruder who had broken into the family home just a week before the trial. She had struggled with the intruder in her own bedroom until her screams had aroused the family and prompted him to flee, the local newspapers reported. She had been briefly hospitalized for shock after the incident.

Less than twenty-four hours after the emotional divorce hearing before Judge John T. Duff Jr., Mrs. Evans was granted an instant divorce decree. The judge explained why he had departed from the common practice of withholding such decrees for at least ten days after a divorce hearing. Mrs. Evans's lawyers had requested immediate action because she was on the verge of physical collapse and had been advised by her physician to leave Pittsburgh for a long rest. "My observations on the bench lead me to agree, and I granted the divorce immediately," Judge Duff said. "I would do it again under similar circumstances for anybody, regardless of their station of life."[37]

Barely two months after his divorce was final, there were published rumors linking Tom Evans romantically to the quiet, dignified Josephine Mitchell, who was reported to be in residence in Lake Tahoe, Nevada, preparing to file for a divorce of her own. By August, they were making plans to be married in Marble Collegiate Church in New York City. His happy anticipation of that event was marred, however, when his growing business reputation finally collided with his insatiable appetite.

During the summer, after the details of his messy divorce had finally moved from courtroom testimony to clubhouse gossip, Evans had set out to acquire the famous old A. Leschen and Sons Rope Company in St. Louis, the second-oldest rope manufacturer in the country. The company had been founded in 1857 by Adolph Leschen, who was a hands-on manufacturer and salesman. His first bonanza was making ropes and horse and mule halters for the Army quartermasters during the Civil War. Leschen ropes became a staple of the Mississippi River waterfront in the construction boom that followed the war. But what catapulted the company to national importance was its Hercules wire rope, rope woven from strands of metal that was strong enough to lift steel girders into place but flexible and elastic enough to be as useful as common hemp rope. Leschen cable was used in the construction of the Panama Canal and the Cathedral of St. John the Divine in New York City.[38]

As Leschen grew, it opened branch offices in New York, Chicago, Denver, San Francisco—wherever cities were striving upward and outward.[39] The founding family had its aspirations too. Adolph Leschen's sons followed him into the business, and their sons followed in turn. Their wives and daughters became important figures in St. Louis society. Their engagement parties and weddings were all described approvingly in the local social pages, their funerals prompted sober obituaries, and the probate of their wills was carefully reported in the local business columns. Their families were large, and their stockholdings slowly became more scattered.

Some of the stock had even fallen into nonfamily hands. An early unsuccessful expansion into the tram railway industry had plunged the company into financial distress, and members of the John A. Roebling family of New Jersey came to the rescue. The Roeblings were best known for designing and building the Brooklyn Bridge, and they had an understanding for how important the Leschen firm was to the country. But their well-timed rescue made them among the largest stockholders in the company, with a representative on the company's board.[40]

And by the summer of 1953, many of the Roebling heirs were ready to sell. Word got out through banking circles, and Tom Evans interrupted his wooing of Josephine long enough to fly to St. Louis with an offer of about $75 a share for the Roebling stake. It was a low price, no doubt about that, less than half the company's book value. But most of the Roeblings promptly accepted. So did several other Leschen family stockholders, including the aging Arthur A. Leschen, grandson of the founder, who was the company's president. Those purchases, which cost Evans just under $1.5 million, gave him 70 percent of the outstanding stock in the family business. Just after the July 4th holiday, the *St. Louis Post-Dispatch* reported that a controlling interest in the venerable firm had been purchased by H. K. Porter of Pittsburgh.[41] A gleeful Evans quickly made plans to combine the old firm with his Watson-Stillman Company, whose products were a perfect fit. He expected to wrap up the deal well before his August honeymoon.

But some Leschen stockholders, and one important Roebling heir, dug their heels in and decided to fight for a higher price. One of those rebels was John A. Leschen II, whose father Elmer had been a grandson of the founder. Elmer Leschen had died in 1936, leaving his widow, Dorothy, largely dependent on the Leschen Company shares for her livelihood. John, a sales executive at Granite City Steel Company in St. Louis, and his married sister Suzanne Leschen Naunheim, also owned a small number of shares. For his mother's sake, young John was determined to investigate the deal thoroughly. He was alarmed when his boss at the steel company, who had moved to St. Louis from Pittsburgh, told him that Evans had a reputation as a hard man and a "family-company predator." His caution was shared by his uncle, William F. Leschen, an older and more substantial shareholder, and several of his older aunts, including Estelle Leschen Leavy and Betty Leschen Phelps, both prominent in St. Louis society.

Besides the concern sparked by the opinions of John Leschen's boss, there was naturally some offended family pride among the older Leschen relatives. The rope company had been the bedrock of the family's identity in St. Louis for generations; its president had long been an important figure in the city's business life and in the rope industry nationally. Was the family heritage to become a mere subsidiary of some unfamiliar Pittsburgh firm? But sentiment aside, what also bothered some of the rebel Leschen relatives was the price they were being offered for this treasured history. "We all thought we were being taken to the cleaners," said John Leschen.[42]

Evans could not absorb the Leschen company into H. K. Porter unless he could acquire all of the outstanding public stock. So in the early fall of 1953, impatient to complete the deal, he traveled to St. Louis and arranged a meeting with the holdout shareholders. It was set for one lovely autumn afternoon at the comfortable Richmond Heights home of Dr. Charles and Estelle Leavy.[43] The family members arrived, and a few took advantage of the light refreshments Aunt Estelle provided. They were gathered in the living room when Tom Evans pulled up in front and got out of his car. He bounded up the walk, a small rotund man with a glowing smile that gave his eyes a cheerful squint. Introductions were made, and he settled into a chair to give his sales pitch. He kept emphasizing that he was making "a very fair offer," John recalled. Some of the aunts questioned Evans about the enormous gap between his offer and the book value of the company. He grew irritated, repeating his arguments and almost willing them to agree with him.

John and his uncle Will took another tack: why didn't Evans throw in some H. K. Porter stock, along with the cash? That would allow the Leschen heirs to share in the future bonanza Evans clearly expected to harvest from the family company. Evans stared at them coldly and promptly answered, "I don't give stock in my companies to anyone." By now, the wide smile had vanished and Evans had become very aloof and more than usually undiplomatic—at one point, he even told the elderly women that they were acting like "spoiled brats" by demanding more money. "We were absolutely incensed, especially the older ladies," John Leschen said. The meeting ended with a chill.

It was the latest in a series of frustrations Tom Evans experienced during that summer of 1953. As he was negotiating with the Leschen family, machinists at the rope company were growing unruly at the bargaining table. Like organized labor everywhere, they were demanding a bigger slice of the postwar profits. Evans's priorities were very different, of course: he wanted to improve profits at the firm, and that required restraining the growth in the payroll. He had made the union what he felt was a fair offer, and like the rebellious Leschen heirs, the union had rejected it. Evans had proposed raising the workers' wage scale by four cents an hour; the machinists wanted a thirty-cent raise, and Evans dug in his heels. In late September, 135 members of the International Association of Machinists walked off the job at A. Leschen and Sons.

Despite the animosity the Leschen relatives felt toward Evans, they might well have given in if they had been contemplating a solo fight. But they were not alone. They were allied with Mary G. Roebling of Trenton, New Jersey, one of the first female bank presidents in the country and a remarkable woman. A substantial block of the Leschen company stock was in a trust fund for her son Paul, and she was determined to get fair value for it. In early November, she and the Leschen holdouts sued H. K. Porter, demanding that it pay them the full value of their stockholdings, which they estimated at $199 a share. Evans sent the lawsuit to his attorneys, and continued with his plans to merge Leschen into Watson-Stillman. A few rich elderly matrons in Trenton and St. Louis were not going to stand in his way.

CHAPTER SIX

YOUNG AT HEART

Tom Evans's methods were pushier than the Establishment preferred and his appetite was far larger than Porter's size would suggest. But he certainly was not alone in his pursuit of growth through corporate acquisitions during the early forties. And in the years immediately after the war, dozens of giant companies purchased hundreds of smaller ones in an orgy of largely amicable acquisitions.

In 1947, the chairman of the Federal Trade Commission informed Congress that "the merger movement has been particularly pronounced since VJ-Day. In the fourth quarter of 1945 it reached the highest level in the last decade and a half."[1] The second most active acquirer between 1940 and 1946, according to the FTC, was the modestly sized H. K. Porter Company of Pittsburgh, which had made seven acquisitions during those years—with Evans's busiest buying years still ahead. The FTC chairman warned that most large companies had emerged from the war with sufficient surplus profits to enable them to go on acquiring smaller firms "for years to come."

This spate of corporate coupling, unlike earlier ones in primary industries like steel and copper, had been especially pronounced in fields that consumers noticed, like canned foods, dairy products, textiles, and clothing. Until the 1920s, these industries had been dominated by hundreds of small, locally owned competitors; now these small firms were being gobbled up by national giants like Borden, Foremost, Textron, and Burlington Mills. It was the same story with small liquor companies and wineries, meat packing companies, grocery stores, and flour mills—companies whose delivery trucks and brand names were familiar to small-town shoppers, and whose bosses were familiar faces across union bargaining tables. Three large liquor companies—National Distillers Products, Schenley Distillers, and Seagram's—had made a total of nearly forty acquisitions during the war years alone.

Federal studies at the time showed that the vast majority of the mergers and acquisitions that reshaped the American business landscape in the first decade after the war were friendly purchases, not hostile takeovers. The heirs of family-owned companies wanted out, or found they could not raise the capital to expand on their own and sold to a better-financed bidder.

These trends meant different things to different people, of course. For economists, they were an inevitable and efficient adjustment to growing urbanization and changing transportation patterns. Most of all, economists said, they reflected a corporate response to America's emergence as the dominant force in the postwar world's shell-shocked economy. Astute financiers, moreover, knew that many small companies were trading on the still-depressed stock market at prices that made it far more attractive for expansion-minded companies to buy their existing factories rather than build new ones, given the postwar shortages of basic construction supplies.

But for politicians, these mergers often were small, local tragedies that demanded explanation and amelioration—or at least, scapegoats.

Congressman Thomas Dodd of Connecticut, an increasingly vocal figure in Congress, had seen several communities in his state bruised and baffled by the consequences of this sweeping economic transformation. For example, Colt's Manufacturing Company, the famed firearms maker in Hartford, had been a reliable local employer for more than a century. In 1948 and 1949, it found itself the target of a group of insurgent investors led by David A. Goodkind, a New York accountant who was identified in some press accounts as "a close associate of Louis Wolfson."[2] By the spring of 1950, Goodkind and two other new directors had been elected to the Colt board. Congressman Dodd blamed them for the company's plan, announced at that time, to repurchase up to $7 million worth of its shares from public investors, a move that Dodd believed was aimed at enriching the Goodkind group itself. The stock-buying campaign cost the company $6.5 million that it could ill afford. As a result, Dodd later complained, "this old reliable and respected firearms company has been substantially weakened. Many longtime, highly skilled workers and their families are in jeopardy, and from a defense production standpoint every citizen in the United States has been affected."[3]

Then there was Torrington, Connecticut, the hometown of the Hendey

Machine Company. In 1952, Hendey was acquired by an investment group led by the young Frederick W. Richmond. Fred Richmond, just twenty-nine, was a precocious young financier, the son of a Boston lawyer. While in high school, he was collecting fees for his advice on filling out income-tax returns; at Harvard in 1942, his aggressive advertising sales helped the popular campus humor magazine, the *Lampoon*, pay off its mortgage. After serving as a Navy radioman during the war, he immediately set himself up in his father's law office in Boston as a business broker, finding buyers for surplus textiles and tracking down scarce industrial machinery for a fee. Soon his business commanded new corporate offices on Fifth Avenue in New York City. In late 1951, at age twenty-eight, he matched Tom Evans's hunger for autonomy and bought control of his first company, W. Ralston and Company of Old Bridge, New Jersey, which recycled industrial paper.[4] Substantial investors began to back him, and with his larger war chest he bought more companies—including Hendey.

Nothing about the brash young man from Boston suggested that he was settling into Torrington, Connecticut, to take his place as a long-term member of the civic elite. Nevertheless, when city officials and nervous employees questioned the takeover, Richmond's representatives were reas-suring. No, the factory would not be shut down, the assets would not be liquidated. Life would go on as it had for decades. But Richmond was developing a knack for finding companies that were worth more dead than alive. Perhaps some struggling company had a well-known brand, some cash in the till, some tax losses that could shelter someone else's future profits, or perhaps just a stock exchange listing. He bought and sold, trad-ing one company's prospects for another company's assets—as he had been doing since he got out of the Navy. For middle-aged men who had worked at Hendey all their lives, 1952 was the year that a good night's sleep became a vanishing memory.

By late 1950, public concern over these early postwar mergers had finally forced Congress to plug a well-known loophole in the nation's antitrust laws.

The original antitrust legislation, the Sherman Act, had been adopted in 1890. In 1914, in the name of further enhancing the competition that big business actually found so troublesome, Congress passed the Clayton Act. The new law made it illegal for one corporation to acquire the stock of another if the result would be to reduce competition between the two firms or within a particular region, or if the acquisition would tend to cre-ate a monopoly.[5] Even a casual reader could see the escape hatch in the Clayton Act, however. If one simply acquired the assets of a rival company, rather than its stock, one had nothing to fear.

Congress was well aware of this defect, and remedial bills were frequently introduced from the mid-1920s onward. But those amendments routinely faltered, amid big business opposition and the distractions of global depression followed by a world war. Finally, on December 30, 1950, Congress enacted amendments to the Clayton Act to bar anti-competitive acquisitions made through the purchase of assets.

But with the federal courts giving little support to the government's antitrust campaign, the amendment did little to deter big American companies from buying up their smaller competitors. Indeed, the number of mergers increased each year after the 1950 Clayton Act amendments, and the nation's largest firms bought up an ever-growing swath of the business landscape.[6]

And while most of those changes in corporate control were the result of friendly deals, there were at least twenty-one full-fledged proxy fights in 1952, according to federal securities regulators, far more than in earlier years. One of them, a battle that continued into 1953, was perfectly scripted to further fascinate and alarm the general public.

Leading the insurgent shareholders was streetwise Charlie Green, that irrepressible proxy fighter whose nose had been bloodied in Minneapolis in 1950 but who had stayed on his feet to defeat a stunned management slate in the United Cigar-Whelan Stores contest in 1951. But unlike the bland businessmen who had squared off against him before, Green's adversaries in this new fight in 1952 were as colorful as he was: Spyros Skouras, an exotic Greek entrepreneur who had risen from immigrant obscurity to become president of Twentieth Century–Fox, the motion picture giant, and Darryl F. Zanuck, the creative head of Fox's Hollywood studios and the company's biggest stockholder.

Green had first become a Fox shareholder—or, as he would have put it, a partner in the moviemaking business—in 1944, when Wall Street was still optimistic about Hollywood. Paying prices as high as $54 a share, he had gradually increased his stake.[7] The motion picture industry was far more glamorous than Green's other investment experiments, but no less troubled. The advent of television was rewriting the script for how America spent its leisure time, just as the automobile had changed the Twin Cities's streetcar business. "The lush business that carried over from wartime into 1947 and 1948 had dried up. The quality of films, by the industry's own admission, was poor. Exhibitors could stand in their silent lobbies watching the public hurry home to catch Milton Berle."[8] Perhaps Green saw possibilities in motion pictures that others did not. Or perhaps the immigrant tailor's son from the rough streets of New York simply wanted to feel that he owned a piece of Hollywood stardom.

Reporters would never tire of describing how the management of Twentieth Century–Fox Film Corporation first attracted Charlie Green's irate attention. In early 1952, long after he had made his first substantial investment in Fox, Green and his wife, Catherine, were in Los Angeles and decided to visit the studio in which they were "partners." By some accounts, Mrs. Green was alone on this fabled studio visit. But in any case, the climax never varied: some low-level studio employee barred the gate. "It was one of the costliest rejections a studio employee ever made," one historian noted.[9] Said another, "It was to cost Twentieth Century close to $1 million to get out from under what was probably the most expensive financial and social gaffe of the decade."[10] More than a mere clash of egos was involved; Green devoutly believed that shareholders should be treated with respect by management. The incident at the studio gate profoundly insulted his sense of how corporate democracy should work.

His anger spurred him to make the train trip from New York to Wilmington, Delaware, to attend the annual Twentieth Century–Fox stockholders meeting later that spring. A member of the Fox management team later described what happened. "All of a sudden this chunky guy gets up and starts asking a lot of questions. He isn't very pleasant about it. He wants to know why we're paying ourselves such fancy salaries. He wants to know why we don't sell off some of the studio properties. He wants to know what about profits. He makes some crack about relatives on the payroll. He mentions a dirty word: television."[11] The assembled executives were stunned by their first look at Charlie Green in action.

People simply did not talk that way to the two towering egos who ran Twentieth Century–Fox. Darryl Zanuck, a small man with a clipped mustache and a taste for health food and polo, had begun his movie career as a scriptwriter for the Rin-Tin-Tin series of canine adventure films. One business writer of the day remembered Zanuck as "swaggering through life as though it were a perpetual Commedia dell'Arte."[12] A creative dynamo, he talked a nonstop line of superlative-studded patter, and seemed to have fifteen ideas before breakfast. "Hollywood offers few more dazzling sights than the diminutive Zanuck in riding breeches in his emperor-sized office slashing away at the air with his [polo] mallet," said a future movie producer.[13]

If Zanuck, who worked out of studio offices in Los Angeles, was what any Hollywood casting director would summon up to fill the role of movie producer, Spyros Skouras, nearly sixty, was more likely to be offered the role of an aging but still potent Caesar. His eyes stared fiercely out of his bullet-shaped head, and his sleek, thinning hair was silver. As a small, powerful youth, he had emigrated in 1908 from Greece with his two brothers, with whom he opened a diner in St. Louis. The diner's profits were chan-neled into the infant nickelodeon industry, which Skouras helped build into a chain of movie theaters. He parlayed his theater chain into a stake in the movie production business, and rose to the presidency of Twentieth Century, overseeing its distribution system from New York City. He was paid handsomely and he lived a lush life at company expense, with a suite of dark-paneled executive offices in Manhattan that included a steam room and massage tables. One of Skouras's associates later recalled the strategy sessions held there in response to Green's challenge. "We all sat around naked as jays listening to Skouras make the kind of conversation you'd expect to find in some boardroom. We'd be telling him why he ought to go through with the cumulative voting idea, for example, while the masseur would be pounding away on him."[14]

The "cumulative voting idea" they were sweating over in Skouras's suite was aimed at taking away one of the key weapons in Green's arsenal, since cumulative voting for corporate directors was the aspect of corporate democracy that most empowered minority shareholders in the early post-war period.[15] Normally, a shareholder has one vote for each share of stock he owns. But a shareholder in a company that permits cumulative voting for directors has one vote per share for every director standing for election. The theory is that an investor with a thousand shares who is voting for a nine-member board is actually casting 9,000 votes; cumulative voting allows him to cast all of those 9,000 votes for a single director, if he chooses. This sort of focused voting gave minority stockholders a sporting chance of winning at least one seat on a corporate board. It had served Charlie Green, and other proxy fighters, extremely well in earlier fights.

Entirely too well, in the view of Skouras and Zanuck, who were alarmed at the threat Green posed to the serenity of the Fox boardroom. Shortly after his undiplomatic debut in Wilmington, Green had in fact demanded a seat on the Fox board of directors. He was turned down—the studio gate, it seems, was still barred. Given Green's background, even men far less astute than Skouras and Zanuck would have seen that a major proxy fight was likely to be waged in advance of the 1953 annual stockholders meet-ing. Since Fox permitted cumulative voting, Green would be able to focus his shareholder votes on a few seats and, just possibly, install himself in the corporate boardroom, within hailing distance of those massage tables. Agi-tated at that thought, the strategists advising Skouras suggested that it was time to eliminate cumulative voting from the company bylaws.

Their cover story for this defensive ploy boiled down to "the Lord giveth, the Lord taketh away." Cumulative voting had been added to the company bylaws in 1935 at the insistence of Zanuck and two partners, when their Twentieth Century Pictures merged with the Fox Film Corporation, Skouras reasoned in a letter to shareholders. "Mr. Zanuck who, with his family, is the largest stockholder of the Corporation, now urges the removal of the provision relating to cumulative voting," Skouras continued.[16] He boldly but illogically asserted that Green planned to liquidate the corporation—no minority board member could do that. And then he reached for the sweeping Hollywood defense of his position: "Management believes that liquidation is contrary not only to the best interest of the stockholders and employees throughout the world, but also that such action would be against the best interests of America." He continued, "Our decision to press for elimination of the cumulative voting provision was made only after every effort had been made to persuade Mr. Green to be patient for another year. We explained that we had tremendous plans afoot and at this time management should not be disturbed. When he refused to understand, we had no alternative but to take this action."[17]

Green played his best hand, sending shareholders a detailed anatomy of the incredibly favorable employment contracts that both Skouras and Zanuck had negotiated with the company, and questioning some of the personnel decisions the two executives had made. "For instance," he wrote, "the current annual report reveals that during 1952 Mr. Zanuck's son-in-law, Robert L. Jacks, was on the payroll as a producer. I understand that he is about 23 years old. The report also reveals that Otto Lange was, until recently, on the payroll as a producer. I understand that Mr. Lange was Mr. Zanuck's former ski instructor and that only a few years ago, he was teaching skiing at Sun Valley."[18] As for any plans to liquidate the company, Green said the idea was "literally ridiculous on the face of it." He was not even seeking *control* of the corporation—merely minority representation on its board of directors. Certain to be out-voted in the boardroom by the Zanuck block, "I couldn't liquidate the company even if I wanted to," he argued.

In any public relations battle, the odds-makers will certainly favor Hollywood over some feisty, tough-talking street kid who learned his social skills at the Madison Avenue Boys Club. And Skouras and Zanuck did not disappoint. First, Skouras recruited an "all-star cast" of director candidates, headed by General James A. Van Fleet, a hero of the Korean War, which was just grinding to its bloody but inconclusive close. The general sent stockholders a letter in which he praised the motion picture industry for "portraying the goodness and decency of America to an ever-growing audience of people who are yearning to know more about freedom."[19]

Skouras had suggested that Van Fleet might prefer to wait out the proxy fight, the war hero continued, but he had decided "that if there was a fight going on, I would not avoid it."

Other candidates on the slate loyal to Skouras and Zanuck included the official biographer of the immensely popular President Eisenhower, the chairman of the board of a nationwide department store chain, and the honorary chairman of the General Foods Corporation, whose brands were familiar to Americans everywhere.

To his perfect casting, Skouras added the essential element of suspense, first introduced with his veiled hint to stockholders that management had "tremendous plans afoot" if Green would only be patient. Seeking to compete with the little flickering box in everyone's living rooms, Fox had been experimenting for years with a new technology that would allow it to shoot wide-angle films that could be projected across a screen far bigger than those familiar to moviegoing Americans. These sweeping wide-screen films would be further enhanced by their stereophonic sound tracks. This great leap forward in moviemaking—called CinemaScope—was the corporation's great hope for stock-market salvation. "The ultimate public acceptance obviously cannot be stated in advance but we have great confidence in our system," Skouras told shareholders. "After only one demonstration, which we held in Hollywood in March, CinemaScope has received the greatest possible acclaim from theater owners as well as producers, directors, writers, newspapermen, business and financial leaders."[20] The message was clear: shareholders should stick with the management team that could make CinemaScope a reality, not with some quick-draw raider like Charlie Green, who had refused to see reason when Skouras had urged him to be patient.

Green, of course, was furious at the suggestion that he was anything but a devoted longterm investor in Twentieth Century–Fox—indeed, he had owned shares since 1944. And he was openly scornful of management's strategy of risking all its chips on the uncertain success of CinemaScope, which seemed to him as unpromising as the gimmicky 3-D films that had audiences watching the screen through flimsy cardboard-and-celluloid glasses. As he wrote: "I hope that Mr. Skouras is right in his confidence as to the future of CinemaScope and not just gambling the assets of our company to impress you stockholders during this contest. If our company is wrong and CinemaScope is not the final answer to the 3-D problem, in my opinion our company will stand to lose many millions of dollars. I believe minority representation on the board is our best insurance against any wild-cat operations in this regard."[21]

Green's fate was sealed when Skouras and Zanuck decided to unveil

CinemaScope to the public—and to shareholders—just before a special stockholders meeting was to convene on May 5, 1953, in Wilmington, to consider management's proposal to eliminate cumulative voting. The company leased the Roxy Theatre near Times Square in New York City, expanded its screen and upgraded its sound system. There were no completed CinemaScope movies yet, but three were in progress: *The Robe*, a religious epic; *How to Marry a Millionaire*, a zany romantic comedy; and *Beneath the Twelve-Mile Reef*, an adventure film. The studio decided to splice scenes from all three into a CinemaScope sampler. "It then invited the financial and theatrical press, its stockholders, bankers, brokers, trustees—anybody who had a vote, or could swing a vote—to a series of showings," wrote proxy-fight historian David Karr.[22]

The new film technique was an enormous success with moviegoers and investors. The studio's gamble had paid off, and Green's lack of faith seemed to somehow disqualify him from hobnobbing in the boardroom with the creative geniuses who had brought CinemaScope to life. When the proxies were counted at the special stockholders meeting, Green lost by a 4-to-1 margin and cumulative voting was deleted from the company bylaws. At the regularly scheduled annual meeting later that month, the Skouras slate of directors scored an even greater victory against Green and his fellow insurgents.

It was to be Charlie Green's last proxy fight. After his loss, he applied himself to the management of United Cigar–Whelan Stores and left takeover battles to others. But even those who defeated him conceded later that Fox executives would probably not have moved as quickly to implement the new CinemaScope technology if Green had not been nipping at their heels. And curiously enough, Green remained a substantial stockholder in Twentieth Century–Fox for years. More curious still, he was treated with increasing courtesy and deference by Skouras. One account, published just a few years after this bruising battle, had Skouras personally escorting Green around studio property as if Green owned the place.[23]

Like Green, most of the other proxy fighters who tried to unseat corporate management in 1953 were unsuccessful. Out of an estimated twenty-two skirmishes that year, the opposition slate won just four, all at very small companies far out of the public eye.[24] But those long odds did not deter Leopold Silberstein, who had managed to revive the prospects of the old Pennsylvania Coal and Coke Corporation by investing in surplus government freighters and who was now ready for some substantial acquisitions.[25]

Silberstein had nibbled up some oil and gas properties but the summer of 1953 was when his corporate shopping spree really got under way. That was when he acquired the Crescent Company in Pawtucket, Rhode Island, from the family that had operated it since 1921. Once a maker of shoe and corset laces, it later specialized in insulated copper wire used in the automotive industry. Silberstein wisely left the family management in place, and Crescent hummed along nicely. The founding family had accepted notes from Silberstein's company in payment for their stake, so he was able to acquire Crescent with very little cash. His knack for building a corporate empire on credit was beginning to make him a figure of controversy on Wall Street. But he was a pragmatist. If people were willing to sell to him on credit, it would be foolish not to take advantage of the opportunity. The Crescent Company deal attracted little attention outside of Rhode Island. But there was considerably more interest when he surfaced as one of the largest stockholders in Industrial Brownhoist Corporation of Bay City, Michigan.

Brownhoist, while unfamiliar to the average American, was the industrial equivalent of a household name, especially in mining and heavy manufacturing circles. At its headquarters on the Saginaw Bay of Lake Huron and at its foundry in Ohio, Brownhoist built locomotives, huge wrecking cranes, and other Godzilla-sized equipment designed to handle monster machinery and mountains of raw materials, especially coal and iron ore. Moreover, it was what one writer called "a rich little plum," with $1.3 million in cash and a line of business that seemed likely to benefit considerably as the American industrial economy adapted to the unprecedented level of peacetime defense spending that characterized what people were starting to call the Cold War.[26]

When Silberstein first began to dream of owning it, Brownhoist was controlled by the vast Alleghany Corporation empire, which in turn was run by the unpredictable Robert R. Young. But by early 1953, "Railroad" Young had made it clear to all but the deliberately obtuse that he was preparing to wage a proxy fight to acquire control of the New York Central Railroad, the famous Vanderbilt line that dominated rail service between New York and Chicago. Silberstein had heard rumors that Young was planning to sell some Alleghany assets to raise cash for the coming campaign, and thought Young might be willing to consider offers for Alleghany's 48 percent stake in Brownhoist.

Silberstein's chance came when one of his well-connected directors, President Truman's former Secretary of the Interior Oscar Chapman, encountered Young at a charity luncheon. Seizing the moment, Chapman said, "'I hear Alleghany wants to sell its Brownhoist stock.' Young said that was so and, when asked the price, he told Chapman $13 a share. Chapman replied: 'I'm with Pennsylvania Coal and Coke Corporation and we'll give $13 a share.' They shook hands" on the deal.[27]

That block of Brownhoist stock would cost Silberstein some $2.9 million. Alleghany was willing to accept three-year I.O.U.s for most of the purchase price, but Young wanted a cash down payment of just over $480,000—considerably more cash than Pennsylvania Coal and Coke had on hand. To close the deal, Silberstein borrowed $500,000 from another of his company directors, David L. Subin, a wealthy hosiery manufacturer who lived in the Philadelphia area.

Although he still owed Alleghany $2.4 million for the stock, Silberstein nevertheless had the right to vote the Brownhoist shares, and in July 1953 he promptly elected himself chairman and chose three other men to sit on the seven-man Brownhoist board with him.

Even with his one-vote majority, Silberstein faced considerable opposition in the Brownhoist boardroom. The other three directors, including company president Hoyt E. Hayes and Alexander C. Brown, a Cleveland industrialist, had been part of the Brownhoist package that Silberstein purchased from Alleghany. And thanks to the company's practice of permitting cumulative voting, these directors were in a strong position to hang onto their seats. "From the start, there was a gulf between the two factions," *Business Week* later reported.[28] The principal bone of contention was Silberstein's plan to merge Brownhoist into Pennsylvania Coal and Coke. The three minority directors were vehemently opposed to the merger, and Alexander Brown soon formed a "stockholders protective committee" that claimed the support of 42 percent of the company's investors. Silberstein had purchased enough shares to turn Alleghany's 48 percent stake into a razor-thin majority. But the commercial laws in Ohio, where Brownhoist was incorporated, required that mergers be approved by two-thirds of the acquired company's stockholders. Silberstein was stymied, and his merger plan was put on hold in October 1953.

But his boardroom opponents could not prevent Silberstein from tapping into Brownhoist's fat bank account. His four votes were sufficient to carry the day when the directors voted on how much Brownhoist should pay in stock dividends. Brownhoist had paid dividends of 90 cents a share in 1952. Silberstein pushed through regular and special dividends that brought the 1953 total to more than $2.30 a share, an amount that Silberstein's opposition argued was excessive since the company had earned only $1.71 a share that year. Pennsylvania Coal and Coke's share of those generous dividends totaled about $800,000—not bad for an acquisition that had so far cost Silberstein only $500,000 in cash, all of which was borrowed.[29]

He also had enough boardroom votes to hire a management consulting firm, Ebasco Services, to undertake a sweeping survey of company operations in late October 1953. And this was perhaps his most brilliant stroke of boardroom strategy. The Ebasco study, conducted by a widely respected industrial engineer named Louis Ralston, was submitted to the Brownhoist board in December. It was full of recommendations on ways to "improve and modernize" company operations. As Silberstein later explained, "Ebasco advised us to strengthen the sales organization, increase plant efficiency, put in a safety program, and make way for the younger men." Who could oppose such a sensible program? Well, Brownhoist's president Hoyt Hayes, for one. After months of argument over the Ebasco recommendations, Hayes threw in the towel and resigned as president and executive committee member. He was resigning "under protest," he said, because "the majority of the board of directors feels that the corporation would get along better without my services."[30] Silberstein shrewdly tapped Lou Ralston of Ebasco to replace Hayes.

In early 1954, Silberstein increased Brownhoist's board to nine members, from seven, but the minority faction led by Alexander Brown retained enough voting power to keep their three seats—confronting Silberstein with continued opposition to his proposal to merge the two companies. Finally, later in 1954, he bought out his troublesome opponents, offering them a premium price for their shares. He promptly merged Brownhoist into his original company, which he renamed the Penn-Texas Corporation—the banner under which he would wage his future proxy fights.

Robert Young's efforts to raise cash by selling assets in 1953 had an unexpected effect on another important proxy fight being waged that year. Once again, the purchaser was bent on taking control of a vulnerable company. But this proxy fighter was very different from Silberstein and Green: he was waging a defensive proxy fight, aimed at fending off another corporate raider. He called it "counter-insurgency." Others described it as "raiding the raider," and they marveled at its originality. The man who devised that novel defense was, in fact, one of the most creative and controversial figures to participate in the proxy wars of the fifties and one of the key strategists in Tom Evans's most ambitious postwar takeover. His name was Art Landa.

Actually, although he was known as both Art and Alfons, his given name was Alfonso Howard Beaumont Landa and he was born in Chicago around 1896. His father, part of a far-flung and socially prominent Hispanic family, died when Landa was twelve. Young Art's education was haphazard, sandwiched between extensive European travel with his widowed mother. He served for a few months in the U.S. Army in 1917, when he was twenty-one or so, but was discharged for medical reasons. The same year, his mother died and left him a substantial legacy of about $200,000, which allowed him to dabble in higher education at various institutions. He tried medicine, drama, even psychiatry by way of a brief apprenticeship with Sigmund Freud in Vienna. Somewhere along the way, according to his son, he acquired a young wife, who soon divorced him. Finally, in 1922, although he still lacked a bachelor's degree, he was accepted at the Georgetown University law school; the next year he transferred to the George Washington University's law school where he buckled down sufficiently to earn a law degree in 1925.[31]

He was nearly thirty, a slim man of medium height with laughing gray eyes set under straight bushy eyebrows. Witty and socially graceful, he was in no hurry to settle into the workday grind. In 1926, after collecting his law degree, he was back in Europe, visiting friends in the privileged circle that would be his preferred milieu for the rest of his life. But while he was in Paris, he met an American lawyer named Joseph E. Davies, who was on vacation from his prominent Washington legal practice, and the two men forged a bond that changed Art Landa's life. When Davies returned to Washington, Landa came with him, joining the law firm that bore his mentor's name—and that would one day bear his own.

It was the Jazz Age in the nation's capital and Landa was perfectly at home in the gossipy dinner-party world that Davies's sponsorship opened to him. Even after the Republicans' New Economic Era had crumbled with the 1929 stock market crash, Landa preserved his privileged position. On an afternoon in late June 1930, most of Washington's "official, diplomatic and resident society" attended his pink-and-white wedding to the daughter of former Wyoming Congressman Frank W. Mondell. He and his bride departed Washington for New York, where they left the Depression behind to sail to Europe for the summer. "Before returning in October, they will spend several weeks in the home of Mr. Landa on the Riviera," the social notice in the New York Times breathlessly concluded.[32]

Soon, most of Washington's political doors were opening to Landa, thanks to well-placed shoves from Davies, a Democrat who worked ardently for the election of Franklin Roosevelt in 1932. Landa, with his elegant manners, urbane chatter, and cultivated European tastes, became a popular addition to lively White House gatherings and a regular presence at presidential aide Harry Hopkins's bridge tables. But his real value to the Democrats was in his fund-raising abilities—he was widely credited with helping to finance and "stage-manage" Roosevelt's second inauguration in 1937. Soon thereafter, his mentor Joseph Davies was confirmed by the Senate as Roosevelt's new ambassador to Moscow, where he would cultivate a brief and woefully undiscerning relationship with Joseph Stalin.

Landa labored on for the Democratic Party in Washington, but by early 1942, his second marriage was on the rocks. Just days after the divorce decree was final, newspapers were reporting that he was to be married again—to Consuelo Morgan Thaw, the eldest of the three Morgan sisters whose beauty and social exploits fascinated a generation.[33] Consuelo's younger sister Thelma, the former Lady Furness, had been romantically linked a decade earlier to the bachelor Prince of Wales, who became the Duke of Windsor after his abdication in 1936. Thelma's twin sister Gloria was Mrs. Reginald Vanderbilt, the widow of an heir to the fabulous railroad fortune and the losing figure in a spectacular legal battle with her husband's family over custody of her young daughter Gloria. Consuelo herself, known as Connie, had been married briefly and unhappily to a French count when she was only seventeen. Her happier second marriage, to career diplomat and socialite Benjamin Thaw Jr., continued until Ambassador Thaw's death in 1937. Her quiet marriage to the amiable Art Landa took place in early May 1942, in the flower-filled living room of her brother Harry's Beverly Hills home. Sister Thelma looked on as sister Gloria served as Connie's matron of honor; brother Harry Morgan was not only host but best man. The new Mr. and Mrs. Landa honeymooned in Havana and Palm Beach.[34]

His sometimes stormy marriage to the well-traveled Connie Thaw brought Landa into an even more glittering social orbit than the Latin and Parisian circles he already occupied. But he already had become something of a celebrity in his own right, at least in the political fishbowl of Washington. He had especially distinguished himself by serving as the defense attorney for an airline pilot who had been charged with destroying records subpoenaed by the Senate in its investigation of air-mail contracts in the mid-1930s. "The case was something of a historic curiosity in that it was actually tried on the floor of the Senate," noted one account. "The numerous lawyers involved had an unparalleled opportunity to perform for posterity." Landa's backstage performance was so impressive, this writer noted, that Louisiana Senator Huey Long "forthwith employed him to serve in a libel action" filed against the senator by one of the victims of his verbal tirades. An assassin soon removed Senator Long from Landa's client roster, but he had other even more impressive names on it: Tom Watson, the founder of IBM; Louis B. Mayer, the motion picture mogul; and Barbara Hutton, the Wall Street heiress.[35]

After the war, Landa formed a real estate venture in Washington, invested in a transit company in the Southeast, and built a substantial portfolio of oil properties. He had always been fascinated by business, he said later, but decided to get involved directly because "I was getting rich clients and large fees, but I had no real money. I looked at these people who pay themselves a million a year and patronized me to the tune of maybe $50,000. I said to myself, 'What's the difference between them and me?' I decided I should move over and become a businessman."[36]

Part fixer, part social butterfly, a meticulous and well-dressed man of great charm, Landa was in high clover while Roosevelt was in office. He had perhaps slightly less pull in the dowdy Truman administration; he would later testify against some of Truman's less worthy associates in subsequent congressional investigations of alleged influence peddling by White House staffers. Although he could navigate Washington's bureaucratic catacombs blindfolded, as the forties ended Landa seemed to sense that the zeitgeist was shifting from bureaucratic America to corporate America. In May 1951, he accepted a seat on the board of directors of Colonial Airlines, a longstanding corporate client of his law firm. Colonial was run by a colorful and charismatic figure named Sigmund Janas, whose careless administration of the airline had provoked the exasperation of the Civil Aeronautics Board, which regulated the nation's domestic airline industry. Just before Landa was to join the board, airline regulators ruled that Janas must resign. "Landa volunteered to take over as president; in the absence of any other contenders he was speedily approved by the C.A.B."[37]

Landa did not pretend that he knew much about running an airline, and his personal diaries reveal that he continued to consult closely with the banished Janas through the summer of 1951. Landa's son recalls that the lawyer did institute one innovation that was soon widely copied: he offered cocktails in the New York departure lounges before Colonial flights. But beyond keeping customers happy, his strategy was to find a buyer interested in Colonial's attractive air routes, which included service to Canada and Bermuda. He inspired a bidding war between National Airlines and Eastern Airlines that dragged on for years. Eastern eventually bought Colonial at $24 a share, compared with the $7.50 that Colonial's shares had commanded when Landa took over.

Running Colonial was not Landa's full-time job, of course. He had other clients and other interests. In February 1951, for example, he met with a group of investors led by that odd Wall Street figure, Jackson Martindell, who had once waged an unsuccessful proxy fight at Bell Aircraft, to discuss a possible stockholders' lawsuit against the *Saturday Evening Post*. He cultivated his friends in Congress, and was politely treated when he testified in March 1951 at Senate hearings examining the operations of the Reconstruction Finance Corporation. He coped with his increasingly rocky marriage to Connie Thaw, which would finally deteriorate into a long separation and a protracted divorce-court battle over alimony. And he made his regular summertime visit to the rustic Canadian vacation home owned by his friend and mentor, Joe Davies.

His loyalty to Davies never faltered, despite the ugly political and media attacks that were increasingly falling on his mentor's shoulders. In 1941, Davies had written a memoir, *Mission to Moscow,* a colorful but naive account of his short tenure as Roosevelt's ambassador to the Soviet Union. The book was full of praise for Joseph Stalin, who was portrayed as "uncommonly wise and gentle," a fatherly giant helping his nation recover from the devastation of the German invasion and prodding his backward people to modernize their agricultural economy.[38]

By 1950, Russia's status as America's heroic wartime ally against Hitler had been thoroughly forgotten. In 1949, China had come under the control of Communist revolutionaries lead by Mao Tse-tung and Russia had broken America's nuclear monopoly by testing its own atomic bomb. A year later, State Department aide Alger Hiss was convicted of perjury, and American troops were fighting Chinese Communists under the United Nations banner in Korea. The nation slid toward an ugly suspicion that hidden Communists were undermining the nation's interests. Soon, Joe Davies had became a common target of scorn among those who now saw the Soviet Union as the summation of all the evil at work in the world. Anytime he was mentioned in the increasingly anti-Communist press, he was referred to as "Joe 'Mission to Moscow' Davies," as if the title of his memoir were some organized crime nickname.

Inevitably, some of the tar from these reckless times was splashed on those business mavericks who stepped out of the conformist mold of the day to challenge corporate management. Landa's frequent travels abroad made xenophobes nervous, and he was "guilty" by association with Davies and with another friend, the controversial columnist Drew Pearson, whom Senator Joseph McCarthy regularly denounced as a Communist mouthpiece. Landa also became friendly with David Karr, an ambitious young public relations man he met one evening at the Pearsons' Washington home. Karr, too, had incurred the public wrath of the Red-hunters, having worked as a freelance writer for the *Daily Worker* in New York and as Pearson's "legman," or research assistant, in Washington. As McCarthyism grew more rabid, Leopold Silberstein—initially portrayed in the business press as a plucky Horatio Alger figure—began to read snide references to his exotic background and his use of foreign banks and extensive credit, with his most vituperative critic being Leslie Gould, the square-jawed business editor of the *New York Journal-American.*[39] Gould raged against Lou Wolfson as well, with what one former colleague said was a thinly veiled anti-Semitism.[40] Gould characterized corporate raiders as "the modern-day version of the buccaneers who sailed the seven seas two hundred years ago," emphasizing the raiders' reliance on "moneylenders, including those operating from foreign sanctuaries, such as Switzerland, Hong Kong and Tangiers."[41]

It was not lost on these isolation-minded conspiracy theorists that many of the young men causing such trouble in the corporate boardrooms, traditionally dominated by old established American Protestant families, were newcomers and outsiders—immigrant Jews, New Deal Democrats, liberal intellectuals, upstart Irish Catholics.

In an America charmed by such banal television fare as *The Adventures of Ozzie and Harriet*, the oft-divorced Landa spoke fluent Spanish and French, and the mercurial Robert Young wrote poetry, entertained the Duke and Duchess of Windsor, and collected modern art, notably that of his iconoclastic sister-in-law, Georgia O'Keeffe. In a largely Protestant business community fueled by inherited money and knitted together by Ivy League friendships, Louis Wolfson was a college dropout whose father had been an immigrant Jewish junk dealer, and Charlie Green was an occasional night-school student whose father had been an immigrant Jewish tailor. In Norman Rockwell's pastel-tinted America, Leopold Silberstein still spoke with a heavy German accent, flippantly answered suspicious questions about his "soldier of fortune" résumé, and collected contemporary French art.

Tom Evans, in contrast to most other takeover players of the day, seemed to be a familiar product of the American heartland, granite-plain and deeply rooted in the conservative bedrock of Pittsburgh. His Main Street image perhaps protected him from the anti-American suspicions that began to settle on the more exotic raiders. And nowhere, in that ugly moment of history, did a corporate raider need protective coloration more than in Pittsburgh. As the Soviet Union installed harsh puppet governments across Eastern Europe, the Polish and Slavic communities of western Pennsylvania were swept by "a violent backlash, a strident assertion of Americanism and a wave of indignation."[42] By one account, Pittsburgh became "the violent epicenter of the anti-communist eruption in postwar America."[43] Militant judges, a fiercely anti-communist press, undercover FBI agents, and various ambitious politicians kept the city in a Red-hunting uproar from 1947 to the mid-1950s. It is doubtful that as controversial and undiplomatic a figure as Tom Evans could have been half so effective in such an environment but for his impeccable mainstream credentials.

But while Evans brandished his Shady Side diploma, Art Landa relied on his charm and his connections. Both were sufficiently impressive that, despite the sour atmosphere of the times, Landa nevertheless found a warm welcome in such heartland communities as Detroit, where he had forged strong personal ties to some members of the Fruehauf family. The Fruehaufs, clients of Landa's law firm for years, manufactured the trucking rigs that independent Teamsters drove around the country's burgeoning network of highways, and their brand was familiar to every Sunday driver.

Landa was invited to join the Fruehauf board in 1950, as the family company was struggling to accommodate the ambitions of the next generation of Fruehaufs. The chairman of the board on which Landa served was Harvey Fruehauf, but his influence was increasingly eclipsed by that of his brother Roy Fruehauf, who was president and chief executive. By the spring of 1953, Harvey had become sufficiently indifferent to the company that he sometimes did not even bother to show up for board meetings. At that time, brother Roy proposed that Harvey pass him the gavel of decision and become "honorary chairman," a plan that Landa and several other Fruehauf directors supported. Harvey somewhat grudgingly agreed, but his pride was clearly injured. He nursed his grievance for several months, and by the time he assumed his honorary title, "he was convinced that he had been treated shabbily."[44]

In July 1953, he expressed his simmering anger in a way certain to attract his brother's attention: he sold 130,900 shares of the company to the Detroit and Cleveland Navigation Company, which was controlled by a scrappy Detroit businessman and budding corporate raider named George J. Kolowich. In 1951, Kolowich had shut down his steamship company's Great Lakes operations and devoted his attention to his other business interest, the Denver-Chicago Trucking Company. But when Harvey Fruehauf sold him a 9 percent stake in one of the best-known brands in the trucking industry, Kolowich understandably asked Roy Fruehauf for Harvey's seat on the board of directors.

Landa would later insist that Fruehauf's reluctance to welcome the company's new shareholder into the boardroom was rooted in Kolowich's background, which included a long-ago prison term in a bank-related embezzlement case. When Kolowich responded to the rebuff by buying additional Fruehauf shares in the open market, Landa realized "the company might have a full-fledged raid on its hands."[45]

Landa's defense of Fruehauf was simply brilliant. First, he measured Kolowich's grip on Detroit and Cleveland, and discovered that it was surprisingly weak. Indeed, a 15 percent block of D&C stock was owned by the ubiquitous Alleghany Corporation. Unlike Silberstein in his Brownhoist raid, Landa could not wait for a chance encounter with Alleghany's

Robert Young. Instead, he took the initiative, notifying Young that the Interstate Commerce Commission might object to Alleghany owning stakes in various railroads and in a steamship line, albeit an inactive one. Landa even nagged the ICC into sending Alleghany a letter questioning this apparent infraction of federal cross-ownership rules, according to one account.[46] The last thing that Young wanted on the eve of his fight for the New York Central was trouble with federal regulators. He promptly but quietly sold Alleghany's D&C shares to Roy Fruehauf and Art Landa.

Next, Landa deftly used his formidable knowledge of how Washington worked to deprive Kolowich of his best defense against a hostile raid, which was simply to issue additional shares of D&C stock and thereby dilute the power of the 15 percent stake Fruehauf and Landa controlled. First, Landa visited the ICC's offices and persuaded the commission that Kolowich was still violating federal rules against cross-ownership because he personally owned both a trucking company and a company with a certificate to operate a steamship service. Pressed again by regulators, the irritated Kolowich decided to give up the steamship certificate, which was virtually the only asset that D&C possessed except for its stake in Fruehauf. Then, Landa marched over to the Securities and Exchange Commission's bleak little offices in Washington and pointed out that D&C now owned nothing but shares of another company's stock. Therefore, Landa argued, Kolowich's company should be considered an investment company, as mutual funds were known in those days. The SEC regulators scratched their heads for moment but then agreed. And under the laws that governed investment companies, Kolowich could not issue new shares without a fresh authorization from shareholders—an electorate that now included Fruehauf and Landa, who had been steadily adding to the 15 percent stake they originally purchased from Young.

But Kolowich's sudden involuntary incarnation as a mutual fund manager did not deter him from scouting out additional Fruehauf shares in the marketplace. There was only one way to block him on that front, and that was to buy Fruehauf shares first and keep the price strong. To get the money for those critical purchases, Fruehauf and Landa turned in September 1953 to David Beck, the powerful new leader who had just risen to the presidency of the rough-and-ready Teamsters union.[47] Beck, who was eager to help his accommodating friend Roy Fruehauf fend off Kolowich, arranged for the union's pension fund to lend $1.5 million to a charitable foundation controlled by the Fruehaufs. The foundation planned to use the money, which was to be disbursed over the coming months, to increase its stake in Fruehauf stock and thereby keep the stock out of Kolowich's hands.

Subsequent congressional testimony suggests that the pudgy-faced Dave Beck was a difficult creditor, demanding better terms and deliberately delaying the delivery of the desperately needed cash.[48] A December 1953 letter that Senate investigators later found in Landa's files offered Beck half of any profits Landa made on the Fruehauf deal.[49] The letter, of course, suggests that Landa and Roy Fruehauf were being shaken down by the corrupt Teamster boss, who would later go to prison for his abuse of his union position. But when the letter was questioned by a Senate committee in 1957, Landa insisted that the offer—a simple expression of his "very lively sense of appreciation" for Beck's timely help, he said—had been politely declined by Beck and promptly forgotten.[50] Senator John F. Kennedy of Massachusetts, whose brother Robert Kennedy was one of the panel's top investigators, fiercely scolded the unruffled Washington lawyer. "I am frankly astonished, Mr. Landa, at your judgment in this matter," Jack Kennedy said. "I don't think that there is any doubt, at least in my mind, that it was highly improper for you to make the offer."[51] The Senate committee that was investigating Beck subsequently agreed with Kennedy, concluding that Landa had "acted in a highly questionable manner by offering to make a kickback to Dave Beck."[52]

Those details did not emerge for several years, however, and they were therefore of no use to George Kolowich as he battled the Fruehauf forces in the months preceding D&C's annual stockholders meeting in April 1954. But as that meeting approached, Kolowich was confident he would win the proxy battle—in part because Landa had mailed in a sizable number of proxies favorable to management. In a proxy fight, only the vote on the final proxy submitted actually counts, and Landa's forces arrived at the annual meeting with new proxies to replace those they had mailed in. These, of course, were not favorable to management. "At the annual meeting Kolowich's dismay was a thing to behold," *Fortune* later reported. "Landa took over as president of D&C and devoted the ensuing months to selling off most of the company's assets."[53] Fruehauf was safe, and Landa and Roy Fruehauf reaped a tidy profit when they liquidated Kolowich's company. Kolowich died a few years later.

Although his dealings with the corrupt Teamster chief would cause Landa considerable embarrassment in future years—indeed, Roy Fruehauf would later go to prison for bribing Beck in a different transaction—the Fruehauf victory in 1953 instantly made Landa's reputation as one of the nation's most creative defenders of corporate management. A business press that had been fascinated by the raiders suddenly saw fresh headlines among the ranks of the defenders and became thoroughly enthralled by the personalities and strategies of these battles for corporate control.

And there was no lack of headline fodder. The year of 1954 brought more than twenty-eight proxy fights, including the biggest one yet, Robert Young's long-expected battle to take control of the New York Central Railroad, a drama in which Tom Evans played a quiet cameo role on Young's behalf.

The fight was a watershed, a battle that briefly drew the general public's attention back to Wall Street for almost the first time since 1933, when bankers and brokers were being grilled by Congress in the aftermath of the 1929 crash. Across the country, everyone was talking about the New York Central fight. It was front-page news, and full-page advertisements filled the nation's leading newspapers; even the adolescent medium of television was enlisted to carry the adversaries' arguments to public stockholders. Robert Young and his publicity-shy rival, Central president William White, were invited to discuss the fight on the popular *Meet the Press* television program, more often a locale for political disputes than boardroom battles. Young even had some of his key advertisements translated into Yiddish and placed in the Jewish *Daily Forward* newspaper.[54] "This proxy war pushed a financial news story onto the front page and converted the term 'proxy fight' into a fixed part of our language," one amateur historian of the battle later concluded.[55]

That Young wanted control of the famous "Vanderbilt line" had been Wall Street's worst-kept secret. But Young made his ambitions official on a bright Sunday afternoon in mid-January 1954. He paid a visit to the home of his Palm Beach neighbor, Harold S. Vanderbilt, to announce that he and his partner, Allan Kirby, together owned 200,000 shares of the Central, on whose board Vanderbilt had served for forty years. Young's demand was simple: he wanted to be named chairman of the Central board, with Kirby at his side as a director. Vanderbilt telephoned Bill White's home in Scarsdale, New York, to deliver the stunning ultimatum.

The only response Vanderbilt and White could devise was to tell Young that his "request" would be considered when the Central board met on February 10 in New York. Young, with an understanding nod to boardroom protocol, agreed. But within days, newspapers had discovered that Young and his allies had severed their ties with the C&O Railroad, freeing them to invest in a different line—most likely, the New York Central. As the Wall Street buzz intensified, Young traveled secretly from Palm Beach to his New York offices in the Chrysler Building and invited White and his second-in-command to lunch at the Cloud Club, the building's private dining room. Young held out an olive branch: if Young were given the chief executive's job, White could stay on as chief operating officer, with a handsome package of stock options. White bristled, and rejected the offer.

Indeed, although he had a long-term contract with the Central, he vowed that he would resign if Young were successful in his takeover attempt.

When the Central directors gathered at the dark, clubby University Club on Fifth Avenue in New York on February 10, they voted unanimously against inviting Young and Kirby to join the board. It was to be war, one of the costliest that Wall Street had seen.

Young handled his financial and legal assault with great skill, fending off efforts by White to block the sale of 800,000 Central shares that had been held in trust for the C&O line. Young found two immensely wealthy Texas oil men, Clint Murchison and Sid Richardson, to buy the shares—largely with loans arranged by Young, and with a guarantee against loss on half the shares. And Young's political allies in Washington blocked White's attempt to persuade the ICC to investigate whether Young had indeed relinquished control of the C&O.[56]

Young was also able to enlist the support of at least one other corporate raider—Thomas Mellon Evans. As the proxy campaign heated up, executives at the New York Central noticed that Evans had showed up on the company's shareholder list as the owner of 3,500 shares. Ignorant of Evans's reputation and misled by that potent middle name, Bill White's team immediately contacted a member of the railroad's board of directors, L. N. Murray, who was president of the Mellon Bank in Pittsburgh. Could Murray get in touch with Evans and "sew up" his proxy for management? Murray immediately advised management that there was "no chance" that Evans would back management in the fight. The Pittsburgh banker was absolutely right: Evans voted the shares for the Young slate.[57]

But Young's most powerful weapon in the fight was his capacity to "merchandise conflict," as one public relations man put it. He cultivated the press, used the new influence of television to tell his story, and drafted most of his own full-page ads. Blithely forgetting to mention his princely residence in Newport and his royal house guests in Palm Beach, the shrewd Texan portrayed himself as the defender of the small shareholder beset by the rich, greedy Morgan bankers who supposedly dominated the Central's affairs. In all, Young spent more than $1.3 million in waging his fight for control, and the New York Central spent at least three-quarters of that amount in management's defense.

On May 26, 1954, about 2,200 stockholders and observers crushed into the Tenth Regiment Armory in Albany, the city which remained the Central's official home office. Young was greeted with cheers when he entered the vast hangar-like hall. Management supporters sported buttons that said "We Want White" while Young's forces had lapel buttons that read "Young at Heart." When a tidal wave of multiple proxies was finally sorted out nearly three weeks later, Young had won control of the Central by more than a million votes. He was generous in victory, remembering those who had helped him even in small ways: about this time, Thomas Mellon Evans became a director of the Central-controlled Pittsburgh and Lake Erie Railroad, a position he held for many years.

The attention that surrounded this remarkable battle would lead many subsequent writers to assume mistakenly that Young's fight for the New York Central was the first postwar proxy fight. It wasn't, by a long shot. But it nevertheless was a remarkable challenge to the entrenched forces of the railroad industry and the Wall Street establishment. The New York Central, with more than $2 billion in assets and more than 90,000 employees, had the backing of the Morgans, after all, and the upstart Young was scathing in his depiction of the powerful investment bankers as the greedy puppeteers of the nation's economy. Of course, his victory provided the best arguments against him.[58] But the lessons of the fight were not lost on American management.

Bill White had almost immediately recognized the essential threat posed by Young's methods. Near the beginning of the battle, he told his staffers, "This could be the beginning of a technique in which we find an astute trader with a certain popular appeal moving in on the professional management of big firms. American business right now has the most widespread ownership that it's ever had in history, and that's a fine, democratic thing. It would be, to say the least, unfortunate if this widespread ownership were allowed to be used as a tool by demagogues." He concluded with a succinct description of his mission: "We're not only fighting to keep control of the Central. We're fulfilling an over-all responsibility to American business."[59]

In an interview with the Associated Press before the final tally, White expanded on those views. "If a campaign of distortion, vilification, misrepresentation and pressure on newspapers and government can displace a sound and progressive management, the stability of every good enterprise can be threatened," he said. "Demagogues are dangerous in our political life. Demagogues in business or industry could, if successful, ruin important sections of our economy."[60]

Young's victory over White turned the corporate world on its head. The outsiders had become insiders. The rebellious shareholders had defeated the professional managers. Like Charlie Green, the "owners" were insisting on being treated with respect.

CHAPTER SEVEN

SOMEBODY ELSE IS TAKING MY PLACE

If Robert Young's victory had been American management's only defeat in 1954, it would still have been highly unsettling simply because it was so visible and so unexpected. But two other bruising and bitterly personal fights for control of major regional railroads were waged in the spring of 1954. While these two fights had been simmering since 1953 and did not attract the publicity of the epic New York Central battle in 1954, their outcomes nevertheless made corporate life seem far more precarious to many professional managers and further elevated the proxy fighter on America's political radar.

Railroad executive Patrick B. McGinnis, who had taken control of the Norfolk Southern in 1947, moved in Robert Young's orbit and generally supported the Texan's condemnation of the industry's "backward" thinking. He was an attractive man with sleek salt-and-pepper hair, a dimpled chin, and dark, angular brows, and he had literally grown up in the railroad business; his father was an Irish immigrant who supported his young family as a workman on the New York Central.

But he was certainly no diplomat. When the ICC criticized his management team at the Norfolk Southern Railway for excessive expenses and lapses in competitive bidding, his response was to grouse bitterly, "You spend a few thousand dollars, they think you robbed a bank." He resigned from Norfolk Southern in January 1953 to take control of the Central of Georgia Railway, headquartered in Savannah. His tenure there was an almost comical collision of cultures. The impatient, back-slapping New

York Irishman routinely insulted his local directors, making speeches that condemned past Central management as "a lot of old fogies dead from the neck up."[1] Two months after he took office, he was forced to resign when even his own allies on the board agreed that he "had probably over-taxed Georgia's hospitality."[2]

That left him free to enlist with a group of disgruntled stockholders of the New York, New Haven, and Hartford Railroad—the New Haven line, on which countless young men in their gray flannel suits commuted to work in Manhattan from expensive suburbs in Westchester County and shoreline Connecticut. The New Haven line had been something of a hobby for McGinnis for years. He had helped Frederick C. Dumaine Sr., one of his Wall Street clients, take control of the road in 1948.[3] After Dumaine died in 1951, however, his son and namesake, known as Buck Dumaine, took over. And by 1953, the younger Dumaine had alienated a substantial block of Canadian stockholders, who recruited McGinnis to help them win representation on the railroad's board. He agreed, on the condition that if he won the fight, he would replace Buck Dumaine as the railroad's president.

The close-fought proxy fight climaxed with a grueling forty-one-hour stockholders meeting in New Haven in April 1954. As the votes were counted, Dumaine tried to conduct a normal meeting; McGinnis shifted restlessly in his seat, tugging at his French cuffs and snapping irritably at questioners. "How long are we going to stay here?" he challenged Dumaine at one point.[4] The final tally showed McGinnis had elected eleven directors, while Dumaine had elected only ten. "Without a word, Buck Dumaine turned and left the room," *Time* magazine reported. Another once-powerful corporate manager had fallen.

Buck Dumaine's reputation was largely borrowed from his father. But Lucian C. Sprague, chairman and president of the Minneapolis and St. Louis Railroad, had been a giant in the industry for decades. His once-bankrupt railroad, known as the M&St.L, had once been a chronic joke in the industry—its initials were variously translated as the "Maimed and Still Limping" line and the "Misery and Short Life" railroad—until Sprague took it in hand in 1935. Tall and commanding, with a shock of snow-white hair, Sprague was a formidable figure who seemed invulnerable to a proxy fight. His railroad had become an important bypass around the busy Chicago bottleneck, he had undertaken massive improvements in track and equipment, and the company had increased its earnings and substantially reduced its debt. What more could shareholders want?

Well, dividends, for one thing. Although the railroad's health seemed robust, it was paying out only thirty-six cents of each dollar of profit to its stockholders. And by this summer of 1953, some stockholders were wondering why.

To get answers, they recruited Ben W. Heineman, a Chicago lawyer who was perhaps one of the most gracious of the men who were labeled "raiders" during this period. Heineman was a balding thirty-nine-year-old, with dark, intelligent eyes, a long, thin nose, and a wide smile. His reputation as a friend to railroad investors had been born in 1950, when he had represented some stockholders who were trying to force the Chicago Great Western Railroad to raise its dividend. Such battles were notoriously difficult to win, and Heineman's victory, in an out-of-court settlement that produced $6 million in dividends for the plaintiffs, quickly became the buzz of the business. He was the logical choice for the dividend-hungry investors in Lucian Sprague's railroad.

Sprague's top executives quickly noticed that "the Heineman group" was buying shares of the railroad's stock in the summer of 1953. Managers had become keenly attentive to such activity, which they tracked through the number of shares being transferred into the names of new owners, and Sprague's team quickly sounded the alarm that a raid was in progress. Heineman calmly denied any such plans, but confirmed that he represented stockholders who held 25 percent of the company's shares. Their principal concern, he explained, was the corporate dividend policy. Shortly thereafter, Sprague's board raised that year's common-stock dividend by forty cents per share. It seemed that war had been averted.

But Heineman raised the stakes and, in September 1953, asked that his group be awarded three seats on the eleven-man board of directors. He also proposed that the board set up a five-member executive committee to oversee management, to cut down on the frequent and costly directors' meetings. And by the way, he added, his group would like to receive certain "operating and maintenance budgets, earnings estimates, and traffic and engineering studies" that management had promised to furnish but had so far not supplied.[5] But while his demands escalated, his tone remained calm and courteous. He was confident, he said, that management would send along the requested information "in due course."[6]

Sprague's response was chilly. "There are no vacancies on the board of directors of this company at this time," he said, and "no director is desirous of resigning from the board." He threw out a challenge: "If Mr. Heineman can prove he has 10 percent of the shares outstanding, he can call a special meeting of stockholders. We rather hope that he will."[7]

Although he engaged in no personal name-calling, Heineman continued to criticize Sprague's management, claiming that expenses were too high. And his group continued to buy stock, strengthening its hand for the proxy fight that both sides knew was coming. In March 1954, it became official when Heineman announced that his group was soliciting support for an independent slate of seven directors to be elected at the annual meeting in New York City two months later.

His first piece of "campaign literature," a ten-page booklet distributed to stockholders, hit hard at the "wasteful, self-serving and inefficient" management practices at the railroad. But the line that became the public's shorthand for Heinemann's accusations was tucked near the back of the booklet. While shareholders had been starved for dividends, it said, "the M&St.L has been a gravy train for its management."[8]

The next mailing to stockholders expanded on the "gravy train" accusation with items drawn from independent audit reports. The theme was simple: The company was incurring a "shocking" number of expenses to support the opulent lifestyle maintained by Lucian Sprague and his wife, above and beyond the tidy salary he collected. According to Heineman, $3,500 of the company's money had been used to pay for a European trip for Mr. and Mrs. Sprague. The company had paid for "medical bills at the Mayo Brothers Clinic, jewelry sent to Mrs. Sprague, meat delivered to the Sprague home."[9] The company maintained two Cadillacs and a chauffeur for Sprague's use in Minneapolis, although he also drew down a $165-a-month car allowance and was out of the city for 237 days in 1952. The company had purchased box seats for the Spragues at leading racetracks, had paid $5,416 for Sprague's personal tax adviser, and had contributed $20,000 to improve the Spragues' island retreat at Rainy Lake, near International Falls, Minnesota. In the war for the hearts and minds of stockholders, the "gravy train" litany was a devastating weapon.

"The precise amount of company money paid for Mr. Sprague's expenses in any year will never be known," Heineman's report warned. "It has been concealed by the failure to keep detailed and proper accounting records and could not be determined by the outside accountants."[10]

One proxy-fight historian called the report a "body blow" to management.[11] Sprague's backers weakly defended the European trip and some of the other expenses as having been made for "good will," in an effort to entertain important business leaders and thereby cultivate new business. Visitors to Sprague Island "would fill the blue book of American trade, finance and industry," management insisted. "It takes money to make money," Sprague told a reporter for the *New York Times*.[12] His company's "welfare depends on the good will generated by the personal contacts made by the officers."

As the annual meeting approached, the exchanges between management and the insurgents grew increasingly hostile. Sprague emphasized the company's solid record and the depth of railroad experience represented on his board. Heineman argued that the company needed to control its expenses, improve its dividends, and elect a board loyal to shareholders, not to the railroad industry. On May 11, 1954, shareholders filled the Chanin Auditorium in New York City—the scene of Charlie Green's victory in the United Cigar–Whelan Stores battle—to cast their votes. When the flood of ballots was finally tallied the following day, just over 52 percent of the shares had been voted against management. Ben Heineman and his backers had defeated Lucian Sprague by more than 88,000 votes. Another towering figure in railroad management had been toppled.

And a few weeks later, thanks to Robert Young, Bill White of the New York Central joined Sprague and Dumaine on the growing list of casualties in the nation's proxy wars. All across America, as the busy proxy season closed and the summer stretched ahead with ample time for contemplation, professional managers began to worry. Were they next?

Thomas Mellon Evans turned worry into reality for J. Douglas Streett, an aggressive young executive in St. Louis. In 1951, Doug Streett, just forty-four years old, had been named president of the Laclede-Christy Company, which had been a fixture of St. Louis industry for more than a century. Its primary product was industrial tile and brick, material tough enough to line the interior of industrial boilers and ovens and to withstand the heat of molten metal. Streett had become acquainted with the young John Leschen when they worked together at Granite City Steel, and had perhaps watched with dismay as John and some of the other Leschen shareholders tried to withstand the Evans juggernaut. Nothing had prepared his generation of executives to expect to live in fear of ambush— indeed, many economists and business experts were convinced that professional managers were the inevitable inheritors of corporate power, given the broad dispersal of stock among largely passive mutual funds, pension funds, and trust accounts.

Streett quickly put his stamp on the company. Right after he was appointed, he announced that the company, which had moved its executive offices to Chicago a year earlier, would return to its birthplace of St. Louis. The rail, barge, and air facilities in the St. Louis area were better suited to the company's needs, Streett informed shareholders. Besides that, St. Louis was "a natural gateway to the Southwest, now the fastest developing industrial section of the country."[13]

Whatever else the move accomplished, it allowed the new company president to remain in St. Louis, where his wife and children lived in the affluent Ladue neighborhood. By the spring of 1954, he was showing newspaper reporters through the handsome new corporate headquarters he had built, adjacent to the largest of the company's eleven manufacturing operations. It was a low, modern one-story building whose decor made abundant and imaginative use of the company's own products. The front facade was decorated with a panel of buff-colored tile normally used to line steam boilers, and the entrance foyer's floor was paved with refractory fire brick. If management life was a pressure cooker, the design seemed to say, then Doug Streett was ready for it.[14]

The boardroom, near the center of the building, was furnished with light, sleek Scandinavian armchairs around a gleaming rectangular wood table with a lighter inlaid edge. But the company directors who gathered repeatedly around that table during the summer of 1954 scarcely noticed the beautiful setting. St. Louis, already shaken by the surprise acquisition of the venerable Leschen firm the summer before, had been buzzing since late spring with rumors that Laclede-Christy was up for grabs. Doug Streett was outraged—and perhaps a bit frightened. When he had been hired away from Granite City Steel three years earlier, he had asked the board for an employment contract but had been turned down. The company's directors had not had good luck with such contracts in the past, they explained; they had wound up paying them off when unsatisfactory executives had been asked to leave before the contracts had expired. Now, however, the rumors of an unfriendly acquisition had the company's top executives and employees in an uproar. In June, Streett renewed his request for some job security, and "to quiet things" the directors granted him a five-year contract at $41,000 a year.[15]

When the company directors again met on August 9, they could talk of little else but the rumored takeover threat. The next day, the company purchased space in the *St. Louis Post-Dispatch* and ran a legal notice under the title "Laclede-Christy Board Statement on Rumors." The directors "took cognizance of reports, rumors and press statements of tentative proposals being made for the possible acquisition of the stock or assets" of the company. But the board was officially announcing that the company "was not for sale, nor was it interested in any consolidations, mergers, or other disposition of its assets." The notice continued, "We have an excellent company and look forth to the future with confidence. No proposals for negotiations or acquisition were submitted to the board that it could recommend to the stockholders." It added, "The board is, of course, not responsible for the reports or rumors of proposals being made or about to be made to it. We intend to conduct our business aggressively and to go ahead without interruption."[16]

In fact, an offer had been made. A large block of company stock, 48,719 shares of the 265,815 outstanding, was held in a trust fund at the Mercantile Trust Company. On August 19, barely a week after the company's legal notice appeared in the papers, Mercantile Trust informed the company and its stockholders that it had received an offer of $20 a share for its trust fund holdings. The offer had come from H. K. Porter, the same Pittsburgh company that had gobbled up A. Leschen and Sons.[17]

To be sure, Evans had bitten off a little more than he could easily swallow in the Leschen deal. Mary Roebling and the Leschen family holdouts had taken Porter to court to seek a higher price than the $75 a share Evans had offered. Theirs was one of the first cases filed under a new Missouri law designed to protect shareholders from being forced to take inferior securities in lieu of "fair value" for their shares. But as the court battle dragged on, Evans had stayed busy. He had purchased Pioneer Rubber Mills, a company that had been founded in San Francisco in 1888 but had moved to the quieter suburb of Pittsburg, California, after the great earthquake of 1906.[18] Closer to home, he had snapped up the Alloy Metal Wire Company in Prospect Park, just outside Philadelphia, and the McLean Fire Brick Company, headquartered in Pittsburgh. But now he was ready for another acquisition, and Laclede-Christy would fit so nicely with his new McLean operation. So he scouted out blocks of stock, and found them at the Mercantile Trust.

At the same moment Mercantile Trust announced his offer it also announced that it and the other co-trustees of the estates placed in its care had agreed to accept it. But that victory only gave Tom Evans about 18 percent of the company. He would have to fight for the remaining 82 percent, and Doug Streett, on behalf of company management, was determined that the battle would not be an easy one.

Streett's first step was to demand the resignation of a vice president and director who was also a co-trustee of the Mercantile Trust estate account; Streett lacked the power to remove him from the board of directors. His next step, with the board's agreement, was to curry favor with investors by increasing the company's dividends. Shareholders would receive an additional share of stock for every four they already owned, and the company planned to pay annual dividends of $1 on each share.[19] That might not stop Evans, but it could make his battle more expensive if it boosted the price of the company's stock. Streett also sought a friendlier buyer. After the stock dividend was approved at an emergency Labor Day board meeting on September 6, Streett informed shareholders that negotiations were under way for a merger with "an established and well-known company," someone who would rescue the company from the predatory Tom Evans. He urged shareholders not to sell to Porter.[20]

He did more: he had the company use nearly $60,000 of its own cash to buy up 2,900 shares of Laclede-Christy stock in the open market, in hopes of forcing up the price. In any case, the purchases kept the shares out of the hands of Tom Evans. Streett explained later that he was fighting Evans because he sincerely believed he was acting in the best interests of the company and its stockholders. Based on what he knew of Evans's reputation, he feared the Pittsburgh industrialist would liquidate the old St. Louis firm the moment it became profitable to do so.[21] What would happen then to its employees? To the neighborhoods where it operated? And, of course, to its executives?

Evans was not deterred. He simply revised his offer to reflect the stock dividend and kept buying. By September 15, he had acquired 51 percent of the stock and the fight for control was largely over. Newspapers reported that "a substantial majority" of the Laclede-Christy stock had been sold to Evans, who promptly requested the resignations of a majority of the company's directors. It was more than a request, of course. In his press release, he added that arrangements were being made to call a special meeting of stockholders to elect a new board, if necessary. And as the majority stockholder, with a stake that by October had grown to 55 percent, he would determine the outcome of that election.[22]

In early October, Doug Streett and four other directors resigned from the board, turning their seats in the brand-new boardroom over to Tom Evans, his faithful Clarence Dobson, and three other Porter executives. Despite his long-term contract, Streett was fired from his executive post. He demanded that the company pay him for the remainder of his contract, but Evans refused. He argued that the board had exceeded its powers under company bylaws when it granted him the five-year contract in the first place. And in any case, as Evans saw it, Streett had violated his contract by using company money to buy up Laclede-Christy stock during the takeover fight. That might have helped management, in Evans's view, but it certainly was no favor to shareholders, and was not a proper use of company funds.[23]

Doug Streett followed the Leschen heirs and Mary Roebling into court, demanding fair treatment from Tom Evans.[24] And Evans? By Thanksgiving, as the national business press was focusing on other proxy fights involving bigger companies, the St. Louis papers reported that H. K. Porter had purchased the one-hundred-year-old Riverside Metal Company in Riverside, New Jersey, Evans's fourth acquisition of 1954. The company had begun life as a subsidiary of the Keystone Watch Case Company, founded in 1853 by James Boss, who held patents on his process for making gold-filled watch cases which were less expensive and more durable than the solid gold cases in use up to that time. Riverside Metal had supplied the alloys that went into these watch cases, and soon grew larger than its parent by manufacturing high-quality alloys for a variety of uses, including the making of pennies and nickels at the United States Mint in Philadelphia. It was a company that, literally, made money.

It is hard to know, looking back, just what impression the small local proxy fights and larger regional battles for corporate control made on the average American, immersed in a kaleidoscope of news, bombast, and brainless entertainment. Certainly, the citizens of each city where management was under attack paid close attention to the fights—as the coverage of Tom Evans's fight for Laclede-Christy demonstrated. And statistically, the odds were still heavily in favor of management in any battle with insurgent shareholders. To be sure, no one could monitor the outcome of battles at small companies like Laclede-Christy, which were not listed on any major stock exchange and thus were not required to follow the SEC's proxy disclosure rules. But among the larger exchange-listed companies, one business publication estimated that management defeated the proxy fighters in all but six of the twenty-seven battles waged at those companies in 1954.[25]

These corporate skirmishes were occurring at an increasingly ugly moment in America's social history. In politics, Senator Joseph McCarthy was squaring off against lawyers for the Army in televised hearings that would leave much of the American public disgusted with the witch-hunts that had dominated politics and cultural life for years. The Cold War had become a grim fact of life, and civil-defense drills and fallout shelters were entering the suburban vocabulary. Organized crime seemed to have become more brazen, and televised congressional hearings a few years earlier had awakened many Americans to the role the underworld played in their local politics. Labor organizations were under investigation for corruption. White bigots were howling in outrage after the Supreme Court struck down the "separate but equal" theory that kept southern schools segregated. Seen from some angles, the entire national stage seemed to have been invaded by thugs and bullies, and the proxy battles of 1954 seemed to fit easily into that ill-tempered pattern.

The worst of the fights of that year, a tar-brush battle for control of Decca Records, had even featured a cameo role by a shady financier and café society figure named Serge Rubenstein, whose nickname on Wall Street was "the Cobra." Aside from his dubious financial interests, Rubenstein was an unrepentant draft-dodger whose appetite for expensive women was matched only by his hunger for easy money. Decca's management and the insurgent stockholders both claimed that the suspicious

Rubenstein was somehow backing their adversaries. Management was more successful at making its smear stick, and the insurgents lost. A few months later, in what may have been an unrelated development, the Cobra was found strangled in his Manhattan townhouse. His murder was never solved.[26]

Much of the public still saw proxy fights in terms of the familiar political hoopla—the "Young at Heart" buttons and the polite debate on *Meet the Press*. But as the Decca contest suggests, the battles for control of American companies were starting to turn as sour as the fights for control being waged elsewhere in the American social landscape.

An "army of experts" was being mobilized by management and proxy fighters alike, one contemporary historian noted with disgust. "Private detectives are recruited to investigate the background of each candidate named as a director on the opposition slate . . . Wire-tappers are employed to listen in on conversations, to snoop around the boudoir as well as the executive suite. One misstep that an opponent may have made, one financial peccadillo or an unsavory affair with a woman may be exploited to blackmail the opposing camp into surrender . . . Whispering campaigns are started about the incompetence, the senility, the venality of the opposition. . . . There are no holds barred."[27]

There is scant evidence that Evans had as yet adopted any of these tactics. He still relied on his internal radar, scouting out undervalued family companies and grabbing them up for less than book value whenever complacent heirs allowed him to. He was his own "bird dog" in the search for likely prospects and—for better or worse—he was his own public relations adviser.

But on the national scene, one of the pioneers in manipulating the public images of these proxy fights was the young David Karr, Art Landa's frequent sidekick and Drew Pearson's former bloodhound. Karr, whose name was originally David Katz, had left Washington in 1948 and moved to New York, where he eventually set up a public-relations house specializing in proxy battles.[28] For all his intelligence and charm, he was a man of great controversy and mystery. During his Washington years, he became a target of Joe McCarthy, who "denounced him on the floor of the Senate in 1950 as Pearson's 'KGB controller.' "[29] Karr managed to clear himself of the Red label, but he was always known for his cheerful ruthlessness. *Fortune* later reported that Karr, while working for Pearson, displayed "vast energy and unlimited nerve, seemingly governed by the maxim that if you see something you want, don't ask for it, just take it."[30] As a public relations man on the proxy-war front, he used his energy and intelligence to cultivate the press and business leaders, but not even Landa seemed to fully trust the judgment of his young protégé, to judge from Landa's personal papers. And a scholarly study published in 1996 cites the stunning allegation—in a 1992 Russian journal citing material from the once-secret archives of the KGB, the Soviet spy agency—that Karr was a "competent source of the KGB" for many years.[31] Whether that claim is true and whether those years included his years on the front lines of the proxy wars is not yet known.

As the proxy wars of 1954 added elements of smoky café society life and dark counter-espionage techniques to the political-convention atmosphere of earlier battles, one takeover suddenly translated the issue of corporate control into a language that redefined the debate, at least for the many Americans who had previously considered takeover battles as Wall Street's form of financial football, a game in which most Americans were merely unaffected spectators.

On August 12, 1954, the Follansbee Steel Corporation of Pittsburgh, the target of that phony takeover raid by the colorful Terry Fahye in the late forties, announced it was selling its assets to a group headed by the young Fred Richmond, whose Connecticut acquisitions had caused such concern to Congressman Dodd.[32] This was no high-voltage proxy fight, like the fight for Decca or the New York Central battle. Rather, it was a complex, uncontested deal in which Follansbee Steel would sell its assets to Richmond and use the cash to purchase two nonsteel businesses from Clint Murchison, one of the Texas stars of Robert Young's proxy fight. Other than that celebrity connection, the deal seemed notable to journalists at the time primarily because it marked the exit of another small steel company from an industry increasingly dominated by giants.

Follansbee Steel's board of directors had approved the transaction, which had the backing of company president Marcus A. Follansbee. It had no doubt been a difficult choice for Follansbee, whose silver hair and gold-rimmed spectacles gave him the air of a pleasant professor of English literature. His father had been president of Follansbee Steel, and his family had founded the company. He had taken over as president in 1948,[33] and had tried to modernize the small company, undertaking a $34 million expansion plan in late 1952. But he felt he was fighting an uphill battle against the escalating wage demands of steelworkers and the continued demands of American industry for one-stop shopping for specialty steel. Follansbee was struggling to keep his company in the black. Indeed, the company had lost money in the first six months of 1954. Nevertheless, he later testified, he was still sufficiently optimistic about its prospects that when Fred Richmond first approached him in June 1954 and offered to buy the company for $20 a share, Follansbee turned him down, although the steel company's stock was trading for just $11 at the time.[34] But Richmond was persistent, and as the weeks went by, Marcus Follansbee became less hopeful about the future, he said, and decided to support Richmond's tempting proposal.[35] The company's directors agreed, and called stockholders to an October 15 meeting in Pittsburgh to vote on it.

A month before that meeting, however, Republic Steel Corporation reported that Fred Richmond had agreed to sell Republic all the equipment and inventory of Follansbee Steel's biggest mill after he took control. That mill was located in the company's birthplace of Follansbee, West Virginia, a town of about 4,500 people located near Wheeling in the state's slender northern panhandle. Republic planned to dismantle the facility and move it south to Gadsden, Alabama, where Republic already operated a plant. Only about 150 of the mill's 740 employees would be invited to move to Alabama, Republic announced.[36]

The announcement hit the little West Virginia town like an earthquake. This was the nightmare that had hovered for years behind the hoopla in all these fights for corporate control. The steel company was Follansbee's only major employer; its workers' paychecks were transformed each week into the revenues of the local businesses, the deposits at the local bank, the Sunday offerings at the local churches. The company's assets were the bedrock of the local tax base. Mayor Frank Basil just did not see how his little community could survive the loss of the steel plant. Marcus Follansbee, in his Pittsburgh office, could only shake his head and tell inquiring reporters that the matter was "out of my hands."[37] Fred Richmond was buying the steel operation; he could do with it as he wished.

But the West Virginia town was the home not only of Follansbee employees, but also of Follansbee stockholders. And in late September, six of them—including Celia M. Humes, the president of the little Follansbee National Bank—hired a lawyer and appealed to their County Court judge for an injunction to block the sale.[38] Soon, forty-one other stockholders who lived in Follansbee had joined the original six.

Their fight to save their little town from the disastrous consequences of the corporate takeovers that had become so routine in corporate America seized the attention of the regional press and touched a tender nerve in Congress. Somehow, for those who paid attention, the Follansbee fight came to symbolize the public's stake in the fights for control that had been, up until then, measured only in terms of stockholder profits, clashing executive egos, and clever legal tactics.

On October 6, lawyers for the stockholders and for the company argued in court for nearly four hours, but the judge withheld his decision and set an additional hearing for October 11.[39] At that hearing, the first witness called was Marcus Follansbee, who explained how he came to support

Richmond's offer. The hearing dragged on into the next week, and was delayed further by local flooding caused by Hurricane Hazel.[40] The stockholders meeting of October 27 loomed closer.

Salvation seemed to have arrived on October 21, when another bidder surfaced for the company. But the town's hopes were dashed the following day when the company's directors met in Pittsburgh and rejected the new proposal, which was for only 51 percent of the stock. At almost the same moment, the local judge in West Virginia announced that he could not find any legal basis under state law for blocking the sale.[41] Neither the marketplace nor the state courts, it seemed, could rescue Follansbee. But perhaps Congress could.

Some congressmen were certainly willing to try. Congressman Wayne Hays, an Ohio Democrat whose district was on the border with West Virginia near Follansbee, released a letter he had written to Attorney General Herbert Brownell Jr., calling for a Justice Department investigation into whether the proposed sale violated the Clayton Act or other antitrust laws.[42] It was the first shot in what would become a barrage of congressional opposition to the sale. And it gave heart to the minority stockholders, who renewed their fight a few days later in the federal courts in Wheeling, where they hoped federal securities and antitrust laws would give them better weapons in their battle.

On the eve of the October 27 stockholders meeting, Federal Judge Herbert Boreman in Wheeling, West Virginia, blocked any vote on Richmond's offer until the judge could conduct a hearing on the minority stockholders' objections.[43] Those objections now included the argument that the company had violated federal securities laws by not fully disclosing to stockholders how the directors and officers of the company would benefit personally from the transaction. For one thing, the stockholders argued, the deal would relieve the company's officers of a possible $6 million liability sought in lawsuits pending against the company. Moreover, they later discovered, the Murchison interests had offered consulting contracts to Marcus Follansbee and one of his vice presidents, worth up to $15,000, as part of the deal.

On October 27, about thirty impatient stockholders gathered in Pittsburgh to hear Marcus Follansbee explain that the court had ordered the company to postpone the scheduled vote on the sale. The same day, new offers for the company surfaced, one from controversial Cleveland industrialist Cyrus Eaton, and one from Mrs. Arlene Warner of Greenwich, Connecticut, the wife of a former Wall Street stockbroker, who was apparently inspired simply by sympathy for Follansbee's plight.[44]

The outrage over his Follansbee acquisition must have baffled the energetic young Fred Richmond. To him, no doubt he was simply making the best economic use of Follansbee Steel's various assets, which included a previous loss that a more profitable company, like Murchison's, could use to cut its future tax bill.[45] Scrambling to put out the fire he had inadvertently started, he announced that Republic Steel had told him it would keep part of the Follansbee mill operating "for at least a year."[46] But that did nothing to cool the political rage now aimed at him by West Virginia governor William Marland; the state's two U.S. senators, Harley M. Kilgore and Matthew M. Neely; and a growing roster of congressmen, including the irate Congressman Dodd.

The court order blocking a shareholder vote on the sale expired on November 1, a Monday. The company's shareholders meeting in Pittsburgh promptly voted overwhelmingly to sell the company's assets to Richmond for $20 a share, without considering the two competing bids, although at least one of those bids seemed to top Richmond's offer. "The board of directors does not feel either of the offers are in such form that we can consider them," Marcus Follansbee told the shareholders who argued against the Richmond proposal from the floor. And besides, he insisted, neither was "substantially better than the Richmond proposal." At least, not better for the shareholders.[47] The sale was scheduled to close November 30.

But the political flak was becoming heavier. On November 11, Senator William Langer, a Republican from North Dakota and the chairman of the Senate Anti-Monopoly Subcommittee, announced that his panel would investigate the sale of the Follansbee plant.[48] The next day, as Judge Boreman in Wheeling set the date for a new hearing on the minority shareholders' challenge, President Eisenhower confirmed that the White House had received "many telegrams" from West Virginia citizens objecting to the deal. The protests had been referred to the office of Commerce Secretary Sinclair Weeks, who directed one of his special assistants to arrange a meeting among the "interested parties."[49] A few days later, Senator Langer issued a statement that suggested a long, difficult examination was ahead. A "preliminary investigation" by his committee suggested that the Follansbee deal with Republic Steel "may well violate various provisions of the antitrust laws." The senator continued, "There is further reason to suspect that the proposed sale has been accompanied by business practices, such as inadequate disclosures to stockholders to obtain their approval, calculated to deceive the interested parties and mask the true nature of the transaction."

He ended with a warning certain to depress Marcus Follansbee and Fred Richmond: his committee would conduct "exhaustive and searching investigations into all these matters," and it had already "urgently requested" that the attorney general and the Securities and Exchange Commission "carry out their necessary supervisory functions."[50] The SEC, under pressure from powerful members of Congress, had been preparing since October 29 to go to court to enforce its proxy rules in the Follansbee case, which officials later said had consumed more of the agency's time that year than even the hotly contested New York Central proxy fight. Fred Richmond was suddenly facing a future of filibuster and red tape.

But the next word on the Follansbee sale belonged to Judge Boreman in Wheeling. On November 29, he blocked the deal and strongly criticized the company for failing to inform stockholders that certain Follansbee officials stood to profit personally from the merger. "It is the conclusion and opinion of the court that inducements were present from the beginning of the negotiations with Mr. Richmond," Judge Boreman said. The company's failure to inform stockholders about those "inducements," he ruled, constituted a violation of federal securities laws.[51]

For Fred Richmond, it was apparently the final straw. A few days after the decision, he announced that Republic Steel had agreed to let him out of the original deal. Instead, he would pay Follansbee Steel's stockholders roughly $20 a share, as promised, and then sell the company's properties in Follansbee, West Virginia, to Cyrus Eaton for an undisclosed sum. From his Cleveland office, Eaton praised Republic for its "business statesmanship," and said that he and his associates were "ready to go forward in preserving employment and prosperity in Follansbee."[52]

The minority stockholders who had fought so long to save their town were jubilant. Labor leaders traded love notes with the Cleveland plutocrat.[53] Even Marcus Follansbee tried to put the best face on the deal. "This comes as a Christmas present to employees and shareholders alike," he said. "This is the type of sale both we and Mr. Richmond tried to arrange as soon as it was apparent the corporation should be sold many months ago." He was only sorry, he added, that "so many weary and costly months of negotiations were necessary" to achieve that end.[54]

The fight had put the proxy wars on Congress's agenda in an emphatic and personal way. But before the lessons of the Follansbee Steel fight had sunk in with the public, the business press was caught up in yet another headline-grabbing, celebrity-studded battle. And this new fight was portrayed as nothing less than a battle between the past and the future, between a Depression-era view of business stewardship and a forward-looking confidence in risk-taking. For good or ill, the face of the future in this fight was the tanned, handsome visage of Louis Wolfson.

Leslie Gould, the raider-hating financial editor of the *New York Journal-*

American, took credit for first breaking the news in September 1954 that Lou Wolfson was planning a raid against Montgomery Ward and Company, the nation's oldest mail-order retailing house. Since the controversy over Capital Transit, Gould had displayed nothing but scorn for Wolfson, whom he routinely depicted as a corporate burglar for whom a proxy fight was merely a crowbar for breaking into a company's cash box. Wolfson, in turn, was scornful of those short-sighted cynics who did not understand his true mission: to restore American companies to their rightful owners, the shareholders, and thus to inspire more Americans to become shareholders.

His target was blindingly obvious. Montgomery Ward was an eighty-two-year-old company that was little more than a cash-stuffed strong box controlled by a bad-tempered, elderly autocrat.

Montgomery Ward's chairman, Sewell Avery, was only two years younger than his company. A lawyer by training, Avery had made his iron-fisted reputation in the 1920s at the helm of the U.S. Gypsum Company. He had been put in the corner office at Montgomery Ward's Chicago headquarters in 1931 by none other than the House of Morgan itself. The Morgans had taken over the troubled business from its prior owners, James B. Duke of the American Tobacco Company and Charles A. Whelan, who founded United Cigar Stores and the drugstore chain that bore his name. The Morgans were so desperate for Avery's expertise, the legend goes, that they summoned him from the fairway at his golf club to offer him the job.[55]

And he amply repaid their confidence. "Within three years [he had] transformed a $9 million loss into a $9 million profit," *Newsweek* noted in its coverage of the proxy fight. As the nation stumbled through a depression, he kept his company's belt tight and its bank account flush. But the wartime prosperity that should have made him a corporate hero instead revealed an uglier side of his management style.

The War Labor Board, which policed labor-management disputes in defense-related industries, had ordered Montgomery Ward to allow fair elections for unions seeking to represent Ward's workers. It was a controversial order. One of President Roosevelt's advisers argued that "since Montgomery Ward was not doing war business, the Army had no right to stick its nose into the labor situation."[56] Another pointed out that three-quarters of the company's customers were farmers whose food production was vital to the war effort. When the anti-union Avery refused to allow the elections, his workers went on strike on April 12, 1944.

A week later, an ailing President Roosevelt signed an executive order directing the Secretary of Commerce to seize Montgomery Ward's executive offices and resolve the strike.[57] As soldiers surrounded the building, Avery refused to budge from his chair in his eighth-floor office. Two soldiers easily lifted the small, scowling man from the chair and carried him into the elevator and out of the building. Photographers captured the scene: the young steel-helmeted soldiers carrying the improbably dignified executive, his craggy face with its thin lips sealed in fierce outrage, his clenched hands extending from the French cuffs of his snowy shirt, his polished shoes dangling several feet above the sidewalk. It was an unforgettable image, one that primarily embarrassed Roosevelt at the time, but one that would surface regularly in later years to underscore Avery's stubborn resolve in the face of opposition.

As the war ended, he steadfastly began to prepare for the next depression, hoarding cash and retrenching at every turn—while his rival, Sears Roebuck and Company, was soaking up the postwar consumer's money like a sponge. Any executive who argued against Avery's strategy was fired—handfuls of presidents, dozens of vice presidents. By the late 1940s, the Morgans had given up and removed their directors from the board.

Even the large mutual funds, theoretically Avery's most influential shareholders, were publicly trying to find some way short of a proxy fight to dislodge him. At the 1949 stockholders meeting, the manager of the Massachusetts Investors Trust, the nation's largest mutual fund, had voted all its shares for directors other than Avery. The fund manager, the urbane and influential Merrill Griswold, explained that he was protesting the fact that, between January 1 and April 13 of 1949, Avery had fired or accepted the resignation of his president and all nine of his vice presidents.[58] Avery ignored Griswold's gesture, as did his directors.[59] The following year, Griswold publicly announced he would not vote for any Ward directors because they "have been responsible for keeping Mr. Avery on as chairman year after year despite the fact that his dictatorial methods are bound to be destructive to the morale of the personnel."[60] Again, Avery ignored the criticism, and continued to shutter stores and accumulate cash for what he believed was the inevitable deluge.

By the fall of 1954, his rainy-day fund totaled nearly $300 million— causing some on Wall Street to dub the company "the Ward's Bank and Trust Company."[61] Since 1945, Ward's profits had grown just 21 percent, compared to profit growth of nearly 230 percent at Sears, Roebuck over the same period. With their company immobilized in the mud of Avery's gloomy pessimism, shareholders got out and walked. Ward's stock sank as low as $56 a share by early 1954. The company had no debt and the cash and government securities in its bank accounts alone were worth $45 a share. At $56 a share, Wall Street was essentially concluding that the rest of the business, the nation's oldest mail-order franchise and a nationwide chain of retail stores and showrooms, was worth just $11 a share so long as Sewell Avery was in charge.

A perfectly logical conclusion, perhaps. But with men like Tom Evans and Leopold Silberstein and Lou Wolfson staying up late at night looking for companies whose businesses and bank accounts were worth far more than their stock market value, Montgomery Ward was a tempting target.

In late August 1954, Wolfson held a press conference in his suite at the New York Biltmore Hotel to announce that he and his relatives and friends had bought more than 105,000 of the 6.5 million Ward shares in circulation, and planned to wage a proxy fight to unseat Avery. Intense and direct, Wolfson gripped his microphone and served up phrases certain to find their way into the next day's newspapers: "Montgomery Ward, as it stands today, is a glaring and notorious example of private enterprise in reverse gear," he said, as the flash bulbs popped and reporters scribbled.[62]

Time magazine sought out Avery in Chicago for his reaction. "Wolfson?" Avery said. "I know nothing about the man. Never heard of him till the other day."[63]

That put Avery in the same boat with most Americans, of course. Although Wall Street and Congress had closely followed Wolfson's empire-building, the average American knew virtually nothing about him. But after he announced his battle against Avery, Wolfson was sought out and profiled by every mainstream publication from *Life* magazine to the *Saturday Evening Post*. He seemed glamorous, with his attractive wife and children, his tanned movie-star looks, his rags-to-riches résumé. "Virtually every [acquisition] has turned into a pot of gold for Wolfson," observed *Time* magazine, mistakenly adding that Wolfson "has never before pitched into a full-blown proxy fight."[64] *Look* magazine did a splashy photo essay showing Wolfson and his family in their sumptuous Biscayne Bay estate in Miami.[65] *Life* and the *Saturday Evening Post* took more careful note of the criticism that had accumulated against Wolfson over the years, exploring his handling of the Capital Transit Company, the frequent congressional investigations, and his sometimes flamboyant methods.[66] *Business Week* allowed Wolfson to explain that his fight for control of Ward was aimed at loftier ends than simply putting Avery's $300 million to "productive" use. He was convinced that the low level of share ownership in America was due "primarily to a profound lack of public confidence in the way U.S. management handles the investor's money."[67] By turning Ward around, he could prove that investors could prosper along with managers. Speaking of himself in the charmingly pompous third-person, he continued, "It may take years, but someday, maybe people will say that Wolfson did more than any other man to breed 20 million U.S. stockholders. Montgomery Ward can save me eight to ten years in this campaign." Cynical reporters might have shaken their heads over such self-important sermons, but Wolfson always seemed to believe himself completely. It was the essence of his considerable charm.

But could he pull this off? Only three of Ward's nine directors were elected each year, so the company's use of cumulative voting was less helpful than it might have been. The most Wolfson could win was a minority voice on the board. Moreover, any long-term investor who still owned Ward's shares after almost a decade of barren retrenchment probably shared Avery's gloomy expectations. To counter that, Wolfson would need the backing of every mutual fund that still bothered to hold any of the lackluster stock, of every bank trust officer who had Ward shares stuffed into widows' accounts, of every union pension fund that might swing some proxies his way.

Wolfson had been popular with labor since his shipbuilding days in Florida. When the influential Teamster chief David Beck heard about the fight, he was determined to put some of his pension fund's power in Wolfson's corner. The Teamsters had been dreaming of organizing the drivers and warehouse personnel at Montgomery Ward for years—indeed, Teamster negotiators had actually been at the bargaining table trying to draft a contract with Ward since 1953. If Wolfson could dislodge Avery, organized labor's nemesis at the company, perhaps things would be different. Other unions might well see things Beck's way. Wolfson's team put the word out on Wall Street that Big Labor was lining up on his side. It was a strong psychological boost.[68]

The heart of Wolfson's public campaign was an expensive series of "kaffeeklatches." He invited shareholders to meet him for coffee in nine cities all around the country—he'd buy the coffee, he said. Avery's chief lieutenant, Ward president Edmund Krider, focused his time on quiet visits with leading citizens and institutional investors, while loyal Ward employees rang doorbells at shareholders' homes.

When the advertising warfare began, the ammunition was predictable. Avery enumerated all the occasions when various government agencies had felt the need to investigate Wolfson's business activities. Wolfson pointed out that none of those investigations had turned up any wrongdoing. Avery decried the fare increases that had followed Wolfson's huge dividend boosts at Capital Transit. Wolfson told of meeting a delicate old woman in Washington who said she lived entirely on the dividends of her Capital Transit stock and was praying for him to stay in charge. Avery insisted Wolfson was a raider, pure and simple, out to grab the company's cash and ride away. Wolfson's allies were shocked: "Lou's never done that, never once," said Alexander Rittmaster, his chief financial aide. "Everything he's gone into, he's built up; everything he touched, he made money. But don't forget, he always made it for the stockholders too."[69]

But Avery was scornful. "It certainly looks as if he wants our money to make attacks on others," he said. "It's purely a raid. He's smelled our money, and he wants to spend it."[70]

From the sidelines, there were complaints that both sides were running roughshod over the SEC's flimsy proxy rules, which had been designed for the polite coronation of incumbent management, not for brawls like these. In February, Avery sent each member of the Senate Banking and Currency Committee a letter condemning Wolfson in scathing terms that the SEC would never have permitted in proxy materials mailed to shareholders; unsurprisingly, someone made the letter public. And the hostile Leslie Gould of the New York Journal-American complained that Wolfson was, in effect, buying votes by insuring some friendly investors against losses, and then by promising that if he won, he would have the company buy back some of its stock at book value, far above its trading price. Two other companies Wolfson controlled also bought Ward stock, most of it with borrowed money, an arrangement that Gould believed was a violation of federal limits on speculating in stocks with borrowed funds.[71]

Less than a month before the annual meeting in Chicago, Wolfson suffered a painfully visible setback. He lost the influential backing of David Beck of the Teamsters, who had originally indicated he would be supportive. The fellow who changed Beck's mind was none other than that wily management defender Art Landa.

Avery had sought out Landa to be part of Montgomery Ward's legal team, but Landa was unable to take on the case. Then he read with disapproval a newspaper report that one of the Teamsters' big regional units had purchased some Ward stock with plans to vote in favor of Lou Wolfson.[72] Soon thereafter, Landa found himself traveling to Washington on the Fruehauf company plane with David Beck. He told the Teamster boss that he was surprised that the union's stock "would be voted in favor of the man who was attempting to, what I call, raid Montgomery Ward," Landa later testified. Beck began to protest that Avery was a foe of labor while Wolfson was a guy you could deal with. Landa quickly hushed him up. "I said that in the event that he supported Montgomery Ward, I felt sure that he could have the opportunity of organizing Montgomery Ward—he had sought to do that often, I had read," Landa continued.

In fact, Teamster efforts to organize Montgomery Ward had been at an impasse because Avery adamantly opposed some of their core demands, especially the demand for a so-called "closed shop," in which employees would be required to join the union. Beck smiled at Landa's suggestion of tying his union's proxy vote to its organizing efforts. "That is a good idea," he said.[73] Before the plane landed in Washington, Landa had agreed to make a call to the Montgomery Ward forces to float the proposal.

He promptly telephoned Richard Nye, who was handling proxy solicitation for Montgomery Ward, and told him that Beck "would be willing to see that stock was voted for management in the event that he had the opportunity to organize Montgomery Ward."

"Okay, I will pass the word on," Nye answered.[74]

On March 31, three weeks before the showdown at the annual meeting, a Chicago newspaper reported that Avery and Beck had met personally and signed a Teamster contract covering 15,000 Ward employees at sixteen locations. At the same moment, Beck and his vice president, Jimmy Hoffa, publicly declared that they would recommend "that all divisions of the union holding Montgomery Ward stock vote their proxies for Avery in his battle with Wolfson."[75]

The Teamsters did not hold a decisive amount of stock, so far as anyone knew. But Beck was influential with unions all across the country, and the earlier rumors that he was supporting Wolfson had helped bolster the insurgent's hopes. Beck's betrayal "was a crushing psychological blow to the reeling Wolfson," concluded David Karr, an admirer of Landa's ingenuity.[76] Immediately after the battle, Ward managers insisted that there had been no quid pro quo in the settlement with the Teamsters. But no one familiar with Landa's Senate testimony years later can take their protest very seriously.

Wolfson recovered a bit of his former momentum on Friday, April 15, when the Illinois Supreme Court agreed with his argument that it was unconstitutional for Avery to put only three of the nine directors' seats up for election each year. Instead, the court ruled, all nine seats should be put up for grabs, so that the victor would control the company. Ward's stock bounced up a bit on the news, and a beaming Wolfson told reporters that the decision was "a tremendous victory for corporate democracy."[77]

At about the same moment, however, another rumor swept through the war zone. It began as a buzz on Wall Street: Avery was privately assuring large stockholders that he would step down as chairman right after the election. The rumor must have seemed like a cold compress on the fevered foreheads of the professional money managers holding Ward shares. Such men traditionally supported management through thick and thin; they were, after all, as firmly embedded in the Wall Street establishment as one could be without a Morgan in one's family tree. But for years, Avery had been sucking the life out of Ward's stock market value. How could any dutiful fiduciary, in good conscience, vote to retain the man who was inflicting such harm on shareholders? But voting for the flamboyant Mr. Wolfson was scarcely something that would produce favorable comment at the monthly partners' meetings. For those caught in this quandary, the Avery-retirement rumor no doubt produced a sigh of relief and a quick check in the box on management's proxy ballot.

Wolfson's forces tried to challenge the rumor—indeed, in public, Avery himself scoffed at the idea that he might step down. "If I retire, I'd have nothing to do," he said. "I saw my father shrivel up and die after he retired. Why, I even get bored after a week of vacation. It terrifies me to think of the day when I won't be able to come down to work."[78] But the hopeful buzz wouldn't go away.

The annual meeting was set for April 22 at Chicago's Medinah Temple on North Wabash Street, a huge hall traditionally used for circus performances. Whatever statement Sewell Avery might have been making with his choice of venue, the building had terrible acoustics and its scale and design made the traditional question-and-answer format of an annual meeting extremely difficult. Indeed, any speaker centered on the vast oval stage could scarcely see, much less hear, a questioner from the audience. But beginning well before 10:30 A.M. on April 22, shareholders poured in, more than 2,500 of them by most accounts. Contemporary photographs show a crowd of well-dressed women in hats, a considerably larger crowd of men in business suits with fedoras to shield them from the bright spring sunshine, and dozens of reporters from around the country. It was, indeed, a circus.

On the oval stage, a boardroom's length from the audience on all sides, nearly two dozen office armchairs were arrayed in two curving ranks facing one end of the auditorium. In front of them was a speaker's rostrum. The light-colored wooden platform was otherwise as bare as a chopping block.

The six-hour meeting was painful for all sides. Sewell Avery, in an old-fashioned navy double-breasted suit, stepped up to the rostrum to open the meeting and was met with "a long, warm ovation," the *New York Times* reported in its front-page coverage.[79] But he promptly turned the gavel over to the corporate secretary, young John A. Barr, a company vice president and a member of the board of directors. Supporters of Wolfson protested. One of them challenged Barr: "I ask if Mr. Avery is physically able to handle the chair at this meeting. If Mr. Avery is unable to carry on, I make a motion we elect someone who can. Is Mr. Avery physically able to serve as chairman?"[80] Wolfson, in a stylish navy suit set off by a pale satin tie, stood up from his spot at the side of the stage and urged his supporters to show respect to the frail chairman. "It seems clear that the chairman is not able to conduct this meeting," Wolfson said. "I would appreciate it if any of my supporters would accept Mr. Barr as the chairman."[81] Avery did return several times to address stockholders, "but he appeared to have considerable difficulty in forming his words and expressing his thoughts," the *Times* reported. "I can't hear," he complained. "Everything they are saying is a jumble."[82]

Eventually, someone asked him directly if he intended to resign as Ward's chairman. He would step down "readily," he said, if stockholders found him "unworthy of the job." But he insisted that he was in "vigorous" physical shape, and that his health was excellent.[83]

His spirits were certainly bolstered when Wolfson conceded defeat, shortly before the ballots began to be tallied. A whiz at numbers, the young industrialist could see that he had nowhere near enough support to control the nine-member board—he had won just 30 percent of the votes cast, as it turned out. He hoped he had allocated his cumulative votes wisely enough to win three seats. He had, but that would not be confirmed for several weeks. As Wolfson and his associates left the hall, Sewell Avery stepped back up to the rostrum and held his arms aloft in a feeble victory gesture, captured by the cameras. The outcome had been just as he had predicted, he said. Ed Krider, his president, was less detached. If management had "another month to expose the background and the financial machinations of the Wolfson group, he would not have elected a single director," Krider said bitterly.[84]

Just seventeen days later, Montgomery Ward answered Wall Street's silent prayers and announced that Sewell Avery was stepping down as chairman, passing the gavel to the young and competent John Barr, who had performed so well in Chicago. Avery remained a director, however, and continued to dominate the boardroom, at least for a time. Of course, he now had to share that boardroom with Lou Wolfson. Wolfson later shared with *Fortune* magazine his memories of that first post-Medinah board meeting. "Everyone looked like undertakers," he laughed. "This man came with a dark blue suit and a high collar, the next with a black suit and a high collar. And they sat down at the table, very properly and very seriously. Each stood up to read his report, then sat down very stiffly. Each report was read to Avery, even though he was just a director by then." He added, "I nearly bust out laughing."[85]

But within months, Avery's young successor had announced plans to implement almost all of the ambitious changes that Lou Wolfson had called for in his proxy fight. A well-known retailing consultant was hired in July, and in September, Barr announced that Ward would open a hundred new catalog-sales offices in the following year and would spend a record $18 million for advertising. A four-year slump in sales was reversed; the stock price rallied. By January 1956, Wolfson and his allies felt comfortable enough to resign from the board and let Barr get on with his renovations—after all, Wolfson's profits on his Ward stock had been more than enough to cover the cost of his battle.[86]

No one gave Lou Wolfson and his expensive proxy fight much credit for the dramatic U-turn in Ward's management strategy, of course; he was simply too controversial for that. "Rightly or wrongly," observed proxy-fight maven David Karr, "Wolfson had got the reputation of being a 'raider.' Or, worse yet, he was regarded as 'a young man in a hurry.' And most newspapers outside of New York City added to this portrait at every opportunity."[87]

As the Ward fight was raging, Leopold Silberstein had been busy adding to his own reputation as a "raider." His target in 1954 was a New England machine tool company called Niles-Bement-Pond, in West Hartford, Connecticut—in the congressional district served by the implacable Congressman Dodd. The company was a paid-up member of the military-industrial complex. Its Pratt and Whitney division made aircraft landing gear, another unit produced aircraft engine accessories, including fuel regulators for jet engines, and a third produced the special lathes used in the manufacture of jet engines and guided missiles. Its wealthy chairman, Colonel Charles W. Deeds, was always welcome at the Pentagon, and its board was equally impressive.

But by 1953, the company's largest stockholder had died, and his estate had been "unable . . . to interest the 'blue ribbon' board in a buyout."[88] So the estate sold its shares to Leopold Silberstein, who gradually nibbled up more stock—using mostly borrowed money, of course. In early 1954, he confronted the company and asked for representation on the board.

Aghast, Deeds refused. The board quickly sought out a friendly deal that would put it beyond Silberstein's reach. It found one with Bell Aircraft, Larry Bell's helicopter company. Bell's managers knew what it was like to be under attack by raiders, having narrowly won that proxy fight led by Ben Graham almost a decade earlier. They quickly negotiated a deal by which Niles would acquire a substantial stake in Bell by issuing approximately 630,000 new shares. After the new shares were issued, of course, Silberstein would own a much smaller percentage of the outstanding stock of Niles-Bement-Pond.

Silberstein went to court in February 1955 and won a temporary injunction blocking the deal with Bell, which he condemned as "high-handed, unlawful, immoral and un-American." A few months later, he defeated the company's management in a proxy fight, in which he was assisted by the energetic David Karr, who used the fight as a sort of post-graduate course in proxy-fighting skills. After taking control of Niles-Bement-Pond, Silberstein changed its name to Pratt and Whitney. (The new name borrowed some luster from the widely known Pratt and Whitney aircraft engine company, which Niles-Bement-Pond had sold off in 1929.)[89]

The attack on Niles-Bement-Pond was the final straw for Congressman Dodd. On March 23, 1955, he rose from his chair in the House of Representatives to demand that Congress "make a full and complete investigation of this increasingly dangerous practice of raiding established businesses in the United States." He continued, "In the postwar years, there has been a plague of such assaults upon well-established and well-recognized management."[90]

Silberstein's acquisition of Niles-Bement-Pond, "one of the finest industries in the United States of America," involved "actions we associate more with the buccaneering days of the 19th century" and was "precisely the kind of case Congress should investigate," Dodd insisted. He drew a tortured and remote connection, via various associates, between Silberstein and the fatally sleazy Serge Rubenstein. He underlined the "obscurity" of Silberstein's refugee past and compared it to the solid American legacy of Charles Deeds. Perhaps both men should be invited to Washington to "establish their respective qualifications to pass judgment on immoral and un-American conduct," Dodd suggested, with an outraged xenophobic huff. After all, the immigrant Silberstein would inherit defense contracts if he got control of Deeds's company, so it was important to know if any unsavory or foreign money was backing him.[91]

Nor was this proxy fight an isolated case, the congressman noted. "The newspapers and business magazines have reported a dozen like it within the past few months," he said. Just five months earlier, *Business Week* had published an extensive examination of these new operators, entitled "They Collect Companies Like Postage Stamps."[92] Pictured in a line-up across the page were Lou Wolfson, engaged in the Ward fight; Leopold Silberstein, who had just started his fight for Niles-Bement-Pond; Fred Richmond, who was battling to carry out his proposed liquidation of Follansbee Steel; and Tom Evans, who was fighting for control of Laclede-Christy in St. Louis.

"Wolfson, Silberstein, Richmond and Evans are but a sampling from a much larger group, known variously as tycoons, industrialists, liquidators, proxy warriors and syndicators," *Business Week* explained. Each of these men controlled several corporations, not just one, and each was better known than his respective company. They "were always fighting to get control of some company, or at least thinking about it." Taking over companies was not merely a way to achieve some business strategy, *Business Week* argued; it was their business strategy.

But did they work beyond the law? Were they somehow breaking the rules? *Business Week* found "a great number of people [who] have the impression that they do, but few can name figures, places, and dates. The fact is that the typical tycoon takes pains to keep his operations scrupulously legal—he has to. Still, there is an atmosphere that surrounds these men, and one that they must continually try to dispel. One New York lawyer says: 'I don't know much about these guys or how they operate, but something in my viscera tells me there is something fishy about them.' " Of course, the magazine noted, the first to cry "buccaneer" typically were the management executives on the losing end of a proxy fight or labor leaders affected by a plant shutdown. "Such talk may fail to impress the stockholders," it observed. "Stockholders, in fact, are prone to go for the tycoon." He usually was fighting a management team that had shortchanged investors—the owners of the business, after all.

There were, of course, a few exeptions, a few cases in which the raiders had shortchanged shareholders. And in May 1955, the Leschen holdouts in St. Louis persuaded a local judge that theirs was just such an exceptional case. The judge ordered Tom Evans to fork over roughly $185 a share for the stock he had tried to buy from Mary Roebling and the Leschen rebels for just $75 a share. These shareholders, at least, had won a round on their own.[93]

Shareholders were far from Congressman Dodd's mind as he pleaded with Congress to investigate the proxy raiders. He did concede that it was important to distinguish between "vulture-like raids which are made to milk a company or to cause its liquidation" and "the normal pushing and hauling among financial interests with perfectly legitimate and constructive purposes." But it was the threat of company liquidations that he emphasized, as those were "felt by employees, their families, and members of the entire community in the area where the industry is located."[94]

Congress, he roared, "cannot sit supinely by and ignore this type of financial hooliganism."

And Congress, it turned out, completely agreed with him. Something quite unsettling was going on in corporate America, in places as obscure as Follansbee, West Virginia, and as center-stage as Chicago's Medinah Temple, from the new Scandinavian-style boardroom at Laclede-Christy in St. Louis to the burnished Vanderbilt boardroom of the New York Central. It was time for the nation's lawmakers to confront the stock market's proxy fighters, face to face.

CHAPTER EIGHT

GRAPES OF WRATH

Shortly after 10 A.M. on June 9, 1955, Senator Herbert H. Lehman of New York entered Room 318 of the Senate Office Building to open that day's hearings in his extensive examination of the nation's recent corporate proxy contests.[1] Senator Lehman, whose family had founded the Wall Street firm that bore its name, was a small square-built man with a gleaming dome of a forehead surrounded by a fluffy fringe of silver hair; despite his seventy-seven years, his bushy, unruly eyebrows were still black as ink, and his wide smile had carved deep furrows around his mouth. He had an appetite for hard work and a passionately liberal record that commanded considerable respect in Congress. While he was not part of the inner circle that ran the Senate—he was far too outspoken and impatient for that—he was part of the surviving New Deal bloc that included his influential friend Hubert Humphrey of Minnesota.[2]

In New York, he had been lieutenant governor under Governor Franklin Roosevelt, and he had succeeded to Roosevelt's Albany office when his mentor became president. Lehman had retired from politics because of ill health in 1946, but he was pulled back into the fray in 1949 to run against Republican John Foster Dulles in a special election to replace the ailing Senator Robert F. Wagner. Lehman won that race, despite Dulles's attempts to smear him as the Communists' favored candidate, and he had become a fearless and unwavering opponent of the character assassinations and witch-hunts initiated the following year by Senator Joseph McCarthy.[3]

As the brisk elderly New York Democrat took his place at the center of the podium, he was joined by Senator Homer Capehart. Nothing in Lehman's nod toward the Republican from Indiana suggested his profound contempt for the support that Capehart had given to McCarthy's career, support which endured right through the summer of 1954, when the Senate finally voted to discipline the discredited demagogue.[4] Capehart was a figure of fun among the members of the press corps; one popular pundit described him as suffering from "pernicious rotundity—fat head, fat body, and fatuousness."[5] He strongly resembled the cowboy comic Andy Devine, with his wide, jowly face and double chins. But Lehman saw no comedy in the pudgy Hoosier. He perhaps remembered that evening in April 1951, when he and Humphrey had joined Capehart for a broadcast of the radio program *Meet Your Congress*. The two Democrats were speaking in support of President Truman's decision, the day before, to dismiss the immensely popular but disobedient General Douglas MacArthur, while Capehart strongly condemned the move. As his fury increased, Capehart shockingly accused his two colleagues of having "Communist sympathies" and wishing to see the Chinese Communists prevail in the Korean conflict—a charge that was virtually an accusation of treason. Humphrey had confronted Capehart the moment the microphone went dead and, by one account, they almost came to blows before Lehman stepped in to separate them.[6]

Capehart was not officially a member of Lehman's subcommittee, although he sat on its parent panel, the Senate Banking and Currency Committee. But he was the sponsor of a bill that would require any investor who owned as much as 5 percent of a company's stock to disclose that investment publicly. The regulations then in effect set the disclosure trip-wire at 10 percent. Capehart seemed to consider Lehman's hearings to be, at least in part, public hearings on his own proposal.[7] Indeed, on several earlier occasions, Lehman had diplomatically but firmly reminded Capehart that he was technically a guest at the hearings.

Robert A. Wallace, the staff director for the parent committee, organized his papers as the committee room began to fill. It was going to be a large crowd. There was a stir by the door, and a moment later, the dapper, diminutive Robert R. Young was standing behind the witness's chair. An assistant set up a chart on an easel behind him; its complexity rivaled the wiring scheme for a guided missile.

Lehman rapped his gavel. "The hearing will come to order. Mr. Robert R. Young is the first witness."

"Good morning," said Young, looking for all the world like a white-haired, elegantly suited leprechaun.

Lehman did not return the pleasantry. Although Young had been an ardent supporter of the New Deal's stock market reforms, his profound, almost obsessive hatred of Communism had made him "an unashamed supporter" of McCarthy, and he had contributed both money and influence to McCarthy's reckless search for government subversives.[8] So the elderly senator got right to business, and simply asked the railroad executive to raise his right hand. He administered the oath, and invited the witness to be seated. "Mr. Young, I believe you have a statement," he said. "You may proceed in the manner that seems most desirable to you."

"Well, sir, if I may, I would like to read the statement and perhaps, in one or two places, interpolate."

Lehman agreed and Young seemed to tighten a bit, like a relaxed hand suddenly taking a firmer grip. His pale blue eyes narrowed slightly. Lehman's study of proxy contests, Young said, gave the Senate "a golden opportunity to sweep away the smoke screen of superficialities and the face-saving froth thrown up by some of the contestants, and to pry into the core of the matter—at least in the New York Central case. You need only look here to find the devices by which a small group of men have assumed control of many of our great corporations."[9]

Someone needed to protect the right of small shareholders to have a voice in the businesses they owned, he continued, warming to his favorite subject. This was especially so when those businesses were run by boards "devoid of any meaningful ownership." And shareholders were not adequately protected at present, he argued, because the nation's regulatory machinery was in thrall to the same Morgan banking interests that Young had battled for so long.[10] (Perhaps it occurred to Senator Lehman that Young used the word "Morgan" the way McCarthy had used the term "Communist.")

"However much this invisible corporate combination of power is denied, and despite the difficulty of putting your finger on it, the public nevertheless persists in the recognition of its existence," Young went on. "I think the proof of this is the tremendous public interest evoked by these proxy fights."[11] He had personal experience with the phenomenon, he said. When he arrived at Pennsylvania Station in New York after announcing his challenge to this secret combine, he said, "I was met not by my assistant, as I expected, but, on the authority of the amazed station-master, by the greatest array of reporters and photographers that had ever gathered in Penn Station to greet anyone, Churchill or Sally Rand not excepted."[12] The audience no doubt smiled to hear the famous statesman and the notorious strip-tease celebrity combined in the same breath.

But in his great proxy fight, Young continued, he had to fight an even bigger army than the Morgans and their minions. "Indeed, we had to contend against the subtle influence of all those large American corporations which for their own quite human reasons sought to discourage revolt by stockholders."[13]

Young offered his recommendations, all of them reflecting his own bruising battles with his adversaries. He urged secret ballots for shareholders but "truth and full disclosure for contestants," and strict limits on management's use of corporate employees, corporate funds, and corporate patronage to solicit proxies. He called for a ban on bystander corporations intervening in a proxy fight—evidence of his still lingering rage over two incidents during the Central fight. First, two large insurance companies had joined the beleaguered New York Central management in urging the Interstate Commerce Commission to investigate Young. And then Morgan, Stanley and Company, J. P. Morgan and Company, and the First National Bank of New York had all run newspaper advertisements disputing his vicious criticism of them and their role at the Central. The "crust" and "effrontery" of his opponents were outrageous, he complained. Young even saw the evil combine's hand in the coverage the proxy fight received from "powerful publishing organizations which as partisans grossly abused the usual high standards of the press," citing as evidence a few mildly unfavorable pieces in *Fortune,* owned by Time Inc. Time's board included a lawyer whose firm had done work for the Morgans—it was obviously a conspiracy.[14] Young also called for tighter controls on the revolving door that connected Washington regulatory offices to the financial establishment. "We cannot have that flitting back and forth and still have justice," Young said, detailing various regulatory decisions against him that showed the evil combine's influence.[15] Young also recommended that commercial banks be forced to spin off their trust departments, an arrangement he thought was far more important than the 1933 legislation that required them to split off their investment banking functions. In a proxy fight, trust departments voted the shares in their control out of loyalty to the bankers, not in the best interests of the trust beneficiaries, he charged.

And finally, he urged Congress to prohibit the interlocking directorships, detailed in his chart, that linked four of the great eastern banks to the boards of some of the nation's largest corporations. Such affiliations were dangerous and wrong, he insisted. "It has got to be stopped or, as I say, our whole economy, political as well as business, is going to fall within their power. And we can lose our freedom to others than the Communists."[16]

With Young's formal statement out of the way, Lehman began his questions. He was curious, first, about who had voted for Young and who had supported management in the New York Central fight. His questioning revealed that, for all Young's Populist bluster, management had polled more votes from the individual shareholders than Young had. Young won on the strength of shares he and his allies owned and shares held in broker's nominee accounts.

Second, Lehman turned his attention to the arrangements which had led to Young's allies, Sid Richardson and Clint Murchison of Texas, acquiring the 800,000 shares of Central stock that Chase Manhattan bank had been holding in trust for the C&O Railroad.

The arrangement had befuddled Wall Street and Washington from the first. On the eve of the proxy fight, Young's Alleghany Corporation had sold its stake in the C&O to Cleveland industrialist Cyrus Eaton, Young's close friend and ally. One of the railroad's assets was a block of 800,000 shares of New York Central, which the ICC had ordered the C&O to place in trust while Young controlled both lines. But there was considerable doubt among Young's legal advisers whether the ICC would allow Eaton, the new C&O owner, to vote those Central shares for Young. So Young recruited the two Texans and helped finance their purchase of the Central stock from the C&O's new owner, a purchase that was made entirely with funds the Texans borrowed from various friendly sources: the Alleghany Corporation itself, Young's partner Allan Kirby, and a Cleveland bank friendly to Eaton.

The arrangement seemed to insulate the Texans from any price risk, because it gave them the right to "put," or sell, the shares to Alleghany at their original purchase price. However, a little-noticed and seemingly contradictory proviso to the deal decreed that the Texans could only exercise that "put" if they also "held Alleghany harmless" for any loss they incurred on the stock, and if they would share half of any profits they made on it. So if the stock price went down, they could sell it to Alleghany for their original purchase price and avoid a loss—except that they could only sell it if they held Alleghany harmless for any losses. The strange and self-negating arrangement, which Young insisted was part of the deal, was so obscure that even Young's lawyer and biographer, Joseph Borkin, was unaware of it and interpreted the agreement as protecting Murchison and Richardson from any loss on the stock.[17]

Now, it was Senator Lehman's turn to try to unravel the perplexing deal. Young promised to explain "the whole story," but he kept skipping key details. The senator would interrupt with astute questions designed to fill the gaps. Young grew more waspish with each interruption.

"As I understand it, Messrs. Richardson and Murchison did not actually put up any of their own cash?" Lehman inquired.

"Well, as you know," Young retorted, "the nation runs on credit, even the housewife, sir."

Yes, Lehman said, but could Young please explain this strange arrangement that allowed the Texans to sell the stock back to Alleghany?

"It is very simple," said Young, with withering scorn. In his machine-gun staccato, he raced through the eye-crossing details. "It was one of the most attractive deals in history," he concluded.[18]

Lehman continued to question the deal, confused by its obscure and contradictory terms. Didn't the right to sell the stock back to Alleghany at $25 a share protect the Texans from any loss?[19]

Young was exasperated. "That is one of those half-truths that I have been talking about, sir. You just have not completed the story." He rattled through the implausible details once more, but to Lehman it still sounded like *Alice in Wonderland*: the Texans had a right to sell the stock back to Alleghany without a loss, but only if they agreed never to exercise that right. When the senator continued to question the terms, the arrogant proxy warrior snapped.

"It's a deal I'm proud of and I'd make with anyone here!" Young, obviously angry, rose from his chair and turned to shout at the spectators who packed the room.[20] "And I would offer any of the gentlemen here the same deal. Anyone in this room! Anyone that will come in with good credit and guarantee me against loss, I will be glad to advance them the money, if they will give me half the profits and 4.5 percent interest. Anyone that would like to, please hold up your hand! Come in! My address is 230 Park Avenue."

An astonished Senator Lehman was pounding the table, trying to restore order. When something approaching silence returned, he said that he still had "very great" questions about the arrangements and then turned the questioning over to the committee's staff aide, Robert Wallace. Wallace got right to the core of the mystery that seemed to baffle everyone but Robert Young.

"Mr. Young, it has been generally understood that Messrs. Murchison and Richardson were in effect guaranteed against loss, and what you are saying is that that is not true, that they were not?"

"It is just the reverse, sir," said Young.

"They were not guaranteed against loss, but the Alleghany Corporation was guaranteed against loss, and if the stock had gone down, as a result of this agreement Alleghany could not have lost but Murchison and Richardson would have lost?"

"You are so correct, sir," Young smiled, as if he had just encountered the only intelligent man in the room.

"Then I think that the confusing point is this $25 'put.' What was the purpose of the put?" Wallace asked. After all, with the proviso that protected Alleghany from loss, the "put" granted to the Texans was "rather meaningless, wasn't it?"[21]

Young stumbled a bit. Well, it did give Alleghany a chance to share in any profits on the upside, he started to explain—but that only raised the obvious question of why the shrewd Texans would have agreed to something that eliminated their loss protection solely to benefit Alleghany. "It gave them a few months to look it over and see whether Young won," the railroad raider sputtered. "It gave them the chance to study the situation."

"It gave them some flexibility?" Wallace asked helpfully.

"Yes, sir: it happens every day in Wall Street."[22]

Then Lehman continued his questioning, and Young grew more insulting with each exchange.

"Mr. Young, you have referred to this deal which you made as a clever deal. Assuming that the facts that you have given are correct—and I am not questioning their truthfulness—it certainly appears to be a clever deal. But have you ever known a deal of this sort to be engaged in, in connection with a proxy fight?"[23]

"Well, to my knowledge, there has really been only one important proxy fight in history, and that is this one," Young said with a lofty scorn for recent history. "Proxy fights are far too rare. . . . on this scale, they are rare and unique. And so is a combination of power such as that," he gestured toward his chart of interlocking directorships. "And when someone has the power to face it, and the stockholders vote for him overwhelmingly, I think that he deserves a hand, sir."

As the hand on the committee room clock moved past noon, Wallace followed up with additional questions about details of the proxy fight. Finally, Lehman moved to close the hearings. He thanked Young for coming, saying that his testimony "has been very interesting and very thought-provoking. You are obviously a skilled businessman and a clever financier. I want to pay you all credit."[24]

Young tried to interrupt, but Lehman stopped him. "May I finish my statement, please?" He said he shared Young's dismay at the small amount of stock held by boards of directors. And then he held out an olive branch, insisting he was not taking sides in Young's long war with the nation's bankers. But he nevertheless had "grave doubts as to the propriety of the deal" involving the Texas oilmen. "That deal, which you described as clever, seems to me to be just a little too clever for my possibly old-fashioned viewpoint."[25]

When Young got a chance to reply, it seemed, at first, that he would end his testimony on a gracious note. He complimented Senator Lehman for his long public service. But then he continued: "I would like to say to the press that, in view of the fact that it has been obvious that Senator Lehman did not understand the transaction that he scored me for, I hope you'll take that into consideration when you report what transpired. Thank you."[26]

"I understand it now," said Lehman, taking the chairman's prerogative of having the last word. "I personally have grave doubts as to the propriety of it."[27]

Young's fiery testimony came on the fourth day of Senator Lehman's hearings into the recent proxy wars. The previous day, Lehman had heard from William White, the man defeated in "the only important proxy fight in history." White had been a careful, reasonable witness, reading from a brief prepared statement. "Although I was a principal in one of the very big proxy contests of recent years—and a loser at that—I would not offer any objections to proxy contests per se," he began. "Our capitalistic profit system must operate in an atmosphere of industrial democracy. Management must always be kept alive to its responsibility to its shareholders, and has no inherent right to become entrenched in its position merely because of the fact that it was once elected."[28]

But he was troubled by the cumbersome role the SEC played in policing what the protagonists in a fight could say to the public. "I should like to see the regulations changed, so that after the initial proxy statement, either side may be free of the requirement to secure SEC approval, though remaining subject to the restrictions imposed by applicable statutes with respect to misleading statements and libel."[29]

But the bulk of the subcommittee's time, since Senator Lehman first called the hearings to order on the first of June, had been spent exploring the Montgomery Ward fight, still fresh in the public's mind.

The aspect of the battle which most alarmed Lehman was Wolfson's use of two other companies he controlled through Merritt-Chapman and Scott—namely Devoe and Raynolds, a widely known paint company, and the New York Shipbuilding Corporation—to purchase Montgomery Ward shares pledged to his slate. The paint company had even borrowed money to purchase the stock. The investments had been profitable, but Lehman nevertheless was shocked that "the funds of one corporation were being used in order to secure control of another corporation unconnected or, if connected at all, very slightly. I believe that is a great evil. I believe it is a great danger."

What was to prevent someone who controlled a "comparatively unimportant corporation" from eventually borrowing enough money to achieve control of much larger and more important corporations? That possibility, he argued over and over during the hearings, "must be made impossible. Otherwise we have opened the door to a kind of manipulation that is evil and I believe unthinkable . . . You can pile one on top of another, you can go on more or less indefinitely." Indeed, if that were to become common, Lehman said with great prescience, "I can see where there is no limit to the empires that a man might build."[30]

Despite his very strong views, firmly expressed on frequent occasions, Lehman denied any partisanship in the proxy fights under study. "This study is not intended to assess blame, to exculpate, to indict, or to accuse any faction in any proxy fight," he said as he opened the hearings. "It is not our purpose to establish who is in the right or who is in the wrong. It is our purpose to ascertain whether there are adequate safeguards, supervision, and rules of fair play, whether by legislation, administrative rule [and] regulation or self-policing, or by a combination of the three."

He continued, "We are approaching a problem of great proportions which has received very little public study or attention. I refer to the problem of corporate democracy." The impact that great corporations had upon the country was "beyond calculation," he said. And in recent years, the ownership of these corporations had become more widespread. "The question then of the control and management of these corporations, and the relationship of that control to the actual owners of these companies and corporations—the shareholders—is one of which must solicit our most earnest interest."[31]

Montgomery Ward, as a company, had been a lightning rod for debates about the changing shape of corporate democracy ever since the late 1940s, when Merrill Griswold of the Massachusetts Investors Trust mutual fund first tried to find some way to balance his role as an injured and outraged shareholder with the traditionally passive role mutual funds and other "fiduciary" investors were expected to play in corporate affairs. Peter F. Drucker, the famed management specialist, decried the consequences of this institutional passivity in an article published on the eve of Lehman's hearings. "The presently accepted policy means that management is essentially responsible to no one," Drucker warned. "By their abstention from voting and control, in the majority of cases, the fiduciary institutions simply confirm the incumbent officers . . . This has been one of the main reasons Mr. Avery could continue to manage without serious opposition to his decision to retrench to a point where his business has been almost in voluntary liquidation." Nor could intelligent fiduciaries "save a competent management from being 'blitzed.' All unwittingly, they invite the attention of any financial sharpshooter or stock market manipulator who wants to get control of the firm in order to milk it. If 40 to 60 percent of the company voting stock is in the hands of fiduciary investors who will not vote," he added, then it was a simple thing to seize control with "a fairly small fraction" of the stock.[32]

As more of corporate America's stock came into the hands of mutual funds and other passive institutional investors, the power of the shareholder—the muscle that had sustained the mighty Mellons and other business barons—had become weaker and less effective. By the 1950s, most chief executives had been essentially liberated from the need to cater to shareholders at all. It was a time when "the subjugation of the shareholder by corporate management . . . seemed to have reached an extreme," one economist of the day observed.[33] In the robustly prosperous 1950s, for example, corporations were paying out substantially less of their profits in the form of dividends than they had paid in the boom years of the 1920s.[34] As another scholar of the period saw it, managers at corporations with widely diffuse ownership "have little or nothing to gain by paying out more than is necessary to keep existing shareholders from complaining in force, to attract any additional capital that may be needed, and in general to build up or maintain the reputation of the firm as a good investment."[35]

And that was what had to change, argued Lou Wolfson when he appeared before Lehman's subcommittee on June 2, 1955. "You realize satisfied stockholders never have a proxy fight," he said in his awkward but sincere patois. "The only time you have a proxy fight is when you have dissatisfied stockholders who are not getting fair returns, that some of the officers are drawing too much money, and a total disregard for the people that are employing them. So that is how proxy fights start."[36]

He had made the same point in his prepared remarks. "Proxy contests are wholesome because, similar to public elections, they serve to focus attention on the stewardship of those holding and aspiring to office. No one enjoys a proxy contest, or undertakes one without some misgivings. But they are a form of surgery sometimes necessary to effect the cure of corporate ills."[37]

And the key illness that Wolfson saw was the failure of American managers to appreciate the importance of the American investor. "Without his willingness to provide the funds to build factories and buy machinery, management would have nothing to manage," he said. "Without his financing of payrolls and operating expenses, labor would be out of a job." He continued, "The nature of the American investor has changed. No longer are our industries owned by a few, or a dozen, wealthy men. A large number of our corporations today are owned by Mr. and Mrs. America." And this new stockholder had to be "reasonably sure of two things: the safety of his investment, and a fair return for the use of his money." Managers who met those needs, he concluded, had little to fear from a proxy fight.[38]

But Wolfson's utopia, in which corporations faithfully served stockholders' needs, failed to include all the others in the American community who had a stake in what large corporations did—people like the citizens of Follansbee, West Virginia. This seemed to be the taproot of the continuing public concern about proxy fights—not whether the fight between management and shareholders was fairly fought, as Lehman was exploring, but how the fight would affect all the hapless bystanders. The tug-of-war between the rights of shareholders and the needs and interests of the broader community had been simmering in the American mind at least since the days of Theodore Roosevelt. In that era, the shareholders effectively were the "dozen wealthy men" that Wolfson mentioned, Rockefellers and Mellons and Vanderbilts and Morgans who expected to pursue their own profit without public interference. Much of the Progressive and New Deal agenda—bans on child labor, support for collective bargaining, full disclosure in the securities markets, food safety legislation—had been aimed at balancing the power of those shareholders against the public's welfare. The gradual transformation of the "shareholder" from plutocrat to democrat did not change that continuing tension between the shareholder's priorities and those of the community at large—as Lou Wolfson would learn just weeks after his appearance before the Lehman committee.

Congress had first called for an investigation of Wolfson's management of the Capital Transit Company in July 1953, after "four years of steadily rising concern . . . as to whether the public interest was being properly regarded."[39] That investigation, carried out by a subcommittee of the Senate Committee on the District of Columbia, had begun in December 1953 and a report had been released in April 1954.

"The public has been unable to reconcile the several requests for fare increases by Capital Transit Company with its substantially increased dividends since its controlling interest was purchased by Louis E. Wolfson and his associates in the fall of 1949," the report noted. The result was a public belief that "absentee owners are stripping Capital Transit Company of valuable assets with a view toward eventually selling the company to the government to be operated under some form of public ownership."

The subcommittee investigators could find little to fault in Capital Transit's operations—it had "done an effective job of controlling costs"—although they raised vague warnings about the company's failure to retain the accumulated capital that had been paid out in dividends. For the most part, the subcommittee had to concede that "the company's financial structure was quite sound. It had $4.6 million working capital and a debt of only $5.7 million. Its equipment was in good condition."[40]

But the subcommittee was "disturbed by the general attitude of the Wolfson group," which seemed to value no one but its shareholders. "Anyone who invests in a public utility does so knowing that the public interest will at least be considered on a par with the private interest," the panel continued.[41]

Moreover, the report criticized the company's "discriminatory hiring policies" and its managers' "refusal to arbitrate a pension dispute with their employees' union." Capital Transit blamed its refusal to employ black streetcar and bus operators on its union's racism, not its own, suggesting that the union might stage a wildcat strike if blacks were hired. But the Wolfson team seemed willing to risk a strike over its continued refusal to arbitrate a pension dispute with the same union. "The inconsistency between the company's refusal to discontinue its discriminatory hiring practices, because of the questionable threat of a wildcat strike . . . and its refusal to submit a pension dispute to the required arbitration, in spite of the serious threat of full-scale strike, is obvious," the subcommittee concluded. "The subcommittee believes that unless the company changes its present attitude, a strike may well be inevitable."[42]

The subcommittee was absolutely right.

On Monday, June 27, 1955, with the strike set to begin at midnight on Thursday, Senator Wayne Morse of Oregon opened his morning newspaper. His eyes quickly found the latest strike developments: J. A. B. Broadwater, the bus company president, was once again refusing arbitration of the long-running wage dispute. It was exactly the same line that Broadwater and the rest of the Wolfson group had taken before the Senate investigative subcommittee eighteen months ago. It was so exasperating! A strike would badly damage the bus company's already feeble public support and would kill any support it had in Congress, he was certain. How, he wondered, could any public utility take the position, in this modern day and age, that it was going to handle its labor problems in accordance with its own will regardless of the public interest?[43]

Senator Morse had long experience as a labor arbitrator. And he knew that the problems that gave rise to the threat of a midsummer bus strike— "what a silly, nonsensical thing it will be!"—were more than problems of attitude.[44] Capital Transit's ridership had declined, its labor and fuel costs had climbed, and it insisted that it simply could not afford the improved wages and benefits that the unions were demanding unless it got an immediate fare increase. All the experts were saying the same thing, Morse knew: "Mass transportation is a losing proposition for the investors."[45] But Capital Transit's plight might have generated more sympathy if it hadn't paid out all that cash to its shareholders between 1950 in 1954. "But now is not the time to thresh that old straw," the senator said. The union contract expired in less than four days. Congress, as the local government of the District of Columbia, had to try to prevent this futile, disruptive strike, if it could.

That afternoon, Morse appeared before the Senate Committee on the District of Columbia and argued that some kind of assistance—a tax benefit or subsidy—had to be provided to Capital Transit or it could not continue providing reasonably priced bus service to Washington's citizens. Perhaps if that were the carrot, the company would submit to the stick of arbitration? But Morse's subcommittee made no progress and the company would not budge. By Thursday, Morse's frustration spilled over on the floor of the Senate. He briefed his concerned colleagues on the stalled talks and fielded some sensible questions. Then he slashed into Wolfson: "I would have the management of the Capital Transit Company recognize and remember that they function and operate under a privilege granted to them by Congress. I think the time has come when that privilege should be taken away . . . I shall have prepared for introduction within the next few days a bill to lift the franchise of the Capital Transit Company." Lou Wolfson "seems to think he is bigger than Congress," Morse said. "I am for cutting Wolfson down to size . . . I am for passing legislation which will say to Brother Wolfson, 'We are going to lift your franchise, because we think your entire conduct has clearly demonstrated very bad faith on your part. You have come here as a sort of economic carpet-bagger, wanting to milk the system. We do not intend to let you get by with it.' "[46]

But angry words and threats had no effect. On Friday, July 1, Washington woke up to a humid and unsettling silence: no wheezing buses, no clattering streetcars.

Morse believed that the key man, the only man who could move Capital Transit in a constructive direction at the bargaining table, was Louis E. Wolfson. He was the man "whose views I want to hear more than all others combined," Morse decided.[47] When he reached the Capitol that morning—the traffic wasn't as bad as he feared; perhaps people had taken their July Fourth holiday early—he asked a staff lawyer, William Gulledge, to call Broadwater at Capital Transit's headquarters. Morse wanted Wolfson to appear before a subcommittee hearing on July 7; surely together they could find some route through this terrible impasse.

Gulledge made the call, but Broadwater was not helpful. Wolfson was traveling and Broadwater did not know where he could be reached.

Gulledge urged Broadwater to inform Wolfson in the clearest terms that his presence was desired by the subcommittee at 10:30 A.M. the following Thursday, but Broadwater remained noncommittal.[48]

Senator Morse was infuriated. Here was the nation's capital immobilized by a transit strike, and the chairman of the transit company not only was not on the scene, seeking a solution, but he could not even be located! The next few days did not improve Morse's mood; a traffic-choked Tuesday came and went, and there was still no word from Wolfson. Fine, Morse decided; the subcommittee would spend Thursday's hearing considering his proposal to strip Capital Transit of its franchise. Perhaps that would get Brother Wolfson's attention.

On Wednesday, July 6, Morse received a breezy wire from Wolfson, somewhere in San Francisco: "Have not heard from you directly, but understand that you want me in Washington in reference to bill dealing with cancellation of Capital Transit Company franchise. J.A.B. Broadwater, president, can testify on this matter if you desire. Would appreciate direct contact from your office if you still want me. Subpoena is not necessary, willing to appear voluntarily. Will be at Beverly Wilshire Hotel, Beverly Hills, Calif., this weekend."[49]

But "direct contact" from Morse's office was impossible, the senator fumed. Even in that era when cellular phones and radio-frequency pagers were undreamed of, Morse could scarcely believe that no one had any idea where Wolfson was at that moment. But there was no return address on the telegram, just a string of symbols. The "weekend" was several days away, and it was a big country. If the president of Wolfson's own company did not know where to reach him, why should the United States Senate "engage in a hide-and-seek performance" to track Wolfson down?

Morse's subcommittee decided late Wednesday afternoon to issue a formal subpoena for Wolfson's appearance, and leave it to the United States marshals to track him down. They sent Wolfson a telegram advising him of this action, directing it to the Beverly-Wilshire Hotel and to the string of symbols contained on his wire from San Francisco. "Your failure as head of a public utility to interest yourself personally by being present and available in Washington D.C. would seem to indicate a lack of appreciation of your responsibility to the public in connection with this emergency," the subcommittee wrote. "We are satisfied that you were aware of the fact that the committee desired your attendance at a hearing set for Thursday, July 7, 1955, in plenty of time to have appeared at said hearing. Your belated . . . wire today raises serious doubts as to your good faith in carrying out the clear responsibility that you owe to the people of the District of Columbia, as well as to your own stockholders."[50]

On Thursday, July 7, the subcommittee gathered at 10:30 A.M. in the grand District Committee room at the Capitol. Senator Pat McNamara of Michigan called the hearing to order—three senators from the full committee had joined the three members of the subcommittee. The transit strike was drawing far greater attention than Senator Lehman's proxy-fight hearings were. As McNamara listened to Morse's recital of his efforts to reach Wolfson, a committee aide hurried over and handed the chairman a telegram. McNamara saw that it was from Wolfson and had been sent at 7 A.M. that morning. He handed it to Morse, who read it aloud.

Wolfson's fury infused every sentence, adding to the staccato syntax in which telegrams were composed in those days. "You may be sure that I recognize my responsibilities to my stockholders, employees, and the public and your committee. . . . As Senators, you are paid by taxpayers such as myself and millions of others. Would seem that you would stop wasteful spending of taxpayers' money and have one subpoena served me at Beverly-Wilshire without too much fanfare. I am making plans to leave for Washington per your request immediately. Will report to your office Monday July 11."[51]

Morse was not intimidated, of course—as an outspoken liberal Republican who had defied his own increasingly conservative party to support Democrat Adlai Stevenson in the 1952 presidential race, Morse was virtually immune to intimidation. "I know that the action of the committee will stand, and the Federal officials will continue today to try to find Mr. Wolfson and see to it that the subpoena is served," he said, laying the telegram aside. "That is not the important issue, Mr. Chairman. The important issue is what if anything can be done to restore transportation service in the district?"

Broadwater had bravely shown up to answer the committee's questions, but when Senator McNamara offered him the floor, he used his public pulpit to stoutly defend his boss. Wolfson was not being elusive, he was simply taking the steps necessary to protect his family from "crackpots." Indeed, Broadwater said, there was not "a more straightforward, fair-minded, upright" man in America. He added, "For my book, he is ace-high."[52] But when asked about the strike, all Broadwater would do was repeat the company line: unless the district's Public Utilities Commission granted the company an immediate fare increase, or some substantial tax break, there was simply no money to increase employees' wages. The company would not use its cash reserves to finance any wage increase. So unless and until the PUC acted—or the employees decided to go back to work empty-handed—the strike would continue.

There matters stood until Tuesday, July 12, when Senator McNamara convened the subcommittee to hear the testimony of Louis E. Wolfson.

There was pandemonium in the hearing room when Wolfson arrived with his advisers and took a seat in the audience. Flashbulbs popped as photographers jostled the cumbersome newsreel camera crews. McNamara pounded the table, calling the meeting to order and urging the "gentlemen of the press" to conclude their work so that the meeting could continue. He invited Wolfson to take his place at the witness table. As the tall, well-dressed executive settled into place, a new outburst of flash bulbs began. McNamara was taken aback when Morse insisted that Wolfson be placed under oath, but he shrugged and agreed. Wolfson raised his right hand, amid another starburst of photography. Finally, Wolfson's attorney urged that the photographers be called off, and McNamara did so.

Once order had been restored in the crowded hearing room, the clerk read Wolfson's prepared statement. Even delivered in the dry, mechanical voice of the clerk, it was no more temperate than his outraged telegram. Apparently, a "scapegoat" for the strike had to be found, and he was it. He chastised the subcommittee for making it appear that he was trying to avoid testifying, when nothing could be further from the truth. "I wish to protest these unfair and unjust attacks made on my integrity in my absence," his statement continued. "I am a responsible businessman, whose honesty is vital to the welfare of more than 100,000 stockholders of the companies with which I am associated and to whom I feel a basic obligation. I resent the wild and irresponsible statements impugning my honor that have been made," he continued. "I reject name-calling as the weapon of the over-emotional."

But, of course he had some name-calling of his own to do. As the clerk read on, Wolfson's statement condemned the district's Public Utilities Commission members as "prejudiced" against his company, and as dishonest and incompetent. If the commission had acted earlier on the company's need for a rate increase, the strike could have been avoided, he insisted. As for his absence from Washington, well, he had delegated responsibility for Capitol Transit to Broadwater, and it was his policy as chairman never to interfere with his operational staff.

The clerk put down the sheaf of papers, and McNamara recognized Senator Morse, who would lead the questioning.

With his curved nose and bushy eyebrows, Morse resembled some great night owl circling a field mouse. He quizzed Wolfson about when he had first learned that the subcommittee wanted to hear from him. On July 4, when he had read it in the newspapers, Wolfson answered.

"You do not recall any conversation with Mr. Broadwater informing you as to a telephone conversation he had with the general counsel of this committee seeking to find out where you could be reached?"

Wolfson hedged, saying he and Broadwater had spoken several times and maybe Broadwater had mentioned that some committee would like to see him, but he really couldn't remember the details. And no, he had not kept Broadwater or the committee posted about where he could be reached, he conceded. He was on vacation. But surely, his office in Washington would have known. Did Senator Morse try there?

"Oh, yes," the senator snapped.

"And they couldn't tell you where I was?"

"It is perfectly clear, the transcript is perfectly clear, Mr. Wolfson," Morse thundered. "We could not find you through Mr. Broadwater, nor could we get any information that would advise us as to how we can get in touch with you." Therefore, he continued, it was simply false for Wolfson to claim, as he had, that the subcommittee knew how to reach him all along and had chosen to subpoena him simply to embarrass him. "We did not know where you were. If we knew where you were we would have been in touch with you."[53]

They sparred for a few more moments over the subcommittee's efforts to reach him, and finally Morse turned to the "substance of this hearing." What efforts had Wolfson made prior to his arrival in Washington to bring about a settlement of the strike?

"No effort, because I didn't get into the situation until I arrived yesterday morning," Wolfson answered.

"When did you first hear that there was a strike on the line?"

"Well, I heard it July 1 through the press. I was very much concerned about it, but I hadn't been in touch directly with officials particularly about the strike," Wolfson replied. But, he continued, he had an excellent operating officer in Broadwater, and an outstanding board of directors at the company, and he had delegated to them the full authority to deal with the strike. That was the way his companies worked.

As for the company's policy toward the strike, Wolfson echoed Broadwater: no fare increase, no wage increase.

Senator Clifford Case of New Jersey gently challenged Wolfson's intransigence. "Proceedings before a regulatory body do take time," he observed. "It is not reasonable for anyone to consider that you can automatically get an increase in rates immediately upon an increase in salaries, or other expenses for that matter. For instance, if you are faced with an increase in electrical power costs, I take it that you would not immediately close down until you got an increase in rates, would you? And I suggest that this is just the same kind of thing."[54]

Wise public utility executives maintained reserves to carry them over such regulatory delays, the courtly senator continued. But Wolfson's management had exhausted its reserve funds through the payment of enormous unearned dividends.

Wolfson had no apologies for the $29 a share in dividends the shareholders had received during his tenure. "I believe in being liberal in dividends; I expect always to be. The only way that you are going to stop my being liberal in dividends, in Capital Transit, is to do it legally, or to get rid of Wolfson as the director and chairman of the board. Because I am going always to be liberal with the stockholders of this company or any company. That has always been my philosophy."[55]

And that, really, was the crux of the conflict. Wolfson believed that shareholders came first, and he did not seem to see that the shareholders might ultimately be harmed by his failure to give equal consideration to the interests of his workers, his passengers, and his regulators—and, of course, his senators. But he had thrown down the gauntlet; Congress would, indeed, "get rid of Wolfson."

The raucous hearings concluded, and the strike continued until July 30. Then, Capital Transit's franchise was repealed, after a Senate debate that reached new heights of animosity toward "the Wolfson wolf-like raiders."[56]

Wolfson had not raided Capitol Transit. He had purchased it peacefully from its former owners, after the rest of wealthy Washington had turned up its nose at the opportunity to buy the cash-rich company. But his response to the strike quickly became one more exhibit in the political brief against the proxy warriors. What was to be done about these new boardroom mavericks?

As Wolfson was grilled over the transit strike, Senator Lehman's committee had continued its examination of the corporate battlefield, listening as proxy raiders and corporate managers who agreed on little else uniformly criticized the Securities and Exchange Commission. The commission had been too lax, or too severe. Its proxy rules were too cumbersome, too vague, too restrictive, too lenient. By June 14, 1955, Senator Lehman had heard enough to persuade him that "new rules are necessary" to regulate proxy contests.[57] He invited J. Sinclair Armstrong, the new chairman of the SEC, to testify before the committee about his agency's experience with proxy battles over the past two years.

The Democrats in Congress had been critical of the Securities and Exchange Commission for years.[58] The agency had been on a starvation diet since 1952. In part this was a result of President Eisenhower's determination to balance the federal budget, but it also reflected the view of Treasury Secretary George Humphrey, a former corporate executive, who believed that American business was overregulated. As a result, the agency that Armstrong had inherited from his predecessor, Ralph Demmler, on May 25, 1955, was operating at a woefully ineffective level.

One of its commissioners had warned in early 1953 that "the Commission is not able to do an adequate job" because of the severe cuts in its budget.[59] By 1954, the enfeebled commission lacked the funds to deal with even the most egregious problems of the booming stock market, which a leading SEC historian characterized as "the most widespread pattern of speculative activity and securities fraud to occur since the late 1920s."[60] The policing of proxy fights had scarcely registered on its radar screen. Indeed, the only recent action it had taken on proxy rules was in 1954, when it curtailed the rights of shareholders to submit questions for inclusion in their company's proxy statements.[61] The assumption underlying these controversial amendments was that shareholders should not be allowed to vote on "any proposal which impinges upon the duties and functions of the management." That pro-management stance perhaps stemmed from the makeup of the commission, which consisted almost entirely of former corporate attorneys.[62]

Under Section 14 of the 1934 Securities Exchange Act, the law that had created the commission, the agency was empowered to set rules to govern corporate proxy elections.[63] In 1942, the SEC strengthened those proxy rules somewhat, despite congressional opposition so fierce that the staff attorney who drafted the proposed rules was accused of having Communist sympathies.[64] "The new rules did not include a proposal earlier considered by the staff to empower non-controlling shareholders to use the corporate proxy machinery to nominate directors," an SEC historian noted. "But the proxy revisions did require certain senior executives to disclose their compensation before seeking re-election or re-appointment; allowed shareholders to circulate 100-word statements at the corporation's expense, proposing changes in corporate charters or by-laws; and directed that an annual report to shareholders accompany or precede the proxy."[65] There were other amendments in 1952, generally dealing with the information that had to be supplied to stockholders before a proxy vote.

That was roughly where things stood at 10 A.M. on Wednesday, June 15, 1955, when Chairman Armstrong took his seat in Lehman's committee room, surrounded by his three colleagues on the commission and six staff aides. He opened with a dry law-school lecture that challenged the eyelids of his listeners on that late spring morning. But attention perked up when he submitted some agency tabulations. Of the roughly 1,800 proxy statements the commission had received, no more than 1.5 percent of them had been filed by challengers to management's slate of directors.[66]

His number showed that fights for board seats or for corporate control had totaled 21 in 1952, 17 in 1953, and 28 in 1954. "Up to March 31, 1955, there were eleven non-management solicitations, of which eight involved election contests," he testified.[67] Those numbers, he cautioned, reflected only those companies listed on a national or regional stock exchange, which were the only companies within the commission's jurisdiction; the vast realm of the over-the-counter market, where Tom Evans had been so active, was an unexplored war zone. Armstrong submitted a study by the American Institute of Management, a curious research organization formed by that Wall Street chameleon Jackson Martindell and run with some assistance from Art Landa. That study, however, showed a half-dozen fewer proxy contests than the SEC's figures.

Still, even those admittedly incomplete tallies showed that there had been nearly twice as many proxy contests in 1954 as in the previous year, and the commission was concerned. Its rules "were designed for the typical uncontested proxy solicitation," Armstrong conceded. The modern proxy battle, with all its public relations trappings, was a new creature and posed new problems.

Armstrong was outraged when Senator Lehman asked him whether the commission "censored" the proxy solicitation materials that were submitted to it before they were mailed out to shareholders. "Absolutely not!" he answered. "We don't engage in any kind of censorship, sir."[68]

Lehman and his staff director, Robert Wallace, persisted. What if statements in materials sent to shareholders were false or misleading? "Do I understand that the SEC allows them to go out unchallenged, and in that way permits the stockholders to be fooled or misinformed?" Senator Lehman asked incredulously.

"No, sir, of course not."

"Well, what do they do?"

Armstrong was insistent that, whatever his agency did, it should never be characterized as censorship. After the senator agreed to substitute the word "review," Armstrong explained that proxy-fight materials had to be submitted to the commission for review at least ten days before they were to be distributed to shareholders. But what if they are flawed? "The commission has only two courses of action," Armstrong said. It could inform the company of its concerns and "rely upon the willingness of the management to cooperate in making appropriate revisions." Or the agency could seek an injunction in federal court, which would block the company from mailing out the materials or, if they have been mailed, from holding the election until the defects in the material had been corrected.[69]

Such injunction requests were rare. In its entire twenty-two-year history, the commission had itself gone to court over proxy issues on just seventeen occasions, and all but three of those cases had occurred before 1950, when the agency was considerably more aggressive. It had intervened as a "friend of the court" in eleven proxy lawsuits filed by private parties. The latter set of cases, again mostly from the 1940s, included a lawsuit that arose during the proxy fight that put Wolfson on the board of Merritt-Chapman and Scott in 1949. Since then, the agency had gone to court only once, in 1954. Defiance of the agency in court, Armstrong added, was extremely rare.[70]

But the SEC chairman emphasized that there was a limit to its review of proxy materials. In possible defiance of public expectations, he insisted that "the commission does not vouch for, underwrite, or defend the accuracy or adequacy of the proxy material." He added, that "is not and cannot be the commission's function."[71]

The modern proxy contest was extremely difficult to regulate, Armstrong explained. First, there was the question of when a "proxy solicitation" actually began. The commission's rules did not come into play until a formal proxy statement had been furnished to shareholders. But that was not the chronology these new fights for control were following. Typically, there were backstage negotiations with mutual funds and other large stockholders followed by some sort of press release announcing a challenge to management. All of this occurred long before any materials were mailed to stockholders. In response, the commission was beginning to take the position that a "solicitation" began as soon as the fight became public.

But the commission's rules never envisioned a world in which fights for corporate control would feature full-page advertisements, campaign buttons, nationwide "kaffeeklatsches," and unscripted appearances on *Meet the Press*. Perhaps "as a result of the application of public relations techniques" or perhaps just accidentally and spontaneously, "statements have been made, promises broadcast, and accusations hurled which, if submitted in writing, would not have met the tests of fairness and truthfulness for proxy material," Armstrong conceded. The commission did require that prepared speeches, press releases, and advertisements be filed with the commission for advance review, but proxy-fight adversaries "frequently depart from the script."

Nor had the commission anticipated proxy campaigns that extended over many months, with constantly shifting levels of stock ownership and changing sources of financing and lists of supporters. It's all very well to require full disclosure—but full disclosure of what? And when? The facts "may change very rapidly" during a proxy fight, Armstrong said.[72] The commission was perpetually trying to hit a moving target.

Then there was the universally acknowledged problem of disclosing the identity of those backing the assault on management. "In almost every major contest, management has challenged the adequacy and accuracy of the disclosures by the opposition on the subject," Armstrong sighed. His staff had spent "a great deal of time" investigating management accusations that some undisclosed puppeteer was pulling the strings in a proxy fight.

The questions managers typically raised about the motives of the proxy raiders were many and troubling: Are they truly seeking control, or are they simply trying to shake management down for a settlement, a sort of blackmail by proxy? Are they truly seeking to benefit shareholders, or simply trying to profit on their own investment in the shares they've recently accumulated? Do they truly own the stock they claim, or have they borrowed it subject to some concealed hedging arrangements? Where did they get the money? What side deals do they have with their backers? And is there someone "who should be identified as a backer or moving force" rather than just a supporter or sympathizer?

Armstrong said that his agency's worst headaches had arisen in trying to police what proxy contestants said about one another. In general, the commission tried to ensure that the material used in a proxy fight did not contain "unsupportable predictions," did not involve character assassination, and was free of "half-truths, distortions, exaggerations, falsehoods, and unsupported or unsupportable opinions and accusations."

But one could scarcely restrict personal information in proxy contests to name, rank, and serial number. There surely could be no more important issue to be considered by shareholders than weighing the character and reputation of those who sought control of their company. And yet the proxy rules required only that the nominees for the board describe their past and prospective dealings with the company, their business experience, and their compensation. Beyond this, there could be no misleading statements of fact, and no important omissions, Armstrong said.

Given that ambiguity, Armstrong said, it was not surprising that there had scarcely been a recent proxy contest in which the contestants had not attempted "to tear down and destroy in the public mind the reputation of individual candidates." Understandably, the victims of these attacks would assert that the attacks violated the commission's rules and would demand that the commission block the distribution of them. If the attacks involved some specific fact—an indictment, or a court judgment—the commission's job was easy. But "more commonly, no specific charges are made." Instead, the attacker uses "artfully worded statements or questions which create in the reader's mind impressions and inferences that a person is an associate of undesirable or criminal characters, is untrustworthy, will steal the corporate assets or is guilty of immoral and improper conduct." Armstrong continued, "These smear tactics have been employed frequently. Seldom have they been supported by factual data. Rarely are they provable."[73]

As a matter of policy the commission had attempted to purge such unsupported "smears" from proxy materials. But sometimes, a clever adversary would simply republish, in his proxy materials, statements about his opponent which had appeared in the press or in some judicial or regulatory proceeding. The commission tried to apply the same standards to such reprinted accusations as it did to original materials, for which it had been strongly criticized by many contestants. But if it had done otherwise, Armstrong insisted, "the administration of the proxy rules would in many cases become a scandalous affair."[74]

Given all these problems, the commission felt its proxy rules needed a thorough overhaul, and its staff was already working in that direction. The key goals were to define "proxy solicitation" more carefully, and to broaden the definition of the term "associate." The new definition would include those who financed a solicitation, lent their name or prestige to such activities, or joined in any joint venture or lending arrangement for buying, holding, or profiting from stock during a proxy contest. Moreover, the rules should specifically prohibit personal attacks unless factual data supporting the accusations had been filed with the commission. And the commission proposed adopting as its own rule the various stock exchanges' rules governing how a broker should handle the proxies on shares held in his name for his customers.

Armstrong's long and occasionally tedious statement finally ended. Lehman was complimentary in his brusque, backhanded way: "Speaking very frankly, I have not felt until today that the commission realized its responsibility and its opportunity in conducting these proxy contests," he said.

Even as Lehman spoke, the commission was being confronted with a new test of its will to enforce its admittedly inadequate proxy rules. Two men, Mitchell May Jr., a prominent New York insurance broker whose clients included several major motion-picture companies, and a friend, Alfred W. Parry Jr., had filed a proposed proxy statement with the commission on May 18. They claimed to be the leaders of the Independent Stockholders Committee, which they said had been formed to challenge the management of Libby, McNeil and Libby, the familiar Chicago-based fruit canning company. The commission's staff lawyers were not satisfied that the materials completely described the "associates" involved in the challenge and details about their stock purchases. On June 6, the SEC staffers had conferred with May and his lawyers, and learned that two other men would soon be added to the list and the materials would be revised.[75]

Thus, when Armstrong testified, it seemed that the Libby problem had been solved. But a week later, May's group filed a new proxy statement with the SEC, one that still did not include the information that the agency had demanded. Over the next two weeks, the negotiations between the would-be proxy fighters and the commission's lawyers grew increasingly testy. By now, the proxy fight had become public, and Libby management had gone on the attack. Charles S. Bridges, the president of Libby, met with reporters on June 28 at the Chicago Club. He showed them a letter he had received from Walter M. Weismann, a well-known company-stalker from New York who had contributed to May's war chest, and a letter he had sent in reply. Weismann had offered to include Bridges and two other senior executives on his proposed nine-man slate of directors; Bridges had rejected the offer as "a threat" and an "inferred bribe." He warned Weismann that management would resist any efforts of "your small coterie to seize and exploit this company."[76]

By Monday, July 11, the insurgent stockholders had drawn their line in the sand: on that day, SEC lawyers received a letter from May's attorney, saying that the committee was unable or unwilling to furnish all the additional information the commission had demanded concerning the finances and the backers of the insurgent group. Nevertheless, it intended to mail its disputed proxy materials, a letter entitled "It's Time for Change," to Libby stockholders before the day was over.

The commission instantly telegraphed May's lawyers, warning them that the proposed letter was inaccurate and misleading and should not be mailed. Two commission staffers followed up with a telephone call to the lawyers, reading them the wire and urging again that the letter not be released until it had been corrected. If the committee persisted, one of the aides warned, the commission might have to go to court.[77] There was further haggling, but on July 14, with the Libby stockholders meeting less than a month away, the offending brochure was mailed—despite the SEC's objections.

On July 21, the commission began a formal investigation, and on August 3, its lawyers went into federal court in Manhattan to seek an injunction against the rebel stockholders.

The same day, Senator Lehman received letters from two of his Republican colleagues, Senator John W. Bricker of Ohio and Senator Wallace F. Bennett of Utah, urging that his proxy-fight subcommittee investigate the Libby battle. Legislation was clearly needed to compel full disclosure of stock ownership in proxy contests "to prevent the deliberate raiding of companies by organized financial manipulators," the letter said.[78]

Meanwhile, the insurgents and Libby management had been bombarding one another with various lawsuits. Charles Bridges had sued the stockholder committee for libel, complaining that the proxy letter had falsely charged that his management was incompetent and that the company had deceived shareholders about the company's finances. His libel complaint echoed one of the SEC's most serious concerns: that the man who was really behind the proxy fight was Bernard Frankel, who had been convicted in 1939 of violating federal securities laws, for which he had been sentenced to two years on probation.

Frankel's role, the commission charged in court, went far beyond the one described in the defective proxy materials. And on Monday, August 15, Federal Circuit Judge J. Edward Lumbard agreed. "The affidavits and exhibits make it clear that Bernard Frankel has been a leading factor in the formation and activities of the Independent Stockholders Committee," Judge Lumbard said. Frankel had enlisted Alfred Parry in his plans as early as the summer 1952, and the two men had gone together to meet with a Libby officer that year to discuss the company's management. Mitchell May, too, had traveled with Frankel to confer with Libby officials in Chicago. Frankel had even been involved in selecting the New York offices from which the proxy fight was being run, Judge Lumbard pointed out. And yet all the offending proxy material had said about Bernard Frankel, beyond disclosing that his family owned Libby stock, was that the leaders of the proxy fight had discussed "their common objectives" with Frankel. That, said Judge Lumbard, was "certainly a misleading understatement" of the role Frankel has played. There was good reason to suspect that this understatement was designed "to minimize the effect of the possible disclosure of his previous 1939 conviction for violations of the Securities Act," the judge continued.

The judge did not buy all of the SEC's other objections to the dissidents' proxy materials. But he did rule that, besides the critical omission involving Frankel, the letter to shareholders had falsely suggested that Libby management had engaged in deceptive or improper financial activities. He ordered the company to delay its annual meeting, scheduled to be held two days later in Portland, Maine, to give the insurgents an opportunity to undertake a new proxy solicitation in compliance with SEC rules. But he invalidated the proxies that the group had already obtained—a devastating setback.

Within a few days, Mitchell May announced his resignation from the stockholders committee. "I have become the center of a smear by management, at odds with government bureaus, both plaintiff and defendant in libel suits," he said. It was enough—he had to get back to his insurance business. His allies promised to fight on, but three of their nominees for directors also resigned.[79]

When the stockholders meeting was finally held on September 7, in a Portland law firm's library, about 30 shareholders reelected the management slate unanimously. The dissidents, with no chance of winning, had "boycotted" the meeting, their lawyer said.[80] A month later, Charles Bridges announced new plans for Libby. It was undertaking a major expansion of its frozen fruit production and enlarging its juice packaging plant in Florida.[81] No one, of course, suggested that the bitter proxy fight was in any way responsible for this more aggressive management strategy.

The SEC had won a controversial victory in the Libby case. But its successes in the proxy wars had been otherwise sparse. It was struggling, in general, to cope with the sweeping social and economic changes occurring in the postwar economy—as were its fellow regulators at the Federal Trade Commission and the Justice Department's antitrust division. Mergers were sweeping the nation, and the hotly contested proxy fights were just one small symptom of the consolidation that was occurring in almost every industry.

Few policymakers felt they understood the forces that were driving this nationwide merger movement, and some thoughtful lawmakers were deeply troubled by the changes being wrought. It wasn't that the nation was gradually being transformed from an economy of small businesses to an economy of bigger businesses; it was rapidly becoming an economy of what Lehman called "giant businesses," those able to utterly dominate their field. This transformation was going on all across the country at what seemed to be an astonishing pace. The Chamber of Commerce of Rochester, New York, found that between 1950 and 1957 "a dozen major independently owned local firms lost their identity in mergers with larger corporations located elsewhere."[82] These mergers had reduced workplace morale, cut corporate contributions to local charities, and cost local banks, insurance agencies, and law firms substantial amounts of business as such services were transferred to the new owners' hometowns.[83] Some academic research suggested that cities whose economy consisted of a few large companies had a less healthy civic life and a greater imbalance of incomes than those where small businesses remained the dominant factor in the local economy.[84]

In May 1955 the Federal Trade Commission released a report examining the trends in corporate mergers and acquisitions between 1948 and 1954. While the merger movement had not yet approached the levels of the frenzied days of the late 1920s, it concluded, "since 1949 the pace of important mergers and acquisitions has been rising."[85] And typically, the nearly 1,800 deals consummated during that period resulted in already big companies getting bigger. Nearly two-thirds of the deals studied by the FTC were made by companies whose assets totaled $10 million or more, and nearly half of those had involved purchasers with assets of $50 million or more. By the yardstick of the day, these were giant companies.

Literally hundreds of companies had made at least one acquisition between 1948 and 1954, but only eight companies made more than ten acquisitions apiece during that period. At No. 5 on that roster was Tom Evans's flagship, H. K. Porter Company of Pittsburgh. Although it had only $50.6 million in assets itself—a small fraction of the assets commanded by the four higher-ranking companies on the list—Porter had made thirteen acquisitions between 1948 and 1954, almost as many as the giant Olin Mathieson Chemical Corporation and the rapidly expanding Borden Company. As a company-shopper, Tom Evans's Porter Company was far ahead of better-known companies like Textron, the General Shoe Corporation, the Continental Can Company, the General Tire and Rubber Company, and the old Mellon mainstay, Koppers Company. Lou Wolfson's primary corporate vehicle, Merritt-Chapman and Scott, had undertaken fewer than half the number of acquisitions that Evans had achieved, the FTC study showed. And Silberstein's Penn-Texas wasn't even on the list yet.[86]

The accelerating pace of acquisitions began to raise worries about the monopolistic consequences for consumers. By 1955, young Senator Estes Kefauver was already thinking seriously about the way increasingly concentrated industries were changing the communities in which Americans lived. What he saw was a world in which economic power rested "in a few hands," one in which monopoly was no longer a potential threat but a real danger. It was a danger that the Justice Department had previously acknowledged: "By 1950, about half of the hundred largest firms had an antitrust suit pending against them," one scholar noted. "The Federal Trade Commissioners also became more active in studying and prosecuting violations of the antitrust laws."[87] That was the year Congress had enacted legislation making it more difficult for corporations to acquire their competitors or their suppliers, raising some barriers to so-called "horizontal" and "vertical" mergers.[88] But those laws proved to be no obstacle at all for diversifying entrepreneurs like Tom Evans, Lou Wolfson, and Leopold Silberstein. Consequently, by 1955, the "upswing in business mergers" had produced "demands both for new legislation and more active enforcement of existing statutes."[89] In December, a House subcommittee headed by Congressman Emanuel Celler, a Democrat from Brooklyn, released a study showing that corporate and bank mergers were at a twenty-five-year high—news that prompted front-page coverage in major newspapers across the country. While congressional Republicans insisted that this was no cause for alarm, the Democrats strongly disagreed. "This is one of the most ominous clouds on the economic horizon, since it is hastening the reduction of competition in many areas and contributing in large measure to the growing concentration of economic power," their party spokesmen warned. More than 3,000 companies in all sectors of the economy had "disappeared in the swelling merger tide," the Democrats observed. They blamed the wave of mergers not on "a normally developing industry" but on "the competitive avarice of certain giant corporate enterprises."[90]

Republican complacency in the face of the merger movement was undermined when President Eisenhower, in his economic address to Congress in January 1956, urged that "all firms of significant size that are engaging in interstate commerce and plan to merge should be required to give advance notice of the proposed merger to the antitrust agencies, and to supply the information needed to assess its probable impact on competition."[91] Unsurprisingly, when Congress began to wrestle with the question of how to control, or at least review, corporate mergers, one of the men it called as a witness was Thomas Mellon Evans, the busy company collector from Pittsburgh.

CHAPTER NINE

THERE'LL BE SOME CHANGES MADE

Tom Evans had moved in from the edges of the proxy battlefields in 1954. His contested acquisitions had not involved large exchange-listed companies with publicly traded stock and he had waged his fights well to the west of the Wall Street–Washington axis, but he was nevertheless getting noticed. In January 1954, *Newsweek* magazine profiled the decidedly portly forty-three-year-old Evans—allegedly less driven than in the past, an entrepreneur who insisted, "I never work at night now, and rarely on Saturdays. What's the use of owning your own company if you have to work all the time?"[1]

He seemed to be playing the role of the wealthy businessman-squire. He and his second wife, Josephine, had settled into a 150-acre farm in Lingonier, near the Mellon family enclave at Rolling Rock. His three sons and her three daughters spent time at that peaceful spot, although Tom's temper and his sons' lingering resentment over the divorce kept the emotional climate in an unsettled state. In addition, Evans traveled abroad at least once a year and kept an apartment in New York's Waldorf Towers so he and Josephine could enjoy the theater and shop for his growing art collection, which he had begun during his years with Betty Evans. He was not yet widely known as a prominent collector, but a few alert art dealers were beginning to cultivate his business. Occasionally, he went fishing at Fisher's Island, off the Connecticut coast.

After the creative turbulence of his first marriage, he seemed to crave an atmosphere of dignified wealth and artistic pursuits in his life with Josephine. Soon, the only hint of the havoc that had gone before was the hostile gulf that divided him from his eldest son. Tom Evans Jr., an athletic young man whose face mirrored his father's youthful beauty, had been kicked out of prep school during the divorce. At age fourteen, he had refused to submit to his father's plans for him—a military academy. Instead, he had moved into a boarding house in the Buffalo area and enrolled on his own in a public high school.[2]

Porter was humming along nicely. As *Newsweek* noted, in early January 1954 Evans had awarded the manager of one of his subsidiary companies a $100,000 bonus check, "several times the manager's annual salary." It reflected how well his decentralized style of operation was serving him. As he accumulated companies, he still relied on the aging Clarence Dobson and his executive staff to prune away dead wood and solve any structural or organizational problems. Then, he gave each manager his head, with the promise of substantial rewards if the executive met Evans's ambitious financial goals. Those divisions that did not meet their goals were sold.

As *Business Week* noted, in another flattering profile published in 1955, the thirteen Porter divisions "boss themselves."[3] In many cases, the magazine noted, Evans and Dobson had recruited the "new management" to run their acquisitions from among the same managers who had worked there when they bought it. When Evans bought the Delta-Star Electric Company in Chicago, Dobson looked around and talked to people and found that two of the veteran executives there were generally credited with the company's success. So Evans made them the top managers of the new Delta-Star division. "We are firm believers in decentralization," Evans told *Business Week*, revealing the lessons he had learned from W. L. Mellon and Colonel Frank Drake at Gulf so many years ago.

But practices were developing at several Porter divisions that reflected a less admirable aspect of the early entrepreneurial lessons Evans had learned from the great Mellon combine in Pittsburgh. For all the lip-service given to free enterprise, the great fortune-builders of the late nineteenth and early twentieth centuries had a profound aversion to unbridled competition.[4] Some of the greatest among them, like John D. Rockefeller of Standard Oil, saw themselves as cultivating order amid chaos through the encouragement of cooperative alliances.[5] Historians saw their efforts, instead, as the pursuit of monopolistic power through the creation of cartels. But the wealth of these early entrepreneurs spoke loudly to future generations of ambitious men about the benefits of such "cooperative" efforts—perhaps more loudly than the stern voice of the federal antitrust laws.

By the early 1950s, the prices that manufacturers charged for most of the nuts-and-bolts commodities of industrial America rarely deviated from those of their competitors by so much as a penny. These so-called "administered prices" would sometimes rise in lockstep, across the industry, even when factories were working at far less than full capacity. Some executives were astonished that congressional investigators later found these circumstances suspicious. "My concept is that a price that matches another price is a competitive price," one leading steel industry executive told a Senate panel at hearings later in the decade. "If you don't choose to accept that concept, then of course, you don't accept it. In the steel industry we know it to be so."[6] As one senator observed, the real question was how those identical prices were determined. "Under genuinely competitive conditions, producers must meet the lower prices of their rivals or lose the business. Under other circumstances, price identity is achieved through lockstep action of sellers, all following the price leader."[7]

In any case, at least by the early 1950s and perhaps earlier, someone in the rubber division at Porter had enlisted in an industry-wide conspiracy to fix the price of flat rubber belting, a ubiquitous material used for factory conveyor belts and for the strong circular belts that helped drive industrial machinery. The price-fixing scheme was remarkably ambitious, involving the Rubber Manufacturers Association and at least ten major rubber companies, from the giant Goodyear and B. F. Goodrich in Akron to the less familiar Quaker Rubber division of H. K. Porter in Pittsburgh. By the time the conspiracy reached its full strength, secret deals to eliminate price competition were affecting more than 95 percent of the market for this critical industrial material, forcing up the cost of building and maintaining factories and distribution centers—and enriching the conspirators' shareholders at the customers' expense.

By 1955, another Porter executive, a man who worked at the Delta-Star electrical equipment subsidiary, was equally active in another campaign to eliminate profit-bruising competition in Porter's markets. The Porter division executive conspired regularly with others in the electrical equipment industry to fix prices and rig bids for two arcane but important gizmos—insulators and distribution lightning arresters—which were sold to various federal, state, and local government agencies and public utilities.[8] The conspiracy also affected power-switching equipment, which was used to interrupt electrical current so that parts of a big power transmission network could be safely worked on, and isolated-phase buses, which were the devices built into generating stations to carry electricity from the generator to the main transformer.

As part of this price-fixing scheme, dozens of executives had "contrived, by an elaborate system involving secret telephone calls, hotel-room meetings, and codes, to defeat the free market by illegally fixing prices on billions of dollars' worth of equipment," one journalist reported.[9] To conceal their activities, the executives had "resorted to such devices as referring to their companies by code numbers in their correspondence, making telephone calls from public booths or from their homes rather than from their offices, and doctoring the expense accounts covering their get-togethers to conceal the fact that they had all been in a certain city on a certain day."[10]

To simplify the price-rigging efforts in the nationwide market for power-switching equipment, the Porter executive and his co-conspirators simply divided the United States into four quadrants, with one manufacturer acting as the "chairman" of each quadrant, responsible for allocating the bidding among the other supposedly competing manufacturers in that region. To rig the government's extensive competitive bidding for isolated phase buses, the executives simply sliced up the government business among themselves. Porter's relatively minor role in the conspiracy is suggested by its share of the pie: it was allocated only 10 percent of the business, while the larger I-T-E Circuit Breaker Company got 42 percent and General Electric and Westinghouse took the remaining 48 percent. Westinghouse and G.E. then divided their share of the bidding, with General Electric getting the bulk of the bids.[11]

The conspiring companies orchestrated the bidding so that the pre-designated winner would quote the low price and his three ostensible competitors would submit higher bids. The position of "low bidder" was rotated among the companies according to a strict system, so that each would win every fourth bid—a simple arrangement that the executives called the "phase-of-the-moon" system.[12] This system was calculated "to establish a price spread that would be sufficiently narrow so as to eliminate price competition among the defendants but sufficiently wide to give an appearance of competition," one account of the conspiracy explained.[13]

Since Tom Evans routinely left such operational details as government bids and sales to his subordinates, he possibly did not know when he agreed to appear before a key antitrust panel in Congress just how much these anticompetitive conspiracies were contributing to Porter's success. That success was certainly dazzling in any case. The company bore no resemblance to the broken-down locomotive manufacturer that Tom Evans had taken over in 1939. Then, the company had less than $1 million in revenues and its net worth was less than $95,000; by June 1955, its sales had been running at an annual pace of well more than $70 million and its net worth was $25 million.

And Tom Evans owned just over 77 percent of the company's publicly traded stock. The ambitious young orphan from Pittsburgh had transformed himself into a multimillionaire, confounding what *Time* magazine called the "modern business folklore" that a man could no longer make a million dollars in the new high-tax, salary-collecting world. Evans was one of ten "new millionaires" the magazine profiled in December 1954, and its sister publication, *Fortune*, gave a glowing report on his success at H. K. Porter in September 1955. "There are no electronics, chemicals, atoms, or pools of oil in Porter," *Fortune* noted, with a wry nod to the "high technology" and energy stocks that were the latest Wall Street fad. Instead, Porter's "interesting growth product" was cool, hard cash.

Some of that cash, no doubt, was the harvest of the price-fixing schemes in which Porter executives had enlisted. But some of it had been generated legitimately by the numerous companies that Evans had acquired over the years. Most recently, just as he was summoned to Washington, he had acquired Henry Disston and Sons, Inc., a 115-year-old toolmaker based in Philadelphia, beating out a rival purchaser in the process.[14] Stocky but confident and beautifully dressed, Tom Evans embodied a one-man merger movement when he appeared to testify before Congressman Emanuel Celler's antitrust subcommittee in January 1956.

Celler's committee was considering a trio of amendments to the Clayton Act, all aimed at preventing the continued growth of giant corporations by somehow restraining the mergers which nourished their growth. Ironically, Tom Evans was heartily in favor of keeping a lid on the growth of already-gigantic corporations—like those powerful companies that dominated the illegal antitrust drama in which Evans's own executives were merely the supporting cast. "It seems to me that this problem of size of corporations is one of the most important Congress should be working on," he testified. "Something must be done about it quite promptly if this country is to be kept away from socialism."[15] But Evans quickly tried to distinguish the strategy he had used to build H. K. Porter from the mergers that were the target of congressional concern. "It was easier and less expensive to buy a small company and develop its potential," he said of his renovation effort at Porter. "We have not in the past, nor have we now, the resources or the desire to buy out an entire industry. Therefore, I do not feel that our mergers in any way restricted trade or injured the competitive system and, of course, [they] have not been in violation of the antitrust laws," he continued, giving the congressman an assurance some of his own conspiring executives must have blushed to hear. "In fact, we believe that in a number of cases we have operated the companies acquired in a more efficient way than they were operated prior to our acquisition and, therefore, strengthened the competitive system."

Celler interrupted. "That is the excuse that is always given when one company merges with another and the merging company is the larger company," he said. The big acquirer always says, "We can make the smaller company more effective, and we can help the employees of that smaller company," Celler continued, adding, "I do not say that by way of criticism of your company, but that general observation is one we are always confronted with."[16]

Evans responded, "I agree with you that there is a limit somewhere that has to be put on it." But the various bills being considered by Celler's committee "do not correct the basic problem or get to the real source of the trouble which confronts our country in the area of mergers and bigness in manufacturing enterprises," Evans insisted. The problem, he said, was that ten of the nation's very largest companies represented nearly 30 percent of the sales and assets of the entire *Fortune* 500. "It will take an extremely powerful, strong union to deal with such gigantic corporations," he pointed out.[17]

But Celler, a veteran politician who understood how difficult it was to rein in human ambition, went right to the point of the problem: "When are *you* going to stop?" he asked Evans pointedly. "Your sales are now, what, $135 million? When do you figure *you* should stop?"

Tom Evans seemed to be taken aback. He had spent his adult life reaching out for more; had he ever considered the point at which he would have enough? He stumbled for an answer. "Whenever the ceiling is put on by Congress," he said, though no such ceiling was under consideration. "My theory is that, when it applies to us, we'll stop." He seemed to be confirming Congressman Celler's own suspicions: merger-driven businessmen would stop only when someone else made them stop. But who should that someone be? A regulator or lawmaker—or a stronger or hungrier competitor who defeats the businessmen in corporate combat?

Evans detoured around the issue of his own ambitions and went on. "It seems to me that the concentration of economic power in such a comparatively few individuals, such as the heads of these giant corporations and the union leaders dealing with them, is not a good thing for the long-term outlook of our country. Most of these giant corporations were formed fifty or sixty years ago by mergers and combinations before antitrust laws were passed. Today many of such mergers or combinations would be illegal."

The committee's chief counsel Herbert Maletz gently corrected the young industrialist, who had always preferred finance to history. "Actually these mergers occurred after the Sherman Antitrust Act was passed," he said. "The Sherman Antitrust Act was passed in 1890. And most of the big mergers to which you refer, I believe, were at the turn of the century."

"I am in error on that," Evans conceded. "But I guess it was not effective then."

"Well, there was an enforcement drive at the turn of the century," Maletz answered. Indeed, there had been an antitrust drive against the Mellon-controlled Aluminum Corporation of America as recently as the recent war, when Alcoa could not meet military needs and was forced to share its technology with competitors who could.

"I'm talking about the nineties, when the [U.S.] Steel, General Electric, and big companies were formed," Evans stumbled on, finding his place in his prepared statement. New antitrust laws or government restrictions "would only complicate business operations and fill up the already crowded courts, without really getting at the root of the problem," he continued.

He and Maletz sparred for a few moments about what the bills under consideration would actually do, with Evans arguing that the requirement that the Justice Department and the Federal Trade Commission be given ninety-day advance notice of pending mergers would be completely unworkable. And then in his characteristically creative fashion, he offered what he obviously considered to be a much better idea—one that seems to catch the committee by surprise.

"It seems to me that taxation is the logical way for both government and business to curb the excesses in the field of mergers, as well as to curb the concentration of economic power and size of corporations," he said. "An individual's income is taxed on a graduated rate according to his earnings. This is done, presumably, to control his economic power. Why shouldn't a corporation have this very same principle applied to it? And for the same reasons."[18] He was proposing, simply, that a graduated income tax for corporations would be "the logical way" to set "a practical limit on the size a company may become."

Congressman Celler was jolted. "How would that stop huge growth? They might so orient their returns as to show very little income."

"How?" Tom Evans asked bluntly. The politician was now on the businessman's turf, and Evans's embarrassing history lesson of a few moments ago was forgotten.

"Well," Celler continued, "they could expand salaries; they could put on more help."

Tom Evans snorted. "Well," he said, "the stockholders would stop that."

In his plan, the corporate graduated income tax would not be imposed until a company's income had exceeded some congressionally established limit, perhaps $100 million or "whatever Congress decides is a reasonable size." Once a corporation was in the highest tax bracket, Evans calculated, "there would not be a reason for that particular company to buy other concerns, or grow from within." Instead, the company might elect to spin off some of its subsidiaries to its stockholders, so that they could operate as independent businesses. "The spin-off provision would give men in large corporations the opportunity to head up their own companies, rather than merely divisions," he explained.

Celler was confused. Wouldn't that create taxable capital gains for the stockholders?

"No," Evans answered. "They would not have any tax, they would just have shares in eight or ten corporations." Congress had passed the tax-free spin-off provisions years ago, he continued, but no major companies had made use of them yet. Evans thought a graduated corporate income tax would encourage giant companies to take another look at the advantages of such spin-offs.

"The effects of such a graduated income tax on corporations would have the same beneficial effects that the dissolution of the Standard Oil Company had in 1911," he concluded. "Today, with the existing laws, we can accomplish the same desired end without setting up any more government bureaus and expenses and without putting any added permanent burdens and expenses on company management." That, he argued, was a far better approach than a rule requiring advance notice and a ninety-day waiting period, given "the difficulty of making extended commitments for financing."

Congress did not embrace his innovative idea, although he returned before a sparsely attended hearing of the Senate antimonopoly committee in early summer to argue for it again. The acquisitions that had allowed H. K. Porter to grow "would have been impossible under the terms of your proposed bill," he told the Senate panel. And yet, he continued, those acquisitions "had helped to keep people in jobs, have given substantial benefits to local and state communities and to the national economy as well as to our stockholders. Anything which hinders this type of merger would, in my opinion, eventually hinder the sound growth of our economy, weaken competition, and penalize smaller companies."

The committee's chairman, Senator Joseph O'Mahoney of Wyoming, was the only committee member present when Evans testified, but he was complimentary. "Your paper has been most interesting and stimulating," he said as he thanked Evans for appearing.

But if Congress ignored Evans's proposal, it also failed to act on the bills he opposed. Requiring advance notice of proposed mergers remained a topic that would receive continued attention but no effective action for years to come.[19] The lack of action reflected the fact that major corporate leaders were opposed to the entire idea of government regulating mergers in any way, beyond the antitrust laws. But the fact that the issue nevertheless remained on the congressional agenda reflected the national unease over the continuing wave of mergers and takeovers. Moreover, a growing body of evidence suggested that the competitive vision of American capitalism, in which firms vied with one another to provide better quality goods to the public at the lowest possible price, was seriously out of focus.

Even before Justice Department investigators exposed the bid-rigging and price-fixing conspiracies in which H. K. Porter was involved, the suspicious pattern of "administered prices" increasingly bothered lawmakers like Senator Estes Kefauver, a thoughtful and intelligent Democrat from Tennessee who would later hold lengthy hearings on allegedly anticompetitive practices by steel manufacturers, pharmaceutical companies, and even large national bakeries. Giant corporations seem to have somehow tilted the competitive playing field against their smaller competitors, the local companies that were accustomed to dominating their own small piece of business turf. Economists might dispute whether consumers were harmed or helped by the emergence of stronger, more efficient national and even international corporations. But there was clearly a sense among liberal Democrats such as Kefauver that Big Business was somehow reshaping American life, and not for the better.

In the summer of 1956, Senator Lehman and the rest of the nation's Democratic leaders gathered in Chicago to build the policy platform on which its standard bearers—presidential candidate Adlai Stevenson and Kefauver, his running mate—would run against President Eisenhower and Vice President Richard Nixon that fall. These merger-driven changes in the nation's economic life were clearly a strong concern among these party policymakers. The Democratic platform of 1956 was harshly critical of the Republican administration for having "allowed giant corporate entities to dominate our economy."[20] The Democrats promised to restore "truly competitive conditions in American industry" by taking "affirmative action . . . to curb corporate mergers contributing to growth of economic concentration." Monopolies and other "concentrations of economic and financial powers" would be prevented. The Democrats charged that "effective administration of the federal securities laws has been undermined by Republican appointees with conflicting interests." And they promised, among other things, to provide safeguards to protect investors from "proxy contest abuses."

The Republican-dominated Securities and Exchange Commission had been struggling since the previous summer to strengthen its own regulatory tools for dealing with such "abuses." In August 1955, the commission had announced proposed changes in its proxy rules. Echoing the arguments the agency was making in the bitter Libby proxy fight, Armstrong said the new rules were designed "to assure that full, fair and adequate disclosure of the basic facts about the proxy solicitation is made available to the stock-holders."[21]

The new rules, which applied only to exchange-listed companies, tried to expose any "behind-the-scenes figures in proxy fights" by more clearly defining those whom the agency considered "participants" in a proxy solicitation. This list would now include not only the nominees for election to the board of directors, but also anyone who helped pick those nominees, oversaw the requests for votes, and organized or financed the fight.

The agency also tried to get a tighter grip on the campaign literature generated by proxy fights. Its new rules would apply to any public statements made in the course of a fight, including those made before the formal proxy statement had been sent to shareholders. The rules also barred specific kinds of "misleading" information from both the campaign literature and from the corporate annual report that was mailed out with management's proxy solicitation material. This banned information included predictions of future financial performance, unsupported accusations that attacked the character or reputation of one's adversaries, and any material likely to confuse or mislead investors. The rules boiled down to the *Dragnet* approach—"Just the facts, ma'am," as Police Sergeant Joe Friday advised witnesses in the immensely popular television series. The new rules also required more of those facts—greater detail about participants' stock holdings and their stake in whatever issue was being voted on by stockholders.

But the SEC proposal, which seems modest in hindsight, ignited a firestorm of unexpected protest. In September 1955, the newspaper industry journal *Editor and Publisher* carried an article charging that the new rules, with their restrictions on what proxy contestants could say in interviews and advertisements, carried a threat of press censorship. The outcry prompted Cranston Williams, the general manager of the American Newspaper Publishers Association, to write the commission in early October seeking an explanation of how the new rules would affect the work of the press in covering proxy fights. Specifically, Williams wondered, would the commission consider an editor who published stories quoting proxy-fight contestants or editorials about the battle, or who permitted such material to be reprinted by the contestants, to be "a participant" in that fight under the agency's new rules?

"Absolutely not," was the answer from Byron D. Woodside, a senior SEC executive.

The SEC already had the right to review proxy-fight advertisements before they were published, but it was the obligation of the proxy contestants, not the newspaper, to seek that review. Nor did a newspaper have any responsibility if such ads were published without SEC review, the editors' group was told.

Chairman Armstrong of the SEC repeatedly insisted that there was "nothing in the proposed revisions of the proxy rules" that would interfere with "traditional American freedom of the press." Adversaries in proxy fights were still free to talk to the press, and the press was still free to ask any questions it wished, he explained. But both the new rules and the old ones required that the adversaries avoid making any comments to the press that were "false or misleading."

Nevertheless, when the commission held public hearings on the proposals in November 1955, witness after witness condemned the proposals as going much too far. One of the harshest critics, surprisingly, was Leslie Gould, the financial editor of the *New York Journal-American*. Although Gould had been a bitter critic of the proxy raiders and had condemned the SEC repeatedly for failing to take action against them, he nevertheless denounced the new rules as "censorship of the press."[22] Adversaries in a fight would most likely refuse to talk to the press for fear of running afoul of the commission's rules, he contended.

Corporations, too, complained about having their annual reports to stockholders subjected to the rules that governed proxy materials, and several witnesses complained about the burden the new rules would impose on management. One Boston lawyer commented, "The question is whether in an effort to prevent an evil you haven't created a greater evil."[23]

The commission bowed to its critics and revised its proposal, limiting its applicability to fights for control, not to other questions being submitted for shareholder votes. Corporate annual reports fell within the new rules only if they contained attacks on an opposition group, in which case only that section would be subject to SEC review. The revisions clearly specified that speeches, press releases, and radio and television scripts did not have to be submitted to the commission in advance, although they did have to avoid any false and misleading statements. And the revisions narrowed the definition of "participants" to apply only to people primarily "engaged in and responsible for the conduct of the proxy solicitation and not to persons only incidentally involved."[24]

This time, the backlash was minimal and the new, less stringent rules went into effect at the end of January 1956. With them, Wall Street's regulators had a slightly clearer rule book to use as they played referee in the coming corporate battles.

Press coverage and analysis of the various proxy fights reflected the same ambivalence that shaped the public reaction to the SEC's new rules. The proxy raiders were fascinating public figures, and their battle cry of

"Protect the Shareholders!" could not be dismissed by any card-carrying capitalist. As Ben Heineman of Chicago told *Fortune* in the summer of 1955: "What a raid amounts to, when the lines of power are drawn, is an effort by a group of investors to take executive directorship into their own hands. You can hardly call the largest investors 'outsiders'; since when is a stockholder an outsider?"[25] A few weeks earlier, *Time* magazine had gotten the same message from stockbroker J. Patrick Lannan, an elegant art collector in Chicago who had acquired an influential stake in at least eighteen companies without a single proxy fight. Lannan did not yet fit the "raider" profile, but he still defended the breed. "This is a rebellion of the owners," he said.[26]

But corporate managers were the bread-and-butter sources of the business press, and management's view of the proxy raiders was uniformly negative. Corporate public relations executive James P. Selvage of Selvage and Lee, a public relations firm that had worked for management teams in several proxy fights waged by Leopold Silberstein, spoke for many when he condemned the new raider. "He is part and parcel of an era we thought had passed—an era the SEC was created to end—the age of financial piracy," he said. "All hands of the business community should be turned against him. He is an economic menace."[27]

So the journalistic gyroscope wobbled between practical tips for defending against or, better yet, avoiding proxy raiders and thoughtful attempts to understand where these men had come from, and why they had suddenly become such an important factor in American business life.

Although share ownership in America remained largely concentrated among the wealthiest 2 percent of the population, several analysts blamed the raider phenomenon on changing stock ownership patterns, the same revolution that Louis Wolfson had discussed before Lehman's committee.[28] Owning stock had long been a rich man's game; now, these theorists argued, corporate shares were far more widely dispersed among "average Americans," offering enterprising men a better chance of winning support.[29] The tax laws certainly played a role in the rise of the proxy raider, since income was taxed far more heavily than the capital gains that even unsuccessful proxy fights could generate. And it was clear to any fair observer that many shareholders could legitimately complain of being ignored by complacent, highly compensated executives who owned very little stock themselves.

But the most common view was that the raiders were primarily a product of the rising stock market—a stock market so remarkably and consistently strong that in early 1955, Democratic Senator J. William Fulbright of Arkansas actually initiated a full-scale investigation into why the market had climbed so high. The answer? "Unhealthy speculation," said the Democrats; "The confidence of the people in the administration of President Eisenhower," answered the Republicans.[30] This historic bull market had continued without interruption since June 1949 and showed no signs of faltering. Raiders who used the stock of their own companies to acquire others found that the rising stock market was putting fresh money in their war chests every day, contributing to the liquidity that has always been essential to the takeover game.[31] By targeting companies whose stocks had lagged behind, the raiders could tap into the understandable concern among the target company's shareholders that they were missing a once-in-a-lifetime opportunity.

The mergers and proxy fights of the early fifties may also have reflected symptoms of a radical shift in the methods used to win the game of corporate survival, as scholar Neil Fligstein persuasively argues.[32] From the late nineteenth century until well into the twentieth century, according to Fligstein, the dominant business strategy was "direct control of competitors" through predatory competition or the creation of cartels or monopolies. "There were only two ways to protect one's firm: attack others before they attacked you or if this failed unite with your competitors to stop competition."[33] When public protest and government intervention gradually made that approach less effective, ambitious corporate leaders tried to compete by controlling every stage of the production process, from raw materials to final distribution. Their goal was to absorb their suppliers and control their retailers—and impose their own prices—to the maximum extent that government authorities would allow. The advertising revolution of the 1920s and the subsequent increase in enforcement of the antitrust laws in the 1930s gave birth to a third competitive strategy: expanding sales by constantly tinkering with the product, diversifying the line of goods offered, advertising heavily, and expanding into new markets.[34] Bigger tail fins and extra helpings of chrome were evidence that Detroit had adopted this competitive strategy with a vengeance.

As corporations became increasingly diversified during the late 1940s and early 1950s, cutting-edge managers began to adopt yet another strategy for winning the game of business competition. The "finance" approach, which Tom Evans mastered when he was running errands for W. L. Mellon at Gulf in the early 1930s, relied on the use of financial tools to measure the short-run performance of each subsidiary, with a strong emphasis on "increasing shareholder equity and keeping the stock price high."[35] That was exactly what successful acquisition-minded managers of the 1950s were doing—and what successful proxy fighters were promising to do.

But at a practical level, both the earlier strategy of expanding sales and the finance-centered approach were feeding the merger mania of the day. The sales-expansion approach usually meant buying or merging with companies that were already selling in coveted markets or making diverse products. Assembling a financial portfolio of businesses and managing it for maximum return inevitably meant buying promising companies and selling those that did not perform.[36] So whether big corporate managers in the 1950s were pursuing sales growth, as they had since the 1920s, or were adopting the financial tools used by the successful newcomers almost did not matter. Both were out there in the marketplace, buying and selling companies. To them, it looked like smart business. To the rest of America, it looked like a revolution.

So Congress and the SEC fretted and tinkered, business writers struggled to understand, and mergers and proxy fights continued unabated. One of the bitterest and most bruising battles for control began to take shape shortly after Tom Evans's testimony in June 1956—and its cast of characters would include men he would soon enlist as his own allies.

Sometime in July, Leopold Silberstein was chatting with Peter Cats, his stockbroker son-in-law and a frequent ally in his raids. Cats mentioned "the possibilities" offered by a Chicago outfit called Fairbanks, Morse and Company.[37]

Fairbanks Morse was a family-dominated manufacturer of diesel engines, electric motors, and other industrial equipment. The company's founder, Charles H. Morse, had died in 1921, leaving two sons, Charles, forty-nine, and Robert, forty-one. Both were active in the management of the family business but they were not particularly compatible. They fought in 1939, and Charles resigned from the board of directors to wage a proxy fight against his brother the following spring; he succeeded in electing two of his candidates to the board. Two years later, the quarrel was mended and Charles returned to the board. In 1950, brother Robert Morse selected his son, Robert Junior, to succeed him as president, but he continued to serve as chairman of the board on which his brother Charles sat as a director.

By late fall 1955, the corporate secretary alerted the board that he had noticed a sharp increase in the amount of company stock registered in the name of a few brokerage houses that Leopold Silberstein had used in the past.[38] Did top executives fear that a raid was being planned? Possibly. In any case, Robert Morse Jr. decided that it would be wise to move ahead with the long-contemplated acquisition of Canadian Locomotive Limited, an Ontario company that had been a Fairbanks Morse subcontractor for many years. The deal made good business sense, Morse argued. The Canadian company had a foothold in foreign markets where Fairbanks Morse was handicapped by quotas or other trade restrictions. But the acquisition would also require Fairbanks Morse to issue between 130,000 and 150,000 new shares. And that would reduce the percentage of the company's outstanding stock that might have been accumulated by any potential raiders.[39] It would also, unfortunately, reduce the percentage of the company's stock owned by Charles Morse, who was firmly opposed to the acquisition. Despite his uncle's objections, president Robert Morse Jr. was determined to go ahead with the deal, and his father, the board chairman, supported him. Old wounds were reopened, and the elderly Morse brothers once again were at odds.

In late January 1956, Charles Morse resigned from the company board and wrote Leopold Silberstein to offer his support for "any efforts you may wish to make in order to improve the management of the corporation with which I have been identified for so many years." He continued, "From your reputation I am certain that when you assume a voice in the management of the company it will redound to the benefit of us all, and I shall try to be of assistance to you in every way."[40] He sold Silberstein 15,000 shares of his stock in the company, and gave him an option on another 27,220 shares.[41]

Silberstein had already acquired a substantial block of Fairbanks stock. He said later that someone had called him in the fall of 1955 to offer a block of about 100,000 shares being sold through a Swiss bank. Penn-Texas purchased the stock for $4.3 million, all but $2 million of which was borrowed. Journalist Leslie Gould was convinced that the purchase of the shares, at a premium price, had enriched the secret sellers to the tune of $1 million, and he was outraged that Silberstein did not disclose who had reaped that profit. "I am not interested in what other men make," Silberstein said. He denied that any of the "secret" profits had gone to him, however.

With Charles Morse's backing, Silberstein decided a proxy fight might be possible, despite the fact that the Morse family controlled nearly a third of the company stock. He went into court in Chicago and sought an injunction to block Fairbanks Morse's acquisition of Canadian Locomotive. This strategy had been successful in the Niles-Bement-Pond fight, when that company tried to slip out of his grasp by acquiring a stake in Bell Aircraft. But his legal challenge did not work this time. Federal District Judge Joseph Sam Parry virtually threw Silberstein out of court.

"I have grave doubts whether Penn-Texas Corporation even had title to the 100,000 shares it claims. It looks like a conspiracy of some type to raid the stock market," the judge said. "This kind of slugging operation has no place in a court of equity and I don't want to see one in my court again."[42]

The judge's ruling left Robert Morse Jr. free to consummate the Canadian Locomotive deal. But that would not be enough to keep Silberstein out of his boardroom; the proxy fighter already had enough stock, it seemed, to elect at least one director to the Fairbanks Morse board, using his rights under cumulative voting rules.

Actually, he did much better than that—but his partial victory was a bitter one. For weeks the proxy fighter had been the target of a vilification campaign in Congress and in the press, with attacks that underscored his German heritage, questioned whether he had fraudulently obtained his citizenship, and hinted at clandestine dealings with shadowy Swiss bankers. Some of the most vicious coverage, in Silberstein's view, had been orchestrated by Leslie Gould. But at least part of the blame should have gone to that ingenious corporate defender Art Landa and his allies, who had enlisted on the side of management. Papers from Landa's files indicate that a member of his law firm used the offices of Senator Olin Johnson of South Carolina, one of Silberstein's harshest critics, as his "Capitol Hill headquarters during the Penn-Texas fight."[43]

When stockholders gathered at the Sheraton-Blackstone Hotel in Chicago on March 28, Silberstein had enough votes to elect four directors to Fairbanks Morse's eleven-member board. It was a foothold, but it wasn't enough to influence company policy, Silberstein knew. After the meeting, while the ballots were still being tallied, Silberstein held a press conference in his hotel suite. He told the thirty or so reporters who attended that he thought Robert Morse Jr. had conducted the meeting fairly. He added that he intended to "work in close harmony with the other members of the board for the betterment of Fairbanks, Morse."

But then Silberstein raised an issue that was obviously troubling him: the ugly charges that had been thrown at him during the proxy battle. At some moments during the press conference, observers wrote, he "appeared on the verge of tears" as he discussed the attacks on his character. He had been the victim of a "smear campaign," he complained. Private detectives had dug into every corner of his life, even traveling to Europe to seek incriminating information. "These agents of Hitler are out to get me," he said, echoing the nightmares of his remarkable past.[44] Leslie Gould looked up from his notebook and challenged Silberstein to identify who had conducted the harassment.

"Yes, I will say who did it—Selvage and Lee," Silberstein said, referring to the prominent public relations firm which had worked for the Fairbanks management. He quickly added, "And you know that, Mr. Gould. You worked with them."

"That's a damned lie," Gould responded hotly.

By some accounts, the two men advanced toward one another as if to trade blows, but Silberstein's senior executives restrained him. He quickly regained his temper and told Gould, "I don't want to offend you. I apologize." They shook hands, but no one believed that the animosity had been buried.[45]

The raider's final comments revealed just how painful the fight had been for him. While promising that Penn-Texas would continue to grow—"after all," he said, "America is the land of growth and possibilities"—Silberstein made a startling vow. "I will never enter another proxy fight," he said.

He was mistaken. As it turned out, he was to be involved in two final proxy fights—first as the raider and, finally, as the prey.

In early 1957, he once again tried unsuccessfully to take control of Fairbanks Morse, a fight which consumed too much of his time and money and tied up too much of Penn-Texas's assets and corporate credit. Then, while that ill-starred battle was under way, he himself became the target of a proxy fight at Penn-Texas.

The dissident shareholders called themselves the Penn-Texas Protective Committee. The committee was organized and led by Art Landa, with public relations assistance from Silberstein's former ally, David Karr—and with the "personal, financial and moral support" of Robert Morse Jr., the president of Fairbanks Morse.[46]

Silberstein, showing flashes of wit, suggested that the committee members "should more properly call themselves the Robert Morse Protective Committee." While Landa's group claimed to be serving the interests of the Penn-Texas stockholders, he continued, it actually was "a stooge for the Fairbanks Morse management."[47]

Still, Silberstein was vulnerable. Penn-Texas had borrowed more than $15 million to acquire Fairbanks Morse stock—Silberstein had acquired just under 49 percent of the outstanding shares—while the price of his own stock had fallen from nearly $20 a share to barely $11 a share in the course of the fight. His sprawling conglomerate encompassed more than fifteen companies and made everything from railroad cranes to pistols—the Colt's Manufacturing Company of Hartford, weakened as Congressman Dodd had feared by its earlier encounter with corporate raiders, had fallen into his net in 1955. But he had borrowed heavily against the company's assets and had raised cash by selling company properties and leasing them back. And he had converted all that generated and borrowed cash into shares of Fairbanks Morse.

He was engaged in an enormous gamble. If he won Fairbanks Morse, he would more than double the size of his empire with a single stroke. But if he failed to take control, his Penn-Texas would find itself the owner of a huge block of rapidly depreciating stock that would be extremely difficult to sell without forcing the price even lower. Moreover, the Fairbanks

Morse management was vowing that it would go to court to prevent him from voting the shares he had obtained largely on credit through his dealings with Swiss bankers in late 1955. That would cut substantially into his voting strength.

Meanwhile, Art Landa and David Karr were irrepressible. They campaigned hard, and Landa invested some of his own funds to buy up Penn-Texas stock. He repeated every ugly allegation hurled at Silberstein in the previous year's fight, and added new ones. Boardroom gossip found its way into print, as Karr cultivated the business press.

As May 1957 approached, Silberstein was pinned down by Fairbanks Morse's court fight to block him from voting all of his shares. With his own Penn-Texas shareholders meeting less than two weeks away, he finally gave up and began negotiating a settlement with his adversaries at Fairbanks Morse. On May 10, an agreement was reached that required Silberstein to refrain from future attempts to take control of the company, and to sell 300,000 shares back to Fairbanks Morse at a price considerably below their market value. In exchange, both he and Robert Morse's team each got five seats on the Fairbanks Morse board, with the eleventh and tie-breaking chair going to a neutral director acceptable to both sides.[48] It was a costly truce, and it came too late.

Four days before the deal was announced, Silberstein had presided over his own stockholders meeting. The gathering was held in the tiny central Pennsylvania town of Cresson, where his original acquisition, Pennsylvania Coal and Coke, had its headquarters. Landa's forces questioned him sharply from the floor about the declining cash dividends and the plummeting stock price. And when the ballots were finally counted, nearly a month later, Landa claimed two of the eight chairs in Silberstein's boardroom.

Landa's nominees, retired real estate executive Robert C. Finkelstein and former hotel and auto executive Wallace S. Whittaker, harried Silberstein through the summer. They got surprising support from a Silberstein ally on the board, the charismatic Major General C. T. "Buck" Lanham, who had been General Eisenhower's immensely popular press attaché in Europe during the war. Silberstein had recruited Lanham to run Colt's Manufacturing, and must have been stunned at his defection. By early September 1957, the three boardroom rebels had tried twice to engineer board approval to remove Silberstein from the presidency of Penn-Texas. Both attempts failed, but the second occurred while Silberstein was hospitalized with severe ulcer problems.[49]

Moreover, the value of his investment in Fairbanks Morse was dropping, along with the price of his own Penn-Texas stock, which had fallen below

$3 share. He had sold off six subsidiaries to raise cash.[50] Wall Street was buzzing with rumors that he was buying more Fairbanks Morse stock in an effort to support its price. But such purchases would have violated his settlement agreement with Fairbanks Morse. He was cornered, and his boardroom adversaries—now including Landa, who had become a director in February—were vowing another proxy battle in advance of the shareholders meeting set for May 1958.

When Penn-Texas stockholders gathered on May 5 at the Biltmore Hotel in New York City, they entered a war zone. "It may have been the most tumultuous corporate annual meeting ever held," one reporter observed. "There was constant shouting by stockholders from the floor."[51] When Silberstein was introduced, he was loudly booed. Not even the opposition was orderly; in the course of the meeting, no fewer than ten antimanagement candidates were nominated for the nine-member corporate board.

Weeks went by, as the competing forces battled in court over the legality of various proxies. Finally, on June 24, 1958, Leopold Silberstein was forced to resign as president of Penn-Texas Corporation, handing the helm over to Art Landa. Silberstein remained a director of the company, and was granted a five-year consulting agreement; but he was not allowed to so much as speak publicly to a reporter about Penn-Texas.[52]

Landa ran the company in the same dashing fashion he had run Colonial Airlines. By the fall of 1958, he had acquired through diplomacy what Silberstein had failed to seize on the battlefield: control of Fairbanks Morse. As part of the settlement of the tangled knot of litigation between the two companies, Landa arranged for Penn-Texas to purchase nearly 300,000 shares of Fairbanks Morse from Robert Morse Sr., whose son had battled Silberstein to a standstill. The block of stock cost Penn-Texas $9.6 million and gave it a 77 percent stake in the Chicago company, which became Penn-Texas's largest subsidiary and eventually one of its biggest headaches.[53]

As for Leopold Silberstein, he withdrew from the public stage of business battles to privately manage his own investments, spending much of his time in Europe. A decade after the summer of 1955, he was virtually forgotten on Wall Street. His death in Europe in the early 1980s went entirely unmarked by newspapers that had avidly followed his financial career two decades earlier.

That mid-decade summer of 1955 also marked the high-water mark for the handsome and complicated Louis Wolfson. He had gotten the last laugh on all the irate congressmen who were wagging their fingers at him during the Capital Transit strike in the summer of 1955. After pulling out

$33 a share in dividends, he sold the company for $13.5 million in 1956, after Congress made good on its threat and refused to renew his franchise.[54]

But he had taken some sort of turn in the road, that hot, bitter summer, and the prestige and public fascination that surrounded him during the Montgomery Ward fight would slowly corrode under the constant drip of poor judgment, shabby associates, and government investigations.

His first big public stumble involved his investment in the American Motors Corporation, whose best-known product was the Nash Rambler, a pioneering compact car. Wolfson started buying AMC shares in 1956; by late 1957, he was the company's largest shareholder and Wall Street was waiting for him to make a bid for control. But then Wolfson met George Romney, the dynamic president who was leading the rescue efforts at the struggling car company—and was charmed. Romney offered him two seats on his board of directors, but Wolfson eventually decided to sell out to spend more time on other business interests.[55]

By mid-April 1958, however, he had not only sold his stock, he had sold the company short by 137,000 shares. (To sell short, an investor borrows shares from a cooperative broker and sells them, hoping the price will fall before he has to buy new shares to return to the lending broker. If he guesses right, his profit is the difference between the price he gets for the borrowed shares and the price he later pays for shares to replace them.) Shorting AMC was a financial disaster, one that Wolfson blamed on a trusted associate. AMC's stock continued to climb under George Romney's management.[56] And each advance of the stock increased the price Wolfson had to pay to cover his short position—a position that he later insisted he had not even known about. The only thing that would salvage the Wolfson group's situation would be a sharp drop in the price of AMC stock.

In mid-June 1958, a Wolfson associate planted an "exclusive" with the New York Times, claiming falsely that Wolfson was selling out of his AMC position because he felt the stock was fully valued. Given Wolfson's prominence as a supporter of AMC, that was news that might spook other investors. The SEC was immediately suspicious—no one as savvy as Wolfson announces he's selling in advance; it would simply drive down the price he would be able to get.[57] The SEC investigated and eventually accused Wolfson of using false and misleading information to drive the stock down to profit on his short sales—market manipulation, under the securities laws. He settled the case without admitting or denying any wrongdoing.[58]

It was the beginning of a dismal downfall. By 1966, Wolfson's Merritt-Chapman and Scott conglomerate was coming unglued and Wolfson had suffered a heart attack.[59] In 1967, in an unrelated case, he was convicted of selling unregistered stock in a small Florida theater-management company he controlled. He insisted later that he had not known of the registration requirements and had relied on bad advice. He was sentenced to one year in prison and fined $100,000—draconian punishment, his many defenders say, for what they consider mere "technical violations" of securities laws. The next year, as his wife was dying of cancer, Wolfson was accused of committing perjury and obstructing an SEC investigation into stock transactions at Merritt-Chapman and Scott. Again, he was convicted on all counts, but that conviction was later reversed on appeal.[60] And while he was serving his jail term in the prior case, shortened to nine months by his good behavior, Supreme Court Justice Abe Fortas was forced to resign after it became public that he had agreed to advise a Wolfson family foundation while he was serving on the nation's highest court—and while Wolfson was under investigation.[61]

Wolfson later achieved considerable fame and success in the world of thoroughbred racing as the owner of the magnificent Affirmed, which won the Triple Crown in 1978. But the way most Americans remember him, if they remember him at all, is as the convicted financier who inadvertently destroyed a Supreme Court justice's career in 1969, not as the charismatic young man who captivated a nation with his daring fight for control of Montgomery Ward in 1955.

In 1955, Ben Heineman, who had taken the Minneapolis and St. Louis Railway away from Lucian Sprague, was recruited by yet another group of dissatisfied railroad investors. Working on behalf of stockholders of the Chicago and North Western Railway, he began preparing for a proxy fight. But by February 1956, the Chicago and North Western was in desperate financial shape. Its president ran up the white flag and agreed to retire. Heineman was named chairman of the board and chief executive—positions which, for him, marked a fork in the road. To devote himself completely to the challenge of saving the desperately ill company, Heineman resigned from the Minneapolis and St. Louis and even disbanded his law partnership.[62] Like Charlie Green before him, he thereafter largely left proxy fights to others, although he made a number of friendly acquisitions and had one more hostile takeover fight ahead of him.

He was a brilliant strategist and his tenure at the Chicago and North Western saw the company—operating under the flag of a new holding company, Northwest Industries Inc.—diversify its business and ultimately sell off its railroad to its employees. In 1985, in the midst of the new generation of struggles for corporate control, Northwest Industries was acquired by Farley Industries for $1.4 billion.

For Patrick McGinnis, too, the year 1955 divided his free-wheeling career into "before" and "after." In March of that year, he consolidated his grip on the New Haven railroad. Having won a bare majority the previous year, he saw his minority opponents resign and he replaced them with his own team. But by February 1956, he had been forced out, as the long-troubled New Haven began to slip down a slope that would eventually lead to bankruptcy.

Commuters on his railroad had simply rebelled. Passenger service declined in the uniquely visible New York suburban market—partly the result of penny-pinching cutbacks in maintenance, compounded by a hurricane, a bad winter, damaging floods, and a trucking strike which forced the New Haven to shift resources from passenger service to freight shipments. Regulators in four states began investigating his management. "I have been a target of abuse and a focal point of attack to a point that defies reasonable explanation," he said in resigning.[63] "There were tears in his eyes when he said his farewell to his close associates on the New Haven a fortnight ago," *Life* reported in February 1956.

Seven hours after his tearful resignation, however, he was named president of the Boston and Maine Railroad, which served northeastern New England. Its stock was trading for nearly $27 a share when McGinnis took over. By April 1963, it had fallen to $5 a share, and he was once again out of a job.[64] Four months later, he was named in a criminal antitrust indictment for allegedly sharing in kickbacks of more than $70,000 from a company that was allowed to purchase some B&M equipment without competitive bidding. He was convicted and was sentenced to eighteen months in prison. He died of a heart attack in March 1973, at the age of 68.[65]

And his close friend Robert R. Young? For him too, that summer of 1955 would later seem the noontime of a golden day. In the year that Young crossed swords with Senator Lehman, the New York Central recorded profits of more than $8 a share and its board of directors voted to pay out $2 a share in dividends, the highest the company had paid since Young took control. To be sure, the pugnacious executive was beset by shareholder suits and other irritations. But he expressed great confidence in the company's ability to fulfill the promises he had made to shareholders during the great proxy fight of 1954.

In reality, his and most other American railroads were desperately ill, hampered by inept government regulation and incapable of competing with trucks navigating along the infant network of federally financed interstate highways that Congress had authorized early in the decade. The New York Central's profits gradually sank, as did its share price. As these troubles mounted, Young's closest associates "became vaguely aware of a languid remoteness" on the part of the usually feisty executive. "On the surface he seemed tired and disinterested but clearly in touch with reality," his biographer Joseph Borkin wrote.[66]

On January 20, 1958, Borkin continued, Young gathered the directors of the New York Central for a special meeting at his ocean-front home in Palm Beach to review the company's finances. The nation's economy had weakened sharply during the previous months and the manufacturers of many big-ticket items like refrigerators and cars were tightening their belts. Unemployment rates were climbing sharply.[67] Against that backdrop, the railroad's earnings in 1957 had been dismal—just $8.4 million, compared to $39.1 million in 1956. "Reluctantly the directors voted not to pay a dividend for the next quarter, the first time this had happened since Young came to power," his biographer reported.

The decision "was shattering to Young's pride. He would find it a problem to face his close friends and associates who at his urging had invested heavily" in New York Central stock.[68] Young was so silent and remote during the troubled board meeting that some of the directors feared he might be facing financial troubles and offered to help. Young reassured them that "his finances were in good order."[69]

On Saturday morning, January 25, Young rose early and had breakfast. After eating, he went to the billiard room at one end of the magnificent twenty-five-room mansion; he was a champion at the game, and always spent the hours after breakfast polishing his skills. When he did not appear at noon to leave for a scheduled appointment, staff members went searching for him.[70] He had not been playing billiards; sometime around 10 A.M., he had taken a double-barrel 20-gauge shotgun from a gun cabinet and carried it to a chair. Then "carefully he set the gun between his knees, placed the barrels against his head, and pulled both triggers."[71]

The enigmatic sixty-year-old proxy warrior left no note for Anita O'Keeffe Young, his wife of more than four decades, but he left her an estate that amounted to a considerable fortune. His finances, at least, had been in good order.

CHAPTER TEN

THE ONE-MAN SHOW

As the fifties moved into their second half, money was rolling into the booming Pittsburgh-based empire controlled by Tom Evans. His diversification efforts, implemented over the past decade, helped Porter navigate the downturn that had such fatal consequences for Robert Young, and Evans was able to invest his abundant energy in developing new parts of his kingdom.

He had bought a beautiful cattle farm in the hunt country of northern Virginia. Buckland Farms had been owned by the family that successfully operated Gallagher's steak house in New York City. Its centerpiece was a beautiful eighteenth-century brick-and-stone manor house whose gracious porches overlooked the rolling fields. Evans insisted it was merely an investment, but Josephine loved entertaining friends in this country-squire setting.

Evans had become a minor philanthropist, setting up a family foundation to make occasional grants to schools and hospitals. Oddly, though, he gave only modest amounts to his friend Larry Mellon's heroic medical mission in Haiti, although he did visit the facility at least once.[1] His art collecting grew more ambitious, too, as he began to search out the first specimens of what would become a sizable collection of American Impressionists and Dutch landscape masterpieces—museum-quality canvases, hanging on his own walls. In the next few years, he would purchase Gilbert Stuart's portrait of Theophilus Jones and a haunting study of a bearded old man attributed to the school of Rembrandt.

And he had staked a claim to a small piece of Wall Street, as well, by setting up Evans and Company, his own securities brokerage firm in the Col-gate-Palmolive Building, one of the starkly modern glass towers rising along Park Avenue just north of Grand Central Station. There, he had his own trading room, where he could sit behind a desk cluttered with corpo-rate financial statements and watch stock prices glide by on the televised ticker tape that filled the screen of a small TV on his desk. Here, too, Evans explained his new venture as a shrewd investment—by owning his own firm, he could pursue his strategies while collecting the trading com-missions he would otherwise pay to someone else. But no one who saw him at work in his trading room, poring through the financial statements that had fascinated him since his high school days, could fail to see the visceral pleasure he felt there. In a very real sense, it was his game room: here, he could scout out the next likely target; here, he could plan his attack.

Other brokerage houses sent Evans their research reports, of course. Every ambitious broker on the Street dreamed of prying at least a small piece of Tom Evans's stock trading business away from his namesake firm. He was always buying and selling, and it was an education just to watch him work. Most of the research reports were a lot of nonsense, in Tom Evans's view, just a lot of puffery about some new chemical process or a nifty new uranium-processing startup that hoped to profit from the night-mare of the nuclear arms race. But in August 1957, one report caught his appreciative eye. It was a list of "undervalued" stocks, shares trading for less than the company's net worth. Those were exactly the situations that Tom "Net Quick" Evans looked for, and he was surprised to see on this list a name that had a prestigious blue-chip pedigree: the Crane Company of Chicago.[2]

The wealthy women in Tom and Josephine's social circle knew the Crane Company for its elegant bathroom fixtures, advertised in the glossy home-decorating magazines of the day. But the men who occasionally lunched with Evans at the Duquesne Club in Pittsburgh thought of Crane as the mother lode of the valve industry. Anywhere in manufacturing America, or indeed in the industrial world, where the flow of some sub-stance had to be controlled, diverted, or rationed—that task was probably performed by a valve manufactured by Crane. It made 40,000 kinds of valves and valve fittings for everything from household toilets to oil refineries.[3]

Historians, too, knew of the Crane Company. It had been founded by Richard Teller Crane, an autocratic self-made man who nevertheless "was possessed of a keen social conscience and sense of civic duty."[4] He began his career in 1855 with a small brass foundry in a corner of a factory site owned by one of his uncles; he died in 1912, a millionaire many times over.

In his will, he left $1 million to be added to his workers' pensions through a charitable trust, and another $1 million to be left in trust for their widows and orphans. "He was one of the first to introduce the eight-hour day in his factories, initiating a 5-cent lunch program with hot coffee and soup for his men, providing free medical care for his workers and their families, and developing liberal profit-sharing and pension plans long before other employers even considered such ideas," one historian noted in obvious admiration.[5] His identically named son joined the family business in 1896 and became president in 1914, leading the company into its glory years of robust growth. He, too, demonstrated "a deep concern for the welfare of the personnel."[6] He donated more than $12 million to aid Crane employees and, like his father, left bequests for his employees in his will.[7]

By 1957, there was still a distinctive corporate culture at Crane, although the Crane family's stake had now been parceled among an increasingly numerous third generation. To be called "a Crane man" was a cherished compliment among the ambitious executives at company headquarters in Chicago. "That expression, as used by Crane people themselves, tends to mean a good fellow, a man who fits, a team player. He almost certainly wears a small service bar in the buttonhole of his lapel with stars or a diamond showing his years—or his decades—of service."[8]

Crane reflected, though perhaps to an exceptional degree, the mild-mannered management that was emerging as the business-school ideal in the postwar years. Increasingly, chief executives portrayed themselves as industrial diplomats. There was a continuing emphasis on "welfare capitalism," that concept from the 1920s that emphasized concern for employee welfare and community relations. Against a backdrop of sometimes hysterical but nevertheless genuine concern about Communist infiltration of the American labor movement, business leaders advocated a strategy of giving workers such a stake in the capitalist system that they would be impervious to socialist seduction. Executive-suite tyrants and lone-wolf entrepreneurs now seemed a throwback to the "robber baron" days. The iconoclastic sociologist, C. Wright Mills, was amused by this altered perception. "When the great moguls were first discovered in print . . . [they] clawed and bit their way to infamy," he observed in his 1956 study, *The Power Elite*. "Just now, with the conservative postwar trend, . . . the colorful image of the great mogul is becoming the image of a constructive economic hero from whose great achievement all have benefited and from whose character the corporate executive borrows his right to rule."[9] It was a trend he had first cited in a scathing 1951 study, *White Collar*: "The image of the big businessman as master-builder and profit-maker, as already noted of the old captain of industry, no longer holds . . . the old entrepreneurs succeeded by founding a new concern and expanding it. . . . the new entrepreneur makes a zig-zag pattern upward . . . by servicing the powers that be, in the hope of getting his cut. He serves them by 'fixing things,' between one big business and another, and between business as a whole and the public."[10] Such managers, he concluded, "are the economic elite of the new society."[11]

They were personified by General Motors' elderly "organizing genius," Alfred P. Sloan, Jr.[12]—majestic, orderly, well-educated, impeccably polite, self-controlled, and respectful of the corporate hierarchy, an efficient corporate Eisenhower, in fact. In the New Deal years, Sloan had incurred liberal scorn by opposing a strike by auto workers while personally avoiding several million dollars in income taxes through the legal but unusual use of a personal holding company.[13] The Sloan school of management was one in which "loyalty among employees was more important than individual brilliance [and] team players were valued more highly than mavericks. . . . The men who ran the corporation . . . were square and proud of it, instinctively suspicious of all that was different and foreign."[14] This new breed of corporate manager, which had begun to arrive on the scene well before the war, was viewed with alarm by some old-timers on Wall Street. A Morgan partner warned as early as 1935 that America was becoming "a nation of hired men," where bookkeepers with slide rules were replacing the distinctive and idiosyncratic corporate founders of the past century.[15] In 1956, writer William Whyte published *The Organization Man,* a sociological study which argued "that the dynamic entrepreneur of old had given up his place to an anonymous, conformist successor . . . [who] got ahead by going along, unlike his plucky forebear."[16] A year earlier, author Sloan Wilson had traveled a different road to the same conclusion with his immensely popular novel *The Man in the Gray Flannel Suit,* whose title quickly became the cultural shorthand for the blandly ambitious junior members of this new "don't-rock-the-boat" managerial class.[17]

At the Crane Company, the team approach of its professional managers meant that company decisions tended to be committee decisions; it took time, but it was an approach that the corporate culture seemed to require. If stockholders grew impatient with the pace of change, that probably was of no great concern to non-stock-holding executives. Chief executives had not yet discovered the charm of stock options and, across the country, stockholders were generally taking a distant back seat to the corporation's other constituents. The postwar corporations displayed "a heightened anxiety to please the companies' customers, employees, even the general public—almost everybody except the stockholders *qua* stockholders," observed business writer John Brooks.[18] After all, a corporation's stockholders were now so numerous and "so different from the old investor stereotype of the hard-bitten coupon-clipper as to be no longer distinguishable from its customers."[19] Corporate reports began to emphasize the company's charitable donations and acts of good citizenship and gloss over the amount to be paid in dividends, Brooks continued.

The young flannel-suited men at Crane rose slowly in the bureaucratic organization, deferring to their elders until they were considered sufficiently seasoned to take on more responsibility. The men at the top were "able though aging." There were lots of talented young men, but there was "an enormous gap in between."[20] Tom Evans no doubt remembered the air-crash tragedy that had hit the Chicago company late in the spring of 1956. As a constant passenger in his own Douglas B-23 prop-jet, he would have noticed the news reports even if they had not originated from Louisville, Kentucky, where his sister and brother-in-law made their home. On May 15, 1956, a small plane owned by Crane had crashed into a field three miles from the Louisville airport, killing the two-man crew and six top Crane sales executives, who had been en route to a sales meeting. The disaster had finally prodded the Crane board to develop a stronger succession plan, and in November 1956, it recruited Neele E. Stearns from Inland Steel Company as president.[21] Stearns, at forty-nine, was a generation younger than the senior directors on his board. Originally a management consultant and educator, he had landed at Inland after working on a consulting project to revise the way that company handled its incoming orders. In 1950, he had taken over a troubled subsidiary and diplomatically straightened it out—a task which commended him to Mark W. Lowell, a vice president of the Continental Illinois National Bank and Trust Company in Chicago and a member of the Crane board of directors.[22] When he arrived at Crane in January 1957, Stearns was the quintessential professional manager.

A quick glance at Crane's performance since 1951 showed Tom Evans that Neele Stearns had his work cut out for him. Crane's sales were strong and its net worth had been rising, but profit margins were less than 3 percent; in 1954, margins had dipped to a dismal 1.9 percent. To Tom Evans, that probably meant that Crane was investing more capital to earn less income.[23] Someone was making stupid decisions about how to use the company's assets, he decided. If the economic experts were right and business activity got worse before it got better, Crane would certainly suffer. All its businesses were strapped to the back of the economic cycle.

And its stock already looked like a bargain—why, it was trading at half the per-share value of the company's total net assets, and darn close to the per-share value of Crane's liquid assets alone. For "Net Quick" Evans, it looked too intriguing to pass up. If the recession got worse, the stock would just get cheaper. When he returned from his Labor Day break in September 1957, Evans told his trading desk to start accumulating shares of Crane stock.[24] As they cautiously bought, recession worries drove the stock lower.

The economy weakened as winter approached. As companies cut back, the nation experienced the most severe drop in employment since the war, with about 5 million people out of work.[25] The stock market was paying little attention to the slump, but that was little comfort in union halls and blue-collar neighborhoods like those that surrounded Crane's 160-acre Chicago Works, where most of Crane's valves and fittings were produced. In Pittsburgh, too, economic stagnation was producing serious hardship, as several major companies pulled up stakes and moved west. Coal mining was in decline, erasing additional jobs. Local jobless rates rose faster and farther than the national figures.[26]

But Evans refused to succumb to the national anxiety. Pittsburgh, with the long-overdue help of its corporate leaders, was struggling to rescue itself from the industrial blight that the corporate fathers of past generations had ignored for so long. New office buildings, rising two dozen stories into the still-sooty air, were being built in the grimy triangle of land where the Allegheny River and the Monongahela River converged.[27] In late 1957, Evans had decided to build, too. For years, H. K. Porter had leased space on the third floor of the Alcoa Building, a tall classic skyscraper near the Mellon Bank. By the spring of 1958, finishing touches were being put on Porter's new 16-story headquarters a few blocks away.[28] It was the first in the area with automatic elevators, in which passengers could select their own floor from a panel of buttons. The building cost $7.5 million, but Porter had more than $13 million in cash, and assets of $72 million. It had thirty-five plants in twelve states and one small operation in Australia—indeed, it almost seemed that the one place Porter did not have a substantial manufacturing presence was Pittsburgh itself. But Pittsburgh was filled with Porter's customers, Evans explained. "We serve industry and where's there a better industrial town?"[29]

Still, the ties that held him to Pittsburgh were frayed. He still owned the house on Oliver Road in Sewickley, the scene of so much unhappiness in the months before his divorce, and he had kept the farm at Lingonier, near the Mellon retreat at Rolling Rock. But the three boys were all away at school. And Evans and Company gave Tom Evans a convenient and undeniably enjoyable base of operations in New York City, a short flight from Pittsburgh in his private plane. Understandably, he and Josephine began to spend an increasing amount of time at their gracious home in Old Greenwich, Connecticut.

When Tom Evans checked in with his trading desk in New York around Christmas 1957, he found he had become the proud owner of 90,000 shares of Crane stock.[30] That made him a substantial shareholder—indeed, the entire Crane board of directors owned only 4,000 shares of the 2.37 million shares of stock that Crane had issued.[31] Tom Evans thought he had a better claim to a chair in the Crane boardroom than any of the current occupants.

He knew one of the directors and asked him to arrange an introduction to Mark Lowell, the banker who was then presiding as chairman of the Crane board. When he got the call, Lowell consulted with president Neele Stearns. Both men had heard of Evans, of course. They had seen the abundant publicity in recent years detailing Evans's spectacular renovation of H. K. Porter. People who knew Evans socially remarked on his wit and charm; those who had encountered him across a negotiating table found him to be blunt, impatient, and demanding.

He was a paradox—at least to anyone who had not followed his awkward social migration from his widowed mother's deathbed to the frugal Rodman home, with those unpredictable excursions into the enchanted Mellon kingdom. Evans's brush with the Mellon family had given him just enough polish to lightly obscure a gritty determination to build his own kingdom, one where he would no longer face the well-meaning humiliations and financial insecurities that had shadowed his childhood.

So far as Lowell and Stearns could see, Tom Evans at forty-nine was still a young man on the make. And Chicago had seen a lot of such men lately. It had seen the handsome but controversial Lou Wolfson come to town, with his loyal disciples and fascinated camp-followers, to do battle for control of Montgomery Ward, one of the pillars of the local economy. It had watched the home-grown Robert Morse Jr. do battle with the exotic Leopold Silberstein for nearly two years; another proxy fight was certainly in store for the spring of 1958, even though Silberstein was under attack by the wily Art Landa. Was Evans just another raider? Another newcomer bent on causing trouble?

The only way to tell was to take the measure of the man in person. So Mark Lowell invited Tom Evans to come to Chicago for lunch. They met in early January 1958. The affair was kept very quiet—a private corporate dining room with only Neele Stearns joining them at the table. Evans was affable, full of energy, almost charming. But his reputation for speaking his mind proved accurate: he bluntly compared the size of his stockholdings to those of the other directors and asked to be added to be the slate of directors who would be elected at the stockholder meeting in April.[32]

His request could not have surprised his hosts. Indeed, they told him they thought it was quite reasonable. "But a pall fell over the luncheon when Evans remarked unblushingly that he hoped the directors would let him set policy," according to one account.[33] Set policy? From one chair around the boardroom table? To both Lowell and Stearns, the remark indicated that Evans expected to be named chairman and chief executive— the positions they currently occupied. The atmosphere grew chilly as the hot coffee was served. Lowell and Stearns would have to discuss his request with the other directors, of course. Of course, Evans agreed, apparently unaware of the shock he had delivered. He was sure something could be worked out.[34]

He returned to New York, resumed his busy trading and travel schedule, and waited for the expected telephone call from Chicago. A week passed, then several more. Finally, at the end of January, Mark Lowell called. It just wasn't going to work out, Lowell explained. There was another interested investor whom the Crane directors had decided to invite onto the board instead of Evans.

Evans was furious. Who was this interloper?

It was Gurdon W. Wattles.

Wattles? Evans was no doubt surprised. He knew of the Wall Street financier, of course. From a wealthy midwestern family, Wattles had made quite a name for himself in New York. He controlled two closed-end mutual funds, Century Investors and Webster's Investors, which gave him access to the best of the brokerage houses' services.

But Evans would certainly have heard if Wattles had been building up a position in Crane—Wall Street was just a small town when it came to gossip like that. So he asked Lowell whether Wattles owned as much stock as Evans did.

"He's going to buy some," said Lowell.[35]

Wattles accumulated nearly 323,000 shares in early 1958, buying largely in the name of Electric Autolite, a company which he controlled through his stake in Mergenthaler Linotype, the dominant newspaper technology company of the day.[36] His purchases triggered Wall Street speculation that he was contemplating a merger between Crane and Electric Autolite.

As Evans fumed in New York and Wattles continued to buy in Toledo, the Crane board met in Chicago in April 1958 and invited Wattles to join their ranks. At the same time, however, they also decided to cut the board down to seven seats, from eleven. In the trading room of Evans and Company, simmering anger became cold, determined fury. Clearly, the move was designed to eliminate any room on the board for Tom Evans.[37]

Crane was not alone in taking defensive steps that season. In 1958, Wall Street saw a record number of proxy fights, and management was being challenged at a host of major companies besides the flamboyant Penn-Texas fight.[38] When Crane stockholders met in April, Tom Evans joined them, causing no trouble but pointedly refusing to vote his shares for the slate of directors that Crane management proposed.[39] Old-timers in Chicago could remember that Merrill Griswold of the huge Massachusetts Investors Trust mutual fund had used the same technique to demonstrate his lack of confidence in Sewell Avery's stewardship at Montgomery Ward a decade earlier.

But if Neele Stearns missed the historic parallels and assumed from this performance that Tom Evans would suffer his rebuff in silence, he soon found he was wrong. In anger, Evans could use his tongue like a blackjack, and Crane's performance gave him ample opportunity to raise some bruises that summer. As part of his reorganization efforts, Stearns decided to sell the Toledo Desk and Fixture Company, a manufacturer of steel kitchen cabinets that Stearns's predecessor, John L. Holloway, had considered a good mate for Crane's plumbing fixtures business. Holloway had valued the business at $2.5 million, but it had not been profitable and Stearns sold it for just $600,000. "Evans immediately blasted the sale as an example of poor management," *Fortune* noted.[40]

His public attacks eliminated any chance that the Crane directors would change their minds and find a chair for him. So as the summer of 1958 progressed, with its hula-hoop mania and the worrisome hostility that greeted Vice President Richard Nixon on his Latin American tour, Tom Evans mapped out the strategy by which he would take control of the Crane Company. He would need an ally, he decided that summer. He would need Art Landa.

It's not surprising that his mind turned to the shrewd Washington power-broker. Most of the business world was following the triangular Morse-Silberstein-Landa battle in Chicago with intense interest. Moreover, Landa had just been portrayed by *Fortune* as an aggressive corporate warrior, although one who had brushed perhaps a little too close to the scandal-smudged world of the Teamsters union through his aggressive defense of the Fruehauf interests.[41] The years had clearly changed Landa's reputation in the corporate world. When the decade opened, he was consistently portrayed as a crafty but loyal defender of managements under siege; now, he was occasionally found advising one of the barbarians at the gates. The ruthlessness of his fight against Silberstein—and his lieutenant David Karr's turncoat role in that fight—had made an impression, even on Silberstein's enemies.

And once Landa had taken charge of Penn-Texas, the company's troubles had required steps which had added the hated "liquidator" label to

Landa's name, as well. Silberstein had so tangled the affairs of the small Liberty Aircraft Company in Farmingdale, Long Island, that Landa decided to enlist Fred Richmond's assistance in finding someone to take the business off his hands for scrap—a step that would affect hundreds of workers in the community. Richmond, sensing another Follansbee in the making, was carefully insulating himself from the transaction. But the effect was the same for Farmingdale, a strong blue-collar community whose union leaders were trying desperately to keep the company open.

Despite his increasingly controversial reputation, Landa still had his charm and his Washington contacts, forged over nearly three decades of cheerful party-going, skillful bridge-playing, and gracious thank-you notes. And there was someone in the old-money world of Washington society that Evans needed to meet. Her name was Emily Rockwell Crane Chadbourne, and she was the daughter of the first Richard Teller Crane, the founder of the company that Evans coveted. Nearly ninety, the elegant and accomplished Mrs. Chadbourne played no active role in company affairs, of course. She was a patron of the arts, having been awarded the French Legion of Honor for locating and reassembling a lost panorama of Versailles by the American Federalist painter John Vanderlyn.[42] Her fortune, in addition to some charming art, several Georgetown homes, and a historic stone farmhouse in upstate New York, included nearly 121,000 shares of stock in the company her father had built, the largest single block in the scattered Crane clan. With Landa's help, Evans introduced himself to Mrs. Chadbourne and exercised his own considerable wit, charm, and artistic interests to persuade her that he could restore her father's company to greatness. Her great-nephew, Robert B. Crane, worked in the company's merchandising department, Evans knew. He agreed to include the young man among his nominees for the Crane board of directors, and Mrs. Chadbourne agreed to give Evans an irrevocable proxy to vote her shares.[43]

Landa's assistance did not come cheap. To secure his help for an attack on Crane, Evans agreed to help finance Landa's purchase of Crane stock, pledging 10,000 shares of H. K. Porter as collateral for the bank loans that he and Landa jointly obtained on Landa's behalf. Landa's shares, of course, were pledged to Evans's interests and were held in an account in Evans's control at Evans and Company in New York. But the arrangement gave Landa the prospect of a hefty capital gain if the Crane shares responded as expected in the course of the upcoming battle. And there might even be some hefty legal fees he could charge along the way, he calculated.

Gurdon Wattles had not been idle since joining the Crane board in April. Through Electric Autolite, he controlled more than 300,000 shares. If Evans could not win his backing, he at least needed Wattles's neutrality.

And with Landa's cunning and diplomatic skills, that neutrality was obtained—through a ploy that remained hidden in Landa's personal papers for four decades.

Those records show that Landa and Evans had quietly threatened to launch a proxy fight against Wattles at Electric Autolite in November 1958, a move that came very close to corporate blackmail. Sometime in early fall, Evans had apparently purchased shares of Electric Autolite in the open market. On November 11, Evans had written F. J. Kennedy, the vice president and secretary of Electric Autolite in Toledo, Ohio, requesting that the list of the company's stockholders be made available for him to inspect. This request, the widely recognized bugle call of the proxy raider, had been drafted by Art Landa. On November 19, Mr. Kennedy wrote back, inquiring about Evans's purpose in making the request. Again, Landa drafted the response and had his secretary telephone it to Tom Evans, who almost certainly sent it out over his own signature. This letter, dated November 25, made Evans's threat perfectly clear: "The purpose for which the request is made is that it is my desire to obtain the names and addresses of the company's shareholders in order that I might communicate with them in regard to the company's affairs, to protect my interests as a shareholder and to act jointly with other shareholders in protecting our common interest as shareholders."[44]

There is no record in Landa's files of Wattles's response. But as 1959 opened, Evans and Landa felt ready to strike at the Crane board, so they must have gotten at least tacit encouragement from their only meaningful rival. By the second week in January, rumors of a proxy fight at Crane were swirling through Wall Street—no doubt, with a little spin from the energetic David Karr, Landa's public relations man. On January 12, a *New York Times* reporter caught up with Art Landa as he was on his way to the airport for a flight from New York to Denver. Yes, Landa confirmed, he was negotiating with the Crane management in an effort to avoid a proxy fight. He and Tom Evans wanted seats on the Crane board, Landa said. And he was optimistic that some sort of compromise could be achieved. He was sorry he couldn't talk further, but he had a plane to catch.[45]

His comments made headlines. Tom Evans had said simply "no comment."

As Evans later described it, "Landa barked once and everything fell into place."[46] He and Landa were invited to sit in on the January meeting of the Crane directors, at which the board would nominate the slate of directors that would be presented to stockholders in April. Chicago in January is a formidable prospect, but Evans and Landa made the trip. In overcoats and mufflers, with their fine fedoras wedged firmly on their heads against the polar winds, the slim Landa and stocky Evans arrived at Crane's headquarters on South Michigan Avenue and were ushered into the boardroom. Introductions were made, and a few routine matters were handled. Then the question of the upcoming slate of directors was raised. The discussions were tense but polite. When they were over, the seven Crane board members had agreed to ask shareholders to restore the board to its original eleven seats. And they had agreed to nominate Evans, Landa, and the young Robert Crane to three of those four new positions. In addition, the fourth new director, Edwin Locke Jr., was added at the request of Gurdon Wattles, who had clearly placed his 323,000 shares in Tom Evans's corner.

It wasn't official yet, but Evans had won his seat at the boardroom table without a proxy fight. His fight for effective control of the company, however, had just begun.

He began by asking Neele Stearns for permission to tour Crane's operations.[47] How could Stearns refuse? Beginning right after the meeting, Evans put thousands of new miles on his private plane, touring Crane properties scattered from Trenton, New Jersey, to Burbank, California. As he did at his own plants, he punctuated each visit with questions, sometimes ignoring his executive tour guides and seeking answers directly from men on the factory floor. He saw the odd mix of antique and modern machinery that worked side-by-side at the Chicago Works. He was tight-lipped and disapproving as he toured warehouse after warehouse, seeing vast amounts of working capital locked up in unproductive inventory. He counted the cost of Crane's sprawling network of 172 sales outlets across North America, where the company sold not only its own products but the whole range of goods needed by plumbing contractors, from copper pipe to caulking compounds. Then he compared Crane's approach to its core business, valve manufacturing, with that of its competitors, many of whom were concentrating on "profitable high-volume items" while Crane continued its commitment "to supplying customers with practically every kind of valve and fitting they require."[48] A third of the valves and fittings manufactured in the Chicago Works were so specialized that they were not even listed in the company's product catalog.

Evans was chafing from frustration, but he managed to restrain himself through February and March, as shareholders received proxy materials from management outlining the proposed changes in the boardroom. He cultivated Mark Lowell, and built up a friendly rapport with the ambitious banker.[49] And he talked regularly with Neele Stearns about the president's reorganization plans, which had included the closing of a small Chicago division in late winter. Here, diplomacy came harder. Stearns was "a quiet, methodical man," trained in modern business methods and at home with Crane's committee-oriented approach.[50] Evans, a few years younger, was a blunt, mercurial man in a big hurry, a man accustomed to being in charge. In another situation, they might have made a good team, complementing each other's skills and compensating for one another's weaknesses. But by March, Evans was apparently convinced that Stearns would simply slow him down, and the Crane boardroom would be too small to accommodate both of them.

Characteristically, he let Stearns know exactly how he felt. Both men knew that Mark Lowell planned to pass the chairman's gavel to someone else on the Crane board in April so that he could devote more time to his new duties as a director at Continental Illinois, where he worked. And Tom Evans intended to succeed him—and to swiftly put in place his own rejuvenation plan for Crane. He offered Stearns a deal: a ten-year consulting contract at $30,000 a year, in exchange for his resignation from the $100,000-a-year presidency. Stearns, accepting the inevitable, demanded $38,500 a year. The negotiations were finally concluded just before the Crane directors gathered in Chicago for the annual shareholders meeting on April 28, 1959.[51]

The negotiations that had been going on between Tom Evans and the Crane management since January, outlined in the proxy materials and reported in the local press, had been watched with growing unease by Crane's workers. Unease turned to alarm when Stearns decided to close that Crane division in Chicago. David McDonald, the ambitious international president of the United Steelworkers union, knew Evans's reputation in Pittsburgh. He was a tough boss, a hard man who demanded profitability from every component of his business empire. Some called him a liquidator. All agreed that he had barely a grudging tolerance for organized labor.

His reputation was not enhanced, in the eyes of some attentive observers, when a federal grand jury in New York City indicted the Rubber Manufacturers Association and ten corporations, including H. K. Porter, on charges of having conspired to fix the price of flat rubber belting. But the case seems to have attracted little public attention in Chicago, and Porter and the other defendant corporations quietly pleaded "no contest" to the charges later that summer, and paid their fines—$10,000, in Porter's case, compared to $35,000 for both Goodrich and Goodyear.[52]

As the April meeting of Crane shareholders neared, McDonald directed union workers in Chicago to print up handbills seeking employee stockholders who would give their proxy vote to McDonald, so he could attend the shareholder meeting and speak out for employee interests. The flyers were passed out in the neighborhoods around Crane's facilities, but none of the nervous workers stepped forward to help.[53]

When the directors met in advance of the annual meeting, Stearns announced his resignation and Evans announced his candidacy as board chairman and chief executive. His fellow directors agreed; whatever private misgivings they may have had about Evans's diplomatic skills, Crane clearly needed new leadership. Control of the company was his—or would be, as soon as the shareholders made his director's status official.[54]

Addressing shareholders for the last time, Neele Stearns assured the hometown gathering that Crane "had no intention of abandoning its Chicago operations." He reported on the company's financial health, blaming the decline in sales in 1958 on the recession that had not begun to lift until the fall. Then, the proxies were tallied and Tom Evans, Art Landa, Robert B. Crane, and Edwin Locke Jr. were officially elected to the board of directors.

It was not until later that day that Art Landa announced the news of Stearns's resignation and Tom Evans's election as chairman and chief executive. Evans told the press that the management change was the result of policy differences, but he repeated Stearns's assurances about Crane's presence in Chicago.[55]

Anyone who thought his reassurance meant that Crane would pursue business as usual was quickly awakened to the new reality. Brushing aside the Crane culture, Evans could not wait to put in place his plans for improving profits at Crane. There were no committee meetings, no task-force reports. His first sixty days were a "whirlwind," according to one industry journal. Inventories had to be cut, and the only way to do that was to cut manufacturing until the existing supplies were sold. So manufacturing was cut back, putting about 700 employees out of work at Crane's huge Chicago plant.

Then Evans tackled Crane's branch sales outlets, which seemed to him to cater more to plumbing contractors and branch managers' egos than to Crane's stockholders. He drew up plans to close or sell forty-three of the branch outlets as soon as possible. To replace them, he signed up 136 independent wholesalers to push Crane's products. He insisted on deep cuts in sales expenses, in corporate overhead, in payroll. Again, his orders came like thunderbolts from Jove, not like gentle nudges transmitted through an elaborate chain of command.

The reaction in the Chicago neighborhoods that relied on Crane for employment was swift and predictable. Tom Evans's name became an epithet, and the local press coverage of his early housecleaning efforts was blistering. The white-collar workers were only slightly less alarmed.

At the time, Art Landa was caught up in other dramas. He had recently determined that Penn-Texas's problems, and its implacable shareholders, imposed too great a burden on his busy schedule and his sometimes fragile health. Retaining the post of chairman of the company's executive committee, he had arranged for proxy-fight publicist David Karr to take over as president of Penn-Texas, whose now-tarnished name was changed to the Fairbanks Whitney Corporation. One article on Karr's elevation credited Landa with single-handedly "engineering" Evans's triumph at Crane.[56] Karr's promotion also prompted Senator Joseph McCarthy, who still haunted the capital in an alcoholic haze, to again denounce him as a Communist, although another senator promptly reported that a House committee had investigated Karr in 1943 and given him a clean bill of health. Behind the scenes, Landa had more serious concerns about Karr's judgment but could see no alternative than to put the presidency of the huge conglomerate in his hands. With the company's divided board and hostile shareholders, it was well-nigh impossible to recruit a more competent candidate from the outside.

So when the busy Washington lawyer got a letter from Tom Evans complaining about the infuriating Chicago publicity, especially the article that had ignored Evans's own contributions to the Crane victory, he casually brushed him off.[57] Then Landa grew expansive about how he saw his own role in the Crane conflict. "When an especially large and valuable diamond is found, the most competent diamond cutter available is usually sought out to determine the cutting," Landa wrote Evans in early May. "He studies the problem and then eventually, he takes a tool and makes a light tap and, as a result, a beautiful stone is produced, or the diamond shatters into many little pieces."[58] Landa, the letter implied, was the master who had turned Evans's rough stone into a jewel.

Evans responded angrily, defending his own importance to the Crane negotiations. "Contrary to the article your people put in the Chicago paper, I did a great deal of work on it also," he complained in a letter he fired off to Landa the following day.[59] And he was continuing to work on making the deal a success, while Landa offered no help and little support.

Evans's controversial policies were already striking sparks when the Crane board met later in May 1959. And he tossed a new firecracker into the boardroom, proposing to use $37 million in cash in the company's coffers to repurchase up to 800,000 shares of Crane stock from public investors at a premium price of $45 share. With fewer shares outstanding,

Crane would report higher earnings per share—a key indicator on Wall Street. And, of course, Tom Evans's block of stock would constitute a larger percentage of the remaining outstanding shares. The balance sheet would be leaner, pruned for growth, he argued.[60] The proposal was approved.

Why would stockholders give up on their Crane investment the moment the company's self-appointed savior had taken charge? The premium price was attractive, *Fortune* magazine noted, "particularly because Evans's management of the company was then under severe attack in the press. It was even being hinted in some quarters that Evans was gutting Crane and would eventually merge it with H. K. Porter. These attacks hurt Evans personally but may well have persuaded some shareholders to sell."[61]

One big stockholder was already persuaded—although he made Evans sweat out his decision until the last possible moment. Gurdon Wattles still had more than 300,000 shares of Crane stock, and controlled two seats on the Crane board. He could see that Evans was single-handedly in charge—the board meetings had become almost painful, with Evans demanding swift change and refusing to pause for discussion. At $45 a share, the stock Wattles owned would produce a profit of about $3 million, and when his stake was sold, he could resign from the embattled board. On July 1, 1959, two days before Crane's repurchase offer expired, the directors of Electric Autolite voted to sell all of its Crane shares back to Crane. Autolite had better uses for the money, its directors announced. And besides, "recent changes in the Crane Company had resulted in the current situation there being materially different from that which existed at the time of Autolite's investment."[62]

Different, indeed. Crane Company had once been treated by the local media with something approaching reverence. Now, it was the subject of one unflattering story after another. Evans seemed unconcerned about the criticism, although his letters to Landa and comments to friends suggested that the attacks stung more than he showed. They were causing pain to other board members as well, and those with interests based in Chicago were growing increasingly uncomfortable with the way the community was reacting to the speed and severity of his changes.

One man on the board who cared considerably about what Chicago thought of the company was young Robert Crane, whose great-grandfather had founded the company. He knew Crane had to change; the issue was how, and how fast. He felt someone needed to restrain the breakneck pace that chairman Evans was setting. He decided to seek the presidency of the company, and he unwisely talked with local newspaper reporters about his plan in late June. Evans was outraged at this affront to his authority. He promptly told the young Mr. Crane to take three weeks off from his job as assistant to the vice president for sales. Perhaps that would give him time to think about the duties of loyalty that a director owed to the man who had put him on the board. To be sure, Robert Crane's great-aunt had helped put Evans himself on the board. But nevertheless, when Robert Crane returned from his involuntary vacation in mid-July, Evans fired him from the company staff.[63]

This time, the angry reaction was not limited to the world outside his boardroom, since Robert Crane remained a director despite his dismissal from his executive post. Art Landa and his lovely young wife, Alexandra, had been vacationing in Paris and Athens when the storm hit Chicago. When he returned, he added his voice to the chorus of protests over young Crane's dismissal, amazed at the amount of unnecessary negative publicity the new Crane chairman was capable of producing.[64] Grudgingly, Evans relented and gave young Crane a new job, overseeing the two charitable trusts that Crane's founder had created with his original $1 million bequests to his workers. The tempest eased, but the board meetings remained acrimonious.

Evans and Landa had already crossed swords in June over Evans's plan to recruit forty-one-year-old Wesley A. Songer to be executive vice president and chief operating officer at Crane. Songer had spent three years at General Electric, working for the fabled Ralph J. Cordiner, who pioneered that company's massive decentralization program in the early 1950s. Evans was determined to decentralize Crane, following the same pattern he had used so successfully at Porter—the pattern, in effect, he had learned from the Mellon example in Pittsburgh. He envisioned a day when the various Crane divisions would "boss themselves" as the Porter divisions did. Songer seemed the perfect choice, since he shared Evans's commitment to this still somewhat novel corporate management approach. Landa was in Europe when Evans proposed Songer's appointment at the board meeting in late June, but the Washington lawyer nevertheless had opposed the choice and had sent cables to the other directors to urge them to join him in his resistance.[65] But Evans across the table was more formidable than Landa across the ocean, and the vote to appoint Songer was unanimous. It did not help Tom Evans's temper when he saw accounts of the closed-door dispute popping up in the press—Landa and Karr at work, he no doubt suspected.

To be sure, Landa was chairman of the executive committee at Fair-banks-Morse, the former Penn-Texas Corporation which had adopted the name of its giant Chicago-based subsidiary. As a result, he was understandably sensitive to Chicago's hostile reaction to the changes going on at

Crane. But Evans expected loyalty from his directors, and Landa was displaying an infuriating amount of independence.

Amid Landa's public criticism, the upheaval at Crane continued through the summer as Evans and Songer pruned away entire branches on Crane's organizational chart. Four of the company's six vice presidents were fired before the end of August 1959, prompting Chicago to once again draw parallels between Evans and the autocratic and unlamented Sewell Avery of Montgomery Ward.[66] About 2,000 lower-level employees also had been cut from the company's payroll, although some of them had lost their jobs as a result of cutbacks and plant closings undertaken by Stearns in 1958.[67] Nevertheless, Evans got the blame, perhaps because he was so candid about the need to shift work from the highly unionized Chicago area to facilities in Tennessee and Arkansas, where labor costs were lower.

The survivors of this crash diet began to see some improvements at Crane. Tom Evans, difficult and ruthless as he was, had looked at Crane with a financial insight that had been missing for years, and he had acted on what he saw. For example, once he was privy to the various sources of Crane's profits, he saw that most of that income in recent years had been generated by the company's relatively small investments in Canada, England, Holland and France.[68] While Landa and other relaxed executives of his vintage traveled to Europe on stately luxury liners and spent long weeks relaxing, Evans rushed over to stake out larger claims on Crane's existing European business.[69] And despite the public criticism that he was "gutting" the business, he began adding new domestic companies that he thought would enhance Crane's profitability, making five acquisitions before the end of the year. The biggest of these acquisitions was his purchase of National–U.S. Radiator Corporation of Johnstown, Pennsylvania, which manufactured products used in boilers, furnaces, and air-conditioning systems and which seemed a good match for Crane's plumbing products. He also acquired a division of the Swartwout Company of Cleveland which specialized in electronic control instrumentation. "By combining its know-how in piping, fittings, and valves with that of Swartwout in instruments, Crane expects to offer complete systems to the process industries, a position it feels is unique in the industry," reported *Chemical & Engineering News*, the bible of the chemical manufacturing business.[70]

Most of these acquisitions were done in a friendly way, with the smaller companies happy to affiliate with their prestigious purchaser. But the aftermath was sometimes a shocking round of staff cuts and belt-tightening— even when the companies were profitable. "You can imagine the pain and suffering this caused many capable people and their families," one veteran of the National–U.S. Radiator deal reported later.[71] Then in September 1959, Evans started using some of Crane's cash to buy a 12 percent stake in Briggs Manufacturing Company, a plumbing manufacturer based in Warren, Michigan, near Detroit. By the end of the year, he was openly proposing to buy up the rest of Briggs's stock for just under its book value of $12.30 a share. His purchases shocked the Briggs's board, as did his casual public comments about how nicely Briggs would fit into the Crane family. Briggs manufactured its china plumbing fixtures at factories in the Midwest, he explained, while Crane's key pottery plants were in California and New Jersey. "It is a good name and has lots of fine assets, but it has been run sleepily for a long time," he told the *New York Times* in December 1959. He added, "We're not planning any proxy fight for control. Our talks with the company have been friendly. Our only request to them is that our proposal be submitted to stockholders to vote upon."[72] The Briggs management, led by Arnold Kohler, quietly began to draw up its battle plan.

Meanwhile, Crane's profits in 1959 were climbing above 1958's dismal levels, but profit margins remained stubbornly low. Crane's stock had soared to $72 a share in the first months of Evans's regime, but had drifted down as a "quick fix" grew increasingly less likely. And in the boardroom, Landa continued to demand a formal "business strategy" from Evans— although it should have been clear that the tireless entrepreneur from Pittsburgh was flying largely by the seat of his pants. As one industry journal observed, under Evans, "long-range planning was redefined in terms of months."[73] It had taken decades for Crane to get into this mess; the solution was likely to take more than six months. But Landa was growing increasingly impatient with the Evans style.

And Evans was no doubt fed up with the Landa style, as well. Since June, the Chicago papers had been studded with articles in which Landa had been openly critical of Evans's methods, conveniently omitting the fact that Landa had voted for the implementation of most of those "methods" when Evans proposed them. Three other directors who had disagreed with Evans's program had simply resigned in 1959, citing the pressures of other business. But Landa seemed to be trying to hedge his bets: condemning Crane's unpopular actions to curry favor in Chicago, but staying aboard to claim credit for what Evans was convinced would be the company's ultimate success. Evans began to fight back with a little press sniping of his own, telling any reporter who asked that he considered Landa to be "disloyal" and wondered why Landa did not simply submit his resignation.

Behind all this public rancor, however, was a far less philosophical dispute. Since early May 1959, Evans and Landa had been bickering over the financial terms of their original alliance. In his letter dismissing Evans's concern about the "disgraceful" publicity about the Crane deal in Chicago, Landa had made a pointed reminder: "I think you should have in mind the settlement of my fee in connection with the Crane situation."

Then he outlined his own assessment of the services he had rendered to Evans. "You sought to obtain the executive control of the company, and it was for that purpose that you consulted with me. By very carefully thought-out moves, you were placed in control of one of the hundred largest companies in the United States. There was no proxy fight. There was no blood. Your associates—bankers, etc.—could have no criticism of the steps taken to accomplish the results." There were other factors that should be considered, as well, he continued. "One, the speed with which the job was accomplished. Two, the amount of your investment involved (in excess of five million). Three, the great opportunity for profit that it presents for you."

He concluded in his characteristically grand manner. "What you desired has been fully accomplished." Then he added, with tongue firmly in cheek, "I always like to determine fees on a basis satisfactory to my clients. I suggest we sit down to arrive at a mutually satisfactory determination of this matter."

Tom Evans was furious at the cool, glib arguments from Washington. Landa's description of their financial relationship was dramatically different from Evans's own recollection. He reminded Landa that when they had first met, "you told me you were making two or three hundred thousand a year in legal fees and could keep very little of it after taxes." In response, Evans had offered to help Landa buy 10,000 shares of Crane stock, and had guaranteed him against any loss on the shares, assuring him he would double his money within three years. "You told me this appealed to you, and [you] would rather do this than have the fee," Evans continued. Now, out of the blue, Landa was talking about legal fees, in addition to the risk-free investment Evans had helped him make. "If you have changed your understanding and are serious about it, I will be glad to talk about it— but it is inconceivable to me that you would not stick to your original agreement," he concluded. His anger tangled his final sentences. "It is my agreement that any business arrangements can be concluded satisfactorily on the basis of integrity. If I am wrong in the understanding I have had with you, will you please then have the stock transfer action canceled and released. We can then sit down to negotiate the matter of fees."

Landa immediately fired back, his arch tone slipping a bit. "I dislike to be critical about other people's comments concerning keeping commitments," he said, before going on to be critical of Evans for having reneged on a commitment he had made to hire Landa's friend David Karr's public relations firm for six months. As to the financial arrangements made at the beginning of the Crane fight, he said, "Your memory is faulty, and I shall be very glad to sit down and discuss the whole situation with you when you are prepared for a calm, dispassionate review of the facts."

Landa's obvious testiness may have been exacerbated by a bout of intestinal trouble that put him in the hospital a few weeks later, or he may have been fretful over a pending visit from two FBI agents, continuing to question him about the Teamster transactions that helped him rescue the Fruehauf trailer company from a hostile raider in 1953. In any case, the correspondence discloses the deep differences between Evans and Landa. By October, Landa had begun to extricate himself from the financial part-nership he had formed with Tom Evans, paying off the loan that the two of them had obtained to finance his purchases of Crane stock. Evans had put up 10,000 shares of his own H. K. Porter stock as collateral for the loan, and he was glad to have the shares unencumbered.

But it was more difficult to unwind their boardroom relationship. Landa's personal papers suggest that Evans may have made some threats in late 1959 about kicking Landa off the Crane board. That would explain why Landa asked his legal staff in Washington to prepare a memo for him describing what provisions the Crane bylaws contained for the removal of a director. The files also suggest that Landa may have been looking for some ammunition of his own to use against Tom Evans. The same staff member had researched the federal regulations that governed loans arranged by brokers for the benefit of their customers—exactly the arrangement Evans and Company had made to help Landa purchase his Crane stock.

In any case, by late January 1960, the two men had parted company, with Evans making the gracious gesture that was more typical of Landa, and Landa making the petulant comments more typical of Evans. Specifi-cally, Evans wrote Landa a "glowing letter of appreciation for his work at Crane and urged him to stay on the board," *Fortune* reported.[74] Landa quoted from the letter in the press release announcing his resignation, but insisted that he and the Crane chairman "differed to such an extent in our business philosophies and methods" that he could not continue to serve.

Soon after Landa's resignation, the director who had originally repre-sented Gurdon Wattles resigned. His was the sixth resignation among the ten men who had started out with Evans on the Crane board in April 1959. Among the survivors as the 1960 stockholders meeting approached was Robert B. Crane, still a thorn in Tom Evans's side and now the last of his former defenders on the board. In late February 1960, Tom Evans announced a proposal to reduce the Crane board to six members whose ranks would not include Robert Crane. When reporters sought him out for comment, Robert Crane said, "It has been apparent over a period of time that I have not been a welcome member of the board." He had not opposed Evans's business policies, he insisted. "But I was not in agreement on methods and procedures."[75]

As for the company's failure to nominate him for another term of the board, he said the move simply proved "that Crane Company is now a one-man show."

CHAPTER ELEVEN

YOU CAN'T GO HOME AGAIN

When Crane stockholders arrived at the company's Chicago headquarters for the 1960 annual meeting in April, they could easily see at least one of the changes that the last year had brought. In April 1959, United Steel Workers leader David McDonald had been unable to find a Crane worker willing to lend his proxy so that McDonald could attend the shareholder meeting. In April 1960, dozens of angry union members assembled at the entrance to the meeting site, carrying signs that condemned Evans for the loss of union jobs. "Money-Mad Evans Has No Heart," one sign proclaimed. Whatever else he had accomplished, Tom Evans had galvanized the local steelworkers into unified action.

Certainly, the Evans approach was a sharp break with the culture that had guided Crane since its founding. But Evans made no apologies for the changes he had made at Crane. "You can't stand still," he told reporters. "You've got to grow. Otherwise, your stockholders lose."[1] His restless recipe for growth was acquisitions—friendly ones if possible, but hostile ones if necessary. He would collect companies, weed out the losers and invest in the winners, and then set them up as free-standing divisions with autonomy over everything but financial policy, which remained firmly in his own hands. That process, repeated over and over again, had produced the Porter empire, a sprawling family of decentralized businesses connected to Evans by the steady back-and-forth flow of money and financial information.

This approach, as one scholar put it, "viewed the central office as a bank and treated divisions as potential borrowers."[2] It had been novel in the early 1940s, when Evans was applying it so successfully. By the late 1940s, other business mavericks—proxy fighters like Leopold Silberstein and less combative empire-builders like Royal Little at Textron—were finding their own way to this diversified, decentralized "financial" model of the corporation.[3] Their initial success attracted new adherents to the philosophy, and by the late 1950s, this "new" way of organizing a firm's operations was gaining attention.

Business Week first noticed the phenomenon in June 1956. These strange new companies, it said, "consist of a host of smaller companies tucked under one corporate umbrella. They muster a wide diversity of product lines, with no apparent logic or relation between them—and they have appeared so suddenly that businessmen still have no name for them. For want of a better name, call them polyglots."[4] Soon, a better name was found: conglomerates.

Their success, the magazine noted, seemed to hinge on "the development of management controls and techniques for handling decentralized operations," including "tight accounting and control, growing use of computers, and the like—and professional managers." These managers had to be willing to think of their skills as generic, not specific to a single industry. The model that *Business Week* found, in case after case, was the model that Tom Evans had introduced at Porter during the war: tight financial controls, but highly decentralized operations.

Before the ink was dry on the magazine's analysis, there were new entries to the "polyglot" club. By 1956, AMF had been built by Moorehead Patterson from a factory-machine shop into a diversified, completely decentralized collection of companies making everything from bowling equipment to guided missile parts. In 1956, James Ling made the first acquisition that would transform his small Ling Electric Company into his highly diversified Ling Industries, which by 1961 was known as Ling-Temco-Vought or LTV.[5] In 1955, a shrewd young Palestinian Jewish immigrant named Meshulam Riklis took over the Rapid Electrotype company; two years later, he merged it with American Colortype to create Rapid-American Corporation. He then used Rapid-American as the basis for his conglomerate empire, which soon included the McCrory dime store chain and Glen Alden, a consumer products company.[6]

But Patterson built his empire by issuing new stock, which he used as travelers' checks on his company-buying sprees. Riklis, a wise-cracking gnome who liked to tease the Ivy League bankers he dealt with, boasted openly of his preference for making acquisitions with other people's money—an approach he called "the effective non-use of cash."[7] James

Ling was even more daring in his financial approach. He issued short-term notes at high interest rates, using the assets of the purchased company as collateral. Then he sold longer-term bonds, at lower interest rates, and used the money to retire the short-term notes. He paid off the bonds by selling off some of the purchased company's assets, if the company did not generate enough cash to service the debt.[8]

Although Ling's approach—borrowing money to buy a company and paying off the debt by selling some of its assets—was exactly how Tom Evans had acquired the Mount Vernon Car Manufacturing Company in 1944, Evans considered most of the newcomers' acquisition strategies foolish because they often came at the expense of real shareholder value. And his measurement, always, was how company policies affected shareholders—he was, after all, his own largest stockholder at Porter, and he was the largest stockholder on the board at Crane. So into the early 1960s, he tended to pay cash when he bought smaller companies. He did not acquire new companies because he was interested in their products or their research—not to mention their workers or their communities. He bought new companies because he thought they would generate strong new profits for himself and other shareholders.

Because Evans's relationship with his business divisions was essentially a financial one—measuring their profits and analyzing their losses so he could maximize the return on shareholders' investment—his management style seemed very strange to the affected workers and executives. It is perhaps not surprising that he seemed "money-mad" to worried factory-floor employees and suddenly superfluous headquarters executives. Paying attention to the money was, in fact, the way he paid attention to the business. He left the small, day-to-day details of how that money was produced to his senior executives, and gave them all the latitude they needed to meet the high financial goals he set for them, by fair means or foul.

That the means had sometimes been foul was demonstrated publicly in February 1960, when a federal grand jury sitting in Philadelphia once again indicted H. K. Porter for violation of the nation's antitrust laws. This time, Porter was named along with eleven other electrical equipment manufacturers, including the giants General Electric and Westinghouse, all of whom were accused of conspiring to fix prices and rig bids for insulators and distribution lightning arresters.[9] Barely six weeks later, federal prosecutors in Philadelphia once again obtained antitrust indictments against the electrical industry, involving different products. And once again H. K. Porter was among the defendants—with top billing in two of the three new indictments announced on May 19, 1960.

Evans might have expected that this latest grand jury embarrassment would be settled as the rubber-belting case had been in 1959—with a quiet "no contest" plea and a fine. But this time, a "no contest" plea simply would not fly. The cases, part of a massive federal crackdown on anticompetitive practices in a variety of industries, ignited a smoldering fire of public and political criticism of the largest defendants, especially General Electric, which was the politicians' consensus nominee for the post of ringleader in what commentators were already calling "the Great Electrical Industry Conspiracy." As one writer noted, "This conspiracy was carried on with all the guilt-conscious cloak-and-dagger techniques known to spies: secret codes, mysterious meetings in hotel rooms, queer notes, guarded telephone calls, concealed records, fictitious names, burned memorandum and the like. . . . Only sinister music was lacking."[10]

Ultimately, twenty-nine companies and forty-five executives in the electrical industry would face criminal charges in the crackdown, and the fines imposed by federal District Court Judge J. Cullen Ganey would total nearly $2 million, a remarkable amount in the antitrust arena of that day.

The magnitude of the case and the attention it received made it impossible for it to be handled in the "business as usual" fashion that had characterized some earlier antitrust cases. Indeed, what made the case so outrageous was the public's suspicion that the behavior outlined in the indictment *was* in fact business as usual—that big business had completely abandoned the rules of fair and competitive markets and simply rigged the game to bolster profits. The president of one of the defendant corporations seemed to admit as much, saying: "It is the only way a business can be run. It is free enterprise."[11] Many of the executives convicted in the conspiracy cases insisted "they had simply inherited procedures carried on by predecessors and were acting under direct orders from higher ups. . . . Top officials denied everything. Judge Ganey clearly did not believe them."[12]

Robert A. Bicks, the Justice Department lawyer in charge of the antitrust division, said the violations were "among the most serious, the most flagrant, the most pervasive that had ever marked any basic American industry."[13]

His eloquence ignored history, of course. Exactly such behavior had been common among the moneyed giants who had controlled American industry earlier in the century. Tom Evans's mentor, W. L. Mellon, would have found the achievement of "price security" to be quite understandable, and perhaps even admirable. The aluminum monopoly had certainly been beneficial to the Mellon family's fortunes.

In any case, Judge Ganey, presiding in Philadelphia, handled the electrical-devices cases in a stern and uncompromising manner. "One would be most naive indeed to believe that these violations of law, so long persisted in, affecting so large a segment of the industry and finally involving so many millions upon millions of dollars, were facts unknown to those responsible for the corporation and its conduct," he said.[14] On March 24, 1960, he refused to permit Porter and the other corporations named in the May indictments to plead "no contest," citing the seriousness of the charges and the "extraordinary" nature of the alleged conspiracy. The companies would have to prepare a genuine defense, or plead guilty. Most of them, Porter included, pleaded guilty on December 8, 1960. Porter was fined $25,000, more than Westinghouse but less than General Electric. One of Porter's senior executives was fined $1,500 and was one of twenty-four executives who were given thirty-day suspended sentences.[15]

Tom Evans, though nowhere near the stature of the top executives at General Electric, clearly had become a noticeable blip on the regulatory radar screen. And the price-fixing and bid-rigging cases, while far more serious and sweeping than the prior year's rubber belting indictment, were not the only antitrust roadblock that regulators were throwing into his path as the sixties opened.

By the time of Crane's annual meeting in 1960, Evans had already made four acquisitions and he was determined that Briggs Manufacturing would be the fifth. A few weeks after the shareholder meeting, he officially opened the proxy fight that he had been hinting at for months. It was the first proxy fight he had waged since stepping onto the national stage, and it attracted attention in the Midwest. Arnold Kohler, the president of Briggs—which newspapers described as "an old-line manufacturer," a sub-tle signal that its recent performance was less than impressive—had not been idle. He and his directors had complained to the Federal Trade Commission, and had gone to court to try to force Crane to back off.

By May, the FTC had issued a complaint asserting that several of Evans's recent acquisitions at Crane may have violated federal antitrust laws. Unlike the price-fixing indictments, this government interference hit Evans at the heart of his business philosophy. Interfering with his managers' efforts to prevent unnecessary price competition in their markets was one thing. But interfering with his own ability to acquire new companies—the activity he enjoyed above all else—was far more serious.

Evans went on the offensive, and succeeded in offending a considerable number of bureaucrats and politicians. At a luncheon talk to the New York Society of Security Analysts, he offered the Wall Street analysts his own theories about what had prompted the government's move against his Crane acquisition strategy. "Somebody came to me several months ago and said, 'If you don't get out of Briggs, one of the family is married to a senator for Michigan, and we're going to stir things up in Washington.'" The public accusation brought a stinging denunciation from Michigan Senator Philip A. Hart, whose wife was the daughter of the man who had founded Briggs but who denied he'd instigated the FTC probe.[16] Evans argued further that the market for plumbing fixtures was largely dominated by American Radiator and Standard Sanitary Company, known as American Standard. Nearly half of all plumbing purchases in the United States put money in American Standard's pocket. "If they want real competition, letting Crane merge with the smaller companies is one way of doing it," Evans said. Combined, they might have a chance at competing with American Standard. "Otherwise," he said, "it will be a race to see who goes broke first."

But his arguments did not persuade a federal judge in Detroit, who in early June 1960 issued a temporary restraining order that blocked Evans from voting his shares at the Briggs annual meeting on June 17. The court found that the takeover might well violate antitrust laws, and Evans promptly appealed, without success.

He was not a man who found government regulators particularly intimidating—indeed, he had already faced down the Internal Revenue Service. In March 1959, the IRS had gone to court in Pittsburgh, asserting that Tom and Josephine Evans still owed the government $170,291 in income taxes for 1954, when he had reported the somewhat staggering sum of $1.06 million in income. The dispute looked simple. In 1954, Evans had made some substantial charitable donations—$700,000 to Yale University and $550,000 to the T. M. Evans Foundation, his personal philanthropy. Instead of giving cash, he donated some public utility bonds that he had purchased a month earlier at a substantial premium to their face value. When he filed his tax return, he took a deduction for the value of his charitable contribution. But he also took a deduction for the premium he paid on the bonds, treating it as a capital loss. The government's tax attorneys condemned this as "double-dipping." But in September 1960, the court ruled in Evans's favor. The industrialist had found a loophole and legally exploited it, the judge ruled.[17] The government appealed, but lost.

So Evans was clearly more than willing to fight over his ambitious acquisition plans at Crane—with the Briggs management, with the FTC, with the courts, if necessary. But unlike the tax case, he did not prevail in his fight for Briggs.

Busy as he was at Crane and Porter, Evans continued his aggressive forays into the stock market, enhancing his reputation as a man whose name on a stock transfer certificate could send a spear of ice into a chief executive's soul. In late 1959, he had heard that a charitable foundation in Montreal wanted to unload a big block of stock in the Brown Company, a mid-size paper and plywood company based in Berlin, New Hampshire. Although it was the nation's leading producer of industrial paper towels, it was a conservative and slightly sluggish firm, a little off Wall Street's beaten track. Evans thus was able to pick up 255,000 of its shares from the Canadian foundation for about $12 a share, or roughly half of the company's per-share book value. Word of his stake hit Wall Street in the spring of 1960 when the company's proxy statement disclosed that management's slate of nominations to the company's nine-member board included two Evans associates: Charles L. Holbert, the new president of H. K. Porter, replacing the retired Clarence Dobson, and William Aldrich Greene, a management consultant to both Crane and Porter.[18] Evans was rumored to have scooted up to Berlin, New Hampshire, in his private plane to tour two of the Brown mills. The company's stock began to scoot upward as well, in the confident expectation that Evans would at the very least stir up the sleepy firm.

Already, his keen eyes had seen that even the company's stated book values probably underestimated the real worth of the company by a substantial amount. Brown owned some 635,000 acres of timberland across New England that its ledgers showed to be worth $2.6 million, an absurdly outdated valuation that was based on an appraisal made in 1904.[19] It also had a strong role in several specialty markets, including synthetic resins for the printing industry and fiber sewer pipes.

But assets and products are one thing, and profits are another. In 1962 the paper market experienced a price war that cut Brown's profits nearly in half. Its stock began to retreat. Evans became impatient—but he still had only two votes on the board. His adversaries in the boardroom included a partner in the Wall Street firm of David J. Greene and Company, which specialized in such offbeat speculations. It controlled about 300,000 shares of Brown, for itself and its customers. Also on the Brown board was Gene Tunney, who had once held the world heavyweight boxing championship but who lately was a director of a coal company that listed Brown as one of its largest customers—a relationship that Evans felt was entirely too cozy.[20]

Brown's president, Leonard A. Pierce, ran the operation but the board had been operating without a chairman for more than a year. That left a power vacuum that the irrepressible Tom Evans was determined to fill—by sheer force of personality, if nothing else.

In December 1962, for example, he completely preempted the Brown management and made an acquisition for the company on his own initiative. The deal was the talk of Wall Street by the Christmas season. In November, Brown's management had made an offer to purchase the American Writing Paper Corporation in Holyoke, Massachusetts. But the

Massachusetts company had "neglected" the proposal, according to Evans, and Brown did not pursue its prey as aggressively as Evans would have done. The Holyoke company's indifference continued even after Evans and Company started buying up about 3,000 shares of American Writing Paper—a little show of force, just to focus their attention.[21] Then Evans heard that Brown's target had opened talks with another buyer. Evans furiously telephoned the president of American Writing Paper to protest. The president assured him that the bidding for his company was still open and he would consider any firm offer submitted by December 11. Evans quickly put together an offer—made in the name of Evans and Company—that was worth about $33 per share, compared to his rival's $28-a-share proposal. Evans and Company wound up owning American Writing Paper as an agent for Brown, whose board simply couldn't meet and act quickly enough, according to Evans.[22] He then sold his new property to Brown, with Evans and Company collecting a $40,000 fee from American Writing Paper in the process.[23]

Wall Street applauded his speed and daring, but the deal may have been the last straw for president Leonard Pierce. In any case, before 1963 was two weeks old, Pierce had announced that Brown had recruited a new chairman, William L. Keady of San Francisco. Keady was sixty-nine years old, and came out of the Sewell Avery mold. He had in fact worked directly under Avery at U.S. Gypsum Company for several decades, and had then run a paper-products company for ten years before his retirement in 1960.[24] To tempt him back into the boardroom, Pierce had proposed a salary of $25,000 and a package of stock options that allowed Keady to purchase nearly 25,000 shares of Brown stock at a price almost $2 below the then-current market price for the shares.[25]

Pierce insisted that Keady would bring the company some "much-needed experience in long-range corporate planning," which sounded to the sympathetic management community like a subtle dig at the blitzkrieg approach employed by Brown's most outspoken shareholder.[26]

Evans was furious over Keady's hiring, but was still in the minority on the nine-man board. Only the two directors loyal to him had voted against the proposal, which Evans said would "saddle the Brown Company with the double expense of two chief executive officers."[27] Evans remained on the offensive, notifying the press that he strongly opposed Keady's election and threatening to sue the company to overturn it. The options grant was outrageously generous, he complained, and Keady was simply too old to give Brown the kind of leadership it needed to pull itself out of its slump. If Pierce couldn't do the job, the company needed a new president, not an additional chairman. On January 11, Evans sued the six directors who had voted for Keady's appointment, filing his lawsuit on behalf of all the company's stockholders.

When the majority of Brown's board stood firmly behind its new chairman, Evans picked up an old familiar weapon: the proxy fight. He quickly enlisted five other Brown stockholders to his cause. In mid-February, he notified the SEC that his group planned to seek shareholder support for a special stockholders meeting to vote on his proposal to expand the company's board from nine members to fifteen. Evans and his five allies were campaigning for the six new seats. With the two seats he already controlled, that would give him a majority on the expanded board. (Although Evans's aborted raid on Briggs had occurred less than two years earlier in Detroit, a number of East Coast reporters mistakenly described the Brown fight as the first proxy fight of Evans's career.)

Explaining his actions to reporters, Evans said, "I have lost all confidence in the management of Brown Company." Profits were continuing to decline—they had shown, Evans said, "an alarming drop." The company was deteriorating so quickly, he insisted, that he simply could not wait until the annual meeting scheduled for later that spring.[28]

That was nonsense, Pierce said. The company's fortunes had begun to improve in the first quarter of 1963, with profits showing almost a twenty-fold increase over the severely depressed levels in that same quarter in 1962. Sales, too, had improved considerably. So there was no reason in the world why Evans should not postpone his battle until the annual meeting—when, of course, management would have the usual home-court advantage.

Evans quickly won enough support to call a special meeting for March 11 in Portland, Maine. But then a very strange ballet began, one that showed how sophisticated management's defenses had become after more than a decade of proxy warfare. Pierce and Keady did not propose their own slate of directors to run in opposition to the Evans team. Instead, they appealed to their loyal shareholders to revoke the proxies they had submitted. This odd strategy reflected the fact that, under the company's bylaws, the meeting was not legal unless just over half of Brown's outstanding stock was represented in the form of submitted proxies. If the special meeting lacked a quorum, obviously no binding action could be taken to expand the board and put the company in Evans's control.[29]

So Tom Evans arrived at the March 11 meeting only to be faced with management's assertions that the meeting was illegal because it lacked a quorum. The session was postponed until March 26. When the March 26 meeting convened in Portland, it lasted all of thirteen minutes. Once again, management stated that no quorum was present, but Evans nevertheless insisted that his proposals be put to vote and accused the Brown management of conspiring to illegally block the meeting. In court, his lawyers argued that revoked proxies should be treated simply as votes cast against Evans—that way, they would still count for purposes of determining whether there was a quorum.

Keady and Pierce tossed some mud balls of their own, accusing Evans of having undermined the company's recent drive to repurchase shares of its stock by going into the marketplace at the same time to buy up shares for himself. The Brown executives were also critical of the $40,000 fee that Evans and Company had collected as part of the daring American Writing Paper acquisition the prior December.[30]

It is intriguing that no one wondered aloud, or in print, about why Tom Evans, who was immensely rich and who already had a full basket with H. K. Porter and the Crane Company, bothered to wage such a bitter, expensive battle simply to take control of a paper company with less than $60 million in annual sales. But he would not give up the fight. In early April, the ballots cast at the March 26 meeting were finally counted. The tally showed that the meeting had been about 193,000 shares shy of a quorum.[31] Management's savvy maneuver was all that had saved it: if Evans had succeeded in persuading the local court to treat revoked proxies as negative votes, he would have won. And so he battled on, asking the court to delay the annual meeting, to give him time to muster additional support. But on April 12, 1963, Maine Supreme Court Justice Walter M. Tapley Jr. refused to permit a delay.[32]

Evans, at last, had to concede defeat. "Like Dewey in 1948, I came in second," he joked to a *New York Times* reporter during an interview ten days after the court ruling.[33] He had lost his two seats on the Brown board, but he remained Brown's largest single stockholder, with 255,000 shares of the company's stock. What would he do? "I frankly don't know what I'm going to do," he said with his big Santa Claus grin. What he ultimately did, in early 1964, was sell his stake to David J. Greene and Company and another Wall Street firm for a profit of just over $2 a share, or about $510,000.

First, the federal antitrust regulators had denied him a victory in the Briggs fight; now, legal technicalities cost him victory in the Brown battle. For a man who had become accustomed to getting what he wanted for more than two decades, these defeats must have stung. Many people would have seen them as a message from the universe that it was time for him to join Charlie Green and Ben Heineman over in neutral territory, far from the muddy frustration of the proxy wars. But Evans seemed to relish the battles, even the ones he lost.

His old ally-turned-foe, Art Landa, would have understood. Landa, too, could not leave the proxy battlefield behind, even if the spoils were meager compared to the fights of the fifties. In 1962, while Evans was revving up his engines for the Brown fight, Landa was challenging John A. Saunders, the new chief executive of the General Fireproofing Company of Youngstown, Ohio, an office-furniture manufacturer that was even smaller than Evans's target. Landa had mustered enough support from shareholders to gain two seats on General Fireproofing's ten-member board in 1961; then he began pushing for two additional seats. Saunders went on the offensive. At a supposedly routine board meeting on January 30, 1962, he pushed through an amendment to the company's bylaws to provide for staggered elections to the board, a sure way to defeat a fight for control. As the annual shareholder meeting approached, management sought approval for the bylaw change and Landa fielded a four-man slate opposing it.

The fight was extremely muddy. In letters to shareholders, Saunders blasted Landa's reputation as a "notorious corporate raider." He cited Landa's "highly questionable" dealings with the Teamsters, complained that he had missed half of the board meetings at General Fireproofing, and recited all his earlier fights for control, including the battle at Crane Company. "Ask your broker, your banker or your financial adviser their opinion of Mr. Landa. Compare it with their opinion of your present management," Saunders wrote.[34] Landa called the attack a management "smear" engineered by "a whole crew of special proxy-fighting aides" hired for the purpose. The management defense team included the firm of Selvage and Lee, Leopold Silberstein's old nemesis, which Landa said was "reputed to be made up of some of the most expert 'hidden persuaders' in the corporate field. It has probably been engaged in more proxy fights than any other single team of press agents in the country."[35]

The team also included a relative newcomer to the game named Joseph Flom, of the upstart New York law firm of Skadden, Arps, Slate, Meagher and Flom. The child of poor Russian-born immigrants, Joe Flom had wiggled his way into Harvard Law School after his wartime military service. Small, stocky, and awkward, Flom had felt uncomfortable at the sleek, richly appointed law firms that courted him at Harvard, but he instantly loved the cheerful hand-to-mouth life at Skadden Arps.[36] The young firm had been formed on April Fools' Day in 1948 by three young lawyers—Marshall K. Skadden, Leslie H. Arps, and John H. Slate—two of whom had failed to win partnerships at a more prestigious firm.[37] In 1956, the firm recruited William H. Timbers, a former general counsel at the SEC who had policed a number of notable proxy fights for the commission. In February 1959, Timbers enlisted the aid of the brilliant young Flom to help defend the management of United Industrial Corporation, a financial holding company in Grand Rapids, Michigan.[38] It was Flom's first takeover fight. A persuasive lawyer—his young son once boasted to a classmate that he was "better than Perry Mason"—Flom had won an ambiguous victory, stalling the raiders long enough to force them to the bargaining table. Among the other lawyers working on that difficult fight was Martin Lipton, a young associate fighting his first battle for corporate control.[39] The two men, decades later, would entirely dominate the legal fraternity specializing in takeover warfare.

Flom was soon enlisted to defend management in the epic 1961 battle for control of the Alleghany Corporation.[40] The business community was riveted by that fight, as the oil-rich Murchison brothers of Texas did battle with the quiet dime-store heir Allan P. Kirby, who had run the company since Robert Young's suicide. Clint Murchison had been Young's ally in the successful New York Central fight, but he turned on Kirby and managed to temporarily wrest control of the corporation from him in what the latest generation of business reporters predictably called the "proxy fight of the century." Joe Flom, whose firm was hired to count the ballots for Kirby, was still only a supporting actor, but he was on center stage.[41]

The battle had the same carnival atmosphere that characterized the big fights of the 1950s, and it provided a sort of apprenticeship for several people who would later come to dominate their specialties in the corporate takeover battalions. Public relations man Richard Cheney, who had just been recruited by Hill and Knowlton and who was then a "total innocent" about proxy fights, signed on as part of the Murchisons' team. "I never had as much fun in my life as I did working on that fight," recalled Cheney, who later became one of the masters of the game.[42] He and the other Murchison advisers would all troop over to one of their homes and stay up all night to write the proxy letters to shareholders. "It was like a political campaign—that's what Selvage brought to it." Jim Selvage of Selvage and Lee, the wily old public relations veteran who had battled corporate raiders like Leopold Silberstein for more than a decade, was fighting opposite him in defense of Kirby's management. Selvage was intimidating, Cheney confessed. "I was humble—but I was learning." Similarly, the lawyer advising the successful Murchison forces was the silver-tongued George C. Demas, another seasoned general of the corporate takeover wars. A former military intelligence officer, Demas was so adept in defense that "he kept special corporate kits in his lower Manhattan office containing samples of the documents a company might need in each stage of a proxy contest."[43] Recalled Cheney, "He was the king of the walk, really." But the young Joe Flom of Skadden Arps was quickly making a name for himself, too.

Flom had his work cut out for him in the fight at General Fireproofing. Landa had some good ammunition and he used it with flair in his public letters to shareholders, insisting that he was not a big-city raider seeking control but only a concerned shareholder seeking a minority presence on the board to serve as "watchdogs" over management. Of the staggered election plan, Landa wrote: "The insiders have the effrontery to claim that their staggered system will be good for you because it will 'assure continuity of management.' That's the reason it's bad!"[44] As for management's claims of record profits, Landa pointed out that they had been achieved only by cutting the standard annual pension fund contribution. Worst of all, he continued, the company's balance sheet showed almost $11 million in cash and government securities, but interest earnings of only $165,000—"indicating the bulk of the cash was idle." He continued, "The undeniable truth is that the insiders at General Fireproofing keep hordes of cash at certain banks in non-interest-bearing accounts. You are losing income!" The largest of those barren accounts was at Union National Bank of Youngstown, which shared three directors with General Fireproofing, including the bank's president.[45]

But the professional proxy-fighters led by Flom easily defeated the Landa forces in the proxy fight—a victory that would be attached to Flom's name by knowledgeable reporters for several years. The earlier Alleghany fight had helped enhance Flom's reputation in the executive suites, but defeating the formidable Art Landa—that was the sort of thing that could get you noticed in the press.[46]

There were a few other proxy fights as the sixties rolled forward, including several widely followed but unsuccessful battles for control of MGM, the motion picture company. The company's defense team included attorney Louis Nizer and public relations veteran Thomas J. Deegan Jr., who had been Robert Young's chief of staff in the famous New York Central fight. Here, too, newcomers to the game learned at the elbows of the veterans—Joe Flom had worked for the insurgent, Philip Levin.

In reality, though, proxy raiders like Tom Evans and Art Landa were the remnant of a vanishing tribe. The methods of war were changing, as Kirby's successful strategy in 1963 demonstrated. A multimillionaire in his own right, Kirby could afford to go into the market and buy up Alleghany shares to strengthen his hand in the proxy fight. From there, it was just a few short steps to the idea of dispensing with the proxy fight entirely, and simply going into the market and buying a controlling stake in the target company from its other shareholders. This new weapon was somewhat redundantly called a tender offer—in Wall Street parlance, "tender" means "a formal offer"—and it brought the warfare for corporate control into the nuclear age. In 1965, there were at least forty-four cash tender offers for exchange-listed companies.[47] If someone had enough money or could borrow enough—or could create some stock certificates or other pieces of paper that people were willing to accept as money—there seemed to be little that management executives could do to prevent him from moving in and kicking them out. "Your only tools really were antitrust arguments and arguments about his creditworthiness," Cheney recalled. "Tender offers were therefore very difficult to fight."

Indeed, they were difficult even to detect until they were almost a fait accompli. People who made tender offers did not have to comply with the disclosure rules that had governed proxy fights since the mid-1950s. There was no way to tell where the would-be acquirer was getting the money to do the deal, or who his backers were, or how much of the stock he already controlled—facts which had to be made abundantly clear in a proxy fight. As one contemporaneous account noted, "The tender offer is designed as a blitzkrieg—move in fast, give an all-powerful appearance, keep up a steady barrage, and establish a solid position before anybody has a chance to think."[48] The managers of the target companies, who probably thought that the world held no evil greater than a proxy raider, gradually discovered they were wrong.

The choice of targets was changing, as well. The government's widely publicized antitrust initiatives, so infuriating to Tom Evans, had made most new company-shoppers more careful. They shunned companies whose business or products resembled their own, and they ignored vendors and distributors who stood upstream and downstream from their own manufacturing processes. The so-called horizontal and vertical acquisitions were considered "either illegal or passé," as one financial writer observed.[49] Indeed, the more unlikely the business, the better these new company-hunters liked it, since the antitrust bloodhounds were not inclined to sniff around the deal. (And they were still on the prowl, as Tom Evans learned in 1965, when H. K. Porter was once again accused of criminal violations of the antitrust laws in a case involving hydraulic hoses made by its Thermoid division in Pittsburgh. It paid a $15,000 fine after pleading "no contest."[50])

The technique of paying for a corporate takeover was evolving in unexpected ways. Some of the conservative big-city banks were still reluctant to allow takeover-minded businessmen to borrow the money they needed for an unwelcome tender offer, but it did not take long before the competitive juices and attractive fees wore down that resistance. It almost didn't matter: the stock market, after a brief, steep stumble in 1962, was roaring ahead, making it increasingly easy to use stock certificates as the coin of the takeover realm.[51] Notes and bonds were almost as easy to sell, and could help immensely in financing a tender offer.

Once again, merger activity went into overdrive and public fascination with the "conglomerateurs" kept pace with their frantic and overheated activity. Almost everyone knew the story of how Jimmy Ling had sold stock at the 1955 Texas state fair to raise money for his Ling Electric Company, the tiny rock on which he built the improbable edifice of the LTV Corporation.[52] Royal Little, who build Textron from a modest textile manufacturer into a highly diversified giant before he retired in 1962, was cultivated for his pithy comments and sound common sense. And as the decade progressed, former accountant Harold Geneen came to be seen as the archetype of the modern scientific manager, capable of managing anything through strict attention to the facts and figures.

Geneen believed in diversification and growth through acquisitions, not because they were exciting but because they were prudent—it was simply less risky to buy an existing business than to try to build one from scratch, as one Wall Street veteran observed.[53] In 1959, Geneen was recruited as the president of International Telephone and Telegraph, or ITT. It had been founded in 1920 and already had a colorful history, but Geneen would transform it. First, he implemented the kind of financial reporting system that the earlier "polyglot" entrepreneurs like Tom Evans had always used to monitor the financial performance of their subsidiaries. Then, he initiated a formal acquisition program, looking for "firms in industries with high growth and potential for continued growth."[54] The currency he used for these acquisitions was the firm's own stock. By 1964, after dozens of acquisitions, Geneen had doubled the revenues and the profits of ITT.[55]

Under the leadership of Charles "Tex" Thornton and Roy Ash, Litton Industries undertook a similar rapid-fire merger program between 1954 and 1966, pushing their annual sales from $12 million to $1 billion.[56] By 1958, they had expanded beyond the electronics industry to acquire companies that made typewriters, packaged foods, and conveyor belts.[57] Similar acquisition-driven diversification was seen by the Eaton Company, Daystrom, and Rockwell Standard, soon to be called North American Rockwell.

The business press was fascinated by the conglomerate-builders, men like Harold Geneen and Tex Thornton, with their impressive grasp of the financial minutiae of their wildly diverse empires. Many of them were vigorous nonconformists who spent their new money in vibrant and noisy ways. Antiques, art treasures, elegant marble mansions provided a delicious counterpoint to their rough and volatile personalities. Like their immediate ancestors, men like Tom Evans and Lou Wolfson and Charlie Green, they were outsiders who thumbed their noses at the polite conventions of corporate America.

And even the Wall Street establishment was captivated by their Topsy-like firms, which soon became the favorite portfolio choices for the high-growth mutual funds that were coming to dominate the burgeoning fund industry. Or, to be more exact, Wall Street was fascinated by the impact that rapid-fire acquisitions were having on these companies' earnings per share. That had become the golden yardstick by which stocks were measured—not return on assets, and certainly not dividends, but simply the annual profits divided by the number of shares outstanding. So long as the conglomerate-builders produced ever-increasing earnings per share, no one looked too closely at the methods they had employed to do so.

The general enthusiasm for conglomerates among analysts, investors, and journalists was part of the fuel that drove the "go-go" stock market to new heights as the sixties advanced. A few Wall Street firms came to dominate the deal-making: the increasingly important Lazard Frères, under the imperious hand of André Meyer and his young lieutenant, Felix Rohatyn; the aggressive young firm of Carter, Berlind and Weill in New York; the irreverent West Coast firm of Kleiner, Bell and Company; and the low-key powerhouse, Allen and Company. In this growth-crazed marketplace, the stocks of the metastasizing conglomerates soared. That provided the eager deal-makers with the very currency they needed to do more acquisitions and report higher earnings per share. To be sure, those earnings were artificially inflated by the flexible accounting techniques that the conglomerate-builders were able to use. But if the SEC did not protest this creative accounting, why should Wall Street complain?

In fact, the accounting profession and its regulators at the SEC were uneasy with some of these accounting techniques long before the merger mania of the 1960s got into full swing. What particularly worried them was the widespread use of the "pooling" method of accounting for mergers, instead of the more conservative "purchase" method.

When an accountant used the purchase method to depict the consequences of an acquisition, he calculated the difference between the book value of the target firm's assets and the price the acquiring firm actually paid for those assets. The difference was assumed to be an intangible asset known as "goodwill," the elusive quality that had prompted the acquiring firm to pay more than the target firm's assets were technically worth. For example, a company acquiring the Brown Company, with its $60 million in assets, might well have been willing to pay $80 million, given the suspicion that the company's timberland was worth far more than the company's books reported. For accounting purposes, that deal would have produced $20 million in goodwill. Like any tangible asset, that goodwill had to be depreciated over time—and there was the rub for the ambitious conglomerateur. Writing off some portion of that $20 million each year would have reduced the acquiring company's reported earnings per share—with grave consequences for its stock price, given Wall Street's fixation.

So any sensible empire-builder in the early 1960s would have simply dismissed that hopelessly stodgy accountant and hired a new one who preferred the pooling treatment. This new accountant would simply ignore the acquisition and behave as if the two companies "had always been together."[58] The book value of the acquired company's assets and its annual earnings were simply added to those of its acquirer. One result of this approach would be that the Brown Company's undervalued timberland could be promptly sold at its real market value, and the difference between that value and the understated book value would be treated as instant earnings.

If the purchase did not involve the issuance of any additional stock—because it was made with borrowed money, for example—the effects of pooling were even happier. Thus, if the hypothetical purchaser of the Brown Company earned $2 million a year and had a million shares outstanding, the pooling accountant would simply have added the Brown Company's annual earnings—let's say, $500,000—to the $2 million earned by the acquiring company to produce total earnings of $2.5 million. That sum would have been divided by the number of shares outstanding, still one million. Presto! The conglomerate's earnings have jumped from $2 a share to $2.50 a share. And that was the kind of earnings-per-share growth that myopic Wall Street was willing to pay for.

Until 1957, the accounting profession's rules had limited the use of pooling to deals in which a firm had acquired another of roughly the same size in a similar industry and had kept its management in place. But a new rule introduced that year eased those restrictions, and pooling became the method of choice among the acquisitive conglomerates. In 1963, a study commissioned by the American Institute of Certified Public Accountants, the profession's standard-setting agency of that day, condemned the widespread application of pooling, and called for new rules that would have substantially eliminated its use in most of the conglomerate mergers of the day. But strident resistance from the corporate community and inaction by both the Institute and the SEC prevented any reform.

The result was an environment in which companies were encouraged to increase their earnings per share by making as many acquisitions as they could, with borrowed money if possible. Indeed, as one corporate attorney of the day observed, "billions of dollars of economic activity" in the mid-1960s "was accounted for in a manner that almost literally everyone knew was an inadequate and sometimes downright misleading method of dealing with the transactions."[59]

Taken together, these favorable accounting gimmicks, widespread antitrust concerns, and the age-old pursuit of the tenderly taxed capital gains unleashed a stampede of mergers that dwarfed the takeovers that had so alarmed Congress in 1955. These deals did not simply erase the small-town companies and sleepy family-owned firms that had been gobbled up in the previous decade. Before the decade ended, one out of every five companies on the *Fortune* 500 had been acquired by someone, occasionally by someone who was a fraction of the target company's size. And every time "a company minnow would successfully ingest a corporate whale," observed business journalist John Brooks, "the other monsters would tremble."[60]

After trembling, they would call their senator, their lawyer, and their public relations agency.

Demands for protection from the tender-offer ambush had become sufficiently loud that in October 1965, Senator Harrison Williams of New Jersey—a state that many *Fortune* 500 companies called home—took action to protect "proud old companies" from this new threat. He submitted a bill that essentially applied the proxy-fight disclosure standards to the hostile tender offer. Under his bill, any shareholder or alliance of shareholders seeking to make a tender offer for 5 percent or more of a public company's stock had to file a report with the SEC at least twenty days in advance. That report had to disclose "the identity of the person making the offer, pre-existing shareholdings, the purpose of the tender offer, and the plans of the tenderer if he won control of the company."[61] The SEC slowly tinkered with the senator's proposal, increasing the threshold amount to 10 percent and eliminating the requirement that the reports be filed twenty days in advance, and even those weaker protections were not adopted until 1968. The new rules were still an improvement over those that had governed the fights for control in the early fifties. But by the late sixties, even a former SEC chairman considered them "obsolete" and "inadequate" in the face of "mid-twentieth-century industrial warfare."[62]

Fortunately for embattled managers, the lawyers and public relations experts acted with greater speed to devise defenses to the unwelcome tender offer. These "chesslike countermoves," as journalist John Brooks called them, included the adoption of less conservative accounting techniques to boost management's apparent performance and the overnight acquisition of some other company whose purchase made the unwelcome acquisition harder and more expensive. "A shrewd variation of this move was to buy up a company that sold products in direct competition with some of those made by the aggressor conglomerate, in hopes of creating an antitrust obstacle to the takeover," Brooks reported.[63] Beyond that, there were the old weapons from the proxy wars: appeals to Congress for protective action, appeals to shareholders to put loyalty above profit, and appeals to Wall Street to place a higher value on the target company's stock.[64]

In many ways, of course, the conglomerate trend was simply an intensification of developments that had been occurring in the outlying districts of American business since soon after the war. H. K. Porter was an industrial conglomerate, as was Wolfson's Merritt-Chapman and Scott and Silberstein's Penn-Texas. Several of the eight "polyglot" companies that *Business Week* profiled in June 1956 would be renamed "conglomerates" less than a decade later. But the new methods of conducting takeover fights and the sheer scale and volume of the takeover activity seemed to brand the conglomerateur as a different breed from the proxy raider of the late 1940s and early 1950s.

To be sure, the target companies had changed in ways that slightly buffered the impact of these corporate games on the lives of workers. The rise of "scientific management" had perhaps made corporation life less individualistic and family-like than it had been under the "founder-owner" model of the prewar years, but there had been major improvements in how workers were treated. "By 1960 some of the larger corporations, such as IBM, offered their employees clean, landscaped places to work in as well as benefits such as employer-subsidized health care, paid holidays, and sick leaves. . . . By the early 1960s millions of American employees could count on annual paid vacations—an unthinkable blessing for most people in the 1930s."[65] These were changes that not even the most iconoclastic cost-cutting takeover artist could entirely erase without labor disruption or an exodus of skilled workers and managers. It was a time of almost unbelievable affluence, extending more broadly than ever before across the population, and new jobs were not excessively difficult for discontented workers and executives to find.

But the rampaging conglomerates nevertheless raised the corporate anxiety level substantially. One witty but sympathetic account of this era, by *New York Times* reporter Isadore Barmash, was entitled *Welcome to Our Conglomerate—You're Fired!* Careers were derailed, and the rewards of long service and loyalty evaporated. Heartland communities were especially affected, since most of the new conglomerates were headquartered in the great coastal cities. "The result was the repeated reduction of mid-American cities' oldest established industries from independent ventures to subsidiaries of conglomerate spiderwebs based in New York or Los Angeles," Brooks observed.[66]

Pittsburgh, Brooks added, had been especially affected, with about a dozen major local corporations being taken over by corporations based elsewhere. "The conglomerate phenomena was like a tornado that left [the city] battered and shaken; it is unlikely to think of itself in quite the old way ever again."[67]

It was a development that Tom Evans had watched carefully from his office in the Porter Building on Grant Street. One by one, local companies that would have been a good fit for some other Pittsburgh-based corporation had been bought up instead by outsiders. And why? Because of the stodgy, unimaginative leadership of his hometown corporations. "If Pittsburgh people do not have the enterprise, you can't blame someone else for coming in and doing it," he said when hometown reporters asked him about the wave of takeovers.[68]

Tom Evans did have the enterprise, but curiously it was not clear that he was still considered to be part of the Pittsburgh business community. Pittsburgh was still H. K. Porter's official headquarters, but Evans had moved the Crane Company's headquarters to New York, where he also maintained an office for Porter. Those offices were tucked on either side of the offices of Evans and Company at 300 Park Avenue, a short walk north from Grand Central Station and within easy reach of the Yale Club. His visits to his hometown had become less frequent, and some local newspaper reporters no longer described him as "the Pittsburgh industrialist" but rather as "the chairman of Crane Company (and H. K. Porter Company, based here)."

His uneasy status crystallized in May 1967, when he arranged a visit with John A. Mayer, chairman of Mellon Bank in Pittsburgh. He had known Johnny Mayer for years, and H. K. Porter kept several million dollars on deposit with old Judge Mellon's institution, located in a magnificent Greco-Roman building a few blocks from Porter's new office tower. But Evans wasn't there on banking business. He knew that Mayer and three other businessmen associated with the bank served on the board of the Westinghouse Air Brake Company in Pittsburgh. Evans already owned a substantial stake in the company and he wanted to do a deal.[69]

Westinghouse Air Brake—or Wabco, as it was known in the business community—had been founded in 1869 by George Westinghouse, the prolific American inventor who separately launched the Westinghouse Electric Company. Wabco seemed to stand in the public mind as a monument to the golden age of Pittsburgh industry, when the building blocks of a burgeoning national economy were fabricated in the city's mills and factories and laboratories. Its fortunes, as its name suggested, had been built on the air brake, which revolutionized the critical process of slowing and stopping several hurtling tons of locomotive steel. Improved brakes allowed trains to travel faster, but their speed soon outstripped the ability of human signalmen to direct train traffic. So George Westinghouse developed new automatic signaling devices and equipment that could keep pace. By 1967, Wabco had added some earth-moving equipment and mining machinery to its product line, but brakes and signals were still the heart of its business. In the Pittsburgh community, 4,000 people were employed at the air-brake factory in outlying Wilmerding and another 2,000 worked at the signal equipment plant in Swissvale.[70] Wabco's top executives had supported Pittsburgh's efforts to renovate its downtown area by signing a long-term lease for space in the new Gateway Center, the centerpiece of the Golden Triangle district. The directors who gathered in the Wabco boardroom were a Who's Who of Pittsburgh's industrial elite, including a former chairman of the U.S. Steel Corporation, a former chairman of Alcoa, and the chairman of Allegheny Ludlum Steel Corporation. At the head of the table was A. King McCord, a handsome, silver-haired figure who at the age of sixty-four was well entrenched in the local business establishment.

But when Tom Evans looked at Wabco he did not see an admirable corporate citizen contributing to the well-being and public infrastructure of its community, under the wise leadership of industrial statesmen. He saw a company that had grown fat and unimaginative, feeding too often on the easy credit provided by its Mellon bank directors, with inadequate financial controls and excessive inventories. He itched to get his hands on the company, to merge it with Crane and put it through his quick-weight-loss regime until it was generating the profits for shareholders he thought possible.

The deal made sense to Evans. Crane manufactured brakes for jet aircraft, and Wabco made train brakes; together, the two companies would be in a position to stop just about anything huge that moved in the American economy. But his warm passion got a cool reception from his old friend Johnny Mayer, a dimpled-chinned man with thinning hair and close-set, piercing eyes. Buddy Evans could not shake his rough-handed history, not even here in the city that had earlier known him as a shy, orphaned boy at Shady Side and a hard-working apprentice at W. L. Mellon's Gulf. So when Evans talked about a "merger," the banker seemed to hear the word "takeover." Although profoundly surprised, he listened to Evans politely— the Porter chairman was, after all, a major customer of the bank. They briefly discussed the skimpy pension plan that the board had put in place for chief executive McCord, and how that might influence his view of any merger that would force him into retirement. Evans was sure some comfortable solution could be found.[71]

John Mayer was less than enthusiastic. Crane's stock market value was just two-thirds of Wabco's, after all. So perhaps Wabco should acquire Crane instead, Mayer said with a challenging grin. In any case, he added, Evans was negotiating with the wrong man, and should take his offer directly to McCord. As he left his old friend's office, Evans knew "we weren't going to receive a warm welcome."[72]

The uneasy, psychedelic summer of 1967 unfolded, and Evans continued to accumulate Wabco stock. In September, he arranged to meet with McCord to discuss his unwelcome merger. His proposal was more fully developed this time, detailing a marriage of the two boards that would give Wabco a majority of the seats. And there was a role for McCord: chairman of a new executive committee. But Evans himself obviously intended to be chief executive.[73]

Evans, his big smile crimping his face into a squint, was calm and pleasant. Unlike the conglomerateurs, he said, he wasn't simply trying to build a big empire for the mere sake of bigness. He truly thought the two companies would both benefit from the marriage, and that it should be explored. McCord agreed to have some consultants study whether the two companies fit together as well as Evans thought they would. Evans smiled, shook hands, and left for New York, where he continued to accumulate Wabco stock.[74]

As Thanksgiving approached, McCord informed Evans that the merger got a failing grade from his consultants—although he declined to identify them, or provide Evans with their report, or explain why they had never contacted Crane for information about its businesses. "There was no material fit whatsoever" between the two companies, he told Evans.[75] And therefore, Wabco's directors had decided that the merger was not in the best interest of the company's shareholders.

Its largest shareholder, Tom Evans's Crane Company, disagreed. But Evans took the news with a calm resignation that would have made anyone who knew him better quite suspicious. And he continued to buy Wabco stock.

On December 13, he met again with King McCord in the Gateway Center headquarters. Evans told McCord how disappointed he was at the board's rejection of his proposal, and suggested that "there were some areas were there could be a reconsideration." For example, with respect to the role McCord would play in the merged companies, no doubt a lifetime consulting arrangement could be set up that would supplement McCord's pension, and a stock option plan could be arranged that would put 5,000 shares of Crane stock into McCord's portfolio.[76]

"I told him that this proposal was improper and I did not wish to discuss it any further," McCord later reported. "Such proposals were inappropriate."

Evans later joked, "I guess they weren't inappropriate enough."[77] He left McCord's office unchastened; after all, he was still Wabco's largest shareholder. On December 14, perhaps not entirely by coincidence, Wabco's stock leaped up nearly $6 a share. Wall Street was whispering: Evans was on the prowl.

Almost as soon as Evans left his office, McCord began preparing to defend the Wabco castle and its Establishment occupants from this "fast-buck artist" who swooped into town on his private plane and threatened to turn life upside down for all of them.

Meeting with the company's lawyers, he and his staff drafted a shareholder letter that would sound the alarm. While Wabco was considering the merger proposal "in good faith," McCord told his stockholders, Evans had been quietly buying up stock behind his back. On December 15, 1967, as the letter reached local investors, the alarm was spread to the broader Pittsburgh community, with headlines announcing "Air Brake Fears Raid on Company." Large blocks of stock had been bought up in the name of nominee accounts, a spokesman told reporters, and the company's efforts to find out the actual owners had been futile. Wabco insisted publicly that it did not know who was behind the buying, but somehow local reporters thought of calling Tom Evans in New York to see if he planned to make a tender offer for Wabco's stock. He had no such plans "at this time," he said. But had he approached the company? "I get to Pittsburgh now and then and I am pretty friendly with all of them and we talk from time to time," he said, grinning from ear to ear.[78]

Without openly invoking the Evans name, Wabco executives explained in their shareholder letter that the company planned to defend itself by adopting a staggered system for electing directors, so that only three members of its nine-member board ran for office each year. Staggered elections had been a favorite defensive ploy for embattled managers ever since the reign of Sewell Avery at Montgomery Ward, of course. But here, as always, the move was described as defending the stockholders—excepting stockholder Evans, of course—not the executives.[79]

Three days later, in a second letter to stockholders, McCord openly accused Tom Evans of attempting a takeover at Wabco. He didn't need to describe the controversy that had surrounded his adversary for more than a decade—everyone knew about the union jobs eliminated at Crane, the pace at which executives burned out at Porter, Evans's relentless demand that people shape up or get out. But McCord did detail his various previous meetings with Evans, the offers that had been made to him and rejected, the consultants' verdict on the merger, and Evans's treacherous stock purchases while the company was carefully considering his offer with an open mind and good grace.

In fact, while rallying Pittsburgh to Wabco's fight for its independence, McCord had been secretly scrambling since November to find some other buyer willing to snatch Wabco from Evans's grasp. Approaches had been made to Willard Rockwell's rapidly diversifying conglomerate, North American Rockwell, but nothing came of them. Then McCord held secret talks with William D. Eberle, the tall genial chief executive of the giant American Standard, Crane's chief rival in the plumbing fixtures industry. The relaxed Eberle, a westerner who had taken over American Standard a few years earlier after distinguishing himself at the Boise Cascade paper company, was interested. And McCord could see that a merger with American Standard would invoke handy antitrust defenses against Crane's continued investment. Eberle seemed willing to leave local management in place and to add McCord and several other Wabco directors to his own board.

But at a time when computers were primitive and slide rules could still be found in any finance executive's briefcase, calculations for a rescue merger of this magnitude would take time. So McCord, with Evans at his gates, settled in for a long siege.

Pennsylvania law allowed any stockholder to inspect his company's list of stockholders for any "reasonable purpose," and in December, Tom Evans asked twice to be allowed to see the shareholder registry. Both times, he was refused—on the grounds that his purposes were not "reasonable."[80] Finally, on January 3, Crane Company went into court in Pittsburgh, demanding access to the shareholder list. Evans used the occasion to emphasize how little stock Wabco's directors and executives owned, compared to his own substantial holdings. He singled out his friend Johnny Mayer, who owned only 100 shares. "We just can't understand why he would be a director if he or the bank does not own any more stock than that," said Tom Evans. "As far as we know, we are the largest shareholder of Air Brake—but of course we do not have the list," he continued. And he hinted that he might make an issue of the company's move to elect only three directors each year. That arrangement "effectively reduces shareholder participation in the affairs of the corporation," Crane had charged in its complaint. "They may have trouble with that," said Evans, his eyes twinkling. "The SEC is very tough on disenfranchising stockholders." [81]

Evans seemed perfectly at ease with the Pittsburgh press corps. He entertained reporters in his office in the Porter building, joking and fencing with them while he lectured them about the rights of the forgotten share-holder—all without ever openly mentioning Wabco. "I've always felt that the stockholders are the true owners of business," he told them at one impromptu press conference. When a reporter bluntly asked Evans about accusations that he had raided companies in the past, he instantly responded, "If a company is well run, it isn't available."[82] He talked exten-sively about how he had restored the health of Crane, hinting broadly that he could do the same at Wabco.

Shortly before the complaint over the shareholder list came to trial in Pittsburgh, Evans heard disturbing news. An executive at one of the big proxy solicitation firms in New York told him that Wabco had hired the First Boston Company, a prominent Wall Street investment bank, to help find a buyer. Two days later, an old friend in Pittsburgh had picked up the same piece of gossip. Evans told his traders to pick up additional Wabco shares whenever they could.[83]

The trial over Crane's demand for access to Wabco's stockholder list opened before a local jury on January 30, 1968. The jurors heard Evans described as an opportunist who was trying to "make a quick killing and a fast buck." He wasn't an investor, Wabco's lawyers argued in court, he was a speculator, trying to milk some $80 million from Wabco to benefit Crane.[84] Evans testified for more than three hours, his restless energy and combative intelligence making him seem like a man in motion even as he sat in the witness box. Pressed to explain why he had continued buying Wabco stock, Evans said, "We didn't buy any more until last week when we heard they were going to peddle the company."[85] As for his business strat-egy, Evans insisted, "We are not in this to make a fast buck. And we can't force a merger without the consent of directors and a majority of the stock-holders." He made no apologies for the offers he had made to McCord, tes-tifying that John Mayer had told him that McCord was dissatisfied with his pension and compensation arrangements. When McCord took offense, "the subject was dropped," Evans told the court.[86]

King McCord led the parade of corporate aristocrats who testified on Wabco's behalf. Remarkably, McCord testified under oath that there was no truth to Evans's suggestions that Wabco was looking for another suitor who would absorb Wabco.[87] John Mayer of the Mellon bank assured the jurors that Evans was trying to swing a takeover, not the friendly merger he described. And Leslie B. Worthington, the former president of the U.S. Steel Corporation, assured the court that Evans's plan would be bad for shareholders. But perhaps the most memorable moment of the four-day trial came when Keith D. Bunnel, the vice president and treasurer of Wabco, said that what Evans was proposing "would be like the canary swallowing the cat" because Wabco was so much larger than Crane, by his measurement.[88]

The local jurors deliberated less than three hours before deciding on February 2 that Evans was not entitled to inspect the stockholder list at Wabco.[89] Evans immediately appealed the verdict to a three-judge panel, and also renewed his demands in a lawsuit filed in federal court in New York. And finally, on February 20, 1968, he revealed that Crane planned to wage a proxy fight to put three of its candidates on Wabco's nine-member board at the annual meeting, scheduled for April 18. McCord said the proxy fight was simply part of Evans's continuing campaign to force a merger, and would be valiantly resisted.[90]

On March 4, resistance took the form of putting the final touches on McCord's secret deal with American Standard, which had just started acquiring Wabco shares on its own to strengthen its hand against Evans. At noon that day, after the details of the merger were settled, Bill Eberle telephoned Crane president Dante Fabiani, and asked to meet with Evans that afternoon. Fabiani told Eberle that he and Evans expected to spend most of the day at the Wall Street offices of Dominick and Dominick, Crane's investment adviser. Eberle arranged to meet them there. But when he arrived at the brokerage firm, Fabiani met him in the reception room and asked if Eberle still needed to meet with Tom Evans. Fabiani added, by way of explanation, "Someone is trying to buy Westinghouse Air Brake and he's busy trying to find out who it is."

Eberle smiled. "That's what I want to see Evans about. We are the people."[91]

Pittsburgh was stunned when McCord announced that afternoon that Wabco had agreed to be acquired by American Standard. Jack Markowitz, the business editor of the *Post-Gazette*, pointedly reminded his readers that McCord had denied any merger negotiations just weeks earlier. Indeed, he said, "McCord's public position until yesterday was that Wabco wanted a merger with no one."[92] While neither side indicated "how long the two firms had been negotiating," Markowitz astutely observed that "yesterday's agreement was sufficiently detailed to be voted by the boards of directors of both companies." And of course there was the obvious question: if Crane, with its plumbing and valve business, was a poor fit with Wabco, why was American Standard, with its plumbing and heating business, a better fit?

Evans raised the same issues. In a statement he released to the press, Evans said, "Because of Mr. McCord's statements under oath in the court case in Pittsburgh—that Wabco had no plans of negotiations for merger with another firm—we are rather surprised at this course of events. We have been advised by American Standard that they have been negotiating with Wabco since last November."[93] There is no indication that either McCord or Eberle ever contradicted Evans on that embarrassing point of timing.

Evans battled on, putting his own proposal to acquire Wabco before stockholders through his proxy fight and increasing his stake in the company. He and Eberle waged a public relations battle in the weeks leading up to the stockholders meeting, which had been rescheduled for May 16 to give shareholders time to review the competing proposals.

On May 16, nearly 500 shareholders gathered at the Carnegie Music Hall in the Oakland area of Pittsburgh to vote on which suitor should marry their company. Evans, dapper in a dark suit and snow-white shirt with his pocket handkerchief perfectly arranged, settled in the second row of the vast auditorium, surrounded by his lawyers and several senior Crane executives. King McCord presided, and he and Evans were "reserved and courteous to each other," by one account.[94] Evans remained cool as stockholders rose to condemn his actions and his reputation. "Many stockholders don't understand mergers and such battles as this one," he told a reporter, as the meeting was adjourned to allow for the proxies to be counted.

But he came face to face with how he was perceived in his hometown when a tiny elderly woman approached him after the meeting, her fists clenched. "I don't like you. I don't like anything about you. I am very much against you," she spat at Evans.

"Thank you," Evans replied gently.[95]

It had been a rough day. At breakfast, Evans had been faced with a highly unflattering profile on the front page of the *Wall Street Journal*. The headlines, stacked up atop the column, set the tone: "Brash Battler: Tom Evans' Take-Overs Build a Vast Fortune, Stir Hot Controversy; Crane, Porter Firms Grow Amid Executive Turmoil; Key Vote at Wabco Today; Make Profits Quick—or Else." The writer had collected all the controversies of his career, except for the criminal antitrust violations, of course; almost every major firm had one or two of those in its closet by then.

Friends described him as "pleasant and even charming," with "seemingly boundless energy" and a wide range of interests. "But his best friends concede that this chatty acquaintance becomes a very different person in business deals," the *Journal* writer continued. "An associate who describes Mr.

Evans as 'quite shy and proper on the personal side' says that 'on the business side he's extremely bellicose—rough, hard-driving, a tough guy.' . . . A confrontation with him can be a nerve-shattering experience for a subordinate, says one former Porter executive: 'He'll call somebody a dumb bastard or an ignorant son of a bitch, and the guy has no choice but to put up with it—until he can find another job.' "[96]

Then there was the meeting in Pittsburgh, and more attacks on his character and methods. Worst of all, perhaps, was King McCord's big smile. He was confident of victory, and he was right. Although Evans controlled 31 percent of Wabco, the final tally in early June showed that American Standard had won the fight.[97]

However much he had been wounded in his last hometown fight, Evans did not pout in public. He simply removed $2 million in Crane and Porter deposits from his old friend Johnny Mayer's bank in Pittsburgh and offered the American Standard shares he'd gotten in the merger to the highest bidder. He sold his huge stake on June 13, in a transaction that "was by far the biggest single trade in New York Stock Exchange history." He pocketed a profit of $5 million, a balm for bruised feelings.[98]

CHAPTER TWELVE

I'LL BE AROUND

The massive transaction that relieved Tom Evans of his unwanted American Standard shares, while a momentary record, was increasingly typical of life on Wall Street. The robust stock market, which had seen the Dow Jones Industrial Average climb from 535.76 at the end of a brief slump in June 1962 to 985.21 by the end of 1968, had generated enormous growth in the securities industry. New branch offices, battalions of young stockbrokers, burgeoning trading desks all sprang up to serve not only the individual investor but also the increasingly aggressive money managers running the nation's mutual funds. Evans and Company was caught up in the expansion, as well, adding branch offices, traders, and salesmen.

What Wall Street had not done during the long string of fat years, however, was tend to the simple paper-pushing details of receiving money from customers and making sure that the customers got their stocks in return. Securities went astray with increasing frequency as the decade advanced. Money that was owed was not collected. Shares were delivered to the wrong accounts. Back-office clerks, their ranks unequal to the task, labored in Cratchit-like conditions, trying to keep track of buyers and sellers with tools that would have been familiar to clerks of centuries past.

In that crisis year of 1968—as America was beset by heartbreaking assassinations and race riots and profound division over the stalemated war in Vietnam—Wall Street was drowning in a sea of unprocessed paper. The stock exchange closed early one afternoon each week to give its own clerks enough time to catch up. Many of its member firms never did catch

261

up with their paperwork, and simply failed, leaving their customers to pick up the pieces. By one estimate, back-office procedures had become so haphazard that somewhere between $100 million and $400 million worth of securities simply vanished from the system, presumably stolen, during the last half of the decade.[1]

Throughout the business Establishment, there was a sense of crisis, of the world having turned upside down. Long-haired college students were picketing in idealistic anger outside the offices of Dow Chemical and other defense contractors, condemning as "killers" the very generals of capitalism whose success had helped finance their own comfortable childhoods. Famous old firms whose executives were among the aristocrats of the Street had been ruined because of the inadequacies of a lowly bunch of clerks in the backroom. Huge, powerful mutual funds were run by arrogant young men who would have been considered little more than apprentices a generation earlier.

This uneasy sense of chaos was confirmed for many Wall Street leaders by the remarkable rise of the Leasco Data Processing Equipment Corporation, the brainchild of an ambitious young man named Saul Steinberg. Started in a Brooklyn loft in 1961, Leasco by 1967 had grown into a substantial supplier of leased computers. That year, with the help of only slightly older investment bankers at the deal-minded firm of Carter, Berlind and Weill, the young Steinberg began looking for ways to put his increasing supply of cash and credit to work. In March 1968, Leasco quietly began accumulating a stake in Reliance Insurance Company, a Philadelphia property and casualty insurer that was more than ten times Leasco's size. In May, Leasco shocked Wall Street by filing an audacious tender offer for Reliance shares—such tender offers had largely replaced proxy fights as the preferred weapon in fights for corporate control, although many among the Wall Street establishment still considered them sneaky and underhanded.[2] By mid-November, the loquacious, outgoing Steinberg had acquired Reliance and was heralded as having "made more money on his own—over $50 million, on paper—than any other U.S. citizen under 30."[3]

But then, having acquired an insurance company, the exuberant young Steinberg thought it would be neat to own a major commercial bank, just to round things out. All through 1968, his financial staff had been quietly buying shares in the $9 billion Chemical Bank of New York, which had been founded in 1824 and had become one of the pillars of the banking community. In February 1969, Steinberg's remarkable ambition leaked out to the press, which seized on its David-and-Goliath aspects with delight. "Can a Johnny-come-lately on the business scene move in on the Establishment and knock off one of the biggest prizes in sight?" asked Robert Metz of the *New York Times*.[4]

The answer, it turned out, was "over the Establishment's dead body." Chemical Bank considered itself under siege—"there was a sense of backs to the wall, of the barbarians at the gates, of time running out."[5] The bank enlisted the help of Joe Flom, by now one of the leading practitioners of the legal arts of corporate warfare. When Flom arrived at Chemical headquarters on a Saturday, he was ushered into an immense conference room that was "simply filled with people." Flom quickly realized he had to get the group down to a manageable size, so he started handing out assignments to the lesser lieutenants: one would organize the public relations staff, another would analyze Leasco's financial statements, and so forth. As they hastened from the room to begin their work, Flom was finally left with a cadre of top executives with whom he could meaningfully discuss a plan to repel the upstart raider.[6]

Steinberg himself understood "that Chemical had the sympathy of a good portion of American industry." After all, he continued, "if a fast-growing company like ours could knock over the country's sixth largest bank, who was safe?"[7] Levers were pulled and legislation appeared in Albany, with the backing of Govenor Nelson Rockefeller, that would empower the state to stop any takeover of a bank by any nonbanking entity where "the exercise of control might impair the safe and sound conduct of the bank."[8] A similar proposal was submitted in Washington, with powerful backers. And mysteriously, the long-healthy stock of Leasco itself began to slump under a wave of selling—sales that many suspected had been orchestrated by Chemical or its sympathizers in an effort to undermine its attacker's power base.[9] Steinberg, who argued that Chemical had been unresponsive to its true owners—its shareholders—found himself "being treated as a sort of business pirate bent on seizing and looting property that did not belong to him. . . . With the realization that the national powers of government as well as those of business were solidly aligned against him, Steinberg decided on surrender."[10] Baffled by the intense hostility of his adversary, Steinberg observed as he left the field, "I always knew there was an Establishment—I just used to think I was part of it."[11]

As the decade ended, established companies found themselves besieged not only by youthful upstarts but by seasoned veterans as well. Ben Heineman, the brilliant Chicago lawyer, had left the proxy-fight arena in 1956 to attempt the resuscitation of the Chicago and North Western Railway. He had succeeded in streamlining and diversifying the line, forging a new conglomerate called Northwest Industries. Then, in the fall of 1968, Heineman retraced his steps as Northwest began to look seriously at B. F.

Goodrich Company, a pillar of Akron and a giant of the tire and chemical industries. To Heineman, Goodrich's management looked flabby and complacent, but he was convinced that stronger hands could produce better profits at the ninety-nine-year-old behemoth. He began to build up a stake of about 2.5 percent of the company's stock, and then discovered that one of his directors, Laurence A. Tisch of the Loew's Corporation in New York, had also recognized Goodrich's potential and owned a matching stake. Then he announced an unwelcome $1 billion tender offer for Goodrich, promising stockholders a package of securities "worth between $75 and $80 for each share of Goodrich, then worth about $55."[12]

Goodrich's president, a former economics professor named J. Ward Keener, instantly mobilized for war. He attacked Northwest in full-page advertisements, pushed through staggered terms for his directors, and tried to establish an antitrust problem by buying an Indiana trucking company that competed with Northwest. He issued 700,000 new shares to buy a stake in an unprofitable synthetic-rubber plant, diluting Heineman's and Tisch's percentage of ownership. Keener even borrowed a page from the New York Central management's defenses and tried, albeit unsuccessfully, to enlist the Interstate Commerce Commission in his battle. He was luckier at the state level. The Ohio division of securities barred Northwest from registering its tender offer in that state, on the grounds that it was unable to evaluate the package of securities being offered in exchange for the Goodrich stock. And in May 1969, the Justice Department announced an antitrust investigation of the takeover attempt.

Heineman fought on, but he was clearly frustrated at the array of weapons Goodrich was marshaling in management's defense. He told one reporter, "There are a lot of frightened, stodgy companies with frightened, stodgy managements. Conservative businessmen are running to the government saying, 'Save me, save me,' and very often it is at the expense of stockholders."[13]

But Goodrich's most imaginative weapon, one that foreshadowed powerful new weapons of corporate defense, was its decision to borrow $250 million from a syndicate of twenty-one banks under terms that provided that the loan would be instantly in default if there were a takeover of the company. Federal Judge Hubert L. Will was briefed on the new financial arrangements during hearings on the Justice Department's antitrust case in Chicago. He was astonished and outraged. "Why would Goodrich voluntarily enter into an agreement under which it threatens to commit financial suicide in the event that this transaction is consummated? [The credit agreement] is a shocking document. It's the worst indictment of Goodrich management of anything in this case," the judge said. He referred to the provision that decreed a default in the event of a takeover as a "Hermann Goering cyanide pill."[14] Later generations would call such self-mutilation practices "shark repellant," and apply the judge's imagery to other, more complex defensive measures. But with the battle in Akron, a new term—poison pill—became common in the patois of the takeover world.

Goodrich succeeded in fending off Heineman, who gave up the fight in the summer of 1969. By then, the stock market had been lagging for more than six months, adding to the pain that brokerage firms were experiencing.[15] The mood in the market was grim, and some of the worst damage was sustained by the once-golden conglomerates, some of which cracked and broke apart, smashing reputations in the process.

As the retail world of Wall Street struggled to stay afloat in the summer of 1969, Tom Evans plowed through the waves from the helm of Evans and Company, watching the horizon for places to put his substantial Wabco profits to work. Some of the money was no doubt used to add to his increasingly important art collection, which by now included *The Martyrdom of Saint Paul* by Rubens, works by Winslow Homer, two fine paintings by the younger Brueghel, and Gainsborough's elegant portrait of Thomas Linley Jr.

He also invested in the Southern Pacific Railroad and Alcan Aluminum. But thanks to his developing friendship with a Wall Street powerhouse named Charlie Allen, Evans put the bulk of his winnings into a controlling stake in CF&I Steel Corporation, originally known as Colorado Fuel and Iron.

The company was a living legend in the mining industry. Originally owned by the Rockefellers, it had been the scene of the infamous Ludlow massacre in 1913, a bloody battle between armed militia and striking miners in which eleven women and children were asphyxiated in a bunker where they had sought safety during the militia attack.[16] Decades later, the Rockefellers sold their stake in the ailing company to Charles Allen, who "converted a sick company into a blooming one."[17]

Charlie Allen and his two brothers, Herbert and Harold, operated Allen and Company more like a British merchant bank than an American brokerage house. The firm picked promising companies, devised the financial structure that would enable them to grow and succeed, invested its own capital and its clients' money in the deals, and usually took a boardroom chair or two to look out for its interests. Allen himself was a graceful, charismatic man, whose world-weary expression sometimes gave him the urbane air of a Left Bank intellectual dawdling in some smoky café. He ran his investment bank the way Tom Evans had built up H. K. Porter, giving his senior staff an enormous amount of latitude to find deals, arrange the financial infrastructure for them, and take them to market. Evans had met him years earlier, and had used him to help oversee his tender offer for Wabco. During that long, ugly fight, the two men forged a foxhole friendship that Evans valued highly. "Both are tough, unsentimental mavericks, accustomed to operating outside of—and in spite of—the business establishment," *Forbes* magazine observed at the time.[18]

It was Allen who overcame Evans's initial reluctance to put more of his money to work in the troubled American steel industry, which was beset by labor strife, outmoded plants, and cheap foreign imports. H. K. Porter's steel division had troubles enough, and it was a small, specialized operation. One of its plants, in Danville, Virginia, had been embroiled in labor conflict for more than a decade as Porter refused to deduct union dues from its workers' paychecks, a practice it had accepted at some of its other plants. Moreover, although Evans may not have known, the Porter steel division had recently begun to violate federal antitrust laws. As the steel market deteriorated, Porter managers had conspired with their counterparts at four other steel companies to rig the competition for the sale of steel reinforcing bars, which are embedded in cement to give strength to the concrete structure. Even if Evans did not know how far across the line his managers went in search of profits, he knew that making steel in America had become a very tough business.

But Allen persuaded him to take a look at CF&I's operations in Pueblo, Colorado. "I changed my mind," Evans said later. "It's an excellent fully integrated mill and it services a booming part of country—Texas, Oklahoma and the Southwest. It would cost $700 million to build a mill like that today. And CF&I owns 360,000 acres of undeveloped land out there, which isn't a bad thing to have in a time of inflation."[19] Not only that, its shares were trading at around $26, or $13 below the company's book value per share—exactly the kind of situation Evans loved. Through Crane, he quietly bought a solid stake and then made a tender offer for the public's shares that ultimately would give him 83 percent of the company. The steel company was shaken, veteran executives recalled.

In May 1970, as he built up his stake, he hopped aboard his plane to meet with CF&I management at the beautiful Broadmoor Hotel in Colorado Springs. Executives of the steel company gathered in one of the private dining rooms at the elegant old mountain resort. The Broadmoor was nearly fifty miles from company headquarters in Pueblo, so most of the management team had booked rooms to stay overnight. The splendor of the Rockies, visible through the dining room windows, was being veiled by dusk as the group of about two dozen nervous managers awaited the arrival of their new shareholder. Then Evans entered, "a round, short man with very bright brown eyes," one executive recalls. "He was a cool cucumber."[20] He seemed to instantly appraise each manager presented to him, "putting each in the proper pecking order," the executive continued. A long banquet table had been set and Evans found his place between Charlie Allen and Frederick Fielder, the president of CF&I. As dinner was served, both Evans and Charlie Allen made a few introductory remarks, but Allen's greeting lacked his usual savoir faire. He was feeling the ill effects of the unaccustomed altitude; later that night, he was taken to the nearby Penrose Hospital as a precaution.

Thus it was that Al Pocius, the top public relations man at CF&I, found himself driving Tom Evans the next morning to the hospital. Evans wanted to visit with Allen before they made the trip to the Pueblo offices where Evans was to sit in on a meeting of the board of directors. Privately, Pocius was relieved at the detour. His boss, Fred Fielder, had called and asked him to delay Evans's arrival as long as he could to allow more time for management to present its case to the board of directors. But when Pocius reached the hospital and prepared to park, Evans told him briskly to just drop him off at the door and wait there. Evans left his beautiful tooled-leather briefcase in the car, and the inquisitive publicist steeled himself against the temptation to inspect its contents. Fortunately he resisted: Evans returned abruptly after ten minutes and retrieved the case before returning to Allen's bedside for a conference that stretched to nearly an hour.

When Evans returned to the car, Pocius still tried to kill time. He dawdled and detoured as subtly as he could en route to Pueblo, but Evans soon noticed they were "going in circles" and put a stop to it. When they finally reached CF&I's facilities, the board meeting was already in progress. Peeved but polite, Evans took his place on the sidelines and listened as management executives outlined a proposed modernization plan. Then he spoke up. Although he was not a director, he was a major shareholder, he said, and he felt he ought to review any proposal to spend such a substantial amount of the company's money. "A chill came over the whole group," Pocius recalls. "Everything froze at that point." The managers soon filed out of the boardroom, leaving the shaken directors to continue their meeting with their aggressive guest.

Evans had done his homework. He earmarked units that could be put on his famous cost-cutting diet, but he also was willing to put money in to modernize and support profitable operations. He could not understand the American steel industry's fixation on the quantity of tonnage produced, rather than the profits generated by that production. Imports were a problem, certainly. "The auto companies have cheaper import competition," he reasoned. "But they make money on the cars they sell." The only way American steel makers could prosper would be if they, too, made money on every ton of steel they sold.

His brisk, sometimes rude manner severely jolted the Colorado management. In a letter submitted as a congressional exhibit five years later, Pocius described Evans's reign at CF&I in extraordinarily harsh terms. "He instituted a management housecleaning, zeroing in particularly on those who had a long service but were still a couple years or so from qualifying for pensions. (I had 17 years of service and about 1 1/2 years to qualify and was dropped with just five minutes notice in the middle of a work week.) Some people were fired summarily. . . . one associate committed suicide; another attempted to do so."[21] But Evans seemed determined to make CF&I repay his confidence in Charlie Allen.

Tom Evans's zest for new challenges was increasingly at odds with the national mood—certainly, at least, the mood on Wall Street. After a rebound in the first two years of the 1970s, during which Evans spun off a subsidiary that made cordless electric products for lawn care, the stock market slumped again at the end January 1973. Then it hunkered down for a vicious bear market that cut the Dow Jones Industrial Averages almost in half over the next two years. Small investors fled, stung once again by the fickle promises of easy wealth and youthful genius. More Wall Street firms closed their doors; major mutual fund companies scraped for sales. But when the dust finally settled and the market began to nudge upward, Tom Evans was still there in his trading room at 300 Park Avenue—ready to do battle for the rights of shareholders and stir up a little management anxiety wherever he could.

To be sure, there was some belt-tightening in the Evans empire along the way. At H. K. Porter, Evans had startled his handful of minority shareholders, and the local press, by announcing in 1970 that the highly diversified company was shedding its industrial rubber and copper operations. "We made the mistake of a lot of smaller conglomerates of getting into too many fields," Evans told reporters. "In some of them, it is awfully hard to compete with the giants."[22] He also arranged to spin off Porter's Disston division, which dominated the nation's hand-saw market, raising approximately $30 million in cash for the parent company.

The pruning and cash infusion helped, and Porter's profits began to recover. But those profit levels were not what they seemed, according to the Justice Department. In April 1972, the department's antitrust division filed a civil suit against H. K. Porter, charging that it had been violating the Sherman Antitrust Act since at least 1956. The division charged that Porter, in addition to fixing prices and rigging bids at its customers' expense, had strong-armed its suppliers, refusing to deal with them unless they in turn agreed to buy only from Porter when they shopped for the products Porter made. These so-called "reciprocal purchasing compacts" were violations of the law although they had no doubt helped bolster Porter's sales. A month after the suit was filed Porter consented, without admitting any wrongdoing, to a court order that prohibited it from pursuing such behavior in the future.[23]

By now, however, the business community and the public in general barely raised an eyebrow over antitrust violations, even criminal ones. What did raise a few eyebrows among the cognoscenti in March 1972 was Porter's assault on the Nicholson File Company in Providence, Rhode Island. Nicholson was the world's largest maker of abrasive metal files. Evans's pursuit of it, which attracted only a little attention, was a template for deals that would soon be sprouting up all over the corporate landscape.

After Porter purchased 7 percent of Nicholson in the marketplace and then announced a hostile tender offer that would raise its stake to 80 percent, management dug in its heels, determined not to be acquired by Evans, whatever the cost. And the cost to shareholders, initially, looked pretty high: Evans was offering $42 in cash for Nicholson's stock, which was trading at about $30 a share, well below its book value of about $53 a share. Nevertheless, Nicholson president George C. Williams appealed to shareholders to stand firm. "It stands to reason that if Porter is willing to pay you $42 per share for your stock, it must see value higher than its offer," Williams wrote to stockholders. Indeed, he assured stockholders that management had been "contacted by a number of substantial corporations" who were interested in Nicholson, although no firm deal had been placed on the table yet.[24]

Evans, in his own letter to stockholders, was skeptical. Other firms had approached Nicholson in the past, he wrote, but "these overtures have been uniformly rejected by Nicholson's management. That Nicholson is now suddenly considering such action raises a serious question as to whether its management is really thinking of your best interests." After all, Evans noted—as he could never resist doing—President Williams himself owned only 285 shares of his company's stock, while Evans already owned 43,806 shares.[25]

Two other bidders surfaced and began to bid against one another. When Nicholson attempted to consummate a deal with one of its suitors, Porter obtained a court order that halted Nicholson's annual meeting in the midst of the election of directors.[26] As one of Nicholson's largest shareholders, Evans would be the primary beneficiary of whatever deal the Nicholson management cooked up—and he thought he could do better than the one management preferred. He was right. By June, Nicholson had agreed to be acquired by Cooper Industries of Texas, and Evans walked away with a big smile and a nice profit.[27]

He had, in fact, discovered other ways to win a takeover battle besides actually taking over the target company. Sometimes it was enough to simply put the company on Wall Street's radar screen by highlighting its obvious value, and then waiting for someone else to win the bidding. No one yet called this "putting the company in play," perhaps because golf and Ivy League football still provided most of the sports metaphors for Wall Street's leaders. But it amounted to the same thing.

Although Evans's success in the Nicholson bidding war in 1972 attracted little attention, a much larger deal followed exactly the same script two years later, in 1974. In July of that year, the International Nickel Company, known as Inco, began a campaign to take control of ESB, a substantial corporation in Philadelphia, where it was still referred to by its former name, the Electric Storage Battery Company.[28] And this time, Wall Street did notice. Indeed, people in the takeover business would come to call it the "first hostile takeover," just as the New York Central and the Montgomery Ward proxy fights were each sometimes called the "first" proxy fights. It may have been the first *successful* hostile tender offer, however. And in any case, it represented a subtle shift in the nature of these fights for control. The battles that were waged during the first two decades after the war resembled the Napoleonic wars, highly personalized campaigns. The earliest raiders were individuals with a capital "I"—Young, Evans, Green, Silberstein, Wolfson, Heineman, Steinberg—and the corporate vehicles they used were almost incidental to the fight. But the ESB fight ushered in a style of warfare resembling the collision of the Allies and the Axis Powers in World War II. These raiders were huge corporations, many of them household names; but the battles were actually fought by largely anonymous armies of investment bankers, lawyers, and senior executives, laboring in the trenches. Reporters in 1972 described how Tom Evans was personally going after Nicholson File; in 1974, reporters followed the fight between the corporate entities of Inco and ESB, with few human faces attached.

The Inco takeover bid for EBS, which mutated into a bidding war with United Aircraft, in fact turned out to be a $200 million disaster. Inco wound up paying far more for ESB than Tom Evans probably would have, and failed to take the early, decisive "rejuvenation" steps that Evans always advocated. "Inco simply seemed ill-matched to manage a consumer goods business," one takeover expert observed.[29] When the market for nickel suffered in the mid-1970s, Inco refused to provide the capital ESB needed to compete against archrivals Duracell and Eveready in the small-battery market, and its automobile batteries lost out to competing products from Sears and Delco that required less maintenance. It is intriguing to speculate whether ESB's fate would have been the same if it had been taken over by one of the old buccaneers.

By 1974, the Crane Company's acquisition of CF&I Steel in 1969 was looking like a brilliant idea. The company's payroll had been cut by thousands of employees, but it was still contributing handsomely to Crane's profits. In fact, Crane itself, which Evans and Art Landa had fought so hard to get in 1959, was running like a well-oiled machine. Sales were strong, profits were stronger, international markets were developing. And in 1974, Crane hired a new vice president: Robert Sheldon Evans, the chairman's youngest son.

Shel Evans, as he was known in the family, was a bright, irreverent young man with his father's ready wit but little of the older man's terrifying temper. After graduating from the University of Pennsylvania, he had earned his MBA at Columbia. He worked briefly at Crane as an assistant to one of the vice presidents, but he soon left to pursue some less than stellar venture capital ideas in the go-go sixties. When those failed, he found a job at Evans and Company, where his older brother Ned was firmly installed.

His oldest brother, Tom Junior, was also well-established on Wall Street, although not at his father's firm. An avid sportsman and athlete, he had little appetite for academic life and had left the University of Virginia after two years. Around 1961, he persuaded his father to lend him enough money to buy a seat on the New York Stock Exchange, and he managed it profitably. Then he became a Big Board specialist, a unique sort of trader required by exchange rules to maintain an orderly market in a specific set of stocks. A specialist was the trader of last resort, buying and selling when no one else would; in exchange for taking on this duty, he received a small commission on every trade involving those stocks. Tom Evans Jr. was one of the youngest men ever to be a specialist on the Big Board—the Evans eye for profitable trades had clearly been inherited. For a year or so in the early seventies, Shel Evans was also working on the floor of the New York exchange, serving as a floor broker for Evans and Company, executing trades for his father and the firm's other customers.

But by 1974, Shel Evans was impatient with work he felt could be better handled by others. He appealed to his father to let him leave Evans and Company—only to be invited to take a post back at Crane. This time, at age twenty-nine, he was to be vice president of international finance, reporting to Dante Fabiani, the strong, competent executive who was

Evans's top executive at Crane. Fabiani proved an excellent mentor to the young man; he was able to stand up to Tom Evans when necessary and could buffer his troops from the worst of the old man's temper. At Crane, Shel Evans quietly distinguished himself for his good manners and good sense. His older colleagues were uncertain, however, of his relationship with his father. He seemed to view the old man with a firm but affectionate detachment, immune after so many years to his tantrums but genuinely admiring of his genius.

And that genius was never in more flamboyant display than it was in 1975 and 1976. With the stock market tentatively recovering from its two-year nosedive, Tom Evans initiated a fusillade of takeover activity that outraged his adversaries, astonished his admirers, and richly educated his young advisers at law firms and investment banking houses up and down the Street. He was doing his lifelong act now on a stage that was almost empty of experienced individual raiders, and the young men who had defied the bear market to seek their fortune on Wall Street were fascinated. Evans was not a patient instructor, so he taught them to deal with the titanic egos they would meet in the takeover arena. He was a bottom-line kind of guy, so he forced them to learn the hard-nosed financial analysis and intricate financing arrangements that drove his deals in those days when a raider's only portable computer was his brain. But Evans was also creative and original, encouraging them to think outside the careful lines that the Establishment had drawn.

In March 1975 he made a run at Inspiration Consolidated Copper Company, jolting its managers into seeking a friendlier acquirer, the giant Anglo-American group of South Africa, whose bid put money in Evans's pocket. Then he went after the Copper Range Company, which immediately rushed into the arms of the larger Amax Corporation, once again giving Evans a profit. These were just target practice, however. In August, he turned his fire on the giant Anaconda Company, the nation's third largest copper producer.

A decade earlier, Anaconda had been the nation's largest copper company, before its copper mines in Chile were seized by a new government there. In 1971, it had recruited a tall, prim banker named John Bassett Moore Place to lead its efforts to recover from that disaster. With his tight-lipped smile, horn-rimmed glasses, and long thin face, Place might have been the model for an illustrator's sketch of Washington Irving's Ichabod Crane. But he had been fearlessly successful at Anaconda, cutting costs and developing interests in aluminum and other manufactured products. By 1975, four-fifths of the company's business was not related to mining.

Profits had slumped in 1975, however, and the company's stock was trading at $15, half the price it commanded a year earlier.[30]

In mid-August, Evans announced that Crane was making a hostile tender offer for just under 23 percent of Anaconda's stock. For each share of Anaconda stock, Crane was offering a package of its own securities worth about $25 a share. That package included an interesting new security dauntingly described as an "eight-percent subordinated sinking-fund debenture." It was, in plain English, a bond that paid 8 percent annual interest. It did not give its owners a first claim on Crane's assets, but to offset the bond's back-of-the-line status, Crane promised to deposit money each year into a fund that would ultimately be used to redeem the bonds. Thus, an Anaconda stockholder could either sell the security for cash, or hold onto it and collect the annual interest. It was imaginative, although some Wall Street analysts thought the company could do better—its shares had already risen to $18 on the strength of Evans's expression of interest. Besides, these novel bits of paper, now widely called "Chinese money," sometimes fared poorly in the marketplace.

But despite Evans's assurances that he was simply making a passive investment in Anaconda and did not even intend to seek representation on the board, John Place reacted to him the way chief executives had been reacting to him at least since Doug Streett's first fight in St. Louis two decades earlier. Place branded Evans's move a takeover attempt, and he battled Evans as if the Crane chairman planned to personally usurp Place's office.

First, he hired Joe Flom at Skadden, Arps. Then, seeking an antitrust buffer, Place acquired the Walworth Corporation, a valve manufacturer that competed directly with Crane. Evans bristled—not only was it a headache, it was a poor use of Anaconda's assets, in his view. He retaliated by dropping his bid for Anaconda stock from $25 to $20—the first time anyone could remember a tender offer being lowered while the bidding was still open. But even the reduced price being offered by Crane was more than Anaconda was fetching in the marketplace, so the shares rolled in and Evans was not deterred.[31]

Then, like other executives before him, Place appealed to Washington. In October, the Senate Government Operations Subcommittee initiated an examination of the antitrust aspects of Evans's offer—a rather remarkable undertaking, since Evans was simply seeking to become a minority stockholder of Anaconda. Place testified that he was certain Evans was intent on taking control. And based on his track record, Place continued, Evans would almost certainly push through his trademark cost-cutting strategies, probably shutting down Anaconda's hard-pressed Montana operations.[32] He was supported in his testimony by Frank Thompson, the genial and popular Democratic congressman from Trenton, New Jersey. Representative Thompson had crossed the Capitol lobby to describe the way his state had been affected in recent years by Evans's streamlining at CF&I and H. K. Porter. Between 1968 and 1973, Evans had shut down five operations, including the John A. Roebling and Sons steel mill in tiny Roebling, New Jersey, on the Delaware River south of Trenton. Under the Roebling family's paternalistic control, it had once turned out the steel that was woven into the Brooklyn Bridge. But its plant was antiquated, and efforts to find a buyer had failed. Evans had sold the equipment and the plant separately, enhancing his profit.[33] The plant closings had put 3,400 people out of work and severely injured Roebling and other Garden State communities dependent on the plants' payrolls.

"In a very real sense," Thompson continued, evoking an image from a suspenseful best-seller of the day, "we have in the Crane Company and its chief executive officer a corporate embodiment of 'Jaws,' the great white shark."[34]

After trying the usual defenses—Skadden Arps's barrage of lawsuits, congressional hearings, and acquisition of one of Crane's competitors—Anaconda tried to rebuff Evans by merging with Tenneco, in a swap of stock that Evans considered a very bad deal. Tenneco already carried a lot of debt, its inventories were rising faster than its profits, and its working capital had shrunk by $113 million the previous year. Its book value was less than half that of Anaconda's.[35] Evans refused to sell his shares to Tenneco. Instead he sought out an old friend, oilman Robert O. Anderson at the Atlantic Richfield Company, and persuaded him that Anaconda was more attractive than Tenneco's bid suggested. Arco stepped forward with an offer to buy 27 percent of Anaconda in a deal worth almost $34 a share—considerably more than Evans's own offer of $20 a share.[36] Arco then moved to acquire the rest of Anaconda, and John Place accepted the inevitable.

The deal gave Crane a profit of $57.6 million on the Anaconda shares it had purchased for $82.4 million less than a year before.[37] Moreover, the fancy new securities Crane had issued to finance its tender offer had declined in value, as some analysts suspected they would, and Evans was able to buy them back at a discount, thus eliminating a dollar of Crane's debt for less than a dollar of cash. "It's one of the best investments I've ever made," Evans told *Business Week* in October 1976, his face breaking into the broad, eye-squinting smile that made people compare him to Santa Claus. The investors who bought those poor-performing debentures were probably less pleased, but they had been under no duty to sell at such fire-sale prices.

By the time he was counting those profits in the Anaconda deal, Evans was at war again, this time through H. K. Porter, where his chief lieutenant was his second-born son, Edward Parker Evans, whom he had named as chief executive at Porter in the fall of 1975.

Ned Evans had dreamed of attending Stanford but bowed to his father's demand that he attend Yale, as generations of Evans men had done.[38] Ned is remembered by classmates at Yale and the Harvard Business School for his devotion to the *Daily Racing Form*, which he would read in class to the delight of bored students and the irritation of his less-inspired professors. One friend recalls the envious stares when he arrived at a campus social event squiring actress Julie Newmar. To some, he was a rascal; to others an endearing scamp. But all agree that he loved business, and was fascinated by the fights for corporate control that his father had waged over the years. As a student, he had watched those fights from neutral territory, and at Evans and Company he had been more like a scout, tracking for shares in disputed territory. But as the new chairman of H. K. Porter, he was on the front lines as his father made his assault on the boardroom of the Missouri Portland Cement Company in St. Louis.

In St. Louis, Missouri, Portland was known simply as "MoPort." It completely dominated the cement market in the Missouri River region. Its huge plants on the edge of the city limits, spewing airborne potash flakes over a broad neighborhood, had been the target of community complaints for two decades, but local officials had been wary of confronting such a powerful taxpayer.[39]

MoPort's president was M. Moss Alexander Jr., whose father had run the business before him and whose family had founded it in 1907.[40] Alexander, an attractive man who somewhat resembled actor Ray Milland, was no stranger to the takeover wars. In fact, his father had been forced into retirement by a takeover attempt led by the Missouri River Fuel Corporation in the late 1950s. His son had succeeded him, and had personally led the company's successful resistance to a later takeover effort by the huge Cargill Inc., the private grain company.[41] That fight had started in December 1973, when Cargill announced a tender offer for MoPort's shares at $30 a share. Alexander stalled through litigation, appealing adverse rulings all the way to the United States Supreme Court.[42] The Federal Trade Commission intervened in November 1974, further delaying Cargill's acquisition. Finally, in late August 1975, Cargill folded its hand and sold its 20 percent stake in MoPort. The buyer was the H. K. Porter Company of Pittsburgh, a name the older members of St. Louis's business community remembered well.[43] Porter had no plans to acquire MoPort, a company spokesman told the local press in St. Louis. "However, observers of the Pittsburgh company's history of operations are skeptical," a local business writer reported. "One informed source in [Pittsburgh] labeled Porter 'something of a corporate vulture.' A local source judged it 'a raider par excellence.' Both sources said it is only a matter of time before Porter acts to swallow the local company."[44] And when that happened, those sources warned, "those [at MoPort] who don't want to work their tails off" might want to update their résumés.

The local skeptics grew more wary in November, when Porter made a tender offer for a half-million shares of Missouri Portland at $24 a share, about $2 more than the stock's trading price but less than the company's book value of about $31 a share. The tender offer, if successful, would give Porter 49 percent of MoPort, but the Pittsburgh company continued to insist that its only interest in the St. Louis giant was as an investment. Besides, Porter noted in its tender offer, Missouri's antitakeover laws—most states had them by now—prevented it from electing even half of the board for at least three years.

Jack Markowitz, the astute business editor at the *Pittsburgh Post-Gazette*, was the first to recognize that a new Evans had stepped onto the takeover stage. " 'Like father like son' will be the inescapable cliché for awhile with respect to this city's H. K. Porter Company," he wrote. "Thirty-three-year-old Edward P. Evans took over as board chairman little more than a month ago and already has a stock tender offer out that the company on the other end hates."[45] The young Evans continued to insist that his interests were benign. "The management out there seems to know how to run the firm," he told Markowitz. "They don't need us to tell them how to mix cement."

Moss Alexander went to court to block this new tender offer, charging that Porter, whatever it claimed, actually intended to dismantle the local company and strip it of its assets. He wrote shareholders, "You should know that not one member of your Board of Directors, or any officer of your company, will tender any shares to Porter at this price." The lawsuit took note of Evans's history: "Under the Evans reign [the] defendants have pursued and continue to pursue an aggressive unrelenting program of corporate control and stripping of assets. Some 43 companies have been absorbed into H. K. Porter alone in the last nineteen years since Thomas Mellon Evans took control of it, many were taken over despite the resistance of their managements, and nearly all have been profoundly transformed under his stern make-money-quick-or-else demands."[46] Shareholders should have been made aware of this history, MoPort's lawyer argued, because "Porter has an unusual record in this area."[47]

Porter's local attorney argued in court that "there is not one bit of evidence in the record that we're going to dismantle this company."[48] From the witness stand, Tom Evans conceded that Porter's passive strategy in the MoPort case was "a complete departure from prior policy, and I'm trying to explain it to you and everyone else."[49] The "everyone else" included the Securities and Exchange Commission, which apparently was also skeptical of Evans's insistence that he was only a passive investor in MoPort and had questioned him about it closely.[50]

But the court hearings and temporary injunction stalled Evans and gave Alexander time to seek a less fearsome purchaser for MoPort. On November 24, he announced that he had found one on his doorstep, the Chromalloy American Corporation of nearby Clayton, Missouri. The deal involved the conversion of Missouri Portland common stock into Chromalloy preferred stock, and was expected to be worth somewhere between $25 and $27 a share for the MoPort stockholders.[51]

Evans was scornful. At a court hearing immediately after the proposed merger was announced, he rattled off figures from Chromalloy's most recent annual report and concluded that the company was making "progress in reverse." The company's accounting methods did not filter out the effects of inflation, an increasing concern in the business community, and the company's promises to its bondholders might leave its preferred stockholders in the lurch. "We feel if Chromalloy got into trouble, there is a question if preferred shareholders would get anything," Evans testified.[52] A federal judge in St. Louis ordered Porter to amend certain misleading portions of its tender offer, giving Moss Alexander even more time to push through his deal with Chromalloy, which was opposed by least one member of his own board, who apparently felt that both pending offers for the company's stock were inadequate. But within weeks, Porter had renewed its tender offer, holding out $26 a share for the MoPort stock. And this time, Alexander was unable to persuade the judge that the amended documentation was anything but perfectly legal.

Indeed, it was Porter's turn to seek an injunction, to block the Chromalloy merger and to seek $20 million in damages from the two companies and their directors for engaging in what Porter called a conspiracy to deprive Porter of its rights as a shareholder. Evans charged that MoPort's response to Porter's offer had been driven by its management's "selfish interests in retaining for themselves the substantial benefits and emoluments of their positions . . . and not by the interests of Missouri's other stockholders, including Porter."[53]

On January 5, 1976, Chromalloy backed out of the deal, noting that Porter's stake of nearly 47 percent of MoPort's stock and the disagreements on MoPort's own board made the deal untenable.[54] But the MoPort board refused to give up. As Porter increased its stake in MoPort to more than 52 percent, the company appealed the adverse rulings in the local courts. The arguments were the same: that Porter actually intended to take control of MoPort, with dire consequences for its employees and stockholders. Indeed, when the appellate judge asked one of Porter's lawyers whether "it is now your intention to exercise control," the attorney replied, "I can't answer that, Your Honor." The waffling only fueled Alexander's conviction that Porter had obtained its controlling stake in MoPort through fraud, by misleading shareholders about its intentions.[55]

Nevertheless, the appeal was unsuccessful, allowing Evans to vote Porter's shares at MoPort's annual meeting on May 25. The lawyers almost outnumbered the stockholders at the meeting. Shortly after Alexander had called the meeting to order, young Ned Evans rose from his seat and nominated himself and his father, and two other candidates, for election to the board of directors. MoPort's attorney immediately sprang to his feet. "I advise you that these nominations are part of unlawful conduct and are improper," he said. But he agreed to let the election continue so that "the court [could] deal with a completed act, not a threat."[56]

With Porter voting its shares, Tom and Ned Evans were easily elected to the board. As the election results were announced, a Porter lawyer rose to ask Alexander whether the Evanses would be allowed to take their seats in the boardroom. Not until a court had ruled that Porter had acquired its shares fairly, Alexander answered. The Evans forces promptly proposed an amendment to the company's bylaws to require monthly meetings of the board, and just as promptly voted their shares in favor of the motion. It was approved.

In hindsight, one is struck by the stately, measured pace at which this and most other corporate struggles of that era unfolded; it is like watching Kabuki theater after a steady diet of hectic action films. Without powerful portable computers, complicated financial calculations took more time, of course, and transportation, telephone service, and paperwork preparation were all a bit more primitive. Outside of a few jurisdictions, court clerks and judges had not yet perfected the "fast-track" procedures that would speed up takeover litigation in later decades. In any case, the slow-motion struggle for Missouri Portland, which had begun around Labor Day of 1975, was still going strong the following summer.

Moss Alexander continued to fight through June and early July, refusing to seat his two new directors and refusing to adopt monthly board meetings until the court had ruled on the legality of Porter's tender offer.

It was at this point, with the takeover fight at a deadlock, that Evans sought the legal advice of a young lawyer named Lawrence Lederman at Wachtell Lipton Rosen and Katz. The firm, already a substantial rival to Skadden, Arps, was the home of Martin Lipton, who had cut his takeover teeth on the same early proxy contest that pulled Joe Flom into the game. Tom Evans "was the first prominent corporate raider that Wachtell Lipton represented," Lederman recalled in a memoir. "Just by working with [him] our reputation as takeover lawyers would be enhanced and others would seek advice. . . . In this new era I had much to learn, but few lawyers were experienced in takeovers, and if I was to master their intricacies, my training would have to come from Lipton and men like Tom Evans and the experience they offered in high-stakes contests."[57] He added, "The lessons learned on offense taught defense."[58]

For Lederman, it was an education simply to follow Evans's train of thought about MoPort. He came to see the value that Evans detected in the way the company was organized, the location of its plants, its distribution network, its competent management—all available at a bargain price because the stock market, in its decade-long slump, could not see the values that Evans did: "The old man was entering (and introducing me to) a new era, the acquisition of undervalued companies, often well-managed. He knew a truth that would eventually fuel an explosion of mergers and acquisitions in this country: it's cheaper to buy going companies than to build them."[59] Although Lederman joined Tom Evans midway through the fight for MoPort, he saw enough of Evans to conclude that "without doubt, he was a financial genius."[60]

His son Ned Evans soon proved that he could play the takeover game with as much skill and fewer bruises than his father. As the elder Evans waged the Missouri Portland fight, the young chairman of H. K. Porter announced an unwelcome tender offer for 85 percent of the shares of Fansteel of Chicago, which manufactured a variety of specialty metals, electrical contacts, and carbide cutting tools. Evans used Solomon Brothers to manage the $17-a-share tender offer for him, giving that firm a chance to further hone its skills in the takeover game. Fansteel tried to escape through a merger with Lear Siegler, Inc., which raised the bidding to $22 a share.[61] Ned Evans countered with an offer of $23.50 a share, and Lear folded its hand, leaving Fansteel braced for the worst. But to everyone's surprise, Ned Evans was generous in victory. He left the top managers in place, and even praised their skill. "The whole thing happened so amicably . . . that observers have had to revise their opinion of the new Evans," *Business Week* reported.[62]

The Fansteel bidding threw a spotlight on the activities of a new breed of Wall Street speculators, called arbitragers. One of them, Ivan F. Boesky, explained to reporters that these arbitragers had bid the price of Fansteel up to $19 share "in anticipation of the second takeover offer long before it was clear that it would materialize."[63] As one market commentator reported in May, "In Mr. Boesky's opinion, the year promises to be a memorable one for acquisitions and mergers of quality companies."

But while Ned Evans was wrestling with the Fansteel fight, Larry Lederman had his work cut out for him keeping the Missouri Portland deal on track. "The impression of Tom Evans in the business community was that he was an American original: a nineteenth-century buccaneer capitalist, unencumbered by altruism."[64] That reputation had been entirely accepted by the MoPort directors, and they were determined to keep his hands off what they saw as their company. Moreover, Lederman found, his new client was a terrible negotiator. "He didn't like adjusting differences and wasn't a good listener. Intransigence seemed inherent in his style: when alternatives were offered, most often they were rejected."[65]

In Evans's view, the MoPort directors had everything to gain by their stalling tactics, and nothing to lose. "If we sued them personally and threatened their personal assets, then they'd have something to lose," he told the young Lederman as they discussed the deadlock. "Pressure is often more effective than reason."[66] So the directors were sued, and as Evans predicted, their lawyers soon contacted Lederman to open negotiations. On July 22, 1976, an out-of-court settlement was reached that allowed the Evans forces to take their seats, although it also required Evans to wait two years to extend his control of the board.[67] He also agreed not to pay less than $26 a share for any additional stock he bought in the company, although he could use either cash or securities to make the purchases. The long battle was finally over, nearly eleven months after it started.

With the boardroom finally open to him, Tom Evans boarded his corporate jet and flew to St. Louis for the first meeting of the newly constituted MoPort board of directors. He was accompanied by his son Ned and by Larry Lederman. The elder Evans dozed often during the flight, Lederman recalled, awakening occasionally to ask a pointed question. After such a long and bitter battle, Lederman was nervous about Evans's first meeting with the MoPort directors. His eyes sparkling above an impish grin, Evans promised to behave himself, but Lederman was not entirely reassured. "Holding his temper was not easy for him," the nervous young lawyer told himself.[68] At least Ned Evans seemed patient and calm, he thought, as the jet touched down in St. Louis.

A hot, sticky taxi ride took the trio to the MoPort offices in suburban Clayton, where they met up with John Kountz, Porter's general counsel, who had flown in from Pittsburgh. They were invited into the boardroom, where the other directors were already gathered. It was Lederman's first look at the men he had sued so many months ago. "Relatively old men, they didn't seem to embody, individually or collectively, the indomitable spirit that had fought to keep the company independent," Lederman recalled. Coffee and doughnuts were provided, and the uneasy group "exchanged pleasantries" while sipping the hot brew from cardboard cups. "As with most well run industrial companies that didn't deal with the retail public, no frills were to be seen."[69] Tom Evans talked enthusiastically about his thoroughbred stable, which he had established at Buckland Farms, his beautiful hunt-country home in Virginia. His sister Elinor and her husband lived in Louisville, and the Evanses were regular guests during the Kentucky Derby. Evans had hopes that someday one of his ponies would shine there.

Finally, as "the social adhesives wore thin," Moss Alexander called the meeting to order. "It was one of those meetings where within the first few minutes you believed it was going to be endless," Lederman later recalled. "Everybody was extraordinarily polite and no one was prepared to be assertive or to advance the meeting. Strangely, the old man sat there with a smile on his moon face, an uncharacteristic pose, and it made me suspect that peace wasn't going to last long."[70] He knew that Evans resented the settlement that required him to sit as a minority director for two years, despite his majority ownership of the company's stock.

Finally, Moss Alexander raised the topic of capital expenditures. The company was considering buying two new barges to ferry its cement to its distribution terminals. There was a silence, as if the board were waiting to see what the feared "corporate raider" would say about this. What he said was, "Why do we own a furniture company?"

The other directors were startled. MoPort had recently acquired a small institutional furniture-maker that "was barely holding its own," Lederman recalled. M. Weldon Rogers III, the youngest of the MoPort directors, flushed angrily and instantly defended the acquisition. "It'll contribute to our earnings," Rogers said.[71]

"Not enough to justify the time," the old man retorted. "The next thing you know we'll be buying a brassiere company because you say it's a good financial move. Cement is our business, not rags or furniture. What do we know about those businesses?"

"There's no point in stripping assets from the company," Rogers answered, ringing the alarm bell that had rallied boardroom opposition against Evans for nearly a year.

Now it was Evans's turn to challenge their assumptions about him. Sell the furniture company, he told them, and "we'll put the money back in the business, where it belongs."

Remarkably, the older directors agreed with him. "Cement is our business," said Alexander from the head of the table.[72]

"And we ought to spend more money on barges," said Evans, returning to the topic at hand and further confounding those who thought of him as an asset stripper. "We have to transport all our cement by river, and we're not fully capable of using our production capacity in meeting our delivery schedules." One way to invest more in MoPort's future production, Evans continued, was to cut the dividend. "The dividend we pay out is too high. Some of it should go back into the business."

This was a difficult moment for Alexander, Lederman could see instantly. The chairman and his family "had a relatively large stock position and a cut in the dividend would sharply decrease their income."[73]

By now, it was clear that the locus of power in the room had shifted, and Evans was now presiding from his seat at the side of the table.[74] And it was Evans, the raider, the "asset-stripper," who was urging that the directors take the long view and invest in the future. But where did that leave the minority stockholders, like the Alexander family, who had invested in a very different MoPort in years past?

"It was no surprise when Moss Alexander asked, 'Tom, why don't you buy the rest of the company?'"

Evans explained that he didn't have enough cash in H. K. Porter to buy the rest of the company, and he didn't want to add additional debt to Porter's balance sheet.

"There was a long silence. He could be comfortable not saying anything, letting everyone contemplate what they faced if he didn't buy out the public shares, all the time waiting as if he were thinking of his alternatives," Lederman wrote of that pregnant moment. "I almost believed that he would let the opportunity pass. His timing, however, was impeccable. Just as I shifted in my chair, he floated a novel idea in a soft voice. 'If you're interested,' the old man said, 'we could use the debt of Missouri Portland to acquire the stock.'"

What he was proposing, which Lederman found fascinating, was to have MoPort issue a new security, a subordinated debenture paying 10 percent interest. Then MoPort—not Porter—could use it as a form of currency, in lieu of cash, to purchase and retire its own minority shareholders' common stock, leaving Porter in sole possession. It "was a boot strap transaction, with the company buying itself. The old man was initiating one of the first leveraged buyouts for subordinated debt, later commonly known as junk bonds," Lederman said.[75]

Such buyouts were still considered mysterious and novel on Wall Street, although they were the specialty of a small boutique that had opened its doors for business a few months earlier. Its name was Kohlberg, Kravis and Roberts, or KKR. The idea sounded like hocus-pocus to some of the men in the MoPort boardroom. But Moss Alexander was intrigued. He gave the nod, and Evans beamed. "I'll take care of it as soon as I get back to New York," he said.

He hurried his team back to the airport, briskly skipping the lunch that was waiting for the board members. As an olive branch, Lederman had invited MoPort's two New York lawyers to return with them on the company jet, but Evans balked at waiting when their taxi was delayed. During ten tense minutes, Evans twice threatened to leave without them—impervious to the difficulty that would raise in the upcoming negotiations over the buyout. Finally the MoPort lawyers arrived, and the ticking bomb of Tom Evans's temper was defused as the plane lifted off for New York.[76]

The transaction was presented to shareholders in March of 1977. A few days later, Moss Alexander was vindicated when the Securities and Exchange Commission went to court against Porter, charging that Tom Evans had indeed misled shareholders about his intentions when he first began acquiring shares of Missouri Portland. With victory at hand, Porter settled the commission's attack on its battle strategy, without admitting or denying any misbehavior.[77] But Alexander did not gloat—he was too busy running Missouri Portland, first as its president, reporting to its new chairman, Edward P. Evans, and then as a well-paid consultant to the firm.

It was in the midst of this long awaited victory that tragedy struck the Evans family. Tom Evans's relationship with his second wife, Josephine, had been deteriorating for many months. His intensive absorption in his successful deal-making, a throwback to the workaholic days of his first marriage, might have seemed reason enough. But it also seems likely that, after twenty-four years of marriage, he had formed an attachment with someone else, a neighbor of theirs in Greenwich.[78] The estrangement weighed heavily on Josephine Evans, and Evans refused to discuss it with her. As spring approached, she became increasingly despondent over the separation from her husband.[79]

On Sunday, May 1, while staying at Buckland Farms, she telephoned a friend in Michigan and spoke about her sorrow. Then, sometime during that humid night, she fetched a single-barrel 20-gauge shotgun from the assortment of game-hunting equipment kept at the farm, and loaded it.

She took it out onto one of the porches that overlooked the serene countryside and she shot herself. Tragically, she bungled the attempt. Twice she inflicted only superficial wounds; the third wound was grievous but not instantly fatal. She tried a fourth shot, but the gun jammed. Somehow, she made her way into the house, fetched another gun, loaded it, and fired a final shot into her neck. She was found, near death, by a maid arriving at the home around 8 A.M. on Monday, May 2. She died soon after arriving at a nearby hospital.

Investigators found that she had taken the time, during her ordeal, to write a note warning others that the first gun she used was loaded but jammed, and should be handled carefully.[80]

The family refused to comment on her death throughout the long investigation that followed. Finally, in late May, local authorities ruled her death a suicide, with the prosecutor attributing "the rather bizarre circumstances" to her inexperience with firearms.[81]

That tragic death and its dark questions were never discussed by Evans, not even with his closest and oldest friend, John Foster. He seemed to have slammed a door on that shocking chapter in his life, shutting up the grief and the anger. He publicly courted Betty Barton Loomis, his slim and vivacious Greenwich neighbor, and as summer progressed, they were making wedding plans. Meanwhile, he scouted the stock market for new deals—an activity that Betty seemed to find as fascinating as he did, friends said. She made frequent visits to his Park Avenue office, and employees could see the couple laughing and talking with happy animation.[82]

By August 1977, Evans had found a new target, Chemetron Corporation of Chicago, for which he made an unexpected and unwelcome tender offer at $40 a share. Although its shares were trading at only about $30 apiece, down from $52 in early 1976, Chemetron had a thriving chemical business, focusing on patented additives for paints, inks, and plastics. It also made industrial equipment, including fittings and valves. Although Evans's offer to Chemetron shareholders was more than anyone else in the stock market had been offering them for a long while, it was still considerably below the company's book value of nearly $54 a share.

"True to Evans's style, Chemetron officials learned of the proposal by a phone call from the New York Stock Exchange," reported the Chicago *Daily News*. The company immediately raised antitrust issues in a lawsuit. "This always happens, doesn't it?" Evans told a Chicago reporter.[83]

And once again, Chemetron sought out a less demanding suitor. By September, it announced a merger agreement with Allegheny Ludlum Industries, the big specialty steel maker in Pittsburgh. "It's anybody's guess who the winner will be," one analyst said as the fight raged. "The merger would fall nicely into Allegheny's plan to reduce its dependence on specialty steel, but then, Thomas Mellon Evans has a reputation for getting just about everything he wants."[84] All he really wanted, of course, was a profit on his investment. And that's what he got when Allegheny Ludlum trumped his bid.

The following spring, Tom Evans's eye fell on the venerable Morrison-Knudsen Company in Boise, Idaho, the giant engineering firm that had helped build the Hoover Dam. He quickly built up a stake of about 10 percent, catching Morrison-Knudsen by surprise. William H. McMurren, the engineering company's president, spoke with Evans after the bid became public, he told reporters. He told Evans it was his "firm belief that Morrison-Knudsen's continued independence is vital to its continued successful operations," McMurren said. Professional engineers, the company's chief asset, were not like cement plants or chemical factories. If they were unhappy, they could walk out the door and not return.[85] But Evans was not deterred, hinting that he might seek control of the Boise giant.

The Morrison-Knudsen directors had a better idea. On Friday, May 19, 1978, the company announced it had purchased Evans's M-K shares from him for $14.3 million, giving Evans a paper profit of almost $4 million on the investment he had made just a few months earlier.[86] Such arrangements were not yet widely called "greenmail," but they were easy money, all the same.

CHAPTER THIRTEEN

FATHERS AND SONS

As the enigmatic seventies came to an end, most Americans paid little attention to the stock market. Despite the well-intentioned efforts of President Jimmy Carter, the nation remained lethargic, anxious, sapped of its confidence. American citizens were being held hostage in Iran. Gold and silver prices were soaring, and oil prices remained high after a decade that had seen long gas lines and skyrocketing home heating bills. High energy prices had sideswiped the economy, afflicting it with the supposedly contradictory forces of inflation and stagnation—"stagflation," in the pundit's parlance. For most small investors, owning a piece of corporate America was far less appealing than owning, say, a gold Krugerrand coin or a few square yards of California real estate.

But on Wall Street, the seeds of change were beginning to sprout. And for Tom Evans, they promised a familiar harvest—though one that would seem wild and strange to newcomers to the takeover field. In April 1979, the increasingly prominent buyout firm of KKR closed on its first major leveraged buyout, or LBO, the purchase of Houdaille Industries, a steel and diversified industrial parts manufacturer that was ranked firmly in the *Fortune* 500. An LBO is a deal in which investors borrow against a company's assets and use the proceeds to buy the company from its previous owners. "News of the Houdaille purchase put the LBO on the map," noted deal-guru Bruce Wasserstein.[1] Other buyouts at smaller companies had been done throughout the previous decade, of course, and Tom Evans had carried out a very similar strategy at Missouri Portland. But this deal seemed fresh, if only because of its ambitious size and the remarkable amount of debt that it added to Houdaille's balance sheet.

Interest rates were starting to climb, as Federal Reserve Chairman Paul Volcker administered the tough medicine that would break the country's inflationary fever. Bonds and other interest-paying securities began to attract investors who had shunned the stock market. Some of these investors, especially large institutional players like mutual funds and savings-and-loan associations, needed a marketplace in which to trade. And Michael Milken of Drexel Burnham Lambert, who had begun as a bond salesman specializing in the convertible debentures and other so-called "Chinese money" generated by men like Evans and by the conglomerate acquisitions of the sixties, was ready to accommodate them. Operating out of his own Beverly Hills offices, he set up the trading desk that would track, analyze, and broker the sale of a new generation of speculative debt securities. Like the earlier purveyors of Chinese money, he and his Drexel colleagues bristled when old-timers called them "junk bonds," but the nickname stuck. Other Wall Street firms set up small speculative-bond trading operations of their own. Gradually, it would become possible for bonds to be traded as easily as stocks, the advocates of debt-based deals predicted.

But there were some new arrivals on the takeover scene who still used the old-fashioned weapons against the traditional prey. Carl Icahn, a successful options trader who had built his own small brokerage business, saw that the long stock market slump of the seventies, like the weak, sparse markets of the thirties and early forties, had left many good companies with undervalued shares. He decided to go after one, and in 1979, he waged a full-fledged proxy fight for control of Tappan, the kitchen-appliance manufacturer.[2] Tappan was rescued from the unknown Icahn when a larger company swooped in and bought it, giving Icahn a $2.7 million profit on his stake in the company. The following year, Icahn tried again, this time with Hammermill, the big paper company. Again, Icahn lost the proxy vote, but retained his troublesome stake in the company. Ultimately, Hammermill paid him to go away, purchasing his stake from him at a price that gave him a handsome profit.[3] The word "raider" was being dusted off by a few experienced journalists, but for most of the reporters who had been drawn into the world of business by the oil shocks and other economic upheavals of the 1970s, the fights for control that had erupted in the 1950s and 1960s were a blank page of forgotten history. It seemed to be a new era on Wall Street, populated by smart young business school graduates with their computer spreadsheets and their textbook knowledge of business law and financial analysis.

For Tom Evans, the nickname "Jaws" had unfortunately stuck among seasoned journalists ever since Congressman Frank Thompson had thrown the "White Shark" epithet at him in congressional hearings years earlier. And he kept stalking new prey, attracting fresh attention from those who had missed his earlier adventures. He was so happy with his cement plant acquisition at Porter that he decided that the Crane Company should have one too. So he went after the Medusa Corporation of Cleveland, quietly buying nearly 140,000 shares while the company's chief executive, Scott A. Rogers Jr., was distracted by a takeover attempt from another quarter. Rogers negotiated a rescue acquisition by another Cleveland company, but Evans did not favor the deal. "I called Scott Rogers and told him I'd have to ask for minority shareholders' appraisal rights if he went through with it," Evans said later, a threat that would stall and possibly derail the merger. Evans also indicated that Crane itself might be a suitable mate, but "Rogers' reaction was typical of executives who have faced a squeeze play from Evans," *Business Week* reported. "Crane's chief executive is known for running a tight ship with little delegation of authority, severe financial controls, and a lean staff, a reputation that could hardly have been palatable to Rogers."[4]

Rogers persuaded Kaiser Cement and Gypsum Corporation to make an offer, but that deal faltered as well, and Evans picked up more than 500,000 Medusa shares in the marketplace as the deal crumbled. Rogers urged the Federal Trade Commission to come to his rescue—after all, Evans owned a competing cement company through his stake in H. K. Porter. But Evans, despite his distaste for negotiations, reached a settlement with the FTC that called for Medusa to sell one of its Illinois plants and for Crane to maintain Medusa as a separate corporation. Rogers accepted the inevitable.

Evans was happy with the deal. "We try to give shareholders a hedge against inflation," he told reporters. "We try to buy value."[5]

The *Business Week* reporter examining the Medusa deal observed that Crane shareholders were "likely to see fewer gains ahead from aggressive acquisitions" because company policy required officers to retire at age seventy, a milestone Tom Evans would reach in 1980. That could leave the way clear for Robert Sheldon Evans, Evans's youngest son and executive vice president at Crane, to step into the top job, the magazine speculated. "Although insiders say that young Evans is a 'chip off the old block when it comes to operations,' his interest in his father's financial legerdemain is still unproven."[6]

Tom Evans, increasingly stout and bald but with the bright eyes and restless energy that had always marked his approach to business, just shrugged off such speculation. Like a short version of the "Daddy War-bucks" cartoon character that he increasingly resembled, he was enjoying the intrigue too much to retire, no matter what the company policy said. While negotiating for Medusa, he made a grab for the Buffalo Forge Company, more than a century old and a substantial manufacturer of industrial fans, blowers, air conditioners, and pumps. The family-dominated company quickly bought his shares back, giving him a profit. Then he bought up a big stake in the Joseph Dixon Crucible Company, familiar to the nation through its pencils and artist supplies but also a manufacturer of graphite and ceramics for industry. Dixon promptly sought the advice of Kidder, Peabody and Company, giving another group of newly minted investment bankers a chance to observe Evans's tactics up close. Then Evans, at the urging of his son Ned, gave the nod for Porter to buy a substantial stake in Macmillan, the giant publishing house.

Then, the media circus really began—although, this time, Wall Street noticed that the starring role was played not by Tom Evans, but by Ned, who was chief executive at Porter and who shared an austere office next to his father's nerve center at Evans and Company on Park Avenue in New York.

While Tom Junior pointedly avoided any but the most perfunctory role in his father's empire, Ned Evans at Porter and his younger brother Shel Evans at Crane had become meaningful members of their father's business team. But their roles were as different as their companies. Shel Evans focused on corporate management and operations at Crane, while the more enigmatic Ned seemed to be following his father's more entrepreneurial, aggressive path. When he first took over at Porter, Ned reminded a few journalists of a stocky version of the actor George Hamilton, but to Larry Lederman, Ned seemed to increasingly resemble his father. "He even had Tom's temper, which sparked and flashed like his father's. Nothing set him apart, and working closely with the old man made any deviation difficult."[7] Ned Evans had gone to war as his father's lieutenant in the fights for Fansteel and Missouri Portland, and the two were skirmishing together with Dixon Crucible. As Pittsburgh's business editor Jack Markowitz had predicted, Ned seemed to be another "Net Quick" Evans, unleashed on the world to harry complacent corporate executives.

So in April 1979, when H. K. Porter announced it had acquired 7.3 percent of Macmillan, the publishing company's top executives assumed the worst: that Jaws and Son were circling management's vessel, preparing to strike. But not everybody aboard at Macmillan was alarmed. Some, indeed, were quite cheerful when the familiar Evans dorsal fin broke the surface of the market, headed in their direction.

Macmillan's boardroom had been the scene of discontent for several years. It was run by Raymond C. Hagel, sixty-three, a former publishing industry consultant who had been recruited to run the company more than two decades earlier. Over the years, he had expanded the company into a variety of educational services, including the Berlitz language schools and the Katharine Gibbs secretarial schools, which had been steadily success-ful, and Brentano's bookstores and C. G. Conn, a band instrument and organ maker, which had been duds. Unlike most corporate boards of the day, Macmillan had several directors who had substantial holdings of its stock, and that stock had declined from a high of $51 to a low of $3 in the mid-1970s. It had inched ahead to around $10 by the time the Evanses were sighted, but that still represented substantial losses for many longtime stockholders. One of the discontented shareholder-directors was the old "kid-glove raider," J. Patrick Lannan of Chicago, who knew a little some-thing about the takeover game and who was outspokenly impatient with Hagel's failure to remedy the company's problems. Lannan was simply delighted when he learned that Tom Evans—that old familiar stalker of undervalued, overweight corporations—was sizing up Macmillan. "Immense joy" was how he later described his reaction. Evans seemed "like an angel rescuing me from the brink of the grave," the eloquent Irishman continued.[8] At the very least, Lannan figured, Evans would spark a bidding war that would drive up Macmillan's stock, which had a book value of $16 a share. And at best, he might frighten Hagel into taking the steps that Lannan had been nagging him to take for years.

"So when Hagel recommended at a special Saturday-morning board meeting that Macmillan fight Evans's takeover, the heavy stockholders on the board had plenty of reason to go along," *Fortune* later recounted.[9]

Hagel brought in Martin Lipton, whose law firm had represented the insurgent Evans in the hostile Missouri Portland fight, but who now spe-cialized in management defense. His strategy was to try to attract a friend-lier suitor—what Wall Street now called a "white knight"—who would step forward with a better offer. But the first one who rode to the rescue after a long worrisome summer was Mattel Inc., the toy company, which in August offered a package of cash, stock, and notes worth about $24.50 a share. The Macmillan directors were less than charmed, for some reason.[10] Fortu-nately, a more attractive suitor arrived within a week: the American Broad-casting Corporation, led by Leonard Goldenson. ABC's offer was "similar in value to Mattel's, except that the securities involved were higher grade, and the deal was structured in a way that would make it tax-free."[11] But the broadcasting network, one of the Big Three that still dominated American television viewing habits, clearly seemed a more prestigious partner, and negotiations began in earnest.

The progress was jerky and small issues seemed to cause big delays. Still, by Thanksgiving eve, the merger agreement was ready to be signed. Suddenly, during an afternoon meeting with a handful of executives who were tepid about Macmillan, Goldenson had second thoughts. "Maybe we better not do the deal," he said.[12] Everyone seemed relieved, and scattered to enjoy their holiday dinners.

When the news of the broken deal was announced, Macmillan's stock fell $4 a share. Ned Evans, as addicted to his office stock-quote monitor as his father had always been, watched the decline with disappointment tempered by a savvy sense of opportunity. The market had clearly given up on Macmillan—it had been wooed once by a toy maker, then left at the altar by a media prince. What were the odds that a better deal would come along? Ned Evans could accept the market's viewpoint and sell out. Or he could hold on, hoping that the market was wrong and another suitor would surface. Or he could become a suitor himself—by buying more Macmillan shares, enough to influence the company from the inside. He was his father's son: ignoring the disapproving grumbles from the old man, he quietly started buying Macmillan shares. Porter accumulated about 15 percent of the company before he was through.[13]

Pat Lannan arranged a private meeting with Tom and Ned Evans, and later recalled that he "took a strong liking to Ned."[14] He suggested the other directors invite young Evans to lunch. They did, and were as impressed as Lannan had been. "He's a first-class guy," Lannan said later. "Tom has called me a few times on this, and I tell him he doesn't have to worry about Macmillan. Ned and I are handling it."

The board meeting on January 7, 1980, was the final showdown between Lannan, now firmly allied with Ned Evans, and Macmillan chairman and chief executive Ray Hagel, whose boardroom supporters "pointed out that he had given the company twenty years of excellent service."[15] Lannan pushed through a reorganization that set up a five-member executive committee, with Ned Evans as its chairman and Ray Hagel as merely one of its members—a role offered as a clumsy concession forced on Lannan by Hagel's supporters. The plan was a cease-fire, not a truce. On February 11, after a five-hour board meeting at Macmillan's midtown Manhattan headquarters, Ray Hagel resigned.[16] Was it fair to say Hagel was forced out? "That's all right, if you wish to say that," Lannan told veteran New York Times reporter Bob Cole. "It's more or less the truth." Ned Evans was elected chairman of the board, and a search was begun for a new chief executive. To Lannan's apparent surprise, however, Ned Evans had no intention of following that script. He intended to run Macmillan himself—on his own, by his own rules.

The successful coup at Macmillan, which carried his middle son beyond the reach of his own domination, was to be Tom Evans's last major hostile takeover.[17] In April 1980, a truce had been negotiated at Joseph Dixon Crucible, with Tom and Ned Evans named to the company's board where they served quietly for little over a year before selling their stake and moving on. After more than four decades, Tom Evans was, briefly, not at war with anyone. The peace would not last; it would be shattered by conflicts with his own children.

Ned Evans shifted his attention from H.K. Porter, where his father was still chairman of the executive committee, to Macmillan. "Ned was able to politely step off his father's ship, H. K. Porter, and take command of his own vessel," observed lawyer Larry Lederman. "That step away from his father's command . . . seemed gracefully executed, without squabble or outward rancor."[18] But appearances were deceptive. Others closer to the scene say that Tom Evans virtually shoved his middle son out of Porter, in the first of several bruising conflicts over the publishing venture.[19]

It could not have been easy for Edward Parker Evans to work for Thomas Mellon Evans, even if he had all the wit and tenacity of the lawyerly grandfather for whom he was named. Nobody found it easy working for Tom Evans. As Ned was just settling in at Macmillan, Tom Evans was included in a *Fortune* magazine lineup of the "Ten Toughest Bosses in America." "Few executives grip the reins so tightly," the magazine reported.[20] Ned Evans must have flushed with anger to read one unfortunate anecdote offered to support the nomination: "Several times recently, while Ned was interviewing candidates for jobs at Macmillan, a side door opened and the sturdy square figure of his father steamed into the room. The father listened for a while, barked out a few questions, expressed his opinion about the candidate's qualifications, and then departed as abruptly as he had entered." Other former executives had felt the same humiliations. One of them told *Fortune* that Evans deserved first place in its rankings. "Peter Grace [of W.R. Grace and Company] is tough. Armand Hammer [of Occidental Petroleum] is really tough. But next to Tom Evans, they are pussycats. He's the toughest man I have ever known."[21]

It was a label that some at Macmillan were soon applying to the younger Mr. Evans. The first president Macmillan recruited lasted barely a year, and the woman who had signed on to run the Gibbs secretarial schools in January 1980 abruptly resigned in May 1981. "My philosophy was a little bit different from the present management," she said in her terse departure statement. As Ned Evans carved his way through Macmillan's flabby businesses, the publishing industry began to whisper about "liquidation," sometimes adding, "like father, like son." With the help of William F. Reilly, a new president recruited from W.R. Grace, Ned Evans "closed or sold 33 lackluster units (including Brentano's bookstores), cut the management team by 66 percent, and repurchased nearly one-third of the company's 13 million shares."[22]

As unprofitable businesses were shed, Macmillan's revenues declined but its profits began to improve. Ned Evans intended to streamline Macmillan into three basic business groups: publishing, commercial education, and information services. And he was prepared to invest to expand and modernize those areas. He looked abroad for new territory that the Berlitz language schools could mine for corporate clients, and he invested heavily in turning some valuable Macmillan advertising-rate tabulations into computer databases. Macmillan was in the right business at the right time, in Ned Evans's view. Its assets were ideas, knowledge, information. It was very different from his father's empire, where the assets were steel mills and cement plants and valve foundries.

And by the spring of 1982, Tom Evans wanted to get back on more familiar ground. Porter owned about 22 percent of Macmillan, and the stock had begun to respond to Ned Evans's methods. Tom Evans had a nice profit, and he wanted to cash out and put his money to work in businesses he understood. "If he sold his block of stock [to someone else], there would be a new owner and Ned would be dismissed, and he'd be working again for his father," noted Larry Lederman. "It was as simple as that, and the old man had relatively little patience: he'd sell, and sell soon."[23]

Tom Evans's determination to sell out of his Macmillan stake must have been a blow to Ned Evans, who tried to persuade his father to take a longer view of Macmillan's prospects. Yes, there were problems facing Macmillan—but there were problems facing Crane and H. K. Porter, as well. The domestic steel industry was in its worst decline since the Depression, with U.S. Steel losing money on each ton it sold. Antiquated plants were closing down, unable to compete with highly streamlined and frequently subsidized foreign producers.[24] Tom Evans had tried to keep CF&I competitive, and its specialty tubular steel was a staple of the domestic oil industry. But staying competitive often meant closing less efficient plants, leaving fewer workers contributing to the company's union pension fund. If it could not escape the industry's problems, it would sink like its bigger rivals. And H. K. Porter's asbestos manufacturing business was being hit by an increasing number of lawsuits filed by former workers claiming that their health had been severely damaged by their exposure to the company's products. A class-action lawsuit had been filed against the nation's asbestos manufacturers in 1978, accusing them of concealing the hazards of handling the material. In addition, thousands of individual lawsuits were pending against Porter and others in the industry.

There were no quick fixes to these gathering problems, and little glamour to tackling them day in, day out. Ned Evans was willing to do that hard, grinding work at Macmillan—if only his father would back him.

But at seventy-two, Tom Evans was accustomed to doing what he wanted, and what he wanted was to play the market as he always had. So in June 1982, he sold Porter's Macmillan shares back to the publishing company for $42.9 million, more than twice what it had originally cost. The transaction consumed money that Ned Evans had hoped to invest in solving his company's problems, but he had no choice if he wished to preserve Macmillan's independence. In effect, he had paid greenmail to his own father.

The dispute cut deeply, friends said. Tom Evans "sulked for two years, like King Lear," said one close associate. But Macmillan continued to improve and expand, almost as if Ned Evans were determined to make his father's exit look as shortsighted as possible in the light of history.

But an appreciation of history was a scarce commodity on Wall Street by 1982. The takeover game was afoot again, and to many forgetful Americans it seemed to have never been played before. A breathless business press, largely ignorant of the postwar history of corporate warfare, provided the play-by-play as upstart takeover players tried to take control of major corporations through buyouts or tender offers financed by the sale of junk bonds.

Mergers and acquisitions, or "M&A," as swaggering young practitioners called it, seized the media imagination for the first time in nearly twenty years. The number of deals—buyouts and takeovers and friendly acquisitions—was exploding, although the annual tallies still fell short of those from the late sixties.[25] In the first year after Ronald Reagan took office, ushering in a laissez-faire approach to antitrust enforcement, the dollar volume of deal activity rose from $44.3 billion to $82.6 billion.[26] Raiders like T. Boone Pickens and Carl Icahn and Bill Farley became instant celebrities, as familiar to the fascinated public as Robert Young and Lou Wolfson had been a quarter-century earlier. Greenmail—"which literally means blackmailing companies with green money," one author helpfully explained—was added to the public vocabulary, along with "golden parachutes" and "poison pills" and "shark repellants."[27] Once again, as the raiders made headlines by grabbing for control of blue-chip companies and indulging in conspicuous enjoyment of their newfound wealth, a growing number of work-day Americans felt the same anxiety and confusion that their counterparts had felt during the earlier outbreaks of merger mania and corporate warfare. Familiar senior executives were swept away, replaced by newcomers determined to shrink overhead and eliminate fat. Some local factories were closed; others were sold off for other purposes. Household names disappeared from the corporate roster, to be replaced by unfamiliar ones.

To business veterans already in retirement, none of this was new. Many of them could remember the dislocations caused by the earlier bands of raiders. But it did seem new to the vast numbers of baby boomers who found themselves, in their early thirties, trying to keep their balance in an increasingly turbulent corporate landscape. Foreign competitors suddenly seemed more agile and efficient than America's heartland industries. Entire layers of middle management were disappearing. The basic business of making things that people used—potato chips, underwear, cold remedies—began to seem stodgy and somehow unimportant. It was the glittering Wall Street business of making deals that suddenly seemed to matter. And that was an activity that most Americans could watch only from the sidelines, however much it might affect their daily lives. As in the past, hostile takeovers and massive mergers could not fairly be blamed for all of these dislocations. But also as before, they became a convenient lightning rod amid the growing storm of public anxiety.

By 1982, Alfons Landa's old technique of counterinsurgency had been rediscovered by a young investment banker who probably had never heard of Landa himself. To be sure, Landa had pursued his "raid the raider" strategy with different weapons, using proxy fights rather than cash tender offers. But the concept was the same. And in early 1982, it was employed memorably in the deal that seemed to ring the starting bell for the decade to come: the takeover battle between Bendix and Martin Marietta.

Bendix, a $1.8 billion conglomerate whose products ranged from auto filters to airplane wheels, was the aggressor.[28] It was led by William Agee, a superficially casual but self-important executive who had already triggered a flashy corporate scandal when he had divorced his wife to marry the attractive and ambitious Mary Cunningham, formerly his top aide at Bendix. His takeover target was Martin Marietta, an aerospace giant headquartered in Bethesda, Maryland. In August 1982, Agee launched a hostile tender offer for Martin Marietta at $43 per share.

Martin Marietta sought advice from its investment banker, the skilled but secretly corrupt Martin A. Siegel of Kidder, Peabody and Company. Siegel ticked off the usual defensive measures, little changed from the 1950s: Martin Marietta could sue on antitrust grounds, or claim that Agee had misled investors. It could buy something Agee would not want, or sell something he was eager to have. It could issue additional shares to dilute Agee's stake, or it could search out another mate more compatible with current management.

But then Siegel added another possible ploy, which he called the "counter-tender." In short, Martin Marietta could defend itself by announcing a hostile tender offer for Bendix. "The counter-tender has been tried before as a defense, but it has never been successful at keeping a company independent," Siegel told the board, apparently unfamiliar with the successful Fruehauf defense in 1953. "In this case I think there is a good chance that it will." As Siegel outlined it, a counter-tender might attract other bidders for Bendix, or force Bendix to negotiate a settlement, or perhaps even drive Agee away entirely.[29] The board accepted his advice, and announced a hostile tender offer for Bendix at $75 a share. "It became known as Marty Siegel's Pac-Man defense," in honor of a computer video game in which a glowing goblin is pursued until it turns and consumes its pursuer, according to one account.[30]

The audacious strategy fascinated journalists this time as much as it had when Landa first used it. Before the battle was over, United Technologies Corporation made a rival bid for Martin Marietta. Allied Corporation ultimately came to Bendix's rescue, but dumped Agee in the process. Martin Marietta emerged independent, as Marty Siegel had hoped it would.

The Bendix four-ring circus just happened to be in full swing when the stock market, in August 1982, finally found its footing after more than a decade of slips and falls. Investment managers abruptly cut short their Nantucket vacations to get back to their desks. The same year, the Supreme Court struck down an antitakeover law that Illinois, like many other states, had enacted in response to the frantic acquisitions of the 1960s. The decision "seemed to mark a death knell for this genre of statute," one legal scholar noted.[31] Under former Wall Street executive John Shad, the Securities and Exchange Commission did little but study the accelerating merger movement, reflecting Shad's belief "that takeovers were good and tampering with the regulatory system to control them would create more problems than it would solve."[32] As the Bendix deal was unfolding, Shad was recruiting the agency's first chief economist, Charles Cox, a University of Chicago alumnus who also "subscribed fervently to the view that free, unfettered markets offered a more efficient and effective means to solve society's problems than government did."[33]

But neither the free market nor the government had any answers for the major corporations that were facing millions of dollars worth of liability claims filed by workers who believe they had been fatally afflicted by their exposure to asbestos. Efforts to derail the asbestos litigation in the courts had failed. On August 26, 1982, Johns Manville, once the dominant giant of the asbestos industry, filed for bankruptcy court protection, explaining that it could not survive the liabilities being claimed in the lawsuits it faced. A few days later, a second major manufacturer also sought bankruptcy court protection. The news was a jolt for Manville's co-defendants, including Porter, which had manufactured and distributed asbestos products since 1958. By 1982, Porter was already facing roughly 8,000 asbestos-related lawsuits. Manville had been paying approximately 30 percent of all the settlements in the asbestos cases so far, and with Manville now protected by the bankruptcy code, the remaining defendants might well find that their burden had grown.

Of course, intractable old problems like asbestos liability, steel industry pensions, and middle-America job security attracted little concern as the new-age stock market took off, lighting the fuse for a new explosive merger movement. Indeed, among the busiest corporate shoppers in 1982 was U.S. Steel, which stunned Washington by spending $6.6 billion—money supposedly essential for modernizing its inefficient steel plants—to come to the rescue of Marathon Oil, facing a hostile bid by Mobil. By then, after a decade of skyrocketing energy prices, it seemed that almost every major oil company was either the target or the pursuer in a takeover fight.

The number of deals and their dollar value began to grow, with the profit-rich oil industry in the forefront. Between January and December of 1983, Wall Street handled nearly 2,400 deals worth $52.8 billion.[34] In 1984, the number of deals would grow to nearly 3,160 and the dollar value of those deals would exceed $126 billion.[35] In April of that year, *Fortune* magazine reported that, during the prior decade, "some 23,000 deals were sealed, including 82 in which *Fortune* 500 companies were swallowed up."

As in the mid-1950s, a backlash was brewing. Corporate executives found some scarce common ground with labor leaders as they both lobbied Congress for some sort of legislation that would curb hostile takeovers and other forms of arm-twisting by the new band of raiders stalking undervalued companies.[36] Once again, as in the salad days of Louis Wolfson and Tom Evans, the rights of shareholders were being championed by those who accused corporate America of forgetting who its real owners were. And once again, many people in the American workforce found themselves wondering, What about us?

In Washington, "Congress considered hundreds of bills aimed at curbing the merger market," but enacted none of them.[37] Reacting to the growing political outcry, the SEC appointed a special committee to examine the effects of cash tender offers on the marketplace and the national economy.

The panel included Marty Lipton, Joe Flom, and deal-maker Bruce Wasserstein, prompting skeptics to assume that the fix was in from Wall Street's corner. Even Wasserstein conceded that the committee's report, released in 1983, "adopted a hodgepodge practical approach that failed to please either side in the debate."[38] The report offered little in the way of broad factual findings, a common failing of the SEC's response to the important policy issues raised by the new merger mania.[39] As in the early 1950s, the commission found itself being swept along by swift and complex changes in how Wall Street did business.

The debate over tender offers raised fundamental policy questions that would have been familiar to any alert congressional staffer in 1955: When should company executives be permitted to resist unwelcome takeovers? Did such deals make the economy more efficient, or did they come at the expense of longer-term investments in research and staff development? And how could the interests of stockholders be balanced against the interests of employees, communities, creditors, and customers? Or, as one scholar put it, "In the broadest sense, were tender offers a 'good' or 'bad' thing?"[40]

Although free-market economists argued passionately that tender offers were merely the market's way of rewarding the good managers and penalizing the bad, state legislatures nevertheless responded to the prodding from their hard-pressed corporate leaders by enacting statutes designed to "frustrate hostile bids."[41] But as the statutes began to fall under Supreme Court scrutiny, the SEC offered little in the way of thoughtful alternatives. The merger movement, far from being deterred by these wrenching debates, simply accelerated.

Underneath the frenzy this time, as in earlier outbreaks, were great amounts of greed and a certain amount of crime. Lawyers and investment bankers were selling their inside knowledge to stock speculators like Ivan Boesky, who sent Marty Siegel briefcases of cash in exchange for tips on pending deals.[42] Corners were being cut, private side deals were being hidden from clients. The sheer scale of the transactions meant that fees calculated at one or two percentage points of the deal would quickly mount to a king's ransom.

One of the rumored takeover targets of 1983 was Macmillan, whose shares were then trading at about $36 apiece. But Ned Evans, having sat at the elbow of one of the great takeover artists of the postwar era, had no intention of becoming a victim of such games himself. In April 1983, he sued David J. Greene and Company, the same offbeat firm that had challenged his father in the fight for the Brown Company in the early 1960s. He charged that Greene was trying to manipulate his company's stock to invite a hostile takeover. His adversary insisted that the younger Evans was overreacting, but Greene sold its Macmillan stock and went away with the profit. Meanwhile, Ned Evans started making acquisitions of his own—but they were all friendly deals, never hostile ones.

The takeover game had changed—indeed, it seemed, all of business life had changed. Porter had a rough year in 1982, when a housing slump driven by sky-high mortgage rates expanded the losses at Missouri Portland. Tom Evans looked for unprofitable operations that could be shed. Of course, his own generation's takeover fights had so reshaped corporate law that nothing could be done without armies of attorneys. And there were few people that Tom Evans disliked more than lawyers.

Indeed, it seemed that there was little to excite him at Crane or Porter. He was almost seventy-four years old, and he was tired of the corporate battlefield. He had other interests. His thoroughbred stables had fulfilled his dreams by producing Pleasant Colony, which won the Kentucky Derby in 1981 in front of a cheering crowd that included his devoted sister Elinor and her family in Louisville. And his magnificent art collection, which he had begun in his days with Betty Parker, had propelled him onto the board of the National Portrait Gallery in Washington, D.C., and into the inner circle of knowledgeable collectors. His collection of old Dutch masters was superb; he owned some heart-lifting Impressionist works, including one of the famous "Flags" series by Childe Hassam; he cherished several lovely Winslow Homers, and his sporting prints were treasures. He and his third wife, Betty, seemed to be having fun—traveling, attending charity events, hosting wonderful Christmas parties for their local church congregation at their comfortable estate on the top of Round Hill in Old Greenwich.

As the rest of America rediscovered the game he had played with such energetic joy all his life, Tom Evans was ready to leave the field. And a path for his exit opened up, courtesy of a formidable Crane board member named William Donaldson. Bill Donaldson, who had an illustrious career in academia, government, and Wall Street, had first come to know Tom Evans through Evans's generous gifts to Yale, where Donaldson had been the founding dean of the business school. Evans had invited him onto the board of Crane, and the astute Donaldson—he was among the founders of the Wall Street firm Donaldson, Lufkin and Jenrette—sensed that his old friend was restless and unhappy. He had a proposal: Why not sell Crane to Donaldson's venture capital firm, which would take the company private? Evans expressed interest.

In an effort to avoid any subsequent criticism that he had used his insider's position to foster his own interests, Donaldson resigned from the Crane board at its January 1984 meeting, without explaining why. He quickly collected an investment group, working out some of the details with the old takeover master. The negotiations were kept extraordinarily quiet, to avoid attracting the raiders who were roaming the landscape. A few members of senior management were approached in confidence, to see if they would be willing to stay on. But among those left out of these discussions was Shel Evans, an executive vice president and member of the board—and Tom Evans's youngest son.

By mid-February 1984, Donaldson was ready to make a presentation to the board on behalf of a group of investors. He proposed to buy all of the Crane Company, except its troubled CF&I Steel unit, for $35 a share, for a total purchase price of $357 million. Evans invited Donaldson to make his offer at the board's scheduled meeting on Monday, February 28, at Crane's headquarters at 300 Park Avenue.

Shel Evans learned officially about Donaldson's proposal the Friday before that meeting when Donaldson called him over to his office. The young Evans was disturbed both by what he heard and what he didn't hear: he opposed leaving CF&I out of any deal, and there had been no future role mentioned for him. He approached his father in his office at Evans and Company, down the hall from Crane's executive suite. The old man, rounded and gray, fidgeted in his chair behind his desk. His son, handsome in a golden casual way that reminded some of the actor Robert Redford, was blunt.

"It looks like I'm not included in the deal," he said.

"Right," said his father.

"What am I going to do?" the younger man asked. He had worked at Crane since 1974, and had worked hard, polishing his management skills and learning the business's day-to-day troubles and strengths. He had been a director for five years, and knew many of the men on his father's board personally. Crane had been a big piece of his life, and now he was being roughly excluded from its future.

"You can go back and work on the floor of the exchange," said his father briskly, relegating his son to the world where he and his brothers had served their apprenticeship so many years earlier.

"I don't think I'm going to do that," answered Shel Evans, angry but unshaken. He turned on his heel and left his father's office.

That weekend, he called all of the directors he could reach to warn them about his father's plans to push through Donaldson's offer at the meeting on Monday. Many of the directors were troubled by the proposal. It seemed that Donaldson was buying the cream of the Crane Company, leaving its soured steel unit's problems for current shareholders to solve.

Besides, the autocratic handling of the matter did not seem fair to the directors, all accomplished men used to running their own businesses—and it certainly did not seem fair to Shel Evans. Even the directors most loyal to Tom Evans were troubled. After all, one said, you don't just sell the company because you want to retire. You plan your succession in conjunction with the board and you bow out gracefully.

Graceful exits had never been Tom Evans's strong suit, however. He had snubbed managers and dismissed critics for years. He hated to negotiate, as Larry Lederman had observed. He had decided to sell Crane to Donaldson. Donaldson had made a fair offer, and that was that. And but for Shel Evans's rebellion and advance warning, the surprised directors might well have gone along with the plan. But in a poignant reversal of roles, the younger Evans was arguing that the deal his father supported actually shortchanged the shareholders his father had always championed.

On Monday morning, February 27, the independent members of the board sent two of their number to Tom Evans's office as ambassadors. They proposed that the board take up the succession issue first, by accepting Evans's resignation in favor of his son. Then, Shel Evans could deal with Donaldson. Evans abruptly rejected the idea and the delegation left to join the other directors in the boardroom.

Bill Donaldson and his team were waiting in an anteroom as the Crane directors assembled, grim and a little nervous. Tom Evans, obviously angry, took his place at the head of the table—and met immediate resistance. Several directors argued that his secret negotiations with Donaldson made him a partisan in the discussions, and that he therefore should not chair the meeting at which Donaldson's offer would be aired. Evans had not faced such a serious boardroom challenge since Art Landa's stormy tenure on the board a quarter-century earlier. But the rebellious directors, with Shel Evans in their ranks, insisted that the first item of business should be selecting a chairman to run the meeting.

Someone called for a voice vote, and a chorus of "ayes" answered. Only two directors held back, one abstaining and one sadly voting against the motion out of deep loyalty to the angry, elderly man at the head of the table.

"If that is the way you feel, I resign," the elderly chairman barked, his fierce brown eyes raking the room. He rose from his chair and, on that day of February 27, 1984, he walked out of the boardroom he had dominated for almost a quarter-century.

Shel Evans was elected to run the meeting—in effect, to run the company. After some discussion about the proposed buyout, he sent one of the directors out to invite Donaldson to make his presentation. Isolated in the anteroom, Donaldson apparently knew nothing of the dramatic generational coup that had occurred behind the boardroom doors. He expected that with Tom Evans's support, the proposal would be welcomed and his presentation would be almost a formality. He learned instead that his old friend had abruptly resigned, and the board was not at all inclined to accept his offer. He made his proposal, fielded the directors' questions, accepted their polite thanks, and left.

He sought out Tom Evans before leaving the building. "Unbelievable, isn't it?" the old man said. Yes, it was unbelievable. Then, some private curtain fell across the topic. There was not a word of blame for his son. Donaldson shrugged, shook his head, and left.

In the boardroom, Shel Evans himself was facing a bit of opposition. His father and Bill Donaldson had both argued that the company had to announce the buyout proposal, to keep the marketplace and Crane investors informed. Shel disagreed, arguing that the offer was "not real," but the more experienced directors overruled him. The board ultimately decided to announce the offer and to hire the investment banking firm of First Boston to evaluate the proposal on behalf of the company.

The announcements were prepared and sent out, revealing both the buy-out proposal and Tom Evans's resignation. "A Crane spokesman said Mr. Evans had intended for some time to step down," the *Wall Street Journal* reported.[43] A reporter for the *Journal* had called Tom Evans directly after reading the press release, and Evans told him he viewed the Donaldson proposal as "a fair offer," but added that he wasn't involved in the buy-out group that Donaldson had assembled. Again, he revealed nothing of the painful battle that had preceded his resignation.

After the announcements were prepared and the directors had left, Shel Evans sought out his father. He tried to explain what had happened, and why he had done what he did. But his father abruptly cut him off. They would not discuss it, not then, not ever. Within days, associates recalled, Tom and Betty Evans left for vacation, leaving Shel Evans and the Crane board far behind them.

For a week, Shel Evans worked with the First Boston team that was negotiating with Donaldson. When the proposal had been fully evaluated, another board meeting was scheduled for March 6. Following their investment banker's advice, the independent directors excluded Shel Evans from this meeting, since he was a company executive with career interests that might collide with his obligations as a director. Meeting without their new chairman, the directors rejected the Donaldson proposal as inadequate, and directed First Boston to advise them on the sale of "selected assets" that would "enhance the value of the company for shareholders, with the view to Crane continuing as an independent company."[44]

Bill Donaldson told reporters that he thought the Crane board had acted in haste, and that he hoped it would reconsider. The deal, he believed, was a good one for Crane shareholders. A spokesman for Crane, however, "later replied that the board had 'carefully considered' the offer and that it would not be weighed again."[45]

The board also voted to repurchase as much as $40 million of its own shares, which were plunging in value as speculators registered their disappointment that the buyout had not gone through. But the first big block of shares that it purchased belonged to Tom Evans. Using company cash and various company pension plans, the board paid its former chairman $8.4 million for his entire stake in Crane. That was about $1.8 million less than their market value at the time, reflecting the difficulty the old man would likely have had if he tried to sell his shares in a nervous, deal-obsessed market.

Tom Evans had left the game for good, but it roared ahead without him. With junk bonds providing the bait and tackle, minnows were once again cruising for whales, and frequently catching them. Mutual funds were buying up the bonds that financed these deals, and consumers were flocking to take advantage of the high yields such mutual funds offered. But corporate defense lawyers were becoming ever more ingenious in devising techniques for repelling the new sharks, and the important chancery judges in Delaware, who presided over most of this era's battles for corporate control, were giving directors a little more room to maneuver.

But still, many Americans were alarmed and outraged at the consequences of this new wave of mergers and leveraged buyouts. As in the earlier battles for corporate control, the people in the trenches seemed to sustain most of the casualties, as less efficient plants were closed and once-comfortable belts were tightened. Much of the anger, and perhaps envy, seem to be aimed at Drexel Burnham Lambert—the Kleiner, Bell and Company of this new day—although by 1985 Drexel had plenty of competition. Takeover battles, a business that had been considered somewhat shameful among the blue-chip barons of Wall Street as recently as the early 1970s, were now considered fair game for any Wall Street investment bank and top-tier corporate law firm.

Practitioners of criminal law would soon find their Wall Street niche as well, as federal prosecutors began to explore some of the dark espionage behind the public takeover wars. Just over two years after Tom Evans stalked out of the Crane boardroom, prosecutors got a tip that would lead to the arrest of Dennis Levine, an investment banker at Drexel. The rest of the decade's deals would be carried out under the shadow of a widening federal investigation and a deepening disdain for Wall Street among the American public.

Back at Crane, Shel Evans settled down to the tasks of running the company and patching up his torn relationship with his father. The former, while difficult, would be a far easier task than the latter. Like his brother Ned, Shel Evans seems to have decided that managing well was the best revenge. And like Macmillan, the Crane Company prospered under the stewardship of another Evans.

For the rest of 1984—indeed, for the rest of his life—Tom Evans's name would be found not in the business pages but in the society columns, where reporters noted his attendance at various glittering charitable events supporting the worlds of art, antiques, and thoroughbred racing. On a beautiful evening in October 1984, he attended a benefit for the Museum of the City of New York's fiftieth anniversary. It was the ultimate in glamour, a gathering of New York's social elite at what was arguably the heart of Manhattan's lush life, the Rainbow Room, high above Rockefeller Center. In keeping with the evening's nostalgic theme, Tom Evans and Betty arrived at the affair in a gleaming antique 1930 Ford. It was the kind of car that the ambitious young Tom Evans of Pittsburgh might have dreamed of owning when it was new, if he had only had the money.

KING SHAREHOLDER

The 1980s roared along without the visible presence of Thomas Mellon Evans, who retreated to a small two-room office suite a block from his old Manhattan headquarters on Park Avenue. There, he traded stocks, oversaw his famous thoroughbred farms in Virginia and Kentucky, and alternately amused and berated his tiny personal staff. He still dressed as befitted a proud tycoon of the 1950s; the concept of "business casual" was utterly alien to him.

Life was less tranquil and formal in the corporate empire that he had built—and in the financial markets where he had once been so feared and influential. With Drexel and its rival Wall Street firms ready to finance almost any conceivable deal, mergers and acquisitions were a national preoccupation. A galloping stock market attracted not only deal-minded entrepreneurs but also millions of upper-middle-class American investors, whose purchases of mutual funds during the decade eclipsed anything that Wall Street had seen in the past. These mutual funds, along with more aggressive pension funds and deregulated banks and savings institutions, provided a ready market for the "deal stocks" involved in takeovers and for the junk bonds and other forms of Chinese money being used to finance those transactions.

As in the 1950s, most companies that changed hands during the 1980s did so in friendly deals, not in noisy boardroom battles. Some were simply purchased back from their public shareholders by their senior managers, in partnership with leveraged buyout funds like KKR. Many friendly mergers were driven by the search for better or bigger markets, more modern facilities, a more profitable mix of products, or a more promising blend of new technologies. But alongside these prosaic realities, the decade also saw the rise of a new generation of individual corporate raiders who alternately fascinated and frightened the American public—media celebrities like T. Boone Pickens, Sir James Goldsmith, Carl Icahn, Ronald Perelman, and the more mature Saul Steinberg. Once again, the demand for "shareholder rights" became a rallying cry for outsiders seeking to wrest control of a public corporation from its incumbent managers, although most newly enfranchised American shareholders still seemed to think of themselves primarily as victims, rather than as beneficiaries, of the raiders' ideology.

Once again, as after the proxy fights of the mid-1950s, there was a sense in America's boardrooms that no chief executive was really safe from an unwelcome takeover, now that formerly fastidious Wall Street firms were competing eagerly to fill the war chests of the new raiders. Once again, as in Follansbee in the 1950s, company towns felt threatened—in tiny Bartlesville, Oklahoma, residents rallied publicly in support of the hometown managers of Philips Petroleum as they fought off first Pickens, in late 1984, and then Icahn in 1985.[1] Movies like *Wall Street* and popular plays like *Other People's Money* once again introduced the mainstream culture to villains and heroes from the world of business. And as before, Washington took up its rhetorical cudgels, prodded by an alliance between job-protecting unions and job-protecting chief executives. Politicians roundly condemned a marketplace in which "almost anyone with a half-baked takeover idea and a few million dollars could persuade Drexel or one of its competitors to help them buy an old-line American company and disassemble it."[2] Subcommittee hearings were held on the impact that mergers were having on jobs, communities, and the American economy, although there was little indisputable evidence to prove the case either way. Newly prominent laissez-faire economists, whose views the Reagan administration had cobbled into a public policy of deregulation and privatization, urged that the market was wiser about such matters than politicians and bureaucrats could ever be. But at least one troubled senator began to publicly refer to the takeover movement as the "corporate killing fields."[3]

Led by creative lawyers like Martin Lipton, the boards and chief executives at major corporations began to craft new, stronger defenses against hostile acquisitions. Indeed, with exquisite irony, that was one of the first tasks undertaken by Shel Evans at Crane Company. In 1984, "golden parachutes" had been created to protect key Crane executives in the event of an unwelcome takeover.[4] Then, in May 1986, Crane's board of directors adopted a "poison pill." It was designed, the board said, to "protect the company's shareholders from abusive takeover practices," including that in which "a raider acquires controlling interest in the corporation through open market purchases" without paying shareholders a premium to reflect the additional value that a controlling block of shares should have.[5] That, of course, had been the young Tom Evans's favorite game.

By then, Crane had spun off its ailing steel operations, CF&I, to its own shareholders, closing the book on the hopeful experiment that Tom Evans took over from Charlie Allen in the late 1960s. The spin-off was approved by shareholders in May 1985. The newly independent steel company took with it a nearly obsolete collection of steel mills and a pension fund insufficient to cover its large and growing responsibilities to retired steelworkers. Crane wanted out of the steel business, and hoped (perhaps beyond reason) that an independent CF&I, which was to be run by a senior Drexel adviser, would be able to attract new credit and develop resources to bring its pension plan into balance.

That did not happen. In November 1990, the legendary Colorado Fuel and Iron filed for bankruptcy. A year later, the federal government's Pension Benefit Guarantee Corporation assumed responsibility for more than $222 million of the company's unfunded obligations to its laid-off and retired employees. For years thereafter, a Crane shareholder in St. Louis—the scene of so many bitter battles during Tom Evans's heyday—struggled unsuccessfully to prove in court that Crane had deliberately understated the steel unit's pension crisis during the spin-off so that it could dump its pension obligations into Uncle Sam's lap.[6] The government pension agency itself never officially supported the shareholder's allegations.

The files in that protracted lawsuit include snippets of testimony by Shel Evans and his father. Shel Evans acknowledged that the difficulties of a CF&I spin-off had been discussed at that tumultuous board meeting in February 1984.[7] Tom Evans himself later testified that CF&I's precarious finances had also been discussed at the December 1983 meeting of Crane's directors, prompting him to conclude that "it was certainly to Crane's advantage to spin it off promptly." The longer CF&I survived as an independent entity the more difficult it would be for the government to hold Crane responsible for the future pension obligations, he explained.[8]

In any case, CF&I Steel also carried into bankruptcy court other potential liabilities, including those arising from pollution problems at the old Roebling steel mill and several other former factory sites.[9] The company ultimately sold its assets to a small Oregon operation, extinguishing a lusty company saga that had spanned a century—and, not incidentally, largely wiping out its shareholders' investment.

No longer burdened with its steel albatross, the Crane Company flourished as the "deal decade" galloped forward. Shel Evans pared the company down to its most profitable, albeit obscure, products and saw his stock price climb with the ambient bull market. On at least one occasion, Shel Evans was the "white knight" who rescued a smaller company from an unwelcome takeover bid. His own acquisitions were almost entirely of a friendly nature. Wall Street analysts began to speak fondly of the now-maturing Evans who occupied the Crane boardroom.

Macmillan, too, prospered under the management of chairman and chief executive Ned Evans. Over the years, he had made sixty-five friendly acquisitions to build up his new empire. By 1987, his company's market value had increased roughly tenfold, to more than $2 billion, placing it among the best performing companies on the New York Stock Exchange during his tenure.

He had aggressively defended Macmillan against two rumored takeovers earlier in the eighties, but as the decade moved past its midpoint the battles for corporate control were becoming more frenzied. One, in particular, alarmed Ned Evans profoundly. In May 1987, the eccentric and controversial British publishing tycoon Robert Maxwell announced a takeover bid for Harcourt Brace Jovanovich, a prominent American publishing house. On May 26, 1987, Harcourt's board approved a plan to frustrate Maxwell's bid through a technique known as a recapitalization. In a recapitalization, a company borrows money, either from banks or by selling bonds, and uses the cash to pay shareholders a substantial dividend or to buy back their shares at a premium. Either step has the effect of making the company more attractive to its own shareholders and, because of its new higher debt burden, less attractive to a potential raider.[10] The day after Harcourt announced its plan to thwart Maxwell's takeover, Ned Evans enlisted the same investment bankers to explore whether Macmillan could use a similar approach to defend itself if it came under attack.[11] He also began increasing his stockholdings in Macmillan, reversing "his five-year practice of selling his Macmillan shares."[12] At the time, Ned Evans and his right-hand man, Macmillan president William F. Reilly, together owned just slightly more than 1 percent of their company's 26 million shares—a state of affairs that Tom Evans in his prime would have condemned.

But despite his meager shareholdings, Ned Evans was determined to retain control of "his" company. His efforts to do so over the next eighteen months appear in hindsight to have been a repudiation of his father's philosophy so thorough and complete that it might have been shaped by a novelist's hand. The fortress he tried to build against the corporate raiders roaming the landscape would expose him to withering scorn and criticism from the nation's foremost business courts and draw the attention of the market's top regulators. And in the end, despite all his effort, the fortress would fall to the raiders who followed in his father's footsteps.

In the year following Maxwell's unsuccessful bid for Harcourt, Ned Evans and his advisers developed a number of different proposals for recapitalizing Macmillan. But through all the permutations, a Delaware judge later observed, "two central concepts remained constant."[13] The first was that Evans and his top executives would control the restructured company. The second, in the judge's view, was that "management would acquire that majority control, not by investing new capital at prevailing market prices, but by being granted several hundred thousand restricted Macmillan shares in stock options."[14]

Through the summer of 1987, as the giddy deal-driven stock market danced higher, Ned Evans proposed and his accommodating directors approved the entire arsenal of modern antitakeover defenses. These included a "poison pill" that would allow existing shareholders to buy more stock at half-price if a raider acquired as much as 30 percent of the company, five-year "golden parachute" severance contracts and substantial stock grants and stock options for Evans and Reilly, and even a $60 million loan to allow the Macmillan employee stock ownership plan (ESOP) to buy 1 million Macmillan shares and tuck them out of harm's way.

But still, Ned Evans apparently did not feel secure. By late summer, he and his advisers had developed a new plan to split Macmillan into two companies, one encompassing its traditional publishing business and the other its newer information-based properties. This "two-company model would be more difficult for a raider to counter," the board was told at its September 22, 1987, meeting. Under the proposal, Evans and his top management would be firmly in control of both companies.

Then came Black Monday, October 19, 1987, when the nation's stock market took its most severe plunge in history. Some shaken observers thought the crash would put the deal-makers and raiders out of business. But the more immediate result was to make the shares of numerous target companies even more affordable. On Wednesday, October 21, 1987, with Wall Street and Washington still holding their breath to see if the market would steady itself, Ned Evans got the news he had dreaded for more than a year. Robert M. Bass, a Texan with a growing reputation as a company collector, had acquired roughly 7.5 percent of Macmillan's stock.[15]

Ned Evans summoned his board members for a special meeting the following Thursday. He warned them about Bass, portraying him as a "greenmailer" who would enrich himself at the expense of other shareholders or use his takeover threat to force Macmillan to let him buy prized company assets cheaply. One judge gently described this characterization as "less than accurate."[16] Indeed, "it was false," another judge wrote.[17] But the Macmillan board, which would itself later be criticized for its docile submission to management,[18] did not independently investigate its new shareholder.

From October into the following spring, as Bass increased his Macmillan stake slightly, Ned Evans continued to work on the plan that he expected would put Macmillan beyond a raider's reach. But on May 17, the day before Macmillan's annual shareholders meeting, Bass wrote to Evans offering to buy the company for $64 a share—a substantial premium to then-current prices. In his letter, Bass emphasized that the offer was a friendly one, open to negotiation, and invited Evans and his management team to participate in the acquisition as his partners.

When Macmillan's shareholders met the following day and approved additional stock grants and options for management, Evans did not mention the Bass offer. But when his board convened immediately after the meeting, he told the directors about the unwelcome bid. Then, in quick succession, he designated a handful of independent directors to be a "special committee" that would evaluate his proposed restructuring plan on behalf of shareholders. He had already lined up Lazard Frères and Company, with whom management had been consulting for many weeks, to serve as the "independent" panel's investment adviser, and had tapped Marty Lipton's firm to be its lawyer. These arrangements, too, would be cited later as evidence that called "into serious question the actual independence of the board."[19]

When the board's special committee first met with its lawyers and investment bankers a week later, on May 24, Evans and his three top executives sat in on the meeting. On the agenda, besides Bass's proposal, was management's proposed recapitalization plan, altered slightly to reduce management's future stake from 55 percent to 39 percent—"so that the restructuring would not be regarded as a transfer of corporate control from the public shareholders to management."[20] But the courts later found that this alteration was "one of form, not substance," since management would nevertheless have "effective control" of both of the two new companies.[21]

Under the plan, valued at just under $65 a share, Macmillan's public shareholders were to receive $52.35 in cash, a bond worth $4.50, and stock in each of the two surviving companies, which were dubbed "Publishing" and "Information." By contrast, Evans and his three top executives would get no cash dividends or bonds. Instead, they would exchange their restricted Macmillan stock and stock options—awarded to them by the board in prior years, and valued at $39 million—for 39 percent of Information's stock and 3.2 percent of Publishing's stock. The ESOP that the executives would control would own 26 percent of Publishing's stock and 4 percent of Information's stock. The management quartet, besides gaining effective control of both new companies, would also receive about $9 million in cash and other benefits as well, under the terms of their compensation packages.[22]

On May 30, 1988, when the Macmillan board assembled to consider the future of the company, Lazard Frères opined that the $64.73-a-share proposal was fair and adequate, despite its earlier view that Macmillan was actually worth somewhere between $72.57 and $80 a share. Furthermore, it was Lazard's official view that the Bass offer of $64 a share was unfair and inadequate. None of the committee's members questioned the extremely elastic logic behind these conclusions. The company's own investment banker, Bruce Wasserstein, said he valued the restructuring plan more generously, at between $63 and $68 a share, but he too dismissed the Bass bid as inferior. On the recommendation of its special committee, the full board approved the restructuring plan and rejected the Bass proposal.

The following day, May 31, 1988, the company announced the restructuring plan in a press release, indicating that it would be implemented ten days later. "The restructuring was not made subject to shareholder approval," a Delaware judge later noted, "and that May 31 press release was the first communication to shareholders that their company would be radically altered."[23]

Then, over the next three days, Ned Evans tried to persuade Robert Bass—who, after all, was one of Macmillan's largest shareholders—to support the restructuring plan. As luck would have it, one of the actors in the drama was Larry Lederman, the Wachtell Lipton lawyer who had counseled Tom Evans in his dealings with Missouri Portland a decade earlier. He later described a meeting between Ned Evans and Robert Bass: "Ned had a simple message, which he'd worked out in the anguish of trying to find common ground for the meeting, which was: 'If you start out hostile, you'll never again do a negotiated transaction.' Ned tried to explain to Bass that he'd abandoned the hostile route for Macmillan because it was very costly and left no assurance that you would get what you were seeking. Ned tried to explain how hard it was to put the image of the hostile raider behind him and how rewarding it had been for Macmillan to do only negotiated, friendly transactions. Bass was not interested in Ned's commentary. It was all beside the point. He acted as if he were waiting for the national anthem to finish and for the ballgame to begin."[24]

Lederman later reflected in his memoirs that "from Bass's perspective, one that I first fully understood from Tom Evans, he was entitled to take a profit wherever he found it, without considering the effects on a flourish-ing company."[25]

Bass went to court in Delaware, where Macmillan was registered, and on July 14, he won a court order blocking Evans's recapitalization plan. The same day, while Macmillan's lawyers prepared to appeal that ruling, Ned Evans opened a second front in his war for control of the company. He began negotiating with Henry Kravis and Michael Tokarz of KKR, the powerful leveraged buyout firm, on a deal in which KKR would buy Macmillan in partnership with Evans and his top executives. "There is nothing in the record to suggest that this was done pursuant to board action," the Delaware Supreme Court later noted. "If anything, it was Evans acting alone in his own personal interest."[26]

On July 18, 1988, four days after his courtroom victory in Delaware, Robert Bass made a public tender offer to buy Macmillan for $73.50 a share. But he almost immediately found himself facing another deter-mined bidder. On July 21, publisher Robert Maxwell, who was still shop-ping for an American publishing property, wrote Ned Evans offering $80 a share for Macmillan. Bass effectively folded his hand.

Ned Evans reacted to the swashbuckling British tycoon the way dozens of chief executives had once reacted to the ebullient Tom Evans. He did not even respond to Maxwell's letter for five weeks, as the negotiations with KKR intensified. When Maxwell made his offer public in mid-August, Wasserstein and Lazard promptly advised Macmillan's board that this unwelcome offer, too, was unfair and inadequate—although it was at the top end of the value they had put on the company less than three months earlier and far exceeded the value of the recapitalization plan that they had previously recommended. The Macmillan board rejected the Maxwell offer.

In early September, Evans and his senior managers met with KKR to finalize KKR's purchase proposal, which would give Macmillan's senior management an ownership stake of up to 20 percent. At this meeting, a critical judge later observed, Evans and his senior managers indicated to KKR that they would recommend the buyout to the board of directors "even though KKR had not yet disclosed to Evans and his group the amount of its bid."[27] KKR said it would have its final bid ready by late in the afternoon of Friday, September 9—which was then set as the deadline by which any other bids for the company must be submitted. On the evening of September 8, at a meeting with Ned Evans, Maxwell was told that he had less than twenty-four hours to prepare his bid, although he had been given only limited access to company information that had been freely sup-plied to KKR months earlier.

Maxwell responded with an all-cash bid for the company at $84 a share. At the end of his letter, he added, "If you have a financed binding alternative proposal which will generate a greater present value for shareholders, I will withdraw my bid."[28] The deadline came and went, but KKR had not yet reduced its bid to paper. Evans and Kravis continued to work on the proposal through the night and into the next morning. The result was a written bid in which KKR offered a package of cash and notes that it valued at $85 share. The company's financial advisers shaved 24 cents off that valuation, before formally advising the board that weekend that the KKR offer was the best deal for shareholders.

Accordingly, the Macmillan board abandoned the company's appeal of the restructuring proposal and approved KKR's apparently superior bid, announcing on September 12 that they would recommend the proposal to shareholders. "An elegant solution, with honor, had been achieved," Larry Lederman later wrote. "Buoyant goodwill was everywhere present in the room. The meeting was adjourned for the board to eat lunch."[29]

But Ned Evans's celebration was cut short on September 15, when Robert Maxwell, unpredictable to the end, stepped forward with a new, higher bid for the company—$86.80 share, in cash. The auction wasn't over yet. The question was, would Kravis increase his bid?

He would, but at a price: Kravis insisted that his bid was conditional on his receiving what investment bankers called a "crown jewel" option, a controversial provision that allowed KKR to buy a prime piece of Macmillan's business even if Maxwell won the bidding. Such "crown jewel options" were designed to effectively end the auction, since no one would reasonably offer more for a company whose "crown jewels" had been promised to another bidder. He further insisted on a "no shop" clause, providing that his bid would be automatically withdrawn if any detail of it were disclosed to anyone except Macmillan's management, directors, and advisers.

Maxwell and KKR both submitted bids by the new deadline, 5:30 p.m., Monday, September 26. Robert Maxwell offered $89 a share, in cash. Kravis offered a new package of cash and notes that he valued at $89.50 a share, and that Macmillan's financial advisers valued at $89.05 to $89.10 a share. It was simply too close to call, the financial advisers decided. Bruce Wasserstein prepared a careful script for his telephone calls informing Kravis and Maxwell that a third round of bidding was necessary.

The Delaware Supreme Court later described what happened next: "Shortly after the bids were received, Evans and Reilly, who were present in the Macmillan offices at the time, asked unidentified financial advisers about the status of the auction process. Inexplicably, these advisers told

Evans and Reilly that both bids had been received, informed them of the respective price and forms of the bids, and stated that the financial advisers were unable to recommend either bid to the board."[30]

Shortly thereafter, at 7 P.M., Evans telephoned KKR's Manhattan office, reaching Mike Tokarz. According to another Delaware judge's recital, Ned Evans told the KKR partner that Maxwell's bid was "$89, all-cash."[31]

"Great, we have won," Tokarz responded happily, obviously assuming that Evans was calling to announce the final results of the auction.

There was, the judge later reported, an "awkward silence." Then, one of the two Macmillan executives responded, "Well, it's a little close."[32] (The judge attributed the remark to both Evans and Reilly; Lederman's memoirs gave the credit to Reilly alone.)[33]

The judge continued, "At that point, Mr. Tokarz suspected that this telephone call was not a legitimate official communication intended formally to announce the results of the auction. He then abruptly terminated the conversation."[34] Ned Evans's back-channel conversation with Tokarz, a Delaware Supreme Court judge later observed, was an "extraordinary act of misconduct."[35]

Shortly after 8 P.M., Wasserstein made his careful calls to notify KKR and Maxwell that "we are not in a position at this time to recommend any bid." He told Maxwell's advisers that if Maxwell had a higher bid, he should submit it by midnight. But he was a bit more forthcoming with KKR, according to the Delaware court, telling the firm that its price should be as high as possible and its demands for a "crown jewel" option should be scaled back.[36]

Maxwell stood pat, but KKR raised its bid slightly, to $89.80, and modified its "crown jewel" option demand to make it slightly less onerous. The final bids were in. It was time for the board to decide.

At 9 A.M. on Tuesday, September 27, Ned Evans and Bill Reilly joined the board members for the report on the auction results. Bruce Wasserstein explained how the option had been conducted, assuring the board that it had been "a level playing field," that both parties "had an equal opportunity to participate," and that "each side was told exactly the same thing, read the same script."[37]

Those assurances, the Delaware courts would later conclude, were simply not true. For one thing, Wasserstein had given KKR more guidance before the final round of bidding than Maxwell had received. But more importantly, KKR also had gotten details about Maxwell's bid from Evans's extraordinary telephone call. Although Wasserstein did not know about the call as he addressed the board, Evans and Reilly did. But neither man spoke up to correct Wasserstein's account. After extensive private discussions, the directors once again voted to accept KKR's proposal.

And once again, on September 29, Maxwell unexpectedly raised his bid, to $90.25 a share. He also went to court in Delaware, joined by Macmillan shareholder Robert Bass, to dispute the granting of the crown-jewel option to Kravis. The same day, Henry Kravis's firm disclosed Evans's telephone call in a routine filing to the Securities and Exchange Commission.

"We were confident of winning, until we found out that Ned had called Henry," Lederman later recalled. Lederman believed the telephone call was immaterial, since there had been another round of bidding thereafter. But he knew that the call, in the hands of Maxwell's skilled attorneys, was certain to make the sparks fly in Wilmington.[38]

Macmillan's attorneys in Delaware urged that the directors be reassembled and informed of what had happened so they could reconsider KKR's offer in light of Evans's indiscretion. Ned Evans at first flatly refused, according to Lederman. But once Lederman told him that he would call the directors together if Evans didn't, Ned relented.

"Ned appeared at the meeting as if the gathering was his idea and an opportunity for him to bring the board current on all events," Lederman later recalled. "He told the board of his call to Mike Tokarz and explained that under the terms of the original contract with KKR (signed when they bid $85) he was obligated to inform KKR of the bid. He hadn't realized there would be a further round of bidding that evening. After he finished speaking there was a long, uncomfortable silence. No one spoke or moved; everyone was waiting for him to leave. His well-tailored suit looked rumpled and his shirt was damp and wilted. When he left, he looked very tired."[39]

The directors decided to stand by their original decision in favor of the KKR bid, and their lawyers prepared to defend that decision in court.

The Delaware chancery court, the preeminent business tribunal in the country, reviewed the messy process and concluded that Maxwell had been given every opportunity to submit his best offer, notwithstanding the many imperfections the judge found in the auction procedure. But Maxwell immediately appealed to the state's Supreme Court.

The senior court's decision was blistering. The entire auction for Macmillan "was clandestinely and impermissibly skewed in favor of KKR," the Supreme Court concluded, overturning the outcome. "The lack of an evenhanded bidding process meant that Macmillan's shareholders did not receive the highest price they might have for their shares." Blame was doled out freely—to Evans, to the passive directors, to the prominent lawyers, to the celebrity financial advisers.[40]

The Securities and Exchange Commission had its own quarrel with how the Macmillan management had responded to the threats of the new takeover era. The commission later filed civil charges against Ned Evans and two other senior Macmillan executives, accusing them of failing to disclose for a year that the company had been developing a refinancing plan to ward off hostile takeovers. Without admitting or denying any wrongdoing, the trio settled the complaint out of court in December 1989.[41]

By then, the bizarre Maxwell had added Macmillan to his increasingly shaky house of cards, which tumbled into bankruptcy and litigation after his mysterious death at sea in early November 1991. If Tom Evans had still owned his 22 percent stake in Macmillan, Maxwell's successful bid of $2.6 billion would have put nearly $490 million in his pocket, compared to the $42.9 million the company paid him for his shares in June 1982. Some estimated it would have doubled his already considerable private fortune, which had been vaguely estimated at between $250 million and $1 billion. Ned Evans, as a Macmillan shareholder, did profit from Maxwell's bid. But he had lost Macmillan to a corporate raider, all the same.

The late 1980s were even more problematical for Tom Evans's old flagship, H. K. Porter Company in Pittsburgh. Its Fansteel acquisition had been a tremendous success—a credit to Ned Evans's stint as chairman at Porter. In May 1983, although the unit might have been auctioned off for a considerable sum, Tom Evans and the other Porter directors voted to distribute shares of Fansteel to Porter stockholders as a dividend. The Evans family received just over 1 million shares of Fansteel stock in this spinoff; about 840,000 of those, with a recorded value of more than $40 million, went to Tom Evans, who remained Porter's largest individual stockholder.

But Porter's prospects were hemmed in on all sides by the uncertainties of litigation filed against it by people who blamed their severe health problems on their exposure to asbestos manufactured by Porter's Southern Textile subsidiary from the late 1950s, when Evans acquired it, to the early 1980s.

By 1986, the steady stream of new lawsuits was becoming a torrent. Since 1983, the number of new cases filed each year had tripled, and the number of pending cases had grown from 9,500 to 25,000. By the end of 1982, three other defendant corporations had already sought bankruptcy court protection under the weight of similar asbestos liability claims. Nevertheless, Porter continued to litigate the complaints, at considerable expense.

In early 1987, as the nation's stock market roared to stunning new highs and Ned Evans began his campaign to defend Macmillan, H. K. Porter began the process of removing itself from the public marketplace. Only 9 percent of the company's shares were still in public hands; Tom Evans, his family, and his top managers owned the rest. But in late 1986, when Porter offered to buy back the public's shares at $65 apiece, less than a third of its shareholders accepted the offer. So this time, the arrangement was structured as a takeover that was being submitted to a shareholder vote—a vote that Evans, of course, could dominate with his own private shareholdings. Only the form of the deal had changed, however: the price was still $65 a share, for a total of $6.4 million. Some shareholders protested, unsuccessfully, that the Evans offer was only about 60 percent of what the company was really worth. But observers shrugged: Tom Evans had always driven a hard bargain.[42]

By the end of August 1987, H. K. Porter had become a private company owned by Evans and his family. As the asbestos lawsuits mounted, Porter began to undergo a remarkable transformation behind the veil of its private status. New holding companies were set up under the Evans family's control, and Porter assets were shuttled into them. In the course of these maneuvers, Tom Evans left the company's board in April 1988 after almost a half-century. When the shuffle was over, the old H. K. Porter—the defendant in the asbestos cases—was left with considerably fewer assets than when it had exited the public arena less than two years earlier.[43] Even its $5 million corporate jet was now the property of a separate Evans family holding company.

Then on February 15, 1991, Tom Evans returned his trusty flagship to the pier from which he had first embarked on his fabulous half-century journey: the bankruptcy court. With assets of approximately $50 million but liabilities that could exceed $500 million, H. K. Porter Company filed for bankruptcy protection in Pittsburgh.[44] Its creditors numbered more than a hundred thousand people, including asbestos plaintiffs, elderly retirees, and government agencies seeking unpaid taxes and environmental cleanup costs.

Porter was scarcely alone. By the turn of the decade, dozens of the frenzied deals of the mid-1980s were collapsing under the weight of the debts that had financed them. Drexel itself filed for bankruptcy in early 1990, sending the junk-bond market into a tailspin that temporarily dampened the enthusiasm of the dealmakers.

In August 1992, the bankruptcy court in Pittsburgh authorized a committee of Porter's creditors to go to court to try to recover some $150 million in former Porter assets from Tom Evans, his family, and other associated defendants. The creditors accused Evans and his co-defendants of having "orchestrated an unlawful plan to strip Porter of substantially all of its assets, without giving fair consideration in exchange, thereby violating the rights of tens of thousands of asbestos disease victims and other legitimate creditors of Porter." As a result of the Fansteel spin-off and other maneuvers, the complaint continued, "by 1988 Porter had been reduced from a healthy industrial conglomerate—which had achieved sales in excess of half a billion dollars per year—to a hopelessly insolvent, non-operating shell company, the remaining assets of which pale in comparison to the enormous liabilities with which Porter has been left."[45]

Lawyers for the Evans family insisted that the various corporate transactions had been legal and appropriate, and that financial advisers had assured the directors along the way that Porter still had enough cash and insurance coverage to handle its asbestos claims for the foreseeable future. But in the summer of 1998, the defendants would settle the case out of court, contributing $31 million to a trust fund that was being created to pay asbestos claims. With other funds wrung out of the bankrupt estate and its insurance carriers, the trust fund would total about $100 million, to be shared among as many as 300,000 ailing people.

Finally, only Fansteel, which Ned Evans had so artfully acquired for his father in 1976 and which had been spun off in 1983, publicly revealed the fragile bridges that had been rebuilt among the Evanses in the 1980s. Fansteel's board included Tom Evans; his third wife, Betty Barton Evans; his son Tom Evans Jr.; and at various points, both Ned Evans and Shel Evans. Shel Evans had continued to run the Crane Company into the late 1990s; in 1994, his father had attended a dinner marking Shel's tenth anniversary as CEO and volunteered that his youngest son had done a very good job. After Ned Evans left Macmillan, KKR backed him and his senior managers in a new publishing venture, now called Primedia, which prospered with publications like *Seventeen* and *New York* magazine. Like his younger brother, Ned had mended his fences with his father and found some common ground in their shared love of horse breeding and racing.

In the late summer of 1995, Tom Evans himself stepped down from Fansteel's board, having served for nearly twenty years. His reason for resigning was simply his age. He was eighty-five.

He still went to his office several days a week. But during the winter of 1996, he fell on an icy driveway, hitting his head against the asphalt. It was the latest in a series of bruising falls that had begun several years earlier. He recovered from the latest injury, but found it difficult to speak and even more difficult to get around. Still, he kept up appearances, arriving at his office less frequently but just as splendidly dressed as ever. On the morning of Thursday, July 17, 1997, he went to be fitted for a new suit. He made some stock trades over the phone in his car as he returned to his glorious two-story apartment at River House, in Manhattan's posh Beekman Place neighborhood. And there, at age eighty-six, he died of what his eldest son termed "heart failure." His obituary in the New York Times, filling nearly a half page, described him as "one of Wall Street's most feared corporate raiders in the 1950s and 1960s."[46]

He left a world remarkably different from the one that saw his rise to power, one that his old mentor, W. L. Mellon, would no doubt have found more congenial than the starchy, highly regulated era in which Tom Evans made his mark. That earlier era of the 1950s, in which Big Labor and Big Government squared off against Big Business, had vanished and been replaced by the age of the Big Stockholder. The values of the raiders, which seemed so threatening and iconoclastic to the American public when Tom Evans and Lou Wolfson and Charlie Green were proclaiming them in the 1950s, had become the creed by which American society operated: the primary responsibility of business was to make money for its stockholders. Labor's duty was to price itself so that business could be competitive and make money; government's duty was to get out of the way of the money-making process.

Gone, too, were the corporate statesmen of the Eisenhower age, diplomatic men who fitted easily into the councils of power and were careful to cloak their corporate priorities in terms of patriotism, "welfare capitalism," and the common good. Across America, self-proclaimed "tough bosses" were thick on the ground, writing memoirs that boasted of their clever incivilities. Even that old epithet "corporate raider" had lost its sting; indeed, the word was scarcely ever used outside the obituary pages. Mutual funds and state pension funds had become as aggressive in dealing with the "entrenched" management at poor-performing companies as Tom Evans and Charlie Green ever were. Even unions had seen the light: their pension funds could be found opposing the "poison pills" that defended corporations from unwelcome takeovers.

What Tom Evans called "corporate rejuvenation" had been rechristened "corporate restructuring," and had become routine. His "quick-weight-loss" approach to producing quick profits, so harshly criticized at Crane in the late 1950s, had become widely adopted as "downsizing," and was resoundingly applauded on Wall Street. Mergers, takeovers, acquisitions, and deals filled the headlines and provided daily fodder for a plethora of business news outlets. A few voices worried aloud about the immense political power vested in the gigantic corporations created by these mergers. "The American economic system is at its best when public and private needs are balanced," warned the dean of the business school at

Tom Evans's beloved Yale. "The sheer magnitude of mergers is skewing the equilibrium."[47] But as the millennium approached, few in Congress even questioned such powerful corporate combinations, which seemed to strengthen American companies for the competitive struggles of a thoroughly global marketplace. Instead, the political debate focused on new ways government could stand aside and let the market work its magic.

In short, the raiders had won and the shareholder was king, treated with as much deference as in Mr. Mellon's day. The early Mellons who dominated the world in which Tom Evans came of age represented perhaps the purest vision of the shareholder—the shareholder as themselves, clear about their rights and privileges, unconflicted by sentimental attachments to worker or city or countryside or even culture, beyond their own art collections. The postwar world took the power of the shareholder, diced it into tiny pieces, and scattered it among Establishment-minded pension funds, passive mutual funds, and small investors who were neither organized nor inclined to assert their power. Tom Evans and his fellow raiders rebelled loudly and colorfully against that arrangement, and in doing so they helped to change it, in ways both admirable and worrisome.

Their efforts may have driven American companies to adapt more quickly to the global competition that was arising from the devastation of world war, as many economists argue. And perhaps, in Lou Wolfson's wonderful phrase, they shook up some clubhouses, allowing youthful daring and new money to gain ground against birthright and privilege and genteel cronyism. Challenged in the mid-1950s to explain what experience his young managers had that qualified them to run his companies, Lou Wolfson responded, "This experience thing does not enter into our scope of operation. Most of us are young, too, and we have not had the opportunity of some of the older men in the business. But we think we have a desire and ambition, and we think we have enough common sense, to go ahead and step into almost any phase of business in any field and be successful."[48]

On the other side of the ledger, Tom Evans and his tribe began to chip away at the bonds of loyalty that had once knitted owner and worker together, and they scorned the notion that a business owed any civic duty to its community. In town after town, they turned the face of economic power into the face of an indifferent stranger.

But, for good or ill, they kept the notion of "shareholder rights" from being drowned out amid the more strident demands of other constituencies—managers, employees, customers, suppliers, neighbors, tax collectors, regulators. And by the century's end, millions of Americans were Tom Evans—owners who expected their corporate investments to produce their future wealth. Newly empowered investors, with their Internet stock trading accounts, had invaded the stock market in proud pursuit of exactly the same "fast buck" that Evans and the other raiders of the 1950s were roundly condemned for seeking.

But one wondered, as the values of the early raiders became the values of America, who would speak for the other silent constituencies of business? Who would challenge the raiders' values on behalf of a society profoundly affected by what companies do in pursuit of shareholder profits? Unlike the smug and isolated business barons who schooled the young Tom Evans, the middle-class shareholders facing the twenty-first century could not hope to ignore the collisions between the profit motive and the kind of world most Americans still pined for, one in which "the stronger does not always take full advantage of the weaker," one in which everything was not for sale to the highest bidder.[49] Immense good had come from the vitality of shareholder-driven capitalism. But as ever, shareholders remained citizens of a community, settlers in a landscape, neighbors and coworkers, consumers and taxpayers. That it was as difficult as ever for shareholders to balance their own profits against the rest of civic life did not make it any less important that they do so.

And what of those other surviving pioneers of the dawning age of the corporate raiders? As Tom Evans breathed his last, Ben Heineman was in retirement in Chicago, although his Northwest Industries had been absorbed years earlier into Farley Industries, which faltered under the weight of its debts in the late 1980s. Lou Wolfson, still successfully engaged in thoroughbred racing and breeding, continued his relentless battle to clear his name, going all the way to the United States Supreme Court in an unsuccessful fight to obtain sealed SEC records that he believed would prove he was unfairly convicted. Frederick Richmond, who added a brief turbulent career in Congress to his exploits as a young raider, was living in quiet seclusion in New England.

Art Landa, long retired, died in the early 1990s. He joined the others— Robert Young, Pat McGinnis, Patrick Lannan, Charlie Green, David Karr, Leopold Silberstein—who had already taken their seats in whatever boardroom nirvana awaited Thomas Mellon Evans at his death. They must have gotten some rich chuckles out of the strange bedmates the modern merger mania produced. After T. Boone Pickens tried to pluck up Gulf Oil, that bastion of W. L. Mellon became a subsidiary of Chevron, once owned by archrival John D. Rockefeller. Montgomery Ward, the missed opportunity that might have changed Wolfson's story, was in bankruptcy, still trailing Sears in the retailing sweepstakes. (Greater ironies were yet to come: in late 1998, Tom Evans's proud acquisition of 1959, the Crane Company, would launch an unwelcome and unsuccessful bid to take control of Coltec Industries, the surviving remnant of solder-of-fortune Leopold Silberstein's turbulent Penn-Texas.)

On July 26, 1997, on a perfectly golden summer day, a memorial service was held for Tom Evans at Round Hill Chapel, where Josephine Evans had been honored two decades earlier. The small trapezoidal chapel was decorated with huge bouquets of blue delphiniums, white lilies, and yellow roses. His widow, in a black dress with a white pique jacket, looked tired but elegant, her silver hair partly hidden beneath a black round-brimmed hat. His sons were all there—Tom Junior, who once so resembled his father's youthful portraits, but now stocky and gray. Ned Evans, taller than his brothers but seeming ill at ease in his rumpled suit. A red-eyed Shel Evans, the youngest and perhaps the most perceptive about his father's legacy.

"It is not always easy to be the son of a great man," Shel Evans told the relatives, friends, former business associates, and other mourners who filled the church. "And he was a great man. His business career was legendary, innovative, and ahead of his time . . . His achievements in sports were of equal distinction but I know he was proudest of being a businessman. He loved the 'hurley-burley' of the marketplace."

Young Evans joked about his father's "sense of urgency," as knowing chuckles rippled softly across the church. "If he were traveling, which he did constantly, he would leave you behind if you were late. He was never late himself. He was decisive and didn't look back."

He continued, "He didn't subsidize us or let us lean on him, but made us independent. In business, he provided the opportunities for us to run three successful New York Stock Exchange companies. He taught us about art, antiques, and good wine. He taught us not to be workaholics, but to have balanced lives."

His voice breaking, he finished quickly: "Dad, we have tried to make you proud of us. We certainly are proud of you."

His pastor knew only by hearsay of Evans's fierce reputation in the world of business, but he knew firsthand of the broader community—the other constituencies—that Evans ultimately seemed to care about. "As tough as he was," the pastor observed, "yet he attended the Christmas pageant here for years."

He added, "Tom Evans was closely a part of who we are."

NOTES

NOTES TO CHAPTER ONE

1 Interview with Sayre Rodman.
2 Interview with Martha Pebbles.
3 Thomas Mellon, *Thomas Mellon and His Times* (Pittsburgh: University of Pittsburgh Press, 1994), p. 436.
4 Pebbles interview.
5 Interview with Elizabeth Parker Kase.
6 Pebbles interview.
7 Rodman interview.
8 Interview with John K. Foster.
9 Ibid.
10 Ibid.
11 Kase interview.
12 "The Pursuit of Excellence: The History of the Holland America Line," a brochure published by the Holland America Line, p. 42.
13 *The Academian* yearbook, Pittsburgh, Shady Side Academy, 1927, vol. 15, p. 45.
14 Ibid.
15 Burton Hersh, *The Mellon Family: A Fortune in History* (New York: William Morrow & Co., 1978), p. 182.
16 Craig Thompson, *Since Spindletop: A Human Story of Gulf's First Half-Century*, published by the company, 1952, p. 11.
17 Ibid., pp. 17-18.
18 Ibid., p. 22.
19 Hersh, p. 56.
20 Foster interview.
21 Hersh, p. 182.
22 Ibid., p. 181.
23 Peter Michelmore, *Dr. Mellon of Haiti* (New York: Dodd, Mead and Co., 1964), p. 24.
24 Hersh, p. 460.
25 Ibid., p. 448.
26 Michelmore, p. 27.
27 Interview with Burton Hersh.
28 Charles J. V. Murphy, "The Mellons of Pittsburgh," Part II, *Fortune*, November 1967, p. 225.
29 Hersh, pp. 182, 184.
30 "The Pursuit of Excellence," p. 43.

31 Kase interview, Foster interview.

32 See Philip H. Love, *Andrew W. Mellon: The Man and His Work* (Baltimore: F. Heath Coggins and Co., 1929); Harvey O'Connor, *Mellon's Millions: The Biography of a Fortune* (New York: Blue Ribbon Books, 1933); Stewart H. Holbrook, *The Age of the Moguls* (Garden City, N.Y.: Doubleday and Co., 1953); the *Fortune* series "The Mellons of Pittsburgh," October-December 1967; Paul Mellon with John Baskett, *Reflections in a Silver Spoon* (New York: William Morrow & Co., 1992); and Hersh.

33 Paul Mellon, pp. 102-3.

34 Holbrook, p. 213.

35 Olivier Zunz, *Making America Corporate 1870-1920* (Chicago and London: University of Chicago Press, 1990), p. 12.

36 Ibid.

37 Rodman interview.

38 Hersh, p. 238.

39 Roy Lubove, *Twentieth-Century Pittsburgh: Government, Business, and Environmental Change* (New York: John Wiley & Sons, 1969), p. 2.

40 Ibid., p. 9.

41 Lubove, *Twentieth-Century Pittsburgh*, p. 6, citing John A. Fitch, *The Steel Workers* (New York: Charities Publication Committee, Russell Sage Foundation, 1910), pp. 214-15, 219.

42 O'Connor, p. 217.

43 Ibid., p. 225.

44 Ibid., 215.

45 Lubove, *Twentieth-Century Pittsburgh*, p. 6.

46 Ibid., p. 1, citing *The Autobiography of Lincoln Steffens* (New York: Harcourt, Brace & Co.), 1931, p. 401.

47 R. L. Duffus, "Is Pittsburgh Civilized?" *Harper's Monthly Magazine*, October 1931, pp. 537-45, reprinted with permission in *Pittsburgh*, edited by Roy Lubove in the Documentary History of American Cities series, edited by Tamar K. Hareven and Stephan Thernstrom (New York: New Viewpoints/Franklin Watts, 1976), p. 160.

48 Frederick Lewis Allen, *The Lords of Creation* (New York and London: Harper & Brothers, 1935 [first edition]), p. 91.

49 Ibid., p. 95.

50 Ibid., p. 96.

51 Murphy, "The Mellons of Pittsburgh—Part I," *Fortune*, October 1967.

52 O'Connor, p. 296.

53 Ibid., p. xii.

54 Ibid., p. 281.

55 Hersh, pp. 311-15.

56 Thompson, p. 53.

57 Ibid., p. 52.

NOTES TO CHAPTER TWO

1 O'Connor, p. 347.

2 Ibid., p. 349.

3 Ibid., p. 348.

4 Ibid., p. 349.

5 Ibid., p. 343.

6 Interview with Burton Hersh.

7 Thompson, p. 51.

8 Ibid., p. 53.

9 Hersh, p. 313.

10 Thompson, p. 54.

11 Foster interview.

12 Kase interview.

13 Elizabeth Parker Kase, *The Extra Wife and Other Stories* (Santa Barbara, Calif.: Fithian Press, 1994), p. 72.

14 Kase interview.

15 Kase, p. 73.

16 Kase, p. 75.

17 Kase interview.

18 Hersh, p. 460.

19 Ibid., p. 462.

20 Thomas Mellon Evans, "A New and Dynamic Concept for Growth: H. K. Porter Company, Inc.," a speech to the Newcomen Society in North America on April 21, 1955, printed for the Society by Princeton University Press, pp. 7-8.

21 Foster interview.

22 Hersh, p. 448.

23 Ralph G. Martin, *Henry and Clare: An Intimate Portrait of the Luces* (New York: G. P. Putnam's Sons, 1991), pp. 112-14.

24 Unsigned article, "Odlum of Atlas," *Fortune*, September 1935, p. 50.

25 Evans described this chain of events repeatedly during interviews in his early career, and his friend John Foster confirmed some details on it. Also see Robert E. Bedingfield, "Personality: A Self-Competent Reorganizer," *New York Times*, December 6, 1959; Alvin Rosensweet, "Financial Wizard in Business," *Pittsburgh Post-Gazette* archives, November 8, 1957; and an unsigned article, "H. K. Porter's Interesting Growth Product: Cash," *Fortune*, September 1955, pp. 114-16.

26 The details of Robert Young's early life were repeated in numerous press clippings about him, and collected in a biography by his lawyer, Joseph Borkin.

27 Joseph Borkin, *Robert R. Young: the Populist of Wall Street* (New York: Harper and Row, 1969), pp. 36-37

28 Ibid., p. 39.

29 Ibid., p. 40.

30 Ibid., pp. 42-43.

31 Ibid., p. 45.

32 Ibid., p. 46.

33 Ibid., pp. 49-50.

34 Foster interview.

NOTES TO CHAPTER THREE

1 Foster interview.

2 Unsigned article, "Young Tom Evans," *Time* magazine, March 27, 1944, p. 79.

3 Ibid.

4 Evans, Newcomen speech, p. 8.

5 "H. K. Porter's Interesting Growth Product: Cash," *Fortune*, op. cit.

6 "Young Tom Evans," *Time*, op. cit.

7 Confidential interviews with Evans relatives.

8 Kase interview.

9 Kase, pp. 27-30.

10 "H. K. Porter's Interesting Growth Product: Cash," *Fortune*, op. cit.

11 "Young Tom Evans," *Time*, op. cit.

12 Ibid.

13 "H. K. Porter's Interesting Growth Product: Cash," *Fortune*, op. cit.

14 Ibid.

15 Ibid.

16 David McCullough, *Truman* (New York: Simon and Schuster, 1992), p. 468.

17 Ibid., p. 469.

18 James T. Patterson, *Grand Expectations: The United States, 1945-1974* (New York: Oxford University Press, 1996), p. 43.

19 McCullough , p. 470.

20 Louis Galambos, *The Public Image of Big Business in America, 1880–1940: A Quantitative Study in Social Change* (Baltimore: Johns Hopkins University Press, 1975), p. 266.

21 Ibid.

22 Eric F. Goldman, *The Crucial Decade—and After: America, 1945-1960* (New York: Vintage Books/Random House, 1960), p. 9.

23 "Columbia Consol. Rys. Orders 15 Mountain-type Locomotives," *New York Times*, December 23, 1946, p. 30.

24 Kase, p. 121.

25 Ibid., p. 122.

NOTES TO CHAPTER FOUR

1 Borkin, p. 12.

2 Duncan Norton-Taylor, "The McGinnis Express," *Fortune*, April 1955, p. 146.

3 "Railroads in the Age of Regulation, 1900–1980," edited by Keith L. Bryant Jr., *The Encyclopedia of American Business History and Biography* (New York: Bruccoli Clark Lehman Books, 1991), p. 194.

4 *Current Biography*, 1962, pp. 199–200.

5 Herbert Brean, "It's Easier to Make a Million Than a Hundred Thousand," *Life*, November 29, 1954, p. 179.

6 Leslie Gould, *The Manipulators* (New York: David McKay Company Inc., 1966), p. 3.

7 Harold H. Martin, "Florida's Fabulous Junk Man," *Saturday Evening Post*, July 24, 1954, p. 30.

8 Ibid.

9 These events were described in most of the numerous profiles of Lou Wolfson, including Brean and Martin, cited above, and Gould, pp. 4–8.

10 Martin, op. cit.

11 "Public Transportation Serving the District Of Columbia," a report of the Committee on the District Of Columbia pursuant to Senate Resolution 140, as extended by Senate Resolution 192, 83d Congress, 2d Session (hereafter referred to as Senate Report No. 1274), p. 6.

12 Ibid.

13 Ibid.

14 Ibid., p. 7.

15 Martin, op. cit.

16 Gould, pp. 8–9.

17 Senate Report No. 1274, p. 8.

18 Ibid.

19 Ibid., p. 10.

20 Transcript of Wolfson's testimony on December 8, 1953, before an executive session of the Subcommittee to Investigate Public Transportation Serving the District Of Columbia, the Senate Committee on the District of Columbia, pp. 27–28.

21 Senate Report No. 1274, p. 11.

22 Brean, op. cit.

23 Richard Hammer, "Why Things Went Sour for Louis Wolfson," *Fortune*, September 1961, p. 132; these events are also described in Martin, op. cit., and Gould, p. 12.

24 Hammer, op. cit.

25 Martin, op. cit.

26 Gould, p. 12.

27 Martin, op. cit.

28 Hammer, op. cit.

29 An unsigned profile of Green in *Town Crier*, March 1952, p. 3.

30 David Karr, *Fight for Control* (New York: Ballantine Books, 1956), p. 64.

31 *Town Crier*, op. cit.

32 Gordon Schendel, "How Mobsters Grabbed a City's Transit Line," *Collier's*, September 29, 1951, p. 30.

33 *Town Crier*, op. cit.

34 Karr, p. 65.

35 Ibid., p. 93.

36 Schendel, op. cit.

37 Ibid.

38 Karr, p. 68.

39 Schendel, op. cit.

40 Schendel gave the most detailed account of these events, but the article prompted Green to sue *Collier's* for libel. *Collier's*, in settlement of the suit, ran a "corrective statement" on January 8, 1954, but that statement in no way retracted or amended the events described here. These events are also described in Karr, p. 69.

41 Karr, p. 69.

42 *Town Crier*, op. cit.

43 Schendel, op. cit.

44 Ibid.

45 Karr, p. 69.

46 "Senate Inquiry Uncertain," *New York Times*, November 4, 1950, p. 10.

47 Karr, p. 75.

48 Ibid., p. 77.

49 Ibid., p. 96.

50 Unsigned article, "Stockholder Assails United Cigar Set-up," *New York Times*, June 20, 1951.

51 Unsigned article, "Company Answers Fight for Control," *New York Times*, August 24, 1951, p. 26.

52 Karr, pp. 100–2.

53 Karr, p. 102.

54 "Charles Green: Corrective Statement," *Collier's*, January 8, 1954.

55 Unsigned article, "300 Stockholders Meet in a Turmoil," *New York Times*, September 26, 1951.
56 Ibid.
57 Dero A. Saunders, "Belligerent Penn-Texas," *Fortune*, March 1957, p. 138.
58 Interview with Clarence George, a stepgrandson.
59 "Gain in Europe Seen Dependent on U.S.," *New York Times*, September 24, 1934, p. 32.
60 Gould, p. 33.
61 Ibid., p. 34.
62 Ibid., p. 35.
63 Goldman, p. 22.
64 Ibid., pp. 25-27.
65 Ibid., p. 42.
66 Daniel Seligman, "Barrier-Breaking Bell Aircraft," *Fortune*, March 1956, p. 125.
67 Ibid.
68 Ibid.
69 Ibid.
70 Unsigned article, "Wall Street Is Puzzled by New Talk of Sale of Follansbee Steel Corp.," *New York Times*, January 13, 1948, p. 35.
71 Unsigned article, "Follansbee Deals Are Traced by N.Y. State Attorney General," *New York Times*, January 17, 1948, p. 21.
72 Unsigned article, "Fahye Arraigned in Stock Scheme," *New York Times*, January 31, 1948, p. 12.
73 Unsigned article, "Fahye Says Deals for Steel Failed," *New York Times*, January 29, 1948, p. unknown.
74 John O'Hara, *From the Terrace* (New York: Random House, 1958), p. 850.

NOTES TO CHAPTER 5

1 Evans, Newcomen speech, p. 9.
2 Ibid.
3 Hersh, p. 467.
4 Ibid.
5 Evans, Newcomen speech, p. 11.
6 Rosensweet, op. cit.
7 Unsigned article, "Louis E. Wolfson: The Man Who Wants Montgomery Ward," *Business Week*, October 2, 1954, p. 172.
8 Evans, Newcomen speech, p. 13.
9 Hersh, pp. 451, 454.
10 Ibid., pp. 465–66, and Michelmore, pp. 34–36.
11 Hersh, pp. 450-51.
12 Ibid., pp. 473-75.
13 Goldman, p. 54.
14 Ibid., p. 55.
15 Kase interview.
16 Howard M. Goldsmith, a notable divorce attorney in Philadelphia, was kind enough to educate the author about the history and terms of a bed-and-board divorce.
17 The divorce was detailed extensively in the pages of the *Pittsburgh Press*, the *Pittsburgh Post*, and the *Pittsburgh Sunday Sun-Telegraph*. Unfortunately, all those clippings have

been merged in the archives of the surviving paper, the *Pittsburgh Post-Gazette*, without identifying marks or, in most cases, page numbers. Therefore, clips will be attributed to the *Post-Gazette*, and will generally be identified by headline and date—in this case, "Mrs. T. M. Evans Files for Divorce," *Pittsburgh Post-Gazette*, October 31, 1952.

18 Confidential interviews with Evans family members.

19 Foster interview.

20 Ferdinand Lundberg, *The Rich and the Super Rich* (London: Thomas Nelson & Sons, 1969), p. 8.

21 "Budget Plagues Millionaire's Wife," *Pittsburgh Post-Gazette*, November 15, 1952, p. 1.

22 "Not As Wealthy As Wife Says, Evans Claims," *Pittsburgh Post-Gazette*, November 13, 1952.

23 "Judge Hints Battling Evans Should Think of Three Boys," *Pittsburgh Post-Gazette*, November 29, 1952.

24 Ibid.

25 "Evans' Alimony Battle to Resume," *Pittsburgh Sunday Sun-Telegraph*, November 16, 1952.

26 "Millionaire's Wife Balked in Hearing for Alimony," *Pittsburgh Post-Gazette*, date illegible, but approximately November 11, 1952.

27 "Steak Sent Marriage to Dogs, Evans Says," *Pittsburgh Press*, November 23, 1952, p. 1.

28 Ibid.

29 "Evans' Alimony Battle to Resume," op. cit.

30 "Evans Offers $866 a Month As Alimony, Estranged Wife Asking $3000," *Pittsburgh Post-Gazette*, November 28, 1952.

31 "Judge Hints Battling Evans Should Think of Three Boys," op. cit.

32 Perry McMahon, "[illegible] Court Decision, Attorneys Conclude Oral Arguments," *Pittsburgh Post-Gazette*, December 5, 1952.

33 Ibid.

34 "Evans Wedded to Job, De-Wedding Wife Says," *Pittsburgh Post-Gazette*, April 8, 1953.

35 Ibid.

36 Ibid.

37 "Quick Divorce Decree Frees Mrs. Evans," *Pittsburgh Post-Gazette*, April 9, 1953.

38 Evans, Newcomen speech, p. 15.

39 "Harry J. Leschen Dies at 63; Rope Firm Head," *St. Louis Post-Dispatch*, August 3, 1942.

40 Interview with John A. Leschen II.

41 "Wire Rope Firm Here Sold," *St. Louis Post-Dispatch*, July 6, 1953.

42 Leschen interview.

43 Ibid.

NOTES FOR CHAPTER SIX

1 80th Congress, 1st Session, Senate Document No. 17, p. 6.

2 *Time*, October 3, 1955.

3 *Congressional Record*, March 23, 1955, pp. 3588–89.

4 John S. Tompkins, "Personality: Big Dealer in Assets and Shells," New York Times, May 5, 1957.

5 Ibid.

6 Harold G. Vatter, *The U.S. Economy in the 1950s: An Economic History* (New York: W. W. Norton and Co., 1963), p. 212.

7 "Proxy Skirmish at Twentieth Century-Fox," *Fortune*, May 1953.

8 Karr, p. 122.

9 Dana L. Thomas, *The Plungers and the Peacocks: 150 Years of Wall Street* (New York: G. P. Putnam's Sons, 1967), p. 257.

10 Karr, p. 121.

11 Ibid., pp. 122–23.

12 Thomas, p. 257.

13 Karr, p. 124.

14 Ibid., p. 127.

15 Carter F. Henderson and Albert C. Lasher, *20 Million Careless Capitalists* (Garden City, N.Y.: Doubleday and Co., 1967), p. 73.

16 Karr, p. 128.

17 Ibid.

18 Ibid., p. 138.

19 Ibid., p. 129.

20 Ibid., p. 135.

21 Ibid., p. 138.

22 Ibid., p. 139.

23 Ibid., p. 140.

24 "The Proxy Contest," *Corporate Director Magazine*, January 1955, published by the American Institute of Management.

25 Gould, p. 36.

26 Ibid., p. 37.

27 Ibid.

28 "Building a Fortune on a Loser," *Business Week*, May 8, 1954, p. 98.

29 Dero A. Saunders, "Belligerent Penn-Texas," op. cit.

30 "Industrial Brownhoist Head Quits 'Under Protest' and Is Replaced," *New York Times*, March 24, 1954, p. 39.

31 Interviews with Alfons Landa Jr.; Daniel Seligman, "Battling Art Landa," *Fortune*, June 1958, p. 146; and a "certificate of non-affiliation with certain organizations" that Landa filed with the Defense Department in December 1958.

32 "Other Weddings: Landa-Mondell," *New York Times*, June 27, 1930.

33 "Mrs. Thaw Plans Wedding on Coast," *New York Times*, April 29, 1942.

34 "Wedding on Coast for Mrs. C. M. Thaw," *New York Times*, May 2, 1942.

35 Seligman, op. cit.

36 Ibid.

37 Ibid.

38 McCullough, p. 418.

39 Interview with Alan Abelson.

40 Ibid.

41 Gould, p. 1.

42 David Caute, *The Great Fear: The Anti-Communist Purge Under Truman and Eisenhower* (New York: Simon and Schuster, 1978), p. 216.

43 Ibid.

44 Seligman, op. cit.

45 Ibid.

46 Ibid.

47 Steven Brill, *The Teamsters* (New York: Simon and Schuster, 1978), pp. 22–23.

48 Proceedings of the May 14, 1957, hearings of the Senate's Select Committee on Improper Activities in the Labor or Management Field, p. 4106.

49 Ibid., p. 4063.

50 Ibid., p. 4092.

51 Ibid., p. 4104.

52 Seligman, op. cit.

53 Ibid.

54 Borkin, p. 167.

55 Karr, p. 9.

56 There are literally dozens of separate accounts of the New York Central fight scattered among newspapers, magazines, and books. The most detailed is contained in chapter 6 of Joseph Borkin's biography of Young, cited earlier; the most entertaining is chapter 2 of *The Seven Fat Years: Chronicles of Wall Street,* by John Brooks (New York: Harper and Brothers, 1954), pp. 5–38. Another account can be found in Dana Thomas's Wall Street history, *The Plungers and the Peacocks,* cited earlier, pp. 263–69. Young's own account of the fight can be found in his testimony before the securities subcommittee of the Senate Banking Currency Committee on June 9, 1955. The transcript is included in the subcommittee's Stock Market Study (Corporate Proxy Contests), pt. 3, 84th Congress, first session, pp. 1457–1505.

57 Letter dated September 12, 1975, from Russell T. Walker of Jackson, Michigan, to John B. M. Place, chairman of the board of Anaconda Company, included in the record of an October 8, 1975, hearing before the Subcommittee on Reports, Accounting and Management of the Senate Committee on Government Operations, 94th Congress, 1st Session, p. 169.

58 Ron Chernow, *The House of Morgan* (New York: Touchstone Books/Simon and Schuster, 1990), p. 511.

59 Brooks, *The Seven Fat Years,* op. cit., p. 12.

60 Borkin, p. 172.

NOTES FOR CHAPTER SEVEN

1 Duncan Norton-Taylor, "The McGinnis Express," *Fortune,* April 1955, p. 146.

2 Ibid.

3 Ibid.

4 "The New Haven Decides," *Time,* April 26, 1954, p. 92.

5 Karr, p. 110.

6 Ibid.

7 Ibid.

8 "Proxy Carries Attack," *New York Times,* March 31, 1954.

9 Karr, p. 113.

10 Ibid.

11 Ibid., p. 114.

12 Robert E. Bedingfield, "Its Prosperity Is Issue in Battle Over Minneapolis and St. Louis Railway," *New York Times,* April 25, 1954, Sec. 3, p. 1.

13 "Laclede-Christy To Move Main Offices Back Here," *St. Louis Post-Dispatch,* October 25, 1951.

14 "Laclede-Christy Gets into New Office Building," *St. Louis Post-Dispatch,* March 7, 1952, p. E1.

15 "Executive Wins $182,050 Lawsuit," *St. Louis Post-Dispatch*, November 15, 1966, p. 9a.

16 "Laclede-Christy Board Statement on Rumors," *St. Louis Post-Dispatch*, August 10, 1954, p. no. illegible.

17 "W. W. Shipley Resigns Top Post at Laclede-Christy," *St. Louis Post-Dispatch*, September 1, 1954, p. 4a.

18 Evans, Newcomen speech, p. 11.

19 "Laclede-Christy Company Votes Stock Dividend of 25 Pct.," *St. Louis Post-Dispatch*, September 7, 1954, p. 4b.

20 Ibid.

21 "Suit for $182,050 in Pay Is Heard," *St. Louis Post-Dispatch*, December 23, 1960, p. C8.

22 "Laclede-Christy Control Shifted," *St. Louis Post-Dispatch*, September 15, 1954.

23 "Suit for $182,050 in Pay Is Heard," op. cit.

24 His battle took nearly a dozen years, but he was ultimately successful in winning a substantial portion of the pay he sought.

25 *Corporate Director Magazine*, op. cit.

26 See Karr, pp. 81–92.

27 Thomas, pp. 253–54.

28 Harvey Klehr and Ronald Radosh, *The Amerasia Spy Case: Prelude to McCarthyism* (Chapel Hill: University of North Carolina Press, 1996), p. 101.

29 Ibid.

30 Daniel Seligman, "Battling Art Landa," op. cit.

31 Klehr and Radosh, pp. 101, 232.

32 "Follansbee Steel Board Agrees to Sell Assets for $9,000,000," *New York Times*, August 13, 1954, p. 23.

33 "Lauson Stone, Head of Follansbee Corp.," *New York Times*, October 9, 1948; "Succeeds to Presidency of Follansbee Steel Corp.," *New York Times*, October 15, 1948.

34 "Follansbee Tells of Offer for Mill," *New York Times*, October 12, 1954, and correction, October 13, 1954.

35 Ibid.

36 "Follansbee Plant May Shift South," *New York Times*, September 14, 1954.

37 Ibid.

38 "Steps Are Taken to Halt Mill Sale," *New York Times*, September 30, 1954.

39 "Follansbee Fights Suit to Block Sale," *New York Times*, October 7, 1954.

40 "Hazel Halts a Suit," *New York Times*, October 19, 1954.

41 "Follansbee Steel Rejects Stock Bid," *New York Times*, October 23, 1954.

42 Ibid.

43 "Follansbee Vote Blocked by Court," *New York Times*, October 27, 1954, p. 41.

44 "Follansbee Gets Offer from Eaton," *New York Times*, October 29, 1954.

45 84th Congress, First Session, House Document No. 169, p. 139.

46 "Follansbee Fight Is Taken to SEC," *New York Times*, October 30, 1954.

47 "Follansbee Sale Voted, Faces Suit," *New York Times*, November 2, 1954.

48 "Follansbee Company Sale to Be Investigated," *New York Times*, November 12, 1954.

49 "Plea Filed to Bar Follansbee Sale," *New York Times*, November 13, 1954.

50 "Senators Assail Follansbee Deal," *New York Times*, November 18, 1954.

51 "U.S. Court to Ban Follansbee Sale," *New York Times*, November 30, 1954.

52 "Eaton Bids Saves Follansbee Mill," *New York Times*, December 4, 1954.

53 "Happy Union, Happy Boss," *New York Times*, December 28, 1954.

54 "Follansbee Sale Gets Green Light," *New York Times*, December 22, 1954.

55 Karr, p. 146.

56 Doris Kearns Goodwin, *No Ordinary Time: Franklin and Eleanor Roosevelt: The Home Front in World War II* (New York: Simon and Schuster, 1994), p. 498.

57 Ibid.

58 Karr, p. 147.

59 "Investment Trust Guns Again for Sewell Avery," *Business Week,* April 15, 1950.

60 Ibid.

61 Karr, p. 149.

62 "The Battle for Ward's," *Time,* September 6, 1954, p. 76.

63 Ibid.

64 Ibid.

65 "The Private Life of a Self-made Millionaire," *Look,* May 3, 1955, p. 44.

66 Brean, op. cit.; Martin, op. cit.

67 "Louis E. Wolfson: The Man Who Wants Montgomery Ward," *Business Week,* October 2, 1954, p. 172.

68 Karr, p. 166.

69 Ibid., p. 159.

70 Ibid., p. 154.

71 Gould, p. 17.

72 Transcripts of the Proceedings of the Select Committee on Improper Activities in the Labor or Management Field, United States Senate, May 14, 1957, p. 4114, hereafter the McClellan Committee.

73 Ibid.

74 Ibid.

75 Article in the *Chicago American,* March 31, 1955, quoted in the McClellan Committee report, p. 4126.

76 Karr, p. 166.

77 "Top Illinois Court Upholds Wolfson," *New York Times,* April 16, 1955, p. 23.

78 Karr, p. 162.

79 Robert F. Bedingfield, "Avery Overcomes Drive by Wolfson to Control Ward," *New York Times,* April 23, 1955, p. 1.

80 Gould, p. 18.

81 Karr, p. 164.

82 Bedingfield, op. cit.

83 Ibid.

84 Ibid.

85 Hammer, op. cit., p. 132.

86 Karr, p. 168.

87 Ibid., p. 167.

88 Gould, p. 39.

89 Ibid., p. 40.

90 *Congressional Record,* House of Representatives, March 23, 1955, p. 3588.

91 Ibid., p. 3590.

92 "They Collect Companies like Postage Stamps," *Business Week,* October 30, 1954, p. 154.

93 Associated Press, "Fair-Value Award Made to Leschens," *New York Times,* May 6, 1955.

94 *Congressional Record,* op. cit., p. 3588.

NOTES FOR CHAPTER EIGHT

1 84th Congress, 1st Session, Senate Banking Committee, Subcommittee on Securities, Hearings on S. 879, pt. 3, Stock Market Study, Corporate Proxy Contests (hereafter Lehman Hearings), Washington, D.C., United States Government Printing Office, 1956, p. 1321.

2 J. Allan Nevins, *Herbert H. Lehman and His Era* (New York: Scribner, 1963), p. 370.

3 Cauté, p. 39.

4 McCullough, p. 766; I. F. Stone, *The Haunted Fifties: 1953–1963* (Boston: Little, Brown & Co., 1963), p. 68.

5 Robert S. Allen and William V. Shannon, *The Truman Merry-Go-Round* (New York: Vanguard Press, 1950), p. 289.

6 Nevins, pp. 402–3.

7 Lehman Hearings, pp. 1326–27.

8 Borkin, p. 8.

9 Lehman Hearings, p. 1457.

10 Ibid., p. 1458.

11 Ibid., p. 1460.

12 Ibid.

13 Ibid., p. 1461.

14 Ibid., p. 1467.

15 Ibid., p. 1468.

16 Ibid., p. 1473.

17 Borkin, p. 173.

18 Lehman Hearings, p. 1489.

19 Ibid., p. 1490.

20 Charles E. Egan, " 'Cleverest Deal' Boasted by Young," *New York Times,* June 10, 1955, p. 29.

21 Lehman Hearings, p. 1491.

22 Ibid., p. 1492.

23 Ibid., p. 1494.

24 Ibid., p. 1502.

25 Ibid., p. 1503.

26 Ibid., p. 1504.

27 Ibid.

28 Ibid., p. 1428.

29 Ibid., p. 1429.

30 Ibid., pp. 1566, 1712.

31 Ibid., p. 1324.

32 Peter F. Drucker, "The New Tycoons: America's Next Twenty Years, Part 3," *Harper's Magazine,* May 1955, p. 39.

33 Vatter, p. 207.

34 Ibid.

35 Edith Penrose, *The Theory of the Growth of the Firm* (New York: John Wiley & Sons, 1959), pp. 27–28, as cited in Vatter, p. 208.

36 Lehman Hearings, p. 1391.

37 Ibid., p. 1420.

38 Ibid., pp. 1420–21.

39 "Public Transportation Serving the District Of Columbia," A Report of the Committee on the District Of Columbia, 83rd Congress, 2d Session, Report No. 1274 (hereafter Capital Transit Report), May 1, 1954, p. 2.

40 Ibid., pp. 21, 40.

41 Ibid., p. 55.

42 Ibid., p. 62.

43 Capital Transit Company Matters, Hearings before the Subcommittee on Public Health, Education, Welfare and Safety of the Committee on the District of Columbia, 84th Congress, 1st Session, June 27, 30, July 7, 12, and 21, 1955 (hereafter Capital Transit Company Matters), p. 2.

44 Congressional Record, United States Senate, June 30, 1955, p. 9581.

45 Capital Transit Company Matters, p. 3.

46 Congressional Record, United States Senate, June 30, 1955, p. 9586.

47 Capital Transit Company Matters, transcript of Senate subcommittee hearings held July 7, 1955, p. 26.

48 Ibid.

49 Ibid.

50 Ibid., pp. 26–7.

51 Ibid., p. 28.

52 Ibid., pp. 36–7.

53 Ibid., pp. 109-110.

54 Ibid., p. 140.

55 Ibid., p. 136.

56 *Congressional Record,* United States Senate, July 30, 1955, p. 12269.

57 "New Proxy Rules Asked," *New York Times,* June 15, 1955, p. 51.

58 Seligman, p. 269.

59 Ibid., p. 267.

60 Ibid., p. 273.

61 Ibid., pp. 270–71.

62 Ibid., p. 275.

63 Ibid., p. 100.

64 Ibid., p. 238.

65 Ibid.

66 Lehman Hearings, pp. 1507–25.

67 Ibid., p. 1526.

68 Ibid., p. 1538.

69 Ibid., p. 1541.

70 Ibid., p. 1543.

71 Ibid., p. 1546.

72 Ibid., p. 1553.

73 Ibid.

74 Ibid., p. 1555.

75 Opinion, Civil Action No. 102-264, U.S. District Court for the Southern District of New York, August 15, 1955, as cited in Lehman Hearings, pp. 1712–21.

76 "Shift in Control of Libby Sought," New York Times, June 29, 1955.

77 Opinion, Southern District, op. cit.

78 "Proxy Study Is Urged," *New York Times,* July 22, 1955.

79 "Libby President Claims Victory," *New York Times,* August 19, 1955.

80 John H. Fenton, "Libby Opposition Boycotts Meeting," *New York Times*, September 8, 1955, p. 43.

81 "Libby Expanding Output," *New York Times*, October 19, 1955.

82 Estes Kefauver, *In a Few Hands: Monopoly Power in America* (New York: Pantheon Books/Random House, 1965), p. 164.

83 Ibid.

84 Ibid., pp. 168–171, 178.

85 "Report on Corporate Mergers and Acquisitions," the Federal Trade Commission, submitted May 19, 1955, to the 84th Congress, 1st Session (hereafter House Document No. 169), p. 2.

86 Ibid., p. 29.

87 Neil Fligstein, *The Transformation of Corporate Control* (Cambridge, Mass.: Harvard Univeristy Press, 1990), pp. 28–29.

88 "Congress and the Nation," *Congressional Quarterly Service*, p. 443.

89 Ibid., p. 448.

90 C. P. Trussell, "Rise in Mergers Called a Menace by House Inquiry," *New York Times*, December 27, 1955, p. 1.

91 "Congress and the Nation," p. 448.

NOTES FOR CHAPTER NINE

1 "Never Works at Night," *Newsweek*, January 25, 1954, p. 76.

2 Interview with Thomas Mellon Evans Jr.

3 "Porter Divisions Boss Themselves," *Business Week*, November 26, 1955, p. 118.

4 Ron Chernow, *Titan: The Life of John D. Rockefeller Sr.* (New York: Random House, 1998), p. 129.

5 Ibid.

6 Kefauver, p. 131.

7 Ibid.

8 "The Federal Antitrust Laws, 1892 to 1951," Commerce Clearing House, pp. 66424–26.

9 John Brooks, *The Great Leap: The Past 25 Years in America* (New York: Harper and Row, 1966), p. 52.

10 John Brooks, *The Fate of the Edsel and Other Business Adventures* (New York: Harper and Row), 1959, p. 139.

11 "The Federal Antitrust Laws, 1890 to 1951," op. cit.

12 Brooks, *The Fate of the Edsel*, op. cit., p. 158.

13 "The Federal Antitrust Laws, 1890 to 1951," op. cit.

14 "Disston Sale Ratified," *New York Times*, November 16, 1955.

15 Hearings before the Antitrust Subcommittee (Subcommittee No. 5) of the Committee on the Judiciary, House of Representatives, 84th Congress, 2d Session, January 16, 18, 20, and 23, 1956 (hereafter Celler Hearings), p. 96.

16 Ibid.

17 Ibid., p. 97.

18 Ibid, p. 98.

19 "Congress and the Nation," op. cit., p. 448.

20 "Text of the Democratic Platform Adopted by Voice Vote by the Convention Delegates," *New York Times*, August 16, 1956, pp. 12–13.

21 William M. Farrell, "New Proxy Rules Proposed by SEC," *New York Times*, August 23, 1955, p. 31.

22 "SEC's Proposed Proxy Rules Draw Fire As Much Too Strict," *New York Times,* November 18, 1955, p. 35.

23 Ibid.

24 "SEC Proposes New Proxy Rules," *New York Times,* December 15, 1955.

25 Dero A. Saunders, "How Managements Get Tipped Over," *Fortune,* September 1955.

26 "The Raiders: Challenge to Management," *Time,* July 25, 1955, p. 80.

27 James P. Selvage, "Pirates by Proxy," *Management Reports,* December 1957, pp. 17–21.

28 Vatter, pp. 36–37.

29 Richard Rutter, "Proxy Wars Shed No Gore, Much Ink," *New York Times,* May 24, 1955, p. 44.

30 Alan Drury, "Senators' Report Asks More Curbs on Stock Market," *New York Times,* May 27, 1955, p. 1.

31 Interview with Joseph Flom, of Skadden, Arps, Slate, Meagher and Flom.

32 Fligstein, p. 12.

33 Ibid., p. 13.

34 Ibid., pp. 14–15.

35 Ibid.

36 Ibid., p. 29.

37 Gould, p. 43.

38 "Financier Silberstein Seeks to Bar Fairbanks-Morse Deal," *Business Week,* February 4, 1956, p. 130.

39 "C. H. Morse Quits As Director of Fairbanks after Stock Sale," *New York Times,* January 28, 1956.

40 Advertisement titled "Senator Wayne Morse Deplores Attempt to Curtail Freedom of Opportunity," paid for by the Penn-Texas Corporation, *New York Times,* March 2, 1956.

41 "Financier Silberstein Seeks to Bar Fairbanks-Morse Deal," *Business Week,* op. cit.; Gould, p. 43.

42 Gould, p. 44; "Slugging Operation," *Time,* March 12, 1956.

43 Letter from Joseph D. Tydings to Alfons Landa, April 1, 1958, the uncatalogued collected papers of Alfons Landa, The American Heritage Center, University of Wyoming (hereafter the Landa Collection), made available to the author through the generous permission of Alfons Landa Jr.

44 Richard Rutter, "Penn-Texas Wins Fairbanks Voice," *New York Times,* May 29, 1956, p. 37.

45 "Bitter Aftermath," *Newsweek,* April 9, 1956.

46 "Penn-Texas Fight Adds a New Twist," *New York Times,* January 15, 1957.

47 Ibid.

48 "Peace Pact Ends Fairbanks Fight," *New York Times,* May 11, 1957.

49 "A Tug and a Tsk," *Newsweek,* September 9, 1957; "Silberstein Foes Vow to Oust Him from Presidency of Penn-Texas," *Business Week,* November 9, 1957, p. 52.

50 "Sidetracked," *Newsweek,* March 10, 1953.

51 Richard Rutter, "19 Vie for 9 Penn-Texas Seats," *New York Times,* May 6, 1958, p. 51.

52 "Sidetracked," *Newsweek,* op. cit.

53 "Penn-Texas Management Meets Irate Minority at Meeting Here," *New York Times,* October 15, 1958, p. 59.

54 Hammer, op. cit.

55 Ibid.

56 Gould, p. 22.

57 Hammer, op. cit.

58 Ibid., p. 25.

59 "Exit for Wolfson," *Time*, May 2, 1969, p. 88.

60 William F. Reed, "A Front-Runner Launches a Comeback," *Sports Illustrated*, June 5, 1978, p. 71.

61 The relationship between Wolfson and Fortas was first disclosed by William Lambert, in "The Justice and the Stock Manipulator," *Life*, May 9, 1969, p. 32. It was subsequently widely reported in newspapers and news magazines, and is described by Bruce Allen Murphy in *Fortas: The Rise and Ruin of a Supreme Court Justice* (New York: William Morrow and Company, 1988).

62 Richard W. Barsness, "Ben W. Heinemann," *Encyclopedia of American Business History and Biography: Railroads in the Age of Regulation, 1900–1980*, edited by Keith L. Bryant Jr. (New York: Bruccoli Clark Layman/Facts on File Publications, 1991), pp. 193–97.

63 Robert Wallace, "The Commuters' Rebellion," *Life*, February 6, 1956, p. 97.

64 "Two Counts against Pat," *Newsweek*, August 26, 1963, p. 62.

65 "Patrick McGinnis, a Rail Executive," *New York Times*, February 24, 1973.

66 Borkin, p. 223.

67 Vatter, pp. 115–20.

68 Ibid.

69 Ibid.

70 "Robert Young, Financier, Ends Life in Palm Beach," *New York Times*, January 26, 1958, p. 1.

71 "End of the Line," *Time*, February 3, 1958, pp. 68-70.

NOTES FOR CHAPTER TEN

1 Interviews with Dr. Mellon's widow, Gwen Mellon, and her daughter, Jennifer Grant.

2 "The Storm That Rocked Crane Company," *Fortune*, May 1960, p. 143.

3 "The Crane Company: Under Repair," *Fortune*, March 1957, p. 125.

4 Kathleen D. McCarthy, *Noblesse Oblige: Charity and Cultural Philanthropy in Chicago, 1849–1929* (Chicago: University of Chicago Press, 1982), p. 91.

5 Ibid.

6 *The National Cyclopedia of American Biography*, pp. 450-51.

7 McCarthy, op. cit.

8 "The Crane Company: Under Repair," op. cit.

9 C. Wright Mills, *The Power Elite* (New York: Oxford University Press, 1957), pp. 94–95.

10 C. Wright Mills, *White Collar: The American Middle Classes* (New York: Oxford University Press, 1953), pp. 105, 95.

11 Ibid., p. 100.

12 John Chamberlain, *The Enterprising Americans: a Business History of the United States* (New York: Harper and Row, 1961), p. 217.

13 Michael Patrick Allen, *The Founding Fortunes: A New Anatomy of the Super-Rich Families in America* (New York: Truman Talley Books/E. P. Dutton, 1987), p. 189.

14 David Halberstam, *The Fifties* (New York: Villard Books, 1993), pp. 488–89.

15 Ibid., p. 122.

16 William L. O'Neill, *American High: The Years of Confidence, 1945–1960* (New York, The Free Press/Macmillan, 1986), pp. 24–25.

17 Ibid., p. 21.

18 Brooks, *The Great Leap,* op. cit., p. 41.

19 Ibid., p. 42.

20 "The Crane Company: Under Repair," op. cit.

21 Ibid.

22 Ibid.

23 Ibid.

24 "The Storm That Rocked Crane Company," op. cit.

25 Vatter, p. 120.

26 Ibid., p. 185.

27 Lubove, *Twentieth-Century Pittsburgh,* op. cit., pp. 123–24.

28 Rosensweet, op. cit.

29 Ibid.

30 "The Storm That Rocked Crane Company," op. cit.

31 Ibid.

32 Ibid.

33 Ibid.

34 Ibid.

35 Ibid.

36 John S. Tompkins, "Crane Company Faces Problem As Five Investors Get Big Holdings," *New York Times,* May 12, 1958, p. 39.

37 "The Storm That Rocked Crane Company," op. cit.

38 "Compromises End Threats of Proxy Fights," *New York Times,* January 11, 1960, p. 73.

39 Tompkins, New York Times, op. cit.

40 "The Storm That Rocked Crane Company," op. cit., and "The Crane Company: Under Repair," op. cit.

41 "Battling Art Landa," op. cit.

42 Achsah Dorsey Smith, "Society," *Washington Post and Times Herald,* February 16, 1952; Mary Van Rensselaer, "Mrs. Chadbourne," *Washington Post and Times Herald,* March 16, 1955.

43 "The Storm That Rocked Crane Company," op. cit.; "The Heirloom Collector," *Time,* May 11, 1959.

44 Unsigned letter to F. J. Kennedy, dated November 25, 1958, the Crane Company file, the Landa Collection, op. cit.

45 John S. Tompkins, "Landa, President of Penn-Texas, May Quit for Crane Proxy Fight," *New York Times,* January 13, 1959, p. 37.

46 "The Storm That Rocked Crane Company," op. cit.

47 Ibid.

48 "The Crane Company: Under Repair," op. cit.

49 "The Storm That Rocked Crane Company," op. cit.

50 Ibid.

51 Ibid.

52 Case No. 1433, p. 66377, "The Federal Antitrust Laws with Summary of Cases," *Trade Regulation Reports,* Commerce Clearing House.

53 "President of Crane Company Resigns; Head of Porter Named Chairman," *New York Times,* April 29, 1959.

54 "The Storm That Rocked Crane Company," op. cit.

55 "President of Crane Company Resigns; Head of Porter Named Chairman," op. cit.

56 Vincent Butler, "Landa to Quit Penn-Texas Presidency," *Chicago Tribune*, May 4, 1959, pt. 4, p. 7.

57 Carbon copy of a letter from Alfons Landa to Thomas M. Evans, May 6, 1959, the Crane Company file, the Landa Collection, op. cit.

58 Ibid.

59 Letter from T. M. Evans to Alfons Landa, dated May 7, 1959, the Crane Company File, the Landa Collection, op. cit.

60 "The Storm That Rocked Crane Company," op. cit.

61 Ibid.

62 "Autolite to Sell Stock in Crane Company," *New York Times*, July 2, 1959.

63 "Crane Dismisses Dissident Aide but He Will Remain a Director," *New York Times*, July 15, 1959.

64 "The Storm That Rocked Crane Company," op. cit.

65 "Landa Rebuffed by Crane Company Board," *New York Times*, June 24, 1959.

66 Robert E. Bedingfield, "Personality: A Self-Confident Reorganizer," *New York Times*, December 6, 1959.

67 "Crane to Close Radiator Shop," *Chattanooga Times*, December 23, 1958, p. 1.

68 "The Storm That Rocked Crane Company," op. cit.

69 Ibid.

70 "Crane Makes It Five," *Chemical and Engineering News*, January 11, 1960, p. 21.

71 Letter from Russell T. Walker to John B. M. Place, dated September 12, 1975, included in the transcript of the Anaconda hearings, op. cit, p. 169.

72 Bedingfield, "Personality: A Self-Confident Reorganizer," op. cit.

73 "Crane Makes It Five," op. cit.

74 "The Storm That Rocked Crane Company," op. cit.

75 "Crane Company Board Declines to Run Director for Re-election," *New York Times*, February 24, 1960.

NOTES FOR CHAPTER ELEVEN

1 "Man in Motion," *Newsweek*, February 15, 1960, p. 74.

2 Fligstein, p. 239.

3 Ibid., p. 242; Fligstein also cited Elmer Bobst of Warner Lambert, Tex Thornton of Litton Industries, Norton Simon, Max McGraw of McGraw Electric, and F. M. Davies of FMC Corp., in addition to Evans, as practitioners of this strategy.

4 "Is This the Coming Thing?" *Business Week*, June 23, 1956, p. 61.

5 Fligstein, pp. 246-7, and Robert Sobel, *The Rise and Fall of the Conglomerate Kings* (New York: Stein & Day, 1984), pp. 81–83.

6 John Brooks, *The Go-Go Years* (New York: Weybright & Talley, 1973), pp. 168–69.

7 Ibid.

8 Fligstein, p. 248.

9 *The Federal Antitrust Laws, 1890 to 1951*, Commerce Clearing House, p. 66424–26.

10 Lundberg, p. 96.

11 Ibid.

12 Ibid., p. 97.

13 John Brooks, *The Fate of the Edsel*, op. cit., p. 140.

14 Lundberg, p. 96.

15 *The Federal Antitrust Laws, 1890 to 1951*, Commerce Clearing House, op. cit., pp. 66424–26.

16 "The Master Plumber," *Time*, June 13, 1960, p. 103.

17 "Evans Wins in $200,000 Tax Battle," *Pittsburgh Press*, September 22, 1960, p. 2.

18 "Brown Company Stock Reported Bought," *New York Times*, March 12, 1960.

19 "Control of Brown Company," *New York Times*, March 29, 1963, p. 9.

20 Ibid.

21 "Fast Deal Nets Paper Maker," *Business Week*, December 22, 1962, p. 61.

22 Ibid.

23 "Control of Brown Company," op. cit.

24 "Evans Battles Keady's Post with Brown," *Pittsburgh Post-Gazette*, January 9, 1963; "Evans Denies Firm Takeover," *Pittsburgh Post-Gazette*, January 11, 1963.

25 "Largest Stockholder Accuses Six on Paper Company's Board," *New York Times*, January 12, 1963, p. 9.

26 "Evans Battles Keady's Post with Brown," op. cit.

27 "Largest Stockholder Accuses Six on Paper Company's Board," op. cit.

28 "Brown Company Proxy Fight," *New York Times*, February 19, 1963, p. 10.

29 "Control of Brown Company," op. cit.

30 Ibid.

31 Clyde Farnsworth, "Evans Loses on Brown Quorum; Asks Court to Reverse Count," *New York Times*, April 3, 1963, p. 59.

32 Vartanig G. Vartan, "Evans Defeated in Brown Ruling," *New York Times*, April 13, 1963, p. 23.

33 Vartanig G. Vartan, "Next Evans Move Waited after Brown Company Defeat," *New York Times*, April 22, 1963, p. 37.

34 Letter to shareholders from John A. Saunders, February 6, 1962, *Proxy Contests, 1959–62*, Skadden, Arps, Slate, Meagher and Flom.

35 David Karr, Landa's own press agent ally, had left the public relations business for corporate management and film production, eventually gravitating to Paris, where he built a small fortune by arranging Western financing for investments in the Soviet Union. He died in July 1979 in Paris.

36 Interviews with Joseph Flom.

37 Lincoln Caplan, *Skadden: Power, Money, and the Rise of a Legal Empire* (New York: Noonday Press/Farrar Straus Giroux, 1993), p. 15.

38 Flom interviews.

39 Caplan, p. 59.

40 Flom interviews.

41 Caplan, p. 43.

42 Interview with Richard Cheney.

43 John J. Goldman, "Lawyer Was in Arenas Where All Contestants Were Goliaths," *Los Angeles Times*, May 25, 1981, pt. I, p. 18.

44 Letter to shareholders from Alfons Landa, February 13, 1962, *Proxy Contests, 1959–1962*, op. cit.

45 Letter to shareholders from Alfons Landa, March 7, 1962, *Proxy Contests, 1959–1962*, op. cit.

46 See Lawrence A. Armour, "Defiant Defied," *Barron's*, December 3, 1962, p. 3; also Caplan, p. 44.

47 Henderson and Lasher,. p. 207.

48 Ibid., p. 211.

49 Cary Reich, *Financier: the Biography of Andrew Meyer* (New York: William Morrow & Co., 1983), p. 223.

50 *The Federal Antitrust Laws, Cases Instituted in 1965,* Commerce Clearing House, p. 52587.

51 Bruce Wasserstein, *Big Deal: The Battle for Control of America's Leading Corporations* (New York: Warner Books, 1998), pp. 56–57.

52 Wasserstein, p. 59.

53 Ibid., p. 60.

54 Fligstein, p. 250.

55 Ibid., p. 251.

56 Ibid., p. 253.

57 Brooks, *The Go-Go Years,* op. cit., p. 155.

58 Wasserstein, p. 555.

59 Seligman, p. 422.

60 Brooks, *The Go-Go Years,* p. 175.

61 Seligman, p. 431.

62 Ibid., p. 432.

63 Brooks, *The Go-Go Years,* pp. 175–76.

64 Ibid.

65 Patterson, op. cit., p. 321.

66 Brooks, *The Go-Go Years,* p. 177.

67 Ibid.

68 Jack Markowitz, "Policy on Wabco Undecided—Evans," *Pittsburgh Post-Gazette,* December 23, 1967.

69 "Escalation," *Forbes,* February 1, 1968, p. 15.

70 William Allen, "Evans Trying Takeover, McCord says," *Pittsburgh Press,* December 18, 1967, p. 1.

71 "Wabco Official Calls Evans' Plan 'Takeover' Try," *Pittsburgh Post-Gazette,* February 1, 1968.

72 "Escalation," op. cit.

73 Ibid.

74 Ibid.

75 Ibid.

76 "McCord Hits Evans' Claim," *Pittsburgh Press,* February 2, 1968.

77 John Barnett, "Tom Evans' Takeovers Build a Vast Fortune, Stir Hot Controversy," *Wall Street Journal,* May 16, 1968, p. 1.

78 "Air Brake Fears Raid on Company," *Pittsburgh Post-Gazette,* December 15, 1967.

79 "WABCO Fights Try on Merger," *Pittsburgh Press,* December 19, 1967.

80 William Allen, "Crane Sues for WABCO Stock List," *Pittsburgh Press,* January 3, 1968, p. 1.

81 Jack Markowitz, "Evans, Wabco Battle On," *Pittsburgh Post-Gazette,* January 9, 1968.

82 Markowitz, "Policy on Wabco Undecided—Evans," op. cit.

83 "Crane Plans Improper, McCord Says," *Pittsburgh Press,* February 1, 1968.

84 "Trial Opens in Wabco Merger Fight," *Pittsburgh Press,* January 30, 1968.

85 "Wabco Eyes Other Buyers, Evans Claims," *Pittsburgh Post-Gazette,* January 31, 1968.

86 "Crane Claims Stock Bought As Safeguard," *Pittsburgh Press*, January 31, 1968.

87 "McCord Hits Evans' Claim," *Pittsburgh Post-Gazette*, February 2, 1968.

88 "[illegible] Improper, McCord Says," *Pittsburgh Press*, February 1, 1968.

89 "Stock List Battle Won by Wabco," *Pittsburgh Press*, February 3, 1968.

90 "Crane Company Will Fight for Three Wabco Directors," *Pittsburgh Post-Gazette*, February 21, 1968.

91 Robert E. Bedingfield, "The Tale of a Westerner Who Came East," *New York Times*, June 16, 1968.

92 Jack Markowitz, "Wabco Picks Foe of Crane For Merger," *Pittsburgh Post-Gazette*, March 5, 1968, p. 1.

93 William Allen, "Wabco Move Shocks Evans," *Pittsburgh Press*, March 5, 1968, p. 1.

94 John Helsel, "Air Brake 'Out' for Long Count," *Pittsburgh Press*, May 17, 1968.

95 Ibid.

96 Barnett, op. cit.

97 Isadore Barmash, "Crane Loses Bid on Wabco Merger," *New York Times*, June 1, 1968, p. 33.

98 "A $5-Million Stock Saga," *Business Week*, June 22, 1968.

NOTES FOR CHAPTER TWELVE

1 Seligman, p. 457.

2 Caplan, pp. 51–53.

3 Brooks, *The Go-Go Years*, pp. 234–38.

4 Ibid., p. 242.

5 Ibid., p. 246.

6 Flom interview.

7 Isadore Barmash, *Welcome to Our Conglomerate—You're Fired!* (New York: Delacorte Press, 1971), p. 192.

8 Brooks, *The Go-Go Years*, p. 253.

9 Ibid., p. 243.

10 Ibid., p. 256.

11 Ibid., p. 259.

12 Barmash, p. 194.

13 Ibid., p. 196.

14 Ibid., p. 197.

15 Birinyi Associates, "Bear Markets: 1945–1990," pp. 2–3.

16 Chernow, *Titan*, pp. 578–79.

17 Ralph G. Martin and Morton D. Stone, *Money, Money, Money: Wall Street in Words and Pictures* (Chicago: Rand McNally & Company, 1960), p. 195.

18 "So I Lost, So What?," *Forbes*, August 15, 1969, p. 44.

19 Ibid.

20 Interview with A. C. Pocius.

21 The Anaconda hearings, p. 169.

22 "Porter To Cut Some Fields," *Pittsburgh Post-Gazette*, April 24, 1970.

23 The Federal Antitrust Laws, 1970-1979, Commerce Clearing House, p. 45,072.

24 Jack Markowitz, "Thomas Mellon Evans Seeks File Firm Stock," *Pittsburgh Post-Gazette*, April 24, 1972, p. 1.

25 Ibid.

26 "Nicholson File Meeting Halted by Court Order," *New York Times*, April 21, 1972.

27 Clare M. Reckert, "Nicholson File Company in Pact with Cooper Industries," *New York Times,* June 14, 1972, p. 65.

28 Wasserstein, pp. 73–74.

29 Ibid., p. 75.

30 Michael C. Jensen, "Anaconda Prepares to Fight Crane's Move," *New York Times*, August 26, 1975, p. 39.

31 Robert Metz, "Market Place: The Tactic of Lowering a Tender Offer," *New York Times*, October 7, 1977.

32 Brendan Jones, "People and Business," *New York Times*, October 9, 1975, p. 61.

33 "Thomas Mellon Evans: A Corporate Entrepreneur Hits the Jackpot; What Comes Next?," *Business Week*, October 25, 1976, p. 80.

34 Ibid.

35 United Press International, "Tenneco Troubled, T. M. Evans Says," *Pittsburgh Press*, February 4, 1976.

36 Michael C. Jensen, "Arco Is Unopposed by Anaconda Company," *New York Times*, March 19, 1976, p. 47.

37 "Thomas Mellon Evans: A Corporate Entrepreneur . . . ," *Business Week*, op. cit.

38 Kase interview.

39 Greg Conroy, "County Is Assailed over Pollution from Cement Plant," *St. Louis Post-Dispatch*, October 3, 1975.

40 Lawrence Lederman, *Tombstones: A Lawyer's Tales from the Takeover Decades* (New York: Farrar, Strauss & Giroux, 1992), p. 81.

41 "Porter To Buy Missouri Portland," *St. Louis Post-Dispatch*, December 21, 1976.

42 Herbert Koshetz, "Missouri Portland Cement and Cargill Inc.," *New York Times*, July 26, 1974, p. 43.

43 Pamela Meyer, "No Takeover of Missouri Portland," *St. Louis Post-Dispatch*, September 2, 1975, p. 7b.

44 Pamela Meyer, "Porter Claims No Acquisition Plan for Missouri Portland," *St. Louis Post-Dispatch*, September 4, 1975, p. 6b.

45 Jack Markowitz, "Young Evans Gets First 'No'," *Pittsburgh Post-Gazette*, November 11, 1975, p. 20.

46 Roy Malone, "Court Order Halts Bid for Missouri Portland Stock," *St. Louis Post-Dispatch*, November 11, 1975, page 6c.

47 Pamela Meyer, "Missouri Portland Hearing Continued," *St. Louis Post-Dispatch*, November 23, 1975, p. 6b.

48 Ibid.

49 Pamela Meyer, "Missouri Portland Seeking Mergers since Porter Offer," *St. Louis Post-Dispatch*, November 21, 1975, p. 11a.

50 Ibid.

51 "Chromalloy, Missouri Portland Announce Plans to Merge," *St. Louis Post-Dispatch*, November 24, 1975, p. 6c.

52 Pamela Meyer, [headline obscured], *St. Louis Post-Dispatch*, December 11, 1975, p. 11b.

53 Pamela Meyer, "Porter Seeks to Ban Missouri Portland Merger," *St. Louis Post-Dispatch*, December 30, 1975, p. 7b.

54 "Chromalloy Calls off MoPort Merger," *St. Louis Post-Dispatch*, January 5, 1976, p. 7b.

55 Pamela Meyer, "Porter's MoPort Goals Are Argued," *St. Louis Post-Dispatch*, February 16, 1976, p. 12a.

56 Pamela Meyer, "H. K. Porter Elects Two Directors to Board of Missouri Portland," *St. Louis Post-Dispatch,* May 26, 1976, p. 14e.

57 Lederman, p. 78.

58 Ibid., p. 101.

59 Ibid., p. 84.

60 Ibid., p. 79.

61 Herbert Koshetz, "Fansteel's Board Backs Siegler Bid," *New York Times,* May 18, 1976, p. 43.

62 "A Young Evans Sets His Own Takeover Style," *Business Week,* June 21, 1976, p. 29.

63 Robert Metz, "Market Place: Takeover Bids Lift Target Stocks," *New York Times,* May 22, 1976.

64 Lederman, p. 83.

65 Ibid.

66 Ibid., p. 87.

67 "MoPort-Porter Settlement," *St. Louis Post-Dispatch,* July 22, 1976, p. 6c; Lederman, p. 87.

68 Lederman, p. 79.

69 Ibid., p. 81.

70 Ibid., p. 85.

71 Ibid., p. 88.

72 Ibid., p. 89.

73 Ibid., p. 90.

74 Ibid.

75 Ibid., p. 92.

76 Ibid., pp. 93–94.

77 "SEC Charges Porter Misstated Its Plans in Buying Cement Stock," *New York Times,* March 22, 1977, p. 64.

78 T. M. Evans Jr. interview; also Eileen Foley, "Industrialist Wife's Death Probed in Virginia," *Pittsburgh Post-Gazette* [date obscured, but likely to be May 15, 1977].

79 Ben A. Franklin, "Questions Remain in Apparent Suicide of Virginia Woman," *New York Times,* May 15, 1977.

80 Ibid.

81 Ibid.

82 Interview with Coleman Abbe.

83 Chicago *Daily News* Service, August 9, 1977, included in the *Pittsburgh Post-Gazette* archives.

84 Winston Williams, "Crane Raises Offer for Chemetron to Block Merger with Allegheny," *New York Times,* September 2, 1977, p. D1.

85 Associated Press, "M-K to Evans: Don't Buy Us," *Pittsburgh Post-Gazette,* May 2, 1978.

86 "Business People: A Company Collector," *New York Times,* May 22, 1978.

NOTES FOR CHAPTER THIRTEEN

1 Wasserstein, p. 96.

2 Ibid., p. 108.

3 Ibid., p. 109.

4 "Crane: Its Acquisition of Medusa Will Give Shareholders a Hedge," *Business Week,* April 9, 1979, p. 116.

5 Ibid.

6 Ibid.

7 Lederman, p. 293.

8 Donald D. Holt, "How Macmillan Learned to Love Edward Evans," *Fortune*, February 25, 1980, p. 98.

9 Ibid.

10 Ibid.

11 Ibid.

12 Ibid.

13 Lederman, p. 295.

14 Holt, op. cit.

15 Ibid.

16 Robert J. Cole, "Macmillan's Chairman Replaced in Management Rift," *New York Times*, February 12, 1980, p. 1.

17 Lederman, p. 294.

18 Ibid., p. 296.

19 Interviews with Douglas Campbell, the Pittsburgh attorney who took possession of Porter's corporate files in 1998, and with T. M. Evans Jr.

20 Hugh D. Menzies, "The Ten Toughest Bosses," *Fortune*, April 21, 1980, p. 62.

21 Ibid.

22 "Macmillan: Back to the School House to Sustain a Textbook Turnaround," *Business Week*, November 28, 1983, p. 68.

23 Lederman, p. 296.

24 Walter Adams and James W. Brock, *Dangerous Pursuits: Mergers and Acquisitions in the Age of Wall Street* (New York: Pantheon Books, 1989), p. 12.

25 Caplan, p. 66.

26 Seligman, p. 578.

27 Ken Auletta, *Greed and Glory on Wall Street* (New York: Random House, 1986), pp. 237–38.

28 Hope Lambert, *Till Death Do Us Part: Bendix vs. Martin Marietta* (New York: Harcourt Brace Jovanovich, 1983), p. 7.

29 Ibid., p. 51.

30 David A. Vise and Steve Coll, *Eagle on the Street* (New York: Charles Scribner's Sons, 1991), p. 103.

31 Seligman, p. 579.

32 Vise and Cole, p. 108.

33 Ibid.

34 Adams and Brock, p. 12.

35 Ibid.

36 Wasserstein, p. 79.

37 Ibid.

38 Ibid.

39 Seligman, pp. 576–77.

40 Ibid., p. 578.

41 Ibid, p. 579.

42 James B. Stewart, *Den of Thieves* (New York: Simon and Schuster, 1991), pp. 96–97, 143, 439–41.

43 Bill Abrams, "Non-Steel Units of Crane Sought for $357 Million," *Wall Street Journal*, February 28, 1984.

Notes

44 Associated Press, "Crane's Directors Reject Buyout Bid," *New York Times*, March 7, 1984, p. D4.

45 Ibid.

NOTES FOR EPILOGUE

1 Wasserstein, pp. 134–37.

2 Sarah Bartlett, *The Money Machine: How KKR Manufactured Power and Profits* (New York: Warner Books, 1991), pp. 257–58.

3 Ibid., p. 265.

4 Crane Company, proxy statement, March 26, 1990, p. 13.

5 Ibid., p. 11.

6 *United States of America ex rel. Stanley Rabushka and Stanley Rabushka vs. Crane Company*, Appeal from the United States District Court for the Eastern District of Missouri, No. 93-3212, The United States Court Of Appeals for the Eighth Circuit, No. 96-3027.

7 Opinion by the Eighth Circuit Court of Appeals in case No. 93-3212, cited above, p. 12.

8 Ibid., p. 16.

9 CF&I Steel Corporation, Form 10k, filed with the Securities and Exchange Commission, March 28, 1991, pp. 9–10.

10 Wasserstein, p. 279.

11 Opinion in *Robert M. Bass Group vs. Edward P. Evans et al.*, in Re Macmillan Inc. Shareholders Litigation, Civil Action Numbers 9953, 9909, Court of Chancery of Delaware, 552 A.2d 1227, July 14, 1988 (hereafter Macmillan I).

12 Ibid.

13 Ibid.

14 Ibid.

15 Ibid.

16 Ibid.

17 Opinion in *Mills Acquisition Company et al., Appellants vs. Macmillan*, Nos. 415, 1988, 416, 1988 Consolidated, Supreme Court of Delaware, 559 A.2d 1261, May 3, 1989 (hereafter Macmillan III).

18 Ibid.

19 Ibid.

20 Macmillan I.

21 Macmillan III.

22 Macmillan I.

23 Ibid.

24 Lederman, p. 300.

25 Ibid., p. 301.

26 Macmillan III.

27 Ibid.

28 Ibid.

29 Lederman, p. 303.

30 Macmillan III.

31 Opinion in *Mills Acquisition Company, Tendclass Ltd. and Maxwell Communications Corp., PLC vs. Macmillan et al.*, Civil Action No. 10168, Court of Chancery of Delaware, 1988 Del. Ch. LEXIS 138, As Revised October 18, 1988 (hereafter Macmillan II).

32 Ibid.
33 Lederman, p. 305.
34 Macmillan II.
35 Macmillan III.
36 Macmillan II.
37 Ibid.
38 Lederman, p. 309.
39 Ibid., p. 311.
40 Macmillan III.
41 "Macmillan Case Accord," *New York Times,* December 6, 1989, p. D19.
42 Bernie Kohn, "After 50 Years, Evans and H. K. Porter Becoming One," *Pittsburgh Press,* August 18, 1987, p. D1; "Porter Shareholders Approved Plan to Take Company Private," *Pittsburgh Press,* August 28, 1987, p. no. unavailable.
43 Complaint, *The Committee of Unsecured Creditors of HK Porter Company Inc. vs. Thomas Mellon Evans et al.,* Civil Division No. G. D. 92-22720, in the Court of Common Pleas Allegheny County, PA; in re HK Porter Company Inc., Debtor, adversary proceedings No. 93-2581, the United States Bankruptcy Court for the Western District of Pennsylvania.
44 Ibid.
45 Ibid., Court of Common Pleas Complaint, pp. 1–2.
46 Nick Ravo, "Thomas Evans, 86, a Takeover Expert, Dies," *New York Times,* July 18, 1997, p. A22.
47 Jeffrey E. Garten, "Megamergers Are a Clear and Present Danger," *Business Week,* January 25, 1999, p. 28.
48 Stenographic Transcript of Hearings, Subcommittee to Investigate Public Transportation Serving the District Of Columbia, Committee on the District Of Columbia, the United States Senate, December 8, 1953, p. 214.
49 Robert Kuttner, *Everything for Sale: The Virtues and Limits of Markets* (New York: Alfred A. Knopf, 1997), p. 61.

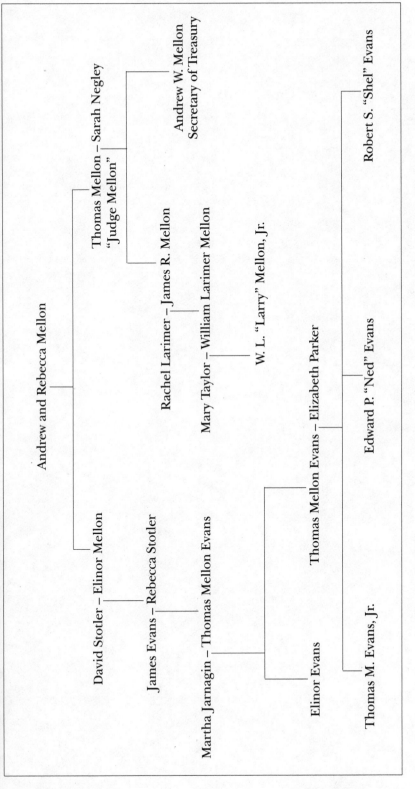

A PARTIAL FAMILY TREE

Andrew and Rebecca Mellon

Thomas Mellon – Sarah Negley
"Judge Mellon"

Andrew W. Mellon
Secretary of Treasury

Rachel Larimer – James R. Mellon

Mary Taylor – William Larimer Mellon

W. L. "Larry" Mellon, Jr.

David Stotler – Elinor Mellon

James Evans – Rebecca Stotler

Martha Jarnagin – Thomas Mellon Evans

Thomas Mellon Evans – Elizabeth Parker

Elinor Evans

Edward P. "Ned" Evans

Robert S. "Shel" Evans

Thomas M. Evans, Jr.